Handbook of Best Practices for Teams, Volume I

Glenn M. Parker, Editor

Published by HRD Press and Irwin Professional Publishing

Published by:
HRD Press
22 Amherst Road
Amherst, MA 01002
1-800-822-2801
1-413-253-3490 (Fax)

Irwin Professional Publishing
1333 Burr Ridge Parkway
Burr Ridge, Illinois 60521
1-800-634-3966

ISBN 0-87425-336-5

Production services by Clark Riley

Cover design by Eileen Klockars

Editorial services by Lisa Wood

Table of Contents

Part VI—ORGANIZATIONAL ISSUES

Part VII—TEAM RESOURCES

Part VIII—CONTRIBUTORS

Part I - Introduction and Overview

1

Introduction to the 1996 Handbook
Glenn M. Parker, Editor

As Bill Dyer points out in his paper, ". . .building effective organizational teams . . . (is) hard work." The purpose of this Handbook is not to help you avoid the hard work but to provide resources to make more productive decisions. Dyer also notes his concern with team building as a "cut and paste operation" where you simply go to a resource book, pull out a few exercises, read a quick summary of a theory, copy an instrument, and off you go to work with a team. It just doesn't work that way or at least it doesn't work very well that way.

Therefore, before you begin using any of the resources in this Handbook, I recommend that you read Dyer's paper, "Essential Conditions for Building Successful Teams." Bill is the author of my favorite book in this field, *Team Building: Issues and Alternatives* (Addison-Wesley, 1977).

Purpose

This Handbook is not intended to be a substitute for a solid grounding in organizational effectiveness, group dynamics, and facilitation skills. Our purpose is to bring together some of the world's leading team builders and ask them to contribute a "best practice." In some cases, it gave them an opportunity to put down on paper a concept they have been developing and using in their practice. Other contributors shared with us a chapter from their new book. Others reached back for a resource previously published, but not widely circulated. Many of our contributors created an entirely new resource especially for this Handbook.

We did not take a "cookie cutter" approach to the format of the contributions. Other similar resource manuals demand uniformity among the contributions resulting in a publication that was described recently as "boring." While we had high quality standards for content and presentation style, there are some fairly wide variations in the resources in this Handbook. Our main format requirement was that each contribution be user-friendly for team building practitioners. While most of our authors have a solid academic background in the field, we insisted that their contributions to this Handbook always address the question: *How can this be used to build teams or create a team-based organization?*

Contents

Team Activities: This section includes six new and creative exercises that can be used to start and build teams. Ed Rose of Harris Semiconductor has contributed one of his favorite activities, developed and honed over the years as he has traveled around the world training teams. It's a quick and fun exercise that can be used as a prelude to a larger team planning session. The internationally respected training firm, Zenger-Miller, has provided us with a simple but powerful activity, *The Team Formation Checklist*, that is used by new teams to get all the relevant questions answered. *The Team Icon Autobiography* is consultant and speaker Bette Krakau's clever ice-breaker for new teams or a team training class. *Team Growth* is a new training game by the master of games and simulations, Sivasailam Thiagarajan. It's a board game that teaches Tuchman's four stages of team development and makes it fun. Dick Kropp's exercise, *Building a Trust-Based* Organization, is an excellent tool to help an intact team increase its level of trust. Stu Noble's *The Site Visit Resource Guide* is not a team building or training activity, but rather a detailed road map for work redesign, process improvement, and other similar teams who visit other companies for learning and benchmarking.

Team Instruments: The section includes new surveys that assess team member and overall team effectiveness. All of the instruments are designed to be a prelude to an action plan. Zenger-Miller's *Quick Check of Team Member Skills* is just what the title implies, a brief self-assessment tool for team members focusing more on behaviors than style. In his instrument, *Measuring the Financial Cost of Team Conflict*, Dan Dana, a specialist in mediation and conflict resolution, has given us a very creative way of estimating the real cost of conflict to the organization. Gayle Porter and Sue Easton have teamed up to provide us with a new way of selecting the right team structure in the *Continuum of Work Structures*. Their instrument works in tandem with their paper on the same subject in the "Practical Theory" section. *The Team Competency Tool* by B. J. and Ken Chakiris and Pat Felkins is an team assessment instrument that builds on the work first published in their book, *Change Management*. Finally, Deborah Harrington-Mackin, author of the popular book, *The Team Building Tool Kit*, has contributed a survey aimed at mature teams who need to reassess and, perhaps, refocus their efforts.

Case Studies: A tried and true method of learning about teamwork is to study how other organizations tried to implement the team process. In this section we have a varied set of contributions. First, we have two cases that are the result of the collaboration of internal and external consultants. In one paper, Tom Buck and Nancy Finley of Prism Performance Systems have teamed up with Mary Rahaim and Lynn Wilson of Amoco to bring us a story of how the company grew a network of multidisciplinary teams. Author, professor, and consultant Glenn Varney and Dan Diers of Rockwell International present a very detailed case with a title that is quite explicit: "A Critical Examination of a Failed Attempt to Implement Self-Directed Teams: How a Success Turned Into a Failure." We are very pleased to have an excerpt from Sylvia Odenwald's new book, *Global Solutions for Teams*. Sylvia integrates two cases into her model for global teams. Internal consultant Lee Royal's contribution is a compact case study of a team charged with the task of developing a peer appraisal system. Lee, an internal OD specialist, does an excellent job of detailing the learnings from the experience. In a similar way, Jerry Klein of Rider University helps us learn about what works and what doesn't from his comprehensive report on a team-based pay-for-knowledge program in a factory.

Practical Theory: In this section we asked contributors to look at an established theory or model and discuss its implications for team building practitioners. The result is a wonderful mixture of ideas and approaches to the practical aspects of team building. In his first publication since the highly successful *Team Handbook*, Peter Scholtes has produced a very thoughtful piece on the Japanese concept of Gemba and the role of teams. In a companion paper to their Continuum of Work Structures in the "Team Instruments" section, Gayle Porter and Sue Easton provide direction on "Selecting the Right Team Structure." On the other hand, Larry Meeker takes the familiar idea of trust and shows how it can be used as a vehicle for team building. Coach Maureen O'Brien has provided us with a new look at team process in an excerpt from her new book, *Who's Got the Ball?* And Ken Thomas and Walter Tymon, developers of several very popular team instruments, present their model of empowerment and its practical implications for developing work teams.

Organizational Issues: Here we opted for wide latitude on the part of our authors. Essentially we were looking for papers that focused on what needs to be done to create a team-based organization. For an overview, start with Dave Jamieson's thoughtful piece, "Aligning the Organization for Team-Based Operation," which explores five major organizational components (structure, systems, vision, practices, culture and strategy) that need to be in alignment. Move on to Steve Phillips' typology of teams and their development needs in his contribution, "Update Your Toolbox for Teams." You may want to compare Phillips' team types with the one in Peter Scholtes' article in the previous section.

If you want to know what team members think about their teams, read the study from the Zenger-Miller research team, Amy Katz, Darlene Russ-Eft, Linda Moran, and Lilanthi Ravishankar, entitled, "The Truth from the Trenches: Team Members Speak Out." It might be useful to compare and contrast their findings with the feelings of team members in your organization. In a more practical vein, Dominick Volini of Block Petrella Weisbord tells us how to help teams make the transition from producing a work redesign plan to the implementation of that plan. Then Jack Zigon tells us "How to Measure the Results of Work Teams," with specific examples from his practice. Finally, in an excerpt from his new book (as yet untitled, but due out in the Spring of 1996 from Jossey-Bass), Jerry McAdams provides us with a very detailed methodology for using the team process to design a group incentive system.

Team Resources: This section begins with a bibliography of recent books and articles on trust in a team setting prepared by Liz Teal of the Center for the Study of Work Teams at the University of North Texas. Liz's bibliography can be used to supplement the paper from Larry Meeker in the "Practical Theory" section and Dick Kropp's instrument in the "Team Instruments" section. In this section we inaugurate a new approach to the review of resources. Instead of reviewing one or two new books, we asked two top team building professionals to examine a variety of different resources on a subject and to indicate how they might be used by practitioners in the field. Jerry Klein of Rider University looks at the area of self-directed teams and assesses several books, instruments, manuals, and videos that can be used by trainers, coaches, and consultants. Similarly, Vic Kline of Princeton Consulting Services reviews a number of resources on empowerment and shows us how to integrate them into a program for team and organizational development.

Questions and Answers: A User's Guide to the 1996 Handbook

Question: How can I use this Handbook? What's in it for ME? **Answer**: What questions do you have about teamwork? What do you want to know or be able to do that will help teams be effective in your organization?

Here are some typical questions and examples of how the 1996 Handbook answers those questions.

1. **New Teams**? I've been asked to help a new team get off the ground. Help me out.

   - Begin with Zenger-Miller's "The Team Formation Checklist" (chapter 5), an activity designed to get all the necessary start-up information out and on the table.
   - Then, use Bette Krakau's "The Team Icon Autobiography" (chapter 6), a very clever exercise designed to help team members get to know each other better.

- Copy and distribute "Every Player Contributes to the Process" (chapter 24) by Maureen O'Brien. Use the article as a basis for facilitating a discussion on the roles of team members.

2. **Mature Teams?** I'm working with an on-going team that is stagnating. What do I do?

- The best place to begin is with a diagnosis and here we have the perfect solution, Deborah Harrington-Mackin's "Team Realignment Tool" (chapter 14). Use the instrument as a basis for assessment and action planning.
- To help the team understand how they got into this situation and have some fun at the same time, try Thiagy's learning game, "Team Growth" (chapter 7). The activity teaches four stages of team development in a very creative manner.
- If you suspect inappropriate structure may be the problem, copy and ask team members to read and discuss "Selecting the Right Team Structure" (chapter 21) by Porter and Easton.
- If stalled implementation is the issue, use Dominick Volini's "Implementation Myopia to Implementation Mania" (chapter 29) as a discussion starter. Copy and distribute the paper to all team members prior to your next meeting.

3. **Trust?** What can I do to develop trust on a team?

- Trust is a complex issue. You should start with Liz Teal's "Bibliography on Trust in Teams" (chapter 32). Do some reading on the subject and then when you find something that seems especially relevant to your team, locate the document and share it with your team.
- Move on to "Trust: The Great Teamwork Enabler" (chapter 22) by Larry Meeker for some specific insight and exercises you can use with your team.
- When you are ready for some direct work with your team, use Dick Kropp's activity, "Building a Trust-Based Organization" (chapter 8), to get the ball rolling.

4. **Empowerment?** How do I develop a course to teach managers and team members about empowerment?

- Begin with Vic Kline's comprehensive review of "Resources on Empowerment" (chapter 34). Vic has assembled and assessed a wide variety of books, instruments and videos designed to help people understand empowerment. Vic also tells you how to use each resource and how to combine them in a program in your organization.
- Look at Ken Thomas and Walter Tymon's practical theory piece, "The Elements of Empowerment" (chapter 25). Thomas and Tymon are also the authors of the *Empowerment Inventory*.

- Since trust is at the core of empowerement, don't forget the trust resources mentioned in the previous section.

5. **Team Building?** What can I do to help ensure that my team building efforts with intact teams are successful?

   - Begin and end with Bill Dyer's insightful paper, "Essential Conditions for Building Successful Teams" (chapter 3). Bill will tell you that it isn't all the exercises and instruments that make team building successful, it's addressing and managing the critical elements of the process.

6. **Conflict?** What can I do to help teams manage and resolve conflict effectively?

   - There is no better resource on conflict than Lois Hart. So, begin with her practical theory paper, "Handling Conflict in Teams" (chapter 23). You can copy and distribute to a team with conflicts and then facilitate a discussion on how they can implement some of Lois' methods.
   - If you want to get management's attention, at their next staff meeting, distribute "Measuring the Financial Cost of Team Conflict" (chapter 11) by Dan Dana. Facilitate a discussion using a recent conflict.

7. **Team Rewards?** What do we do to develop rewards program that recognizes the work of successful teams?

   - Look no further. Read Jerry McAdams' "How to Design a Group Incentive Plan" (chapter 31). Jerry is the world's leading expert on reward systems. Everyone in a leadership position in your organization should also read the paper.
   - An important part of the rewards process is measuring team results and for a how-to approach to the subject, read Jack Zigon's "How to Measure the Results of Work Teams" (chapter 30). Once again, copy and distribute copies to key people in your organization.
   - A related methodology that some organizations are experimenting with is peer appraisals. For a case history of how one organization did it, look at Lee Royal's "The Performance Appraisal Team: A Peer Appraisal Case Study" (chapter 17).

8. **Quality?** What is the role of teams in the quality process? Our total quality effort is in trouble—what should we do?

   - A wonderful resource for your organization is Peter Scholtes' "Teams in the Systems Era" (chapter 20). Peter, a student and protégé of Dr. Deming, makes a useful distinction between different types of teams and indicates when each type should be used. Use the paper as a basis for a discussion with key people in your organization responsible for the quality process.

9. **Reengineering?** We're going through reengineering now. What is the role of teams in business process reengineering?

- Once again Peter Scholtes's paper, "Teams in the Systems Era" (chapter 20) is THE resource on the role of teams.

10. **International Teams?** I'm working with a team composed of people from different countries. What should I know about this type of team?

- Read Sylvia Odenwald's "A Model for Global Work Teams" (chapter 18). Copy and distribute the paper to members of the team. Facilitate a discussion on the four phases of team development and which stage their team is in and what they need to do to go forward.

11. **Needs Assessment?** I have to develop a training program for team members. Are there tools available to help me with this process?

- An excellent tool is Zenger-Miller's "Quick Check of Team Member Skills." This tool will provide you with data on areas for improvement among team members. You can use the results to identify key areas for your program.
- Another useful instrument is "Team Competency Tool" (chapter 13) by B. J. Chakiris, Ken Chakiris and Pat Felkins. You can ask team members to complete the tool and when you compile the results you will have a list of the areas where training is needed.
- After you have used these tools, take a look at Steven Phillips' paper, "Up-Date Your Toolbox for Teams" (chapter 27). Phillips provides some concrete ideas for training programs for various types of teams.

12. **Self-Directed Teams?** I have been asked to help start self-directed teams in my area. How should I get started? What tools are available?

- Begin with Jerry Klein's comprehensive review of "Resources on Creating Self-Managed Work Teams" (chapter 33). He has reviewed and recommended a number of videos, instruments and books on the subject.
- It will also help to look at Thomas and Tymon's paper, "The Elements of Team Empowerment" (chapter 25).
- Another useful resource for a start-up process is Porter and Easton's analysis tool, "Continuum of Work Structures" (chapter 12).

- For a telling story of an organization that tried to implement self-directed teams, read Glenn Varney and Dan Diers' case study, "A Critical Examination of a Failed Attempt to Implement Self-Directed Teams: How a Success Turned into A Failure" (chapter 16).

13. **Developing A Team-Based Organization?** How do we move from a functional organization to a team-based organization?

- Begin by reading and sharing with your management team Dave Jamieson's excellent work, "Aligning the Organization for Team-Based Strategy" (chapter 26).
- It will also be helpful to read the results of the Zenger-Miller survey, "The Truth From the Trenches: Team Members Speak Out" (chapter 28).
- And finally, read about a success story at Amoco written by two internal Amoco consultants and two external consultants from Prism Performance Systems, "Large Scale Change at Amoco: Becoming Team-Based" (chapter 15).

Do You Want to Be a Contributor?
If you would like to submit a contribution for publication in the 1997 Handbook, please contact me at:

Glenn M. Parker Associates
41 Woodlane Road
Lawrenceville, New Jersey 08648
Phone: 609-895-1920
Fax: 609-895-1920
E-Mail: 72202.3676@Compuserve.com or glennparker@ASTD.Noli.com

Before you submit a manuscript, ask for a copy of the *Guidelines for Authors*.

Acknowledgments
I would like to thank Chris Hunter of HRD Press for his support and help throughout the development and implementation of this project. Chris provided specific ideas as well as a supportive ear. The Center for the Study of Work Teams of the University of North Texas was encouraging of the concept of the Handbook and helped identify and access contributors.

Finally, I want to thank the authors whose work appears in this first Handbook. Many are personal friends, some are professional colleagues, while others are people whose work I admired. To all, I say "thanks" for wanting to be part of this new venture and be willing to adhere to some challenging quality standards and submission deadlines.

About the Editor

Glenn M. Parker comes to the position of Editor of this Handbook with some 30 years of experience in the development of individuals and teams. His experience includes work with unions, community groups, government agencies, and businesses. He is the author of two books from Jossey-Bass, *Team Players and Teamwork* (1990; paper, 1995) and *Cross-Functional Teams* (1994); co-author of two manuals published by HRD Press, *50 Activities for Team Building*, volume 1 (1992) and *50 Activities for Self-Directed Teams* (1994); developer of *The Team Kit* (HRD Press, 1995), *Parker Team Player Survey* (Xicom, 1991), and the *Team Development Survey* (Xicom, 1992). A video based on his team player concepts, *Team Building II*, is available from CRM Films. Glenn does more than just write about teams; he works full-time as a consultant, trainer, and speaker helping organizations create and sustain high-perfoming teams.

11

2

History of Work Teams
Michael M. Beyerlein

Work teams come in many forms. Barry Macy (in press) has identified eleven such forms that range from natural work groups through self-managed teams to virtual teams that only connect via computer (see also Scholtes, 1988). Work teams are not new. The term was first used in the 15th century to refer to a team of horses; a century later it was used to refer to people working together. People have always worked together. You can't build pyramids without some form of teamwork. However, the way that people work together has been taking on some new forms. And in the United States and a number of other countries, those new forms seem to be part of a revolution in the way work is organized.

"There is nothing new under the sun" is an old cliche. It is fairly accurate. And it suggests that there is usually a history to whatever we are working on that warrants a check, so we do not have to reinvent the wheel when we reinvent the corporation. In this preface, I briefly review a few of the many events, ideas, and trends from the past that form the foundation we are building on now with work teams. I define work teams very broadly as groups of people collaborating together to achieve some purpose that requires their interdependence, such as satisfying a common customer, jointly producing a product or providing a service.

The contributions to our foundation for work teams come from both research and practice. Over the past 75 years, researchers and practitioners have shared enough with each other to provide "a leg up" to one another, in a kind of zipper effect. For example, Kurt Lewin, known as the father of social psychology, worked with other major contributors, such as Kenneth Benne, Leland Bradford, and Ronald Lippitt (French & Bell, 1978) in the 1940s to start National Training Laboratories. They took what they had learned in the lab studying groups and made it available to managers in intense, short-term learning experiences. It was the beginning of the group movement and provided an important part of the foundation of the organizational development movement.

1920-1960

Social psychologists had been working in the 1920s and 1930s on a number of research questions dealing with social interaction, communication, and group dynamics. Lewin, known for his emphasis on the applied side of social and behavioral science, including the invention

13

of action research and principles of participative management, was an outstanding leader in applying the answers to research questions to public problems. Others contributing important work at that time included Moreno and Ash in the United States and Bion, Trist, and Bamforth in England.

Between 1927 and 1934, Elton Mayo and his associates at Harvard worked with engineers at Western Electric in Cicero, Illinois in an intense study of work groups (Roethlisberger & Dickson, 1939). The results of their work triggered the human relations movement in management and woke up managers and researchers to the fact that employees were more than machines and that psychological and group influences could motivate more than pay.

Many people believe that work teams were discovered by Trist (who met Lewin in the 1930s) and Bamforth in the 1940s. They do deserve a great deal of credit for identifying and writing about autonomous work groups, beginning with their observation of coal mining teams in England, which were quite similar to the self-managed work teams of today. In addition, Trist and his colleagues laid the groundwork for the sociotechnical systems approach to work design, an emphasis on quality of work life, and the idea that the people actually doing the work should have more authority, control, skills, and information than was traditionally available, in order to perform at high quality levels (Weisbord, 1991).

1960-1980

Other early examples of team implementation include Non-Linear Systems in California from about 1958 to 1968, Procter & Gamble from the early 1960s to the present, Volvo in Sweden from the late 1960s, the failure at British Leland in attempting to copy Volvo, and the Gaines Pet Food Plant in Topeka, Kansas in the early 1970s. There were other examples during those early years in the United States, Europe, Australia, and India. Of course, the Japanese implementation of Deming's work contributed another major influence to the growing trend to use teams in the workplace. Between 1973 and 1987 an increasing number of leading-edge organizations began to use teams, including Cummins Engine; GM; DEC; Ford; Tektronix; LTV Steel; GE; Champion International; Caterpillar; Boeing; and A. O. Smith (Orsburn, Moran, Musselwhite, & Zenger, 1990). Many of these companies have continued to expand the use of teams, but some have scaled back. For example, DEC acquired some fame for use of teams in its Enfield, Connecticut plant in the 1980s, but a couple of years ago the plant was closed.

While the above research and implementation events were happening, management philosophies and organizational designs were evolving through a number of stages. Ray Miles (1995; Miles & Snow, 1994) describes the historical pattern as theories of management changed from traditional to human relations to human resources to human investment models. At the same time organizational forms evolved through several stages: (a) owner-manager, (b) functional design with vertical integration, (c) diversified and divisionalized, (d) matrix, (e) network, and finally (f) spherical. Miles suggests that true teams are only possible at the later stages, implying that the organizational context of the teams is critical to their survival. Only a few organizations have begun to use the human investment model and network or spherical forms for organizing work.

In the 1960s and 1970s important books and articles were published that provided foundation material for thinking about work teams, but there was a limited amount of information and much of that was written for an academic audience. Major contributions included Katz and Kahn's (1966) book applying systems theory to organizations, the initial publications in the Addison-Wesley series on organizational development, including Bill Dyer's book on team building (1987), the initiation of the annual series for group facilitators by Pfeiffer and Jones (1970), and articles describing teams in a few companies (e.g., Walton, 1974).

1980-1996

1987 may be classified as a watershed year, because that year Lawler and his associates at the Center for Effective Organizations at USC published their first survey of Fortune 500 companies to determine the extent to which teams were being used. They published subsequent surveys in 1992 and 1995. The survey results show a continual spread of team-based forms for organizing work. The latest survey shows that over 50 percent of Fortune 500 companies are trying or using teams, but that only 10 percent of the work force is actually in teams (Lawler, 1995). Others have done related surveys since 1990 that also support these findings.

In 1988, 1989, and 1990 several publishing events happened that seemed to be milestones and that both represented a culmination of developments in practice and a critical mass of published material. In 1988, Peter Scholtes published *The Team Handbook*. Chuck Manz and Hank Sims (1989) published the first book focused on a new theory of empowering leadership: *SuperLeadership*. Business magazines finally brought work teams to the general business audience with articles in *Business Week* (Hoerr, 1989) and *Fortune Magazine* (Dumaine, 1990). Jack Orsburn et al. (1990) led a team at the Zenger-Miller consulting firm in publishing the first widely disseminated "how to" book for implementing self-directed teams and Glenn Parker (1990) published his description of team player styles. The Association for Quality and Participation (AQP) and the Center for the Study of Work Teams held their first conferences on work teams. There was so little written material available to practitioners before 1990 that many considered the presentation papers collected in the Proceedings from the Center for the Study of Work Teams' conference a significant resource.

AQP and the Center for the Study of Work Teams are still holding annual conferences on work teams. And now a number of other organizations are doing similar things; the number of small workshops on teams has proliferated to the point that the readers of this book probably receive somewhere between one announcement per week and one announcement per day for such "educational opportunities."

Current Trends

Reviewing the history of teams provides an awareness of trends that are still valid. Examples include the recognition in the 1930s of the influence of the group, the value in cross-functional mixes of employees in the 1960s, the emergence of facilitation and team building in the 1970s, and the increasing focus on the role of the team member (e.g., Parker, 1990).

Based on changes in attendance at the Center's conferences, several other trends seem to have emerged in the past five years. First, attendance at the conference has increased from 320 to 1,200, suggesting that interest in the use of work teams continues to grow as more success stories stimulate interest. Second, in the first couple of years at the Center's conference, manufacturing organizations dominated attendance; their numbers have continued to increase at a steady rate, but more rapid increase has occurred for service organizations, vendors to the manufacturing organizations, and government agencies. Consequently, the use of teams seems to be spreading from manufacturing to technical professionals, service, health care, professionals, sales and retail, and managers, in that order.

The latest shifts seem to be toward virtual teams. For many years, definitions of the term "team" included the statement that the team members had to be co-located, i.e., working in the same physical location. With the increasing ability to utilize the Internet for communications, a growing number of teams are only linked electronically and share cyberspace rather than physical space. New questions for research and practice emerge as a consequence of the invention of this new kind of teaming. So, although we have learned a lot in the past 75 years about how to make teams effective ways to organize work, changes in the business environment continue to drive the need to learn and discover more answers. Other changes that seem to be emerging include the shift from a focus on teams to a focus on team-based organizations (Lawler, 1995; Mohrman, Cohen, & Mohrman, 1995); from self-managed work teams to self-managed development (Elden & Gjersvik, 1995); from self-managed teams to self-governing teams (Hackman, 1992) or self-organizing teams (Elden, 1994); and from a sociotechnical systems implementation process to a search conference implementation (Elden, 1994; Emery, 1993; Weisbord, 1992).

Conclusion

This overview of the history of research and practice with work teams provides a brief sketch of the foundation on which current practices are built. The philosopher Santayana wrote that those who do not remember history are condemned to repeat it. That means, if we don't know what we have in the warehouse, we are likely to invest an enormous amount in reinventing it. The contributions to this book and its subsequent companion volumes are written by people who know a lot about the relevant history. They base their work on a substantial foundation of reading, thinking, and experimenting. Their contributions will remind you of some of the history, guide you to resources, translate the research into useful tools, and present new tools based on the foundation work of the pioneers. Three of the key pieces for staying in business will be new ideas and perspectives, new awareness and sensitivities, and new tools for learning and working. The contributions to this series will provide help with all three for managers and other leaders, trainers and educators, change agents, team members, and students.

Members of each of these groups are struggling with important issues, striving to solve significant questions, and hungering for new learning opportunities that will enhance their competencies in an increasingly dynamic and uncertain work world. The articles, exercises, and instruments in this series will provide a variety of contributions for them. Each new volume will provide new insights, and as volumes accumulate, the old ones will become familiar references that can be visited again and again when tackling new challenges in growing teams and a team-based work culture.

I believe we are going through a revolution that is becoming worldwide. The revolution is economically driven, but the solution is based on employee empowerment and involvement. The revolution first impacted manufacturing, then knowledge work, then government. It is now moving into the schools and the healthcare and retail industries in the United States. It is also moving into Pacific rim countries and Europe in new places and new ways. We have only seen the tip of the iceberg. Once people have the opportunity to experience empowerment at work, they won't give it back. And the organizations that invest in their human resources will reap magnified contributions from their employees and excel.

References

Dumaine, B. (1995). The trouble with teams. *Fortune, 130 (5)*, 86-92.

Dumaine, B. (1990, May 7). Who needs a boss? *Fortune,* pp. 52-60.

Dyer, W. G. (1987). *Team building: Issues and alternatives.* Reading, MA: Addison Wesley.

Elden, M. (1994). Beyond teams: Self-managing processes for inventing organization. *Advances in Interdisciplinary Studies of Work Teams, Volume 1,* 263-289.

Elden, M., and R. Gjersvik (1995). Back to the future? or Is Norway really 15 years ahead of America in thinking about team based organization? Presentation at the annual meeting of the Academy of Management, Vancouver, B.C.

Emery, M. (1993). *Participative design for participative democracy.* Centre for Continuing Education, The Australian National University.

French, W. L., and C. H. Bell, Jr. (1978). *Organizational development: Theory, practice, and research.* Dallas: Business Publications, Inc.

Hackman, J. R. (1992). The psychology of self-management in organizations. In M. S. Pallak and R. Perloff (Eds.), *Psychology and work: Productivity, change, and employment.* Washington DC: American Psychological Association.

Hoerr, J. (1989, July 10). The payoff from teamwork. *Business Week,* pp. 56-62.

Katz, D., and R. Kahn (1966). *The social psychology of organizations.* New York: John Wiley.

Lawler, E. E., III (1995). Discussant remarks for the symposium: A retrospective on work teams: Lessons from research and practice or "back to the future." Presentation at the annual meeting of the Academy of Management, Vancouver, B.C.

Macy, B. A. (in press). *Successful strategic change.* San Francisco: Berrett-Kohler Publishers.

Manz, C. C., and H. P. Sims, Jr. (1989). *SuperLeadership.* New York: Berkley Books.

Miles, R. E. (1995). The role of teams in organizational development. Presentation at the annual meeting of the Academy of Management, Vancouver, B.C.

Miles, R. E., and C. C. Snow (1994). *Fit, failure, and the hall of fame: How companies succeed or fail.* New York: The Free Press.

Mohrman, S. A., S. G. Cohen, and A. M. Mohrman, Jr. (1995). *Designing team-based organizations.* San Francisco: Jossey-Bass.

Orsburn, J. D., L. Moran, E. Musselwhite, and J. H. Zenger (1990). *Self-directed work teams: The new American challenge.* Homewood, IL: Business One Irwin.

Parker, G. M. (1990). *Team players and teamwork: The new competitive business strategy.* San Francisco, CA: Jossey-Bass.

Pfeiffer, J. W., and J. Jones (1970). *Structured experiences for human relations training.* Iowa City: University Associates.

Roethlisberger, F. J., and W. J. Dickson (1939). *Management and the worker.* Cambridge, MA: Harvard University Press.

Scholtes, P. T. (1988). *The team handbook.* Madison, WI: Joiner Associates, Inc.

Walton, R. (1974). *Using social psychology to create a new plant culture.* Working paper 73-12, AR 4. Boston: Harvard University.

Weisbord, M. R. (1991). *Productive workplaces: Organizing and managing for dignity, meaning, and community.* San Francisco: Jossey-Bass.

Weisbord, M. R. (1992). *Discovering common ground: How Future Search Conferences bring people together to achieve breakthrough innovation, empowerment, shared vision, and collaborative action.* San Francisco: Berrett-Kohler Publishers.

About the Contributor

Michael Beyerlein, Ph.D., is Director of the Center for the Study of Work Teams and Assistant Professor of Industrial/Organizational Psychology at the University of North Texas. Mike's work focuses on the implementation and development of work teams. His research interests include all aspects of work teams, organizational change and development, cognitive styles, job stress, decision-making, and measurement.

3

Essential Conditions for Building Successful Teams
William G. Dyer

Over the years I have been haunted by the following question: "Why do some teams fail to improve their effectiveness in collaborating and functioning together, despite my best efforts to help them?" I wondered if there was something I could have done differently. Should I have used a different exercise, a new instrument for gathering data, a different theory or model about what a team is and what a facilitator does? I have found myself reading or hearing about what another person did that was successful and wondering if I should try this new approach the next time around.

After going through this self-examination process for the more than thirty years I have been doing team building, I have come to the conclusion that my ineffective efforts have been the result of certain critical conditions that must be addressed and hopefully managed if team building is to be successful. I believe that the absence of managing one or more of these conditions resulted in every failure experience I have had. Here are the key conditions that I think are essential to understand.

Adequate Diagnosis

Since I am an external consultant, a common experience for me is to receive a phone call from a human resource person from a company asking if I would be willing to come and help a particular group in that organization do some team building. I usually ask, "What are the problems this team is having?" If the HR person has any data about the team, he/she shares it with me, but I know this may not be accurate or adequate. I usually then ask for a chance to spend time talking with the team leader and, at times, team members to get their perspective on the team's difficulties. Sometimes I do a decent job of diagnosing the real problems facing that team, but sometimes my diagnostic processes have been inadequate. When I am called to help a team, they usually want help immediately and I feel pressured to take action before a thorough diagnosis has been made.

21

Here are some of the questions I ask to diagnose the scope of the problem: (1) Is this a real team in the sense that people must work together to achieve common goals or are they just a collection of people who work for the same boss and whose work really does not intersect? (2) Is this a work team, i.e., jobs are interconnected, or a decision team, wherein their major collaboration is to make decisions—about strategy, budgets, programs, policies, etc. (3) Accepting the assumption that team building can be time consuming and expensive, are their problems those that only some kind of team building effort will solve? I remember vividly the experience of Dr. Jerry Harvey, of Abilene Paradox fame, who was asked to do team building with a manager and his production foremen of a paper plant in New England. The symptoms were that work was not getting done on schedule or at appropriate production levels and people were blaming each other. Jerry met with this group several times over a period of months and production and morale problems did not improve significantly. One day a visiting engineer walked through the plant, listened, and said, "It sounds like your major drive shaft is not functioning properly."

The drive shaft was examined and found to be defective. Once the shaft was replaced the entire plant began to function properly. Productivity and morale improved. People then asked, "Why did we do all that team building when what we really needed was a new drive shaft?"

There is also the famous case of William Foote Whyte (Whyte, 1948) in the restaurant where a major problem was conflict between the waitresses and the chefs. These two groups were constantly haggling as waitresses put pressure directly on chefs to get their orders done immediately, and in the manner the waitresses wanted. A natural diagnosis would be that these two groups needed to get together and work out their differences. Whyte's solution was simpler: Eliminate the interaction between waitresses and chefs by putting up a spindle and have orders rotated from waitress to chef. Any problems were to be handled through the assistant manager.

Another time I was asked to do some team building with an academic department in a university. Their problem, as they saw it, was the inability to make necessary decisions fast enough. As I talked with and observed them in action, it was clear that they needed some training or instruction in decision making, not a total team building program. They were afflicted with "consensusitis," that is, they felt that all decisions, large and small, should be made by consensus and they felt that consensus meant everyone in complete agreement. I introduced them to Vroom's model (Vroom & Yetton, 1973) and examined the departmental decisions that should be made by the chairperson alone, the ones that needed consultation between the chair and members, and those decisions that should be made by consensus. We also defined consensus as a "hammered out" decision where all were committed to implementation even though they may have had some reservations. This diagnosis led to training and instruction, not a total team building program.

It takes time to do a thorough diagnosis. It may mean watching the team members interact over time, looking at their assignments, watching the dynamics as well as looking at the organizational conditions and constraints. A survey instrument that does not take into account the technical system, the culture, and the organizational demands and procedures and only focuses on the social system represented by team dynamics may miss some very important factors affecting team performance.

System Support

Some years ago I spent time training managers of a major oil company in the methods of doing team building. After several of these sessions, I asked for a follow-up survey to see how many of these managers were, in fact, doing any team building. The data gathered indicated that less than 25 percent had engaged in any of the processes I had been teaching. When asked "why not?" the primary response was: "In our yearly performance review there is nothing about team building activities. If I want to get a good review and subsequently the raises and promotions that are connected, I must pay attention to those factors my bosses (via the rating system) deem important."

This company had a forced ranking system. One third of all employees, including supervisors and managers, had to be ranked at the bottom, one third in the middle, and one third at the top. Managers knew that if they wanted to be in the top third they had to be seen as highly effective on the evaluation criteria. Since team building was not part of the criteria, it received little or no attention. I have generally found that unless the performance review system, and the reward system itself, identify team building as important, people who manage teams see it as interesting but unprofitable to spend time in this activity. Additionally I find that very few pay systems have found ways to reward the team. Team building may be seen as important and even one of the performance criteria, but often the reward system acknowledges only individual merit and contribution. Team members see time and energy spent on building the team as a nonprofitable expenditure of effort. Part of the diagnosis includes an examination of the performance review and reward systems of the organization asking for team development.

Culture Congruence

Several years ago, I did a piece of research asking American companies if they were doing team building, how much, and if not, why not (Dyer, 1994). Two of the reasons given for not doing team building were: (1) Bosses at higher levels did not see it as important; (2) While team building was listed as important in company statements of values and goals, there was no commitment at the highest management levels, hence no real allocation of time and resources for this activity.

I have found this incongruity in a variety of organizations. It is seen as popular or the "in" thing to be seen as being team oriented, but the long-term culture of the organization has never been team focused. I have worked in a number of companies where the cultural norms about management have been: A successful manager is one who is bottom-line oriented, shows real results (usually short term), is decisive, runs a tight ship, and is a good soldier. The latter means that one does what one is told, supports one's boss, and fits in to the acceptable pattern of management.

When such a company pretends to adopt team building, the managers are good soldiers and they do what they are told. But everyone gets the message that if one is a good team member in this organization, he/she finds out what the boss wants, keeps quiet, and goes along with what is expected. In real teams there is high trust, open communication, joint problem solving, and real (not pretended) commitment.

I have found two ways to understand something of the culture of an organization. One is to ask people, "What kind of behavior gets you in real trouble in this company?" Another is to ask employees, including managers, "What does this company say it believes in but what does it really see as important?" I then get them to identify the "espoused" culture and the "culture in practice" or in other words, the "real" versus the "ideal" culture. Again, this must be part of the diagnosis.

Commitment

There are those organizations where management does honestly support the idea of teamwork, and collaboration is part of the culture but team building efforts still struggle and often die out. Often this has to do with ongoing priorities. Team building is seen as useful, but it is a low priority effort.

When downsizing occurs, it is the budget for team development that is cut and the HR department responsible to spearhead the effort that is reduced. (This, incidently, is another barrier to team building, when the HR department and not line management is responsible for team building activities. However, it is symptomatic of priorities when HR departments are cut back.) In light of more pressing priorities, managers and team members will engage in some team building, but the real energy is focused elsewhere. Unless those responsible for pushing team development can see that team building is connected to high priority issues, they put team development on a back burner. It is part of the competency of the facilitator (to be discussed next) to help power people see the connection between team building and high priority strategic goals like profits, expanded markets, reduced costs, market share, etc.

Some years ago a vice-president of human resources from a major American food company came to see me and asked if I would be willing to do some team building with a new CEO and his staff. The CEO had a day and a half open on his schedule and wanted team building done at that time. When I asked for time to visit with the CEO to review the entire process, I was told there was an hour available on a particular date for a meeting. At that point I declined to participate in the project. I told the vice-president that there was not enough apparent real commitment to engage in a team building program that had a reasonable chance for success. The vice-president responded, "Well, you know I *can* find someone who will do team building on this schedule." I agreed that he probably could, but it would violate my sense of ethics to engage in a project I did not feel could be reasonably successful.

Competency of the Facilitator

I have found that most organizations will not commit real resources to team building unless someone is trying to facilitate this effort. I use the term "facilitate" to refer to a total process of moving a team building effort from acceptance by the power people to start the activity, then provide a consistent follow-up program. Sometimes this facilitation can be done by a person inside the system, sometimes by an outside expert, and often by a combination of both. I know that the most effective work I have done as an outside consultant has been a result of my collaboration with competent internal change agents.

Someone must help key decision makers see the connection between team building and the strategic future of the organization. This means the facilitator must understand something about strategic planning and the place the human factor has in business plans.

The facilitator must have a vision about the critical connection of human effort and business or organizational results and must be able to communicate this vision to others. In a broad sense, team building should probably be seen as part of a total organization development process—a way of looking at the social, technical, and management systems to see how the creative and productive efforts of human beings at all levels can be released, so organizational goals and human needs are consistently met.

At the actual team building level of action, the facilitator needs to help the team identify their goals and to help the team see how more effective collaboration, creative problem solving, conflict reduction, and commitment building will help the unit achieve their important goals.

I started doing team building in the early 1960s when the model for team building was the T group. The idea was that if you could put a working unit through a T group experience with its emphasis on interpersonal behavior and giving and receiving feedback, the team would somehow benefit. This was a very inadequate model for it did not connect the process with the goals of the group, its long-term history, the culture and systems that were connected, nor make any provision for long-term follow up.

As part of the team building process itself, the facilitator must be skillful, competent, and personally comfortable dealing with an authoritarian leader, handle emotionality, deal with conflicts, confront inappropriate actions, and generally model useful teamwork behaviors.

One person does not have to have all of these competencies, but these skills must be part of a facilitation team where different individuals may play different roles.

Turnover

One of the great bug-a-boos of team building efforts is the turnover of personnel. I have spent time and achieved real results helping a unit get molded into an effective work or decision team and then see the team leader transferred or a key member or two reassigned or leave for some reason. New people came in and the remaining members did not know how to integrate the newcomers, especially if one is the leader, and the team effectiveness quickly diminished.

It is important to have a commitment for team development in the organization because a new leader or member who joins a group in a truly team oriented culture, where management at all levels has bought into the process, knows that he/she is joining an existing team and there are expectations that time will be allocated for successful integration. This integration process will be supported by the boss to whom the team leader reports when time is spent in rebuilding the team.

The integration process in most units is superficial and inadequate. Usually the new member is asked to introduce him-/herself, give something of a background and the existing members give their names, ranks, and serial numbers. Nothing of the team's background, history, or norms are shared. In a productive integration session, the team explains its history and how it is functioning. The new member is asked for his/her reactions to this, and how that person would like to function in the team. As in Alcoholics Anonymous, the new member might even be assigned a "buddy" to meet one-on-one to explain the team's processes and help the member deal with team dynamics. It is also important that the existing members be flexible and allow the new member to make some changes or additions to the team's activities.

A new team leader must be willing to take time to understand the background of the team into which one is coming, share one's own experience and preferences, and work through some accommodations with the team members. All of this is part of what should be one of the guiding principles about team development: Team building is a process, not an event!

Follow Up

An effective team is characterized by having shared goals, a deep level of trust, a willingness for people to support and help each other, open communications, decisions that result in commitment to implement, clear assignments, and roles that relate to the goals, supportive leadership, and team structures and actions that facilitate teamwork. These are complex, sensitive, and often difficult conditions to achieve and maintain. They are not accomplished in one two-day initial team building session.

I feel discouraged when a manager tells me, "We did team building in 1989." I would like to hear, "We started team building in 1989 and we are still working at trying to function as an effective team."

Follow up takes a number of different forms. It can mean having a regular time after team meetings to critique what went well during the meeting and what needs to be improved. It may mean reviewing the team's goals and looking at current assignments and processes to see if the goals are accepted and are being accomplished. It may mean having an outsider come in and observe the team's actions and give the team some feedback.

Wayne Boss of the University of Colorado says it may also mean having follow-up sessions, one-on-one between boss and subordinate to deal with issues and concerns that each individual may have and help each member set personal goals and plans to achieve them (Boss, 1983). It may also mean involving the team leader in subsequent training programs on team leadership, strategic planning, conflict management, or dealing with diversity.

It should be part of the team's mentality, vision, and plan that working on maintaining the team includes constant attention to the critique and review of team functioning to see what has been going well and what still needs to be improved.

Conclusion

It has been my concern with this book on best practices for teams that people involved in facilitating team building may be seduced into thinking that effective team building is a cut and paste proposition. That is, one may think you can build effective teams by selecting a new theory or model, a new exercise or game, or a new instrument and put this altogether and find instant success. I have found building effective organizational teams to be hard work. It is a long-term procedure that requires understanding and dealing with a range of conditions that are much more than just helping a team deal with its own internal processes.

References

Boss, R.W. (1983). Team building and the problem of regression, *Journal of Applied Behavioral Science 19*, No. 1.

Dyer, W. G. (1994). *Team building: current issues and new alternatives*, Reading, MA: Addison-Wesley.

Vroom, V. H. and P. W. Yetton (1973). *Leadership and decision making*, Pittsburg, PA: University of Pittsburgh Press.

Whyte, W. F. (1948). *Human relations in the restaurant industry*, New York: McGraw-Hill.

About the Contributor

William G. (Bill) Dyer received his Ph.D. from the University of Wisconsin in 1955. Bill has combined teaching, administration, research, writing, and consulting in his professional career. In 1958 he attended his first NTL T group lab and worked extensively with NTL programs.

For the next ten years he was involved in T group training while holding an appointment at Brigham Young University. He found the T group did not lead to organizational change and shifted to an Organizational Development (OD) emphasis. He wrote the first book on team building in 1977 (*Team Building: Issues and Alternatives*) and has written fifteen books and sixty-five articles. He founded the Organizational Behavior department at BYU in 1970 and was Dean of the School of Management from 1979 to 1984. His consulting has taken him around the world with a wide variety of organizations. His last two books deal with improving the spiritual/interpersonal effectiveness of families and church groups.

Part II - Team Activities

4

It's Those Little Problems That Are Hard to Figure Out
Ed Rose

Overview
This exercise allows teams to experience group dynamics in a fun and nonthreatening environment. Participants are faced with a challenge to "save" a company by solving problems to keep pace with the competition. The focal points of this exercise are the value of team synergy; breaking down invisible walls within the company; internal benchmarking; effective communication; creativity; and lateral thinking. The exercise can be useful for self-discovery learning for any of the above listed learning points. The procedure outlined was created to deliver as a warm-up for a goal setting session.

The goal of the exercise is to allow participants the self-discovery that solving the problems would be easier if the departments worked together. In most cases the five problems are solved by the collective group but it's highly unlikely that one team solves all five problems.

The key to the success of the exercise is the initial set-up and the debriefing. It's a great way to get the participants energized for the working session.

Objective
Participants will attempt to solve problems that will save the company from failure. They will discover that there are benefits to working together as a team, and learn that team members sometimes place restrictions on themselves that block success.

Materials
1. Handout of the exercise, Attachment 4-A.
2. 3-foot piece of rope for each department
3. 6 toothpicks for each department
4. 1 "T" puzzle for each department. (Prepare puzzle pieces in advance using cardboard or construction paper. Use answer key to trace outline of "T.")
5. 1 envelope to hold toothpicks and "T" puzzle

Number of Participants

Ten to 40 people depending on the skill of the facilitator. Consideration should be given to the size of the room and ability to manage the group dynamics.

Physical Set-Up

One large conference or training room and, if possible, break-out rooms for each department. At the very least, separate areas in the room where groups can meet undisturbed.

Time

45 minutes: 20 minutes for the exercise and 25 minutes for debriefing.

Groups (if more than 20) will take more time for debriefing.

Process

1. The facilitator informs the participants that they are going to learn firsthand about team dynamics and have some fun.

2. The participants are separated into departments. A group of two to six people in a department works best. It's better to have four departments with two in each department than fewer departments and more people on a team. The goal is to create a traditional company structure.

3. If separate rooms are available, the facilitator should use them. If not, the departments should be separated based on space available.

4. Each department selects a department manager and asks that person to report to the facilitator.

5. The facilitator conducts the meeting with the department managers, stressing the importance of solving the problems. Emphasize they must produce (the facilitator can "slip" in that everyone is in this together, but doesn't force the statement). They are to leave with a mission to succeed and under time constraints (15 minutes).

   - The facilitator distributes one handout per department.
   - While the meeting is going on, the employees and team members should occupy themselves as real employees would do without directions.

6. If the facilitator is using a participant that has gone through the exercise, identify him/her as the plant manager. Let the individual conduct the meeting with the facilitator acting as the CEO of the company. The plant manager should walk around and ask how things are going, if the department is going to make the schedule, and if they need any help. If the plant manager is asked to help, have him/her ask questions that will lead the team to the answer—the plant manager is *not* to give the answer. The facilitator must explain expectations clearly to the plant manager. The facilitator should play the role of plant manager if no participant is identified for the role.

7. The facilitator checks each group on a regular basis and takes notes for debriefing, listing specific behaviors that can be used for discussion in the debriefing.

   Note: The facilitator stops after 15 minutes regardless of the number of problems solved.

8. The facilitator has each department answer the following questions while separated from the entire group.

   A. Were you successful as a team?
   B. How did you define your team?
   C. How would you rate your teamwork on a scale of 1 to 10?
   D. What do you do well?
   E. What could be improved?
   F. How did the department manager affect your behavior?

9. The entire group is brought back together (all the teams/departments) and they review questions A through F.

   Note: The idea of this exercise is that the plant manager conducted a meeting with his/her managers to inform them of the problem and task that needed to be accomplished to save the company. Most likely, they went back to their groups and continued as individual departments with separate goals. The point is that if the company fails, then they all fail. During the problem-solving activity, teams will display various behaviors that promote building walls and destructive competitive behaviors.

Key Question

Once the group realizes they have a common goal, the facilitator asks them if that awareness changes their answers to questions A through F.

The facilitator should take notes of both negative and positive team building behavior and use them during the debriefing, and ask the participants:

"What can be learned from this exercise that will benefit your future team project(s)?"

Variations

If some participants have experience with any of the problems, the facilitator should use that in the debriefing and determine who took advantage of that knowledge.

If the facilitator knows in advance that a manager has been through this activity, the manager can be the plant manager in the exercise. He/she can run the meeting with the department managers. The manager is an "expert" and experience shows that no one will ask him/her for help, which provides great material for debriefing.

It's those little problems that are hard to figure out

FY '96 Sector Goals:

All departments must solve four of the following five problems during FY '96 (which ends in fifteen minutes). All department managers should submit their answers to the plant manager (the Facilitator) at the end of FY '96.

Message from the plant manager:

"Our competitors have already solved these problems, and for us to be successful as a company, we must find the answers. Good luck in your problem solving."

Dept. A

Dept. B

Dept. C

FY '96 Goals

Solve four out of the five problems

1. Problem: Create four equilateral triangles with the six toothpicks you have in front of you.

2. All members of the team should be able to perform this task. Objective: Take hold of each end of the rope. Once you have hold of the ends of the rope, you can't let go. Now make a knot in the rope.

3. Solve the "T" puzzle by forming the four pieces in the envelope into the letter "T."

4. The fallen sign: A man was walking in a country unfamiliar to him. He came to a crossroads where he found that the signpost showing the directions of the roads had fallen over. How did he find out which way to go?

5. An odd story: Three men went into a diner and each had a single cup of coffee. Each put an odd number of lumps of sugar into his coffee. In total they put 12 lumps of sugar into their cups. How many lumps did each consume?

Explanation of the puzzles:

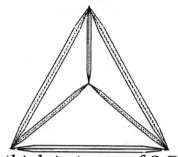

1. The toothpicks — think in terms of 3-D.

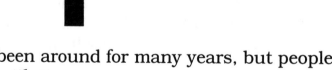

2. The key here is to break your paradigm and fold your arms as shown before grabbing the ends of the rope. When you pull your arms apart, you have a knot. There are others ways of doing this, too. The facilitator should make the final judgment call comparing your method to the world-class technique above.

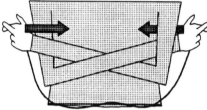

3. The "T" puzzle has been around for many years, but people still have problems with it.

4. The fallen sign: The man put the sign up facing the direction he came from, thus the other direction would be correct.

5. How many lumps?: 1, 1, and 10. The 1's are odd numbers, and 10 lumps of sugar is certainly a very odd number of lumps to put into a cup of coffee.

About the Contributor

Ed Rose, Training Manager for Harris Semiconductor in Palm Bay, Florida, has over 30 years experience with teams and teamwork, both in industry and the world of sports. He has presented internationally on the subject of self-directed work teams, and he has published numerous articles and papers on self-directed work teams in technical journals and magazines. Ed has played on five world championship softball teams. He is also a member of the International Brotherhood of Magicians.

5

The Team Formation Checklist: A New Team Activity
Zenger-Miller, Inc.

Objectives

The purpose of this activity is to help members of a new team gather information about the team and their role in the team. More specifically, the activity will help team members develop a clear understanding of:

1. Why the team was formed.
2. How the team and its work fit into the larger organization.
3. What the performance expectations are for the team.

Participants

An intact team of under 12 people.

Time

One to two hours.

Physical Setting

Chairs around a conference table.

Materials and Resources

A copy of Attachment 5-A for each team member.

Process

1. Prior to the meeting, provide a copy of the Checklist to the team leader or senior manager who will be responsible for answering the questions. Ask this person to prepare his/her answers in advance of the meeting.

2. Open the meeting by reviewing the objectives and the format of the session. Emphasize the importance of asking questions if an answer is not clear.

3. Distribute copies of the Checklist. Ask team members to take notes on their copy.

4. Ask the team leader or senior manager to read each question and provide the team's answer. As team members proceed through the Checklist, stop and ask for questions from the team.

5. Conclude the session by summarizing the key points and thanking the team leader or senior manager.

6. Ask one of the team members to prepare a summary of the answers for distribution to the other team members and to other key stakeholders.

7. Meet with the team after the team leader or senior manager leaves to review the session, the answers provided, and to identify any areas requiring additional information.

Variations

1. The Checklist may be used when the team:

    -   is starting a new project
    -   needs to adjust to a change in direction or plans
    -   has difficulty meeting deadlines
    -   has a new leader
    -   is clarifying roles and responsibilities
    -   changes its focus

2. The Checklist can be given to a new team member to help him/her get oriented to the team.

Team Formation Checklist

Directions: Complete this checklist with your team in mind. As you listen to the team leader or senior manager, write their answers in the space provided. Then indicate if you have enough information in each area to go forward with your work as team.

Enough Information?

Yes　No
☐　☐　1. What is the team's mission or purpose?

☐　☐　2. How does that mission fit into the larger organization mission?

☐　☐　3. What are the expectations for this team? What specifically are we to accomplish?

☐　☐　4. What specific goals or milestones already exist?

Enough Information?

Yes No

☐   ☐   5. If goals or milestones don't already exist, what is the time frame for developing them?

☐   ☐   6. What is the time frame for results?

☐   ☐   7. How will we get the information we need?

☐   ☐   8. What resources will be available to us?

☐   ☐   9. Will we be doing activities that we don't currently know how to do? If so, how will we get the training we need?

Enough Information?

Yes No

☐   ☐   10. What process will we use to connect with the larger organization?

☐   ☐   11. What time commitment will participation on this team require from each of us?

☐   ☐   12. What is each team member's specific role? long-term responsibilities?

Enough Information?

Yes	No	
☐	☐	13. What are the limits on our authority to make decisions?
☐	☐	14. Who approves decisions that are outside our limits?
☐	☐	15. What is our budget?
☐	☐	16. When will this team disband?

About the Contributor

Zenger-Miller, Inc. is an international consulting, educational, and training company that specializes in measurably improving individual and organizational performance by helping organizations focus on customers, involve employees, manage processes, and develop leaders.

Zenger-Miller offers a full spectrum of consulting, educating, and training for all organizational levels. Executives, managers, individual contributors, team leaders, and members all benefit from the knowledge, enhanced skills, and useful, practical tools that Zenger-Miller provides.

6

The Team Icon Autobiography: A Get Acquainted Exercise

Bette Krakau

Objectives

The purpose of this activity is to help team members learn more about each other by opening up and sharing about themselves. Through this exercise, participants will be able to identify similarities and differences among team members. This activity is particularly useful during the early formation of team development when building trust and open communication is important.

Participants

This activity is suitable for any natural or intact work team, cross-functional, or project team.

The ideal size of the team is four to eight members to ensure full participation by each person. This exercise can be facilitated easily with four to six teams.

Time

Allow 10 to 15 minutes for every team member to individually share information about their life and 15 to 20 minutes to develop the "team icon autobiography," approximately 5 minutes per team for debriefing, and 5 to 10 minutes to discuss the application of the information. **Total time:** 40 to 50 minutes (add 5 minutes for each additional team for the debriefing).

Physical Setting

Round tables or participants seated in a circle around a flipchart stand.

Materials

Each team will need a full piece of flipchart paper, a variety of colored markers (the scented kind are preferred by participants), and masking tape or push pins for posting on the wall if flipcharts are not available for each team.

Process

1. Prepare ahead of time on a flipchart an example of a "team icon autobiography" to share with the group to help them visualize the end result. Use eight to ten icons, pictures, or symbols.

2. Introduce the exercise by asking the group, "What is an icon?" [An icon is a pictorial representation of something.] Next ask, "What is an autobiography?" [Remind participants that it is the story of a person's life written by the person.]

    Explain to the group that each team will be developing their own "team icon autobiography," or story of their life in pictures or symbols.

3. Show the group the example you have developed, Attachment 6-A, of a team icon autobiography.

4. Explain that you would like each team member to share information about their life to identify similarities and differences among team members. This may include facts about where they were born, family and educational background, hobbies, interests, and career or work history.

5. Suggest that the team start by going around the table or circle and ask everyone, individually, to share two or three pieces of information about their life. Inform participants that they will have 10 minutes for this sharing. (If you have a large group of seven to eight participants, you may want to add 5 minutes.) Let them know when 5 minutes are up.

6. Next, ask the participants to identify the similarities and differences on the team. For example, a similarity might be that all team members were born in a different state than the one they presently live in. A difference might be that each member started their work history at a different company.

7. Explain that as a team they will depict these similarities and differences in eight to ten pictures or symbols on the flipchart paper. Encourage the group to be creative using a variety of pictures, symbols, and colors. Allow 15 to 20 minutes depending on how many people there are on each team.

8. When the entire group comes back together, ask for a team spokesperson to share the "team icon autobiography." The facilitator and participants from other teams can ask questions for clarification.

9. When each team has shared their icon autobiography, review the exercise by asking these questions:

   • What did you learn about your team from this exercise?
   • Were there any surprises?
   • Before this exercise, did you think you knew everything there was to know about your teammates? Do you think there is still more to learn?
   • How did you feel when you were first asked to do this exercise?
   • What concerns did you have?
   • How do you feel now about the exercise?

10. Finally, ask the teams to discuss how they can apply this information on similarities and differences back on the job to enhance team effectiveness. Allow 5 to 10 minutes for this discussion.

11. Encourage teams to take their icon autobiography back to their work area and post it on the wall or bulletin board.

Variations

Prior to the activity, the facilitator develops four to five specific questions and team members share the answers with each other to develop the team icon autobiography.

Some examples are:

   • What city, state, or country did you grow up in?
   • What classes did you like the best in school? the least?
   • What did you do on your last vacation?
   • What is your favorite location for a vacation?
   • In what aspect of your job do you feel the most knowledgeable? least knowledgeable?
   • What do you like to do in your spare time?

- What is your favorite sport? least favorite?
- What kind of music do you like? dislike?
- What is your favorite way to spend a Saturday afternoon?
- What adjective would you use to describe yourself?
- What is your favorite television show?
- Who is your hero?

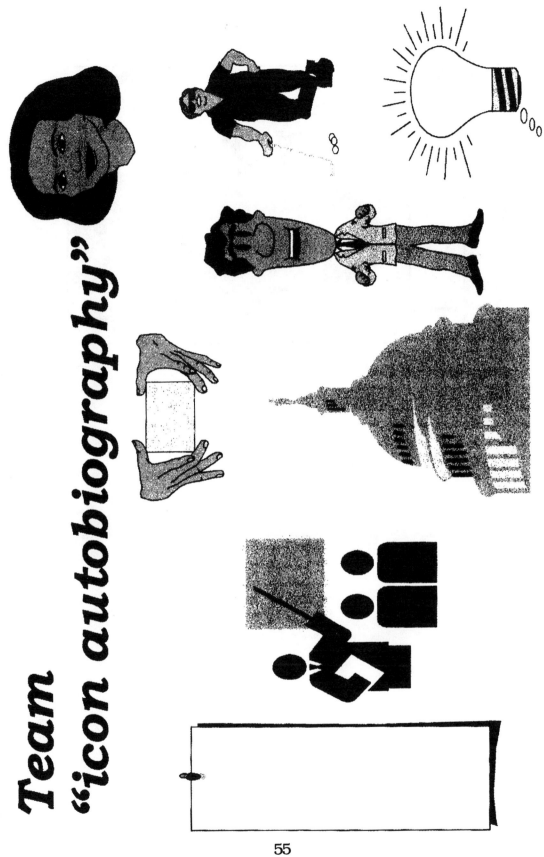

Team
"icon autobiography"

Explanation of Symbols

1. *Woman's face:* this is a team of all women.

2. *Hands:* team members like to "show their cards" and be open in communicating with others.

3. *Flipchart/group discussion:* they like to lead meetings and facilitate discussions.

4. *Capital:* all team members are from the state capital.

5. *Man:* they are married.

6. *Golf:* this is their hobby and they enjoy playing with their husbands.

7. *Light bulb:* they are creative and have many ideas to contribute to the team.

Reference

American Society for Training and Development. (1992, December). How to build a successful team. *INFO-LINE,* p. 2. Reviews the stages of team development (forming, storming, norming, performing) proposed by M.A.C. Jenson and B.W. Tuckman in *Group and organization studies* (1977).

About the Contributor

Bette Krakau's background includes more than 20 years of organization and management development experience as both an internal and external consultant. This experience has been with a broad range of organizations including The Gillette Company and National Computer Systems (as an internal consultant); 3M; BMW; General Electric; Mettler-Toledo; State of South Carolina; and Agricultural Cooperative Development International (as an external consultant). Bette provides consulting services in the areas of team development and effectiveness, leadership development, strategic planning, and customer service. She is a frequent speaker at major conferences including the American Society for Training and Development International Conference where this exercise was presented in a session entitled "Shazam! You're a Team: Demystifying Team Development."

7

Team Growth: A Learning Game
Sivasailam Thiagarajan

Tuckman's model of developmental stages in a small group, first published in 1965, has definitely withstood the test of time. His constructs of forming, storming, norming, and performing elegantly explain the stages in the growth of a team and help its members understand why certain things happen the way they do. While most teams are familiar with Tuckman's sequential labels, few take the time to explore the details of exactly what is involved in each stage. The board game, *Team Growth*, which is described below encourages extensive exploration of the four stages. If played after a brief introduction to the developmental stages, it can result in an effective understanding of what to expect during different stages of a team's development.

Objective
To identify attitudes, behaviors, perceptions, expectations, problems, tactics, and strategies associated with different stages in a team's development.

Time Requirement
30 to 45 minutes

Participants
Any number can play, divided into groups of two to six at each game board.

Supplies
Game cards. Statements about different attitudes, behaviors, perceptions, expectations, problems, tactics, and strategies associated with different stages in a team's development are printed on 80 different cards. Each statement is related to at least one of the four stages in a team's development. Each card also contains a random three-digit number for identification purposes. There are also ten blank cards in the set.

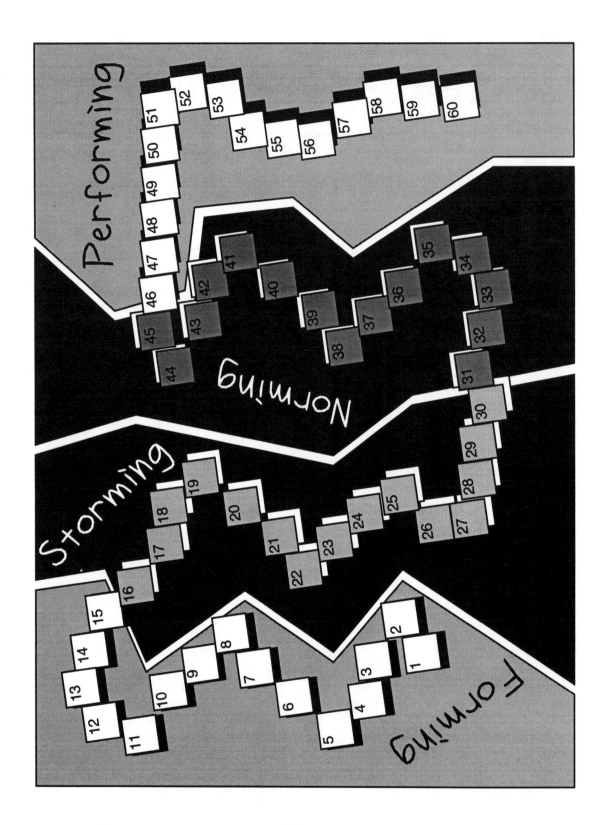

To prepare a set of game cards, type the 80 statements given in Attachment 7-A on cards. If you are planning to produce several sets, divide pieces of 8 1/2" x 11" paper into eight equal parts. Type your master set centered on each of the eight areas on ten sheets of paper. Photocopy on card stock and cut the copies to produce the cards.

Game board. This board has 60 spaces, divided into four stages of 15 spaces each. The boxes are labeled according to the stage: forming, storming, norming, and performing.

A reproducible game board is provided on the previous page. For best results, have this page enlarged 200 percent at your local photocopy shop, photocopy on card stock, and cut to produce the cards.

Game pieces. Each player chooses a plastic pawn of a different color. These pieces are moved across the game board to reflect the progress of the player.

Feedback sheet. This sheet lists the card numbers and the correct stage (or stages) associated with them. The feedback sheet is used for settling disputes during the play of the game.

Photocopy Attachment 7-B to produce the feedback sheets for your games.

Flow of the Game

Preliminaries. Ask each participant to choose a piece and place it at the starting position on the game board.

Dealing the cards. Ask a player to shuffle the packet of cards and deal seven to each, including her/himself. Ask all players to study their cards and separate those that are associated with the first stage in a team's development.

Showing the cards. Beginning with the player to the left of the dealer, each player shows his/her selected cards associated with the first stage. If the other players agree that these cards are associated with the first stage, then the player moves his/her counter the number of spaces on the game board equal to the number of cards.

Blank cards. If a player received a blank card, he/she can use it as a part of the collection by making an appropriate statement associated with the first stage. This statement should not duplicate any statement found on the other selected cards.

Challenge. Immediately after a player has read a card (or made a statement for a blank card), any other player may challenge that statement if he/she believes that it is not associated with the first stage. The first player to yell, "Challenge!" is designated to be the official challenger.

Persuasion. The challenger tries to convince the player that the card is not associated with the stage. The player, in turn, attempts to convince the challenger to take back his/her challenge by proving that the activity is definitely associated with the stage.

If the challenger convinces the player, this is what happens:
- The player removes the card from the selected set for the round. He/she advances according to the number of remaining cards.
- The challenger advances his/her piece by one space for being successful.

If the player convinces the challenger to withdraw the challenge, this is what happens:
- The player advances his/her piece by one space. (This is in addition to advancing the piece according to the number of selected cards.)
- The challenger moves back his/her piece by one space. (If the challenger does not have his/her piece on the board yet, there is no penalty.)

Settling disputes. Sometimes neither the challenger nor the player may be able to convince the other. In this situation, someone checks with the feedback sheet for the official verdict.

- If the challenge is valid, then the incorrect card is removed from the player's set of selected cards for the round. In addition, the player moves his/her piece by one space. (If the player's piece is not on the board yet, this penalty does not apply.)
- If the challenge is invalid, then the challenger moves back his/her piece by two spaces. (If the challenger's piece is not on the board yet, this penalty does not apply.)

Continuation of the round. The player sets aside his/her cards (including those which were not selected) on a face-down discard pile. The round is continued with each player taking a turn to read the cards (and to make a statement for a blank card).

Continuing the game. At the end of the round, the next player shuffles the original pile of cards and deals seven to each, including her-/himself. The new round is conducted as before.

Stage Change. Whenever a player's piece advances to, or beyond, the first space of a new stage, he/she will select cards associated with that stage in the future rounds. Thus, if the player's piece is on spaces 1-15 at the beginning of a round, he/she will look for cards associated with the *forming* stage; if it is on spaces 16-30, he/she will look for cards associated with the *storming* stage; if it is on spaces 31-45, he/she will look for cards associated with the *norming* stage; and if it is on spaces 46-60, he/she will look for cards associated with the *performing* stage.

It is possible for different players to be selecting cards associated with different stages—if their pieces are in different sections of the board.

Using the discard pile. If the dealer runs out of activity cards during a deal, he/she picks up the discard pile, shuffles the cards, and continues the deal.

Conclusion. Any player who lands on, or advances beyond, the last space on the board wins the game. However, this round is continued, and if more than one player reaches or crosses the last space, they are all winners.

Debriefing

To get the maximum value from the play of *Team Growth*, be sure to debrief the players after the game. Begin by inviting the participants to discuss their experiences with the game. After this open-ended discussion, structure the review with a few questions. Some suggested questions are listed below. Read each question and ask the participants to silently think of the response. After a suitable pause, invite the participants to share their responses and to discuss them.

- Can you recall a statement that is clearly associated with *each* of the four stages of team development?
- Can you recall a statement that is associated with several different stages of team development?
- If you are forced to make only one statement about each of the four stages, what would they be?
- Which of the four stages do you feel is the most frustrating one? Which stage is the most rewarding one?
- What would be a logical stage to follow the performing stage? What could be some statements associated with this stage?
- Think back on what happened to your group as you played the game. Did your group go through different stages of team development? What behaviors indicated your passage through different stages?
- Think of one of the teams that you belong to. At what stage of development is this team? What evidence do you have to support your conclusion?

Variations

Time requirement. You can easily adjust the playing time by specifying how long the game is to be played. For example, you can play the game for 15 minutes. In this situation, change the rule for winning the game: the player who is farthest along the game board at the end of 15 minutes is the winner.

Number of participants. You can play this game with two to six players. If you have more players, divide them into teams of equal size and have the team members make joint decisions. For example, if you have 20 players, organize them into five teams of four players each.

Settling disputes. In this version, we used the feedback sheet for settling disputes. Instead, the facilitator or the instructor can act as the judge. Alteratively, you can have the uninvolved players (other than the original player and the challenger) act as the jury and decide who has more logical arguments.

Spaces on the game board. If you want to spice up your game board, mark a random set of spaces with these labels:

- "Double": If you land on this space, you advance the number of spaces equal to twice the number of selected cards—during the next round.
- "Miss a Turn": If you land on this space, you don't get to play the next round.
- "Wild Stage": If you land on this space, you can select cards associated with any one of the four stages—during the next round. For example, space 18 is usually associated with the storming stage. But if it is marked "Wild Stage," you can select cards from the fourth stage, if it has the most number of cards.

Reference

Tuckman, Bruce W. (1965). "Developmental sequence in small groups." *Psychological Bulletin, 63 (6)*, 384-399.

Statements for Game Cards

101. All members participate in all team activities.
102. Disagreements become more civilized and less divisive.
103. Feelings of *us-them* increase.
104. Groundrules become a second nature to team members.
105. If there is a formal leader, team members tend to obey him/her.
106. Leadership is shared among different members.
107. Leadership role is rotated among appropriate members.
108. Members are anxious and suspicious of the task ahead.
109. Members are more committed to their subgroups, not to the team as a whole.
110. Members are more friendly toward each other.
111. Members are not committed to the group's goal.
112. Members are not fully committed to the team's goal.
113. Members are proud to be chosen for the team.
114. Members are relieved that things are progressing smoothly.
115. Members are satisfied about the team's progress.
116. Members argue with each other—even when they agree on the basic issues.
117. Members attempt to figure out their roles and functions.
118. Members begin to enjoy team activities.
119. Members challenge, evaluate, and destroy ideas.
120. Members choose sides.
121. Members compete with each other.
122. Members deal with each other with greater confidence.
123. Members develop great loyalty to the team.
124. Members don't have enough information to trust each other.
125. Members feel comfortable about their roles in the team.
126. Members feel confident about disagreeing with each other.
127. Members feel empowered. They take initiative without checking with the leader.
128. Members feel excitement, anticipation, and optimism.
129. Members form subgroups who get into conflicts.
130. Members freely ask questions and express their frustrations.
131. Members have a better idea of who to trust and who to distrust.
132. Members have a realistic sense of trust based on their experiences with each other.
133. Members have clear understanding of the strengths and weaknesses of each other.
134. Members take a "wait-and-see" approach.
135. Members tend to avoid the tasks and argue about groundrules.
136. Members tend to be polite to each other.
137. Members tend to become complacent.
138. Members understand the team processes.

139. Members' feelings and attitudes keep fluctuating.
140. Most conversations are directed to and from the team leader.
141. Most discussions are about getting the task done.
142. Most discussions are shallow.
143. No groundrules established. Members depend on their previous team experiences to decide how to behave.
144. Regular team meetings are replaced by a variety of as-needed communications.
145. Several conflicts develop.
146. Some members become bored with the routine and begin looking for new challenges.
147. Some members demonstrate passive resistance.
148. Some members dominate team discussions.
149. Some members still dominate team discussions.
150. Status of members inside the team is based on their status outside.
151. Team activities become more informal.
152. Team becomes creative in accomplishing its goal.
153. Team begins celebrating its success.
154. Team begins to receive payoffs.
155. Team demonstrates greatest levels of flexibility.
156. Team establishes groundrules for interactions among the members.
157. Team generates solutions that are acceptable to all members.
158. Team goal is unclear.
159. Team groundrules are clearly established.
160. Team holds abstract discussions of concepts and issues.
161. Team is able to prevent potential problems.
162. Team is likely to suffer from *groupthink* and lack of objective evaluation.
163. Team is not very productive.
164. Team members are committed to the goal and to the task.
165. Team members are more natural and less self-conscious in their interactions.
166. Team members attempt to understand their goal and task.
167. Team members complain about organizational barriers.
168. Team members disagree and argue with each other.
169. Team members disagree with the leader.
170. Team members don't participate fully.
171. Team members resolve conflicts easily.
172. Team members seek clear guidance.
173. Team members talk and argue with each other.
174. Team spends more time on task and very little time on groundrules.

175. The team becomes increasingly productive.
176. The team has a better understanding of the goal, but still needs to guided.
177. The team's commitment to itself extends to commitment to the organization.
178. There is a clear understanding of the goals and roles among team members.
179. Trust is at the highest level.
180. Trust level increases.

Feedback Sheet

Card Number	Stage	Card Number	Stage	Card Number	Stage	Card Number	Stage
101	p	121	s	141	n,p	161	p
102	n	122	n	142	f	162	n,p
103	n	123	n,p	143	f	163	f,s
104	p	124	f,n	144	p	164	n,p
105	f	125	p	145	s	165	n,p
106	n,p	126	n,p	146	n,p	166	n
107	n,p	127	p	147	s	167	f
108	f	128	f	148	f	168	s
109	s	129	s	149	s	169	s
110	n,p	130	s	150	f	170	f,s
111	f	131	n	151	n,p	171	n,p
112	f	132	n	152	p	172	f
113	f	133	p	153	p	173	s
114	n	134	f	154	p	174	p
115	p	135	s	155	p	175	n,p
116	s	136	f	156	n	176	n
117	n	137	p	157	p	177	n,p
118	p	138	p	158	f	178	n,p
119	s	139	s	159	n,p	179	p
120	s	140	f	160	f	180	n

About the Contributor

Dr. Sivasailam "Thiagi" Thiagarajan designs and delivers public and in-house workshops on different aspects of performance technology, OD, team building, and management. He is the designer of more than a hundred training games and simulations, including BARNGA, which simulates cross-cultural conflicts and TRIANGLES, which simulates the costs and rewards of focusing on the customer. Thiagi has been the president of the National Society for Performance and Instruction (NSPI) and of the North American Simulation and Gaming Association (NASAGA).

8

Building a Trust-Based Organization
Richard P. Kropp, Jr.

Purpose and Introduction

Cross-functional teams have become, and will continue to be, a key element in the ability of the organization to achieve its goals and objectives. This is largely due to the fact that the growing need for innovation and responsiveness requires that managers from various areas pool their collective knowledge, resources, and expertise to meet competitive challenges. And, in order for these cross-functional teams to operate effectively, efficiently, and productively, they require a baseline of trust—meaning that all team members must be willing to share resources and information. Consequently, cross-functional team members must exhibit a high level of trust.

This high degree of trust is usually absent in the traditional bureaucratic organization where decision making is often centralized, with few cross-functional interactions at lower levels, and influence is often unilateral and exercised in a top-down manner. It is in this type of organization where a large part of the manager's role is devoted to managing vertical dependencies, that is, directing and monitoring the work efforts of subordinates and acquiring control.

In contrast to the traditional bureaucratic organization, flatter organizational structures allow for the creation of team structures where there is a requirement for a great deal of interaction and trust among and between workers and their manager. And, unlike the traditional bureaucratic organizations, in the flatter organizational structure, where there are trust-based teams, managers are required to spend an increased amount of time interacting with individuals outside their vertical chain of command. And, due to this requirement, the manager's effectiveness is contingent upon his/her ability to influence those over whom he/she has no formal authority.

Trust-based teams also place high premiums on involving employees in decision making and increasing the operational autonomy of individuals and work groups, with the result being the manager shifting his/her role from one where he/she gains control of employees to one where he/she gains commitment and cooperation.

Thus, managers in trust-based organizations, as they attempt to influence peers and co-equals, must alter their influence tactics to account for the unique dynamics that exist in these critical relationships.

With this background, the following activity is designed to help intact work groups build the basis for a trust-based organization.

Objectives

- To provide the participants with a vehicle for understanding the concepts of trust and its role in cross-functional teamwork.
- To examine the dynamics of building trust.
- To develop an awareness of the need for interpersonal trust among and between members of cross-functional teams.

Time

90 minutes; may vary depending on the number of team members

Number of Participants

Any number but is ideally suited for an intact cross-functional team. It may also be used in a training session as an opening to a longer term session.

Materials and Equipment

- Paper and pencil
- A copy of Attachment 8-A for each participant

Procedure

1. You should begin the activity by giving a short lecture on the nature of cross-functional teams and the critical role that trust plays in the ability to make them successful. You should suggest that trust is developed along a continuum extending from open sharing of information to a closed environment in which little information is shared.

2. Ask the group members to form two or three groups and generate a list of descriptors for each end of the continuum. The open end might be characterized as direct, free, and honest, while the closed end might be characterized as hidden, unwilling, and tentative.

3. Having processed this discussion you should tell the group that the degree of trust in the cross-functional group depends upon the responses to the following questions or statements:

A. Is behavior directed toward achieving goals held in common or directed toward achieving personal goals?

B. Is the environment open or closed?

C. Do team members have an accurate personal understanding of their own needs or are they hidden/misrepresented?

D. Is behavior predictable yet flexible and not designed to take other members by surprise?

E. Threats and bluffs are not used in the team process.

F. Logical and innovative processes are used to support team member views and not irrational defensive arguments.

G. Success demands that stereotypes be dropped and ideas are considered on merit.

4. You should either form several small groups or keep the large group intact and pose each of the questions in relation to the cross-functional team under discussion, having the group use the "Analysis Matrix," Attachment 8-A, to capture the product of the discussion. Once the groups have completed their work, reconvene and process the activity using the following question:

   • Is there a way to develop action steps to resolve issues that result from the answers to these questions?

5. Having developed a list of possible alternatives, bring the activity to a close by reminding the group that trust must be developed if cross-functional teams are to help the organization achieve its goals.

ANALYSIS MATRIX

Question/Statement	Response	Alternative
A. Is behavior directed toward achieving goals held in common or directed toward achieving personal goals?		
B. Is the environment open or closed?		
C. Do team members have an accurate personal understanding of their own needs or are they hidden/misrepresented?		
D. Is behavior predictable yet flexible and not designed to take other members by surprise?		
E. Threats and bluffs are not used in the team process.		
F. Logical and innovative processes are used to support team member views and not irrational defensive arguments.		
G. Success demands that stereotypes be dropped and ideas are considered on merit.		

About the Contributor

Dick Kropp has over 20 years of experience as an internal HRD consultant and manager with such companies as AT&T, First National Bank of Boston, and Wang Laboratories. He is currently Assistant Professor in the Department of Organizational Communication at Suffolk University in Boston. He holds a Ph.D. in Human Resource Education from Boston University.

Dick is also Managing Partner of The Davies Group, Inc., a tactical human resource consulting firm in Nashua, NH. He has conducted team building sessions, designed human resource systems, and developed management development strategies for a variety of organizations.

He is also co-author of the best seller, *50 Activities for Team Building,* Volume 1 (HRD Press, 1992) and *50 Activities for Self-Directed Teams* (HRD Press, 1994).

Dick is a former President of the Massachusetts Chapter of ASTD and was formerly Region 1 Director.

9

The Site Visit Resource Guide
Stu Noble

Introduction

A key strategy for maintaining a competitive edge in today's rapidly changing marketplace is learning from other organizations. Task forces, reengineering teams, work redesign teams, process improvement teams, or management groups seeking to expand their perspectives, are routinely visiting companies to accelerate their learning of new ideas.

There is little question of the potential value of organizations providing learning opportunities to each other as a "regular way of doing business." Certainly, today's emphasis upon building learning organizations has challenged assumptions and begun to break down even the strongest "*not invented here*" traditions.

However, the ultimate value of these visits is often limited in several different areas, such as:

- Failure to identify the *specific* aspects most relevant to value added learning.
- Lack of *advanced preparation* to maximize the value of the time and resource investment.
- The inability to *clearly summarize* and fully articulate to others what has been learned.

In addition, it is not uncommon that large companies have multiple teams visit the same sites without knowledge of each others' activities.

To address the needed for more focused, efficient, and effective use of site visits as a learning strategy, the material provided in this *Resource Guide* is intended to be used by teams as a tool to aid in planning, collecting, organizing, and condensing useful information gained during site visits. This *Guide* has been designed to be used as a stand alone resource or as a complement to *Innovative Site Visits: A Planning and Preparation Guide for Success* (William O. Lytle, Block Petrella Weisbord, Inc. Publishing, 1991) and other resources.

Note: This *Guide* is not intended to be a "how to" approach to benchmarking, although it can be useful for benchmarking trips as well as *any* other team approach, both formal and informal, to access learning from their site visits to other organizations.

The Site Visit Process

After the *Key Areas of Focus* are identified, follow these steps.

Step 1: ⇒ Research, brainstorm possible site visit locations.

Step 2: ⇒ Prioritize locations; assure that all focus areas are covered.

Step 3: ⇒ Assign team members to each site. Assure preparedness.
- Conduct training, as required.

Step 4: ⇒ Make initial contact.

Step 5: ⇒ Develop, send visit confirmation letter.
- Include questions and/or topics of specific interest.

Step 6: ⇒ Research, if available, background of location to visit.
- Contact others in your company familiar with this organization?
- Articles, journals, conferences and seminars, etc.

Step 7: ⇒ Develop and organize questions for visit; be clear about desired outcomes.
- Be sure to take information about *your company* if asked.

Step 8: ⇒ Visit site.
- Who asks what? How will you record information received?

Step 9: ⇒ Organize, discuss information received.

Step 10: ⇒ Prepare concise summary report.

Step 11: ⇒ Send a "Thank You."

Selecting Site Visit Locations: (Steps 1 and 2)

A. Define criteria for selection based on project requirements, typically including aspects such as:

- Products or service
- Technology
- Size
- Geographic location
- Type of industry
- Nature of the work
- Union/non-union
- Specific features (i.e., work teams, pay-for-skill, gain-sharing, employee involvement programs, TQM or reengineering experience, etc.)

B. Brainstorm list of potential candidates.

- Internal Sources: organizations or functions within the company
- External Sources: Other organizations or competitors

C. Research, gather data.

- Evaluate.
- Assure coverage of all key areas of focus.
- Refine and/or consolidate the list.

D. Prioritize final choices.

- Review to assure list meets pre-determined criteria.

Defining Areas of Focus

Critical to the success in obtaining value from a team's site visit are:

- the clear definition of the purpose of their project
- clarification of project or research boundaries
- defining the areas of focus, and their key elements to guide data collection and analysis

These areas of focus usually fall into one of many categories, such as:

- Core process(es)
- Key functions or operations
- Organizational practices or characteristics
- Organizational "whole system" design

Begin by identifying the critical areas of focus in your team's project then, in each area, define the key elements or aspects for pinpointing data collection and analysis. Conclude by developing questions that enable you to obtain this information from chosen site visits to other organizations (or within your own company).

Examples of Area of Focus and Key Elements for the "Core Process" category:

Area of Focus   (Core Process): Delivering timely data to our customers

Key Elements: Technology; response or cycle time; work flow; continuous improvement; customer satisfaction; staff motivation and morale

Sample Questions: (Technology, Continuous Improvement, Customer Satisfaction)

1. What technology do you use that helps you get information back to your customers?

2. How long have you had this technology? How effective is it? How is this evaluated?

3. Any plans for improvements or enhancements?

Sample Site Visit Confirmation Letter

Date:
Contact name:
Address:

Dear _____,

Thank you for agreeing to arrange for the site visit by the _____
team from _____. This letter is to confirm these plans as
well as provide you with some information, in advance, as to how we
would like to focus our visit.

The _____ team has been chartered to _____
_____.
Several high caliber organizations, such as your own, have been
contacted that have operations, functions, and/or processes that we
anticipate can greatly add to our learning. The purpose of our visit is to
_____
_____.

The following team members are currently scheduled for the trip to your
location:
_____, _____, _____,
_____, _____, _____.

As discussed, we will arrive on _____.

Attached you will find a list of topics and some questions that we hope to
ask during our visit. If you have any questions of your own or need
clarification, please feel free to contact us immediately.

Once again, thank you for providing our team with this opportunity. We
are looking forward to our visit to _____.

Sincerely,

Basic Guidelines for Questions

1. Prepare several questions in each area of focus, as well as various ways to ask a similar question.

2. Use short, simple, and clear questions. Rely on the basics: what, where, when, who, how, why, how many, how often, etc. For example,

   - *What* is your current organizational structure?
   - *Where* are your backup files stored?
   - *When* did you implement this change?
   - *Who* is responsible for safety?
   - *How* is information collected?
   - *Why* did you change your strategy?
   - *How many* managers do you currently have?
   - *How often* are performance evaluations given?

3. Don't raise several issues in a single question.
   Example: What are your biggest problems and how have you addressed them?

4. Don't ask *leading* questions or questions that are actually thinly veiled statements of your own opinion.
   Example: Don't you *really* think that . . .?

5. Ask the same questions of people from different groups (i.e., departments, divisions, levels of management, line employees, etc.); see where they agree or disagree.

6. Place major emphasis upon *active listening* and *probing* for more information; avoid having the interviewer also record responses.

   Examples of active listening:
   - "What you seem to be saying is. . ."
   - "It sounds like you're still not sure. . . is that so?"

   Examples of probing questions:
   - "Could you say more about that?"
   - "Is there anything else?"

Examples of probing comments:
- "Continue. . ."; "Uh, huh. . ."

Examples of probing non-verbal cues:
- Nodding
- No comments made

7. Search for *the facts*, differentiate between opinions and feelings.

8. Use both positively and negatively worded questions. For example,

- "What are the advantages of. . .?"
- "Is there anything that people do not like about. . .?"

SITE VISIT QUESTIONNAIRE (Cover Sheet)

Project:_____

Visit Location   _____
Date   _____

Site Visit
Team Members   _____

    _____

    _____

    _____

Guidelines for Use of Worksheets

The following worksheet formats have been developed in order to help facilitate the efficiency and effectiveness of your site visit data collection and analysis. However, the value in organizing your data collection activities is *not* in making your efforts "fit" these forms. Therefore, use them as designed, *or better yet,* adapt the format to meet your specific needs and team working style.

Site Visit Planning Worksheet

This worksheet has been designed to assist in the site visit planning process. It can also be helpful as a project management tool for tracking data collection progress and as a communication vehicle to assure that all team members are kept informed of team activities.

Instructions

Identifying key elements of each area of focus defines more specific aspects to research. Be sure to address these aspects in the "Data to Collect" column.

Data Collection Worksheets 1 and 2

These two worksheet formats have been provided to help in documenting your plans to collect information in each defined area of focus of your data collection. It can also be used as a cross-reference for organizing and analyzing the information gathered from all site visit activities.

Instructions

"Research Categories" can be defined as areas of focus, key elements, or any other appropriate heading that assists in providing a focus for your data collection.

Data Collection Worksheet 3

To assure the accuracy of your data collection during your site visit, it is recommended that a minimum of three people attend a site, with one person asking the interview questions and two recording responses.

Instructions

This worksheet is designed to assist in collecting data in a focused and organized way to record information on your site visit. Prepared questions will assure an informative and value-added trip.

Example:

Area of focus: COMMUNICATION & SHARING INFORMATION

Core questions

1. *What are your current vehicles for sharing information in your department?*
2. *Which of these are more effective, which don't work very well? Explain.*
3. *What improvements have you made in this area?*
4. *What has been planned or is currently underway to improve communications?*
5. *How has (or will) effectiveness be measured?*

Follow-up questions
1. *What has been the role of technical solutions to your communication problems?*
2. *How did you justify your investment in this?*
3. *Have these changes lived up to the expectation?*
4. *Do you provide any training for employees in this area?*
5. *How are decisions made to address improvements in communication?*

Data Analysis Worksheets 1 and 2

This form is to be used in conjunction with the *Site Visit Planning Worksheet* and the *Site Visit Data Collection Worksheet 5*. Using these formats will help focus the consolidation, summary, and analysis of information collected from site visits and is helpful in establishing justifications for ultimate team recommendations.

Site Visit Summary Report

This form has been designed to address the site visit team's need to consolidate their learning, organize it to assist in presentations and sharing information with other team members, and provide a reference for future team data collection.

Instructions:

Assure that responses to the "Other Resources" and "More Information Needed" sections of this report are addressed to determine any additional data collection activities required.

SITE VISIT PLANNING WORKSHEET

Area of Focus	Key Elements	Data to Collect	Where	Who	When	Contact

SITE VISIT DATA COLLECTION WORKSHEET 1

RESEARCH CATEGORIES ⇒ *SITE LOCATIONS* ⇓	______ ______	______ ______	______ ______	______ ______	______ ______

SITE VISIT DATA COLLECTION WORKSHEET 2

RESEARCH CATEGORIES ⇑
SITE LOCATIONS ⇒

SITE VISIT DATA COLLECTION WORKSHEET 3

Area of focus   _____

Core questions

_____
_____
_____
_____
_____

Follow-up questions

_____
_____
_____
_____
_____
_____
_____
_____

Notes

_____
_____
_____
_____
_____
_____
_____
_____
_____
_____
_____
_____

SITE VISIT DATA ANALYSIS WORKSHEET 1

AREA OF FOCUS OR TOPIC	KEY ELEMENTS	OBSERVATIONS OR CONCLUSIONS	IMPROVEMENT IDEAS OR RECOMMENDATIONS

SITE VISIT DATA ANALYSIS WORKSHEET 2

TOPIC, PROCESS, OR KEY ELEMENT	SOURCE OF INFORMATION	WHAT WORKS?	WHAT DOESN'T WORK?	RECOMMENDATIONS, SUGGESTIONS, IMPROVEMENT IDEAS

SITE VISIT SUMMARY REPORT

Company: _____   Date of visit:

Location: _____   Visited by:

(Team members)

Contact person:

Title or role:

Mailing address:

Background information:

_____

_____

_____

_____

Specific areas of focus: Key learnings or information:

_____   _____

_____   _____

_____   _____

_____   _____

_____   _____

_____   _____

_____   _____

_____   _____

_____   _____

_____   _____

_____   _____

Other resources, companies to contact mentioned during trip?

_____

_____

More information needed from this source?   Yes _____   No _____

If yes, what is still needed?   _____

_____

Additional comments (use other side if necessary):

_____

_____

Bibliography

This Resource Guide has been designed and developed by Stu Noble, Block Petrella Weisbord, Inc., and is based upon the various experiences of teams conducting site visits.

Some material has been excerpted or adapted from the following:

Lytle, William O. (1991). *Innovative site visits: a planning and preparation guide for success*, Block Petrella Weisbord Publishing, 1991.

About the Contributor

Stu Noble, M.Ed., is a Senior Consultant with the firm of Block Petrella Weisbord, Inc., which for the past 25 years has specialized in consulting that is practical, system focused, client empowering, and results oriented.

Stu brings to his practice a diverse background that has integrated his experience in human resources management, organizational development, training and education, and Total Quality Management.

Stu's experience in socio-technical work design, team development, training design, and facilitation skills has been successfully applied in the fields of health care, manufacturing, engineering, transportation, financial, and other service organizations. In addition, he is the co-developer of The Flying Starship Factory®—Quest for Quality™ simulation.

Among Stu's recent clients are United Airlines, St. Vincent Hospital and Health Care Center (Indianapolis), Shared Medical Systems (Malvern, PA), Ashland Chemical Co., Textron Lycoming, Harrah's (Atlantic City, NJ), and the U.S. Postal Service.

Part III - Team Instruments

10

Quick Check of Team Member Skills
Zenger-Miller, Inc

Objectives
1. To identify team member strengths and areas in need of improvement.

2. To provide the basis for an individual development plan for each team member.

Participants
This activity can be used with an intact team of under ten people. It can also be effective in a class of up to 20 participants with people from different teams.

Time
45 minutes to two hours depending on the amount of time devoted to analysis and discussion of the results. To reduce the amount of class time, the instrument can be completed by the participants prior to the session.

Physical Setting
Chairs set up around a conference table or a set of tables arranged in a U-shape.

Materials
A copy of Attachment 10-A for each participant.

Process
1. Open the session by reviewing the objectives and explaining the importance of self-development by team members.

2. Distribute a copy of Attachment 10-A to each person.

3. Ask each person to complete the instrument. Emphasize the importance of honest answers. Point out that no one outside of the

class will see their answers. Allow 15 to 20 minutes to complete the form. Make sure that everyone transfers their scores to the analysis sheet.

4. At this point you may present a brief lecture on the importance of the five areas (e.g., Honor Team Values and Agreements). Alternatively, you can facilitate a discussion among participants on the five areas and their importance for their team.

5. Ask team members to meet with another participant (e.g., the person that knows them best on the team) to discuss their results and, where possible, to get some feedback on these skill areas.

6. Conclude the session by asking each person to prepare an action plan for personal development as a team member using the data from the instrument and the discussion.

Variations

1. With an intact team, you can ask members, individually, to present their scores and the key points from their action plan to the total team.

2. With an intact team, you can create a team score for each of the five areas by adding the individual scores of team members. Then, use the results to facilitate a discussion on team strengths and weaknesses.

3. To save class time, ask each person to complete the instrument before class. Participants can also do their action plan for personal development as "homework" and bring it in to the next session or meeting of the team.

Quick Check of Team Member Skills

Instructions:

This quick check will give you a snapshot of your actions as a team member over the past several months. Answer the questions the way you think other members of your team would if they were describing your actions.

Using the scale provided in the left margin, rate how often other team members would say you perform these activities.

Total your score on each page. Then transfer all totals to the boxes in the large circle on the "Analysis of the Quick Check" sheet.

For this chart, I will focus on my relationship with the following team:

I. Honor team values and agreements

Scale:

1 = Almost never
2 = Seldom
3 = Sometimes
4 = Usually
5 = Almost always

As a team member, I:

a. Show appreciation for other team members' ideas.

b. Help other team members cope with change.

c. Encourage others to use their strengths.

d. Help the team develop a productive relationship with other teams.

e. Willingly assume a leadership role when needed.

Your score:

_____

_____

_____

_____

_____

Total: _____

105

II. Promote team development

Scale:

1 = Almost never
2 = Seldom
3 = Sometimes
4 = Usually
5 = Almost always

As a team member, I: *Your score:*

a. Volunteer for all types of tasks, including the hard ones.   _____

b. Help orient and train new team members.   _____

c. Help organize and run effective meetings.   _____

d. Help examine how we are doing as a team and make any necessary changes in the way we work together.   _____

e. Help identify milestones and mini-successes to celebrate.   _____

Total: _____

III. Help make team decisions

As a team member, I: *Your score:*

a. Analyze what a decision entails.   _____

b. Ensure that the team selects and includes the appropriate people in the decision process.   _____

c. Clearly state my concerns.   _____

d. Search for common ground when team members have different views.   _____

e. Actively support the team's decisions.   _____

Total: _____

IV. Coordinate and carry out team tasks

Scale:

1 = Almost never
2 = Seldom
3 = Sometimes
4 = Usually
5 = Almost always

As a team member, I: *Your score:*

a. Help identify the information, skills, and resources necessary to accomplish team tasks. _____

b. Help formulate and agree on a plan to meet performance goals. _____

c. Stay abreast of what is happening in other parts of the organization and bring that information to the team. _____

d. Find innovative ways to meet the needs of the team and of others in the organization. _____

e. Maintain a win-win outlook in all dealings with other teams. _____

Total: _____

V. Handle difficult issues with the team

As a team member, I: *Your score:*

a. Bring team issues and problems to the team's attention. _____

b. Encourage others on the team to state their views. _____

c. Help build trust among team members by speaking openly about the team's problems. _____

d. Give specific, constructive, and timely feedback to others. _____

e. Admit when I've made a mistake. _____

Total: _____

107

Analysis of the Quick Check

Instructions: **Transferring Scores**
Enter your total scores for each of the pages of the quick check in the boxes provided below:

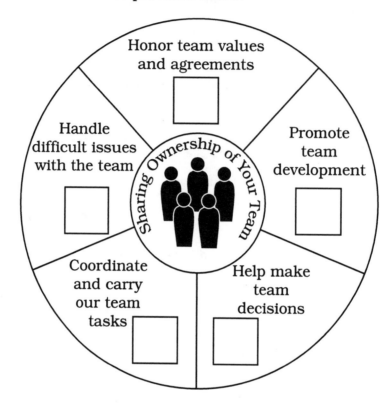

Interpreting Scores
- A score of 20 *or above* in any activity indicate an area of strength.
- A score of 20 *or below* in any activity indicate an area that needs more attention.

Looking over your scores, which activities are currently areas of strength?

_____

_____

Which activities need more attention on your part?

_____

_____

About the Contributor

Zenger-Miller, Inc. is an international consulting, educational, and training company that specializes in measurably improving individual and organizational performance by helping organizations focus on customers, involve employees, manage processes, and develop leaders.

Zenger-Miller offers a full spectrum of consulting, educating, and training for all organizational levels. Executives, managers, individual contributors, team leaders, and members all benefit from the knowledge, enhanced skills, and useful, practical tools that Zenger-Miller provides.

11

Measuring the Financial Cost of Team Conflict
Dan Dana

Objectives
1. To enable managers and team leaders to assess the hidden costs currently being incurred by conflict within their team(s).
2. To provide a cost-justification for team consultants and internal decision makers to conduct conflict-reducing interventions in teams.

Participants
This instrument may be self-administered by individuals on their own, as well as facilitator-administered in training, consulting, and conference events. When facilitator-administered, an unlimited number of people may participant. It may be used with intact teams as well as large audiences of unrelated participants.

Time
15 to 30 minutes

Process (self-administered format)
1. Make a photocopy of Attachment 11-A.

2. Follow the "Facilitator Instructions" to estimate each cost factor.

Process (facilitator-administered format)
1. Distribute one copy of Attachment 11-A to each participant.

2. Explain the objectives of the exercise, tailored to the particular situation in which it is being used.

3. Briefly discuss the idea that conflict is not simply an unpleasant annoyance or irritant in the workplace, but actually incurs financial costs that can be estimated, if not precisely measured. Consequently, team conflict should be regarded as a bottom-line relevant factor that can and should be strategically managed.

4. Ask participants to privately and individually think of one specific conflict in which they have either been a participant or a close observer and, therefore, have intimate knowledge of its consequences. Ask them to jot a key word or phrase on their worksheets that will not reveal the conflict they have in mind, but that will keep each participant focused on the specific conflict being used for reference.

5. Read aloud or paraphrase the "Facilitator Instructions," pausing long enough for participants to calculate the dollar amount of each cost factor and record their figures on their worksheets.

6. Once each cost factor has been estimated, ask participants to total their figures and enter the total cost on their worksheets.

7. Gather the participants' data by asking for a show of hands indicating the number of "total cost" figures that fall into each of the following ranges (a flipchart may be prepared to display the frequency of figures in each range):

   - Below $100 (expect few if any)
   - $100-$1000 (expect few)
   - $1000-$10,000 (expect many)
   - $10,000-$100,000 (expect several)
   - $100,000-$1,000,000 (expect some, depending on levels of management responsibility of participants)
   - Over $1,000,000 (very possible; the highest recorded figure is $6.2 million)

   Remind participants that this is the cost of just ONE conflict, and that over the course of a fiscal year it is likely that several such conflicts may occur. Therefore, the cost of conflict per budget year is no doubt a multiple of the total-cost figure recorded on their worksheets.

8. Explain that the cost of conflict cannot be reduced to zero, and that even a very effective team conflict management strategy may only reduce the annual cost by 10 to 50 percent. Nevertheless, one tenth to one half of that figure represents a significant and unnecessary expense. Consequently, investing some resources to effectively manage team conflict may be a cost-justifiable decision.

Estimating the Cost of Just ONE Team Conflict

Key word/phrase to privately identify a conflict: _____

COST FACTORS	*ESTIMATED COST*

1. Wasted time $_____
   - your time plus others' time
   - salary/benefits per hour/day (150%)

2. Reduced decision quality $_____
   - any decision made by you and/or others, independently or jointly, affected by the conflict

3. Loss of skilled employees $_____
   - a factor in voluntary/involuntary termination?
   - cost of loss of human resource (150% of total annual compensation)

4. Restructuring $_____
   - inefficiency of work redesigned to accommodate conflict

5. Sabotage/theft/damage $_____
   - equipment, work processes, reputations

6. Lowered job motivation $_____
   - reduced performance/productivity
   - % reduction × salary

7. Lost work time $_____
   - absenteeism, illness
   - number of days at prorated daily salary

8. Health costs $_____
   - stress related
   - insurance premiums linked to rate of claims

                                            _____

TOTAL COST (total items 1 through 8): $_____

Facilitator Instructions

Estimating the Cost of Just ONE Team Conflict

We will use your worksheets to produce an estimate of the financial costs that a particular team conflict incurs, aside from its impact on quality of work life and other similar concerns. By repeating the analysis for other conflicts, or by multiplying the resulting figure by the number of conflicts that have occurred, we may gain fuller appreciation of conflict as an **expensive** organizational process that can and should be **strategically managed**.

First, identify one conflict that you have intimate knowledge of, either by having been a participant or close observer. This may be a conflict that is still current, or one that happened in the past. Jot down a key word or phrase to help you stay targeted on that particular conflict.

The "cost factors" listed on the worksheet indicate the primary means by which financial cost is incurred. Not all cost factors are relevant to every conflict, but every conflict incurs cost by several of these means. We will analyze your targeted conflict by asking ourselves, with regard to each cost factor in turn, "Did/does the conflict I am analyzing have the effect of . . .?" If you answer *Yes*, estimate its dollar cost in the ways suggested below, and enter your estimate in the space provided. When you are finished, total the column to derive an estimated total cost. I will talk us through each of these cost factors, allowing a few moments for you to mentally calculate a dollar cost for each one.

Factor 1: Wasted time
Conflict inevitably distracts team members from otherwise productive use of time. A classic management study revealed that up to 30 percent of a typical manager's time is spent dealing with conflict. Estimate the amount of time wasted by each person who is/was affected by the team conflict. Then calculate the financial cost as a fraction of monthly or annual salary or wage, including the value of insurance and other fringe benefits (typically 50 percent of gross salary).

For example, let's say each of four team members wasted 40 hours during a six-month period in which a conflict disrupted their team's work. And, let's say the annual salary of the employees is $40,000. Forty hours is one week of work time, which is one-fifty-second of one year's salary, and a year's salary is typically about two-thirds of the total compensation package paid by employers. So, the dollar value of the four team members' time that was wasted by the conflict is $4615.38.

114

Factor 2: Reduced decision quality

Decisions made under conditions of conflict are **always** inferior to decisions made under conditions of cooperation. This is true for two reasons. First, we know that good decisions are necessarily based on an optimum quantity and quality of objective information. If individuals who provide information withhold or distort that information (which virtually always happens when those people are in conflict with the decision maker), then the individual who makes the decision does so with defective information.

Second, if conflict is present between people who share decision-making authority, as in the case of team-based decisions, the resulting decisions are likely to be contaminated by the power struggles between those people. A precise estimate of cost is probably impossible here, but you can ask yourself, "What opportunities were lost by poor decisions that were affected by this conflict, and what might have been gained if a better decision had been made?"

Considering these influences on decisions made by your team, estimate the dollar cost of the conflict you have in mind and put the figure on the line provided. Place a conservative figure there (i.e., on the low side of the range of its potential financial impact), even though the actual cost may be highly variable and very uncertain. *Guideline:* 50 percent of the dollar impact of decisions made by the team while it was affected by the conflict (e.g., estimate $2500 if the team was disputing whether to purchase a $5000 piece of equipment).

Factor 3: Loss of skilled employees

Organizations invest in employee skills by paying premium compensation upon hiring and by providing training thereafter. Exit interviews, which ascertain reasons for terminations, reveal that chronic unresolved conflict acts as a decisive factor in at least 50 percent of all such departures. Conflict accounts for up to 90 percent of involuntary departures, with the probable exception of staff reductions due to downsizing and restructuring. Raytheon Corporation determined that replacing an engineer costs 150 percent of his/her total annual compensation. This determination was reached by accounting for lost productivity, recruiting fees, interviewing time, staffing department employee salaries, orientation and retraining costs, etc. So, replacing an employee whose salary is $40,000 per year incurs a cost of $90,000. If one or more team members departed at least partially because of the conflict you are analyzing, calculate the dollar cost to your organization.

For example, using conservative estimates, let's say that one team member voluntarily resigned, and that his/her decision to leave was only 50 percent due to the conflict. Using Raytheon's figures, the dollar cost of this factor is half of $90,000, or $45,000.

115

Factor 4: Restructuring

Often, design of workflow is modified in an effort to reduce the interdependency between conflicting employees. Unfortunately, the restructured work is generally less efficient than the original design, which would be quite satisfactory if the team members were able to work cooperatively. As with Factor 2 above, it is impossible to precisely calculate the resulting inefficiency, but your subjective assessment will produce a reasonable estimate. Again, be sure to enter a conservative (low side) figure on your worksheet, even though it is an uncertain estimate. *Guideline:* 10 percent of the combined salaries of employees whose relationship was restructured for the time the restructuring is in effect. *Example:* Estimate $8000 if four team members, each of whom is paid $40,000 annually, were reassigned to different task groups for a six-month period, i.e., ($40,000 × 4)/10)/2. Rationale: The financial value of employees (i.e., "human resources") to an employer for performing specified work is, by definition, roughly equivalent to their salaries. If that work must later be restructured to control interpersonal conflict, the redesigned work relationship is probably not the most efficient allocation of the human resources.

Factor 5: Sabotage/theft/damage

Studies reveal a direct correlation between employee conflict and damage and theft of inventory and equipment. And, covert sabotage of work processes and of management's efforts usually occurs when employees are angry at their employer. Much of the cost incurred by this factor is hidden from management's view, often being excused as "accidental" or "inadvertent" errors. This cost is almost certainly greater than you may realize. Again, enter a conservative figure for this cost factor. *Guideline:* 10 percent of the acquisition cost of equipment, tools, and supplies that conflicted employees use in performing their jobs. *Example:* $2500, if an operator of a $20,000 machine in a work-team manufacturing environment is angry with his/her team leader ($2000 for careless operation and maintenance of the machine, plus $500 for unnecessary scrap and waste of raw materials).

Factor 6: Lowered job motivation

Everyone has experienced, from time to time, the erosion of job motivation resulting from unrelieved stress from chronic conflict with someone with whom it seems impossible to get along. Consider as a base line the productivity that would have occurred in the absence of conflict, and estimate a percentage decline of that productivity. Multiply that percentage times the dollar value of the total compensation of the person(s) affected to derive a figure for Factor 6.

For example, let's say that the productivity of three team members was eroded by 20 percent for a period of three months. Using similar calculations as we have previously, the total compensation of the three employees cost the organization $3 \times \$60,000$ or $180,000, of which one-fourth was earned during the three-month period ($45,000). Consequently, the conflict cost the organization $9000.

Factor 7: Lost work time

Absenteeism has been shown to be positively correlated with employees' anger and disaffection toward others in their workplace. This stress, combined with no concern for the impact of one's absence on others, results in employees' choices to take time off, sometimes excused as a "sick day." And, medical science has determined that nearly every physical illness and injury, from viral infections to cancer to workplace accidents, are partially "psychogenic," meaning that they are caused *in part* by psychological or emotional conditions. Although the portion of lost work time resulting from your targeted conflict is largely hidden from your direct view, with the possible exception of your own absences, you can subjectively estimate the amount of time and calculate its cost as a proration of daily or monthly compensation. Again, be sure to enter a conservative estimate on your worksheet, despite the difficulty of an exact calculation. *Guideline:* 10 percent of annual salaries of employees in conflict. *Example:* $18,000 if all six members of a team, each of whom is paid $25,000 annually, are in ongoing conflict with their team leader (who is paid $30,000) throughout the year $(\$25,000 \times 6)/10 + \$30,000/10$.

Factor 8: Health costs

As mentioned under Factor 7 above, illnesses and injuries that require medical attention are partially psychogenic, and conflict contributes to their psychogenesis. Since the rate of claims affects the premium paid to the insurer by the employer, insurance is an indirect cost of workplace conflict. To derive a numerical figure, estimate the percentage of the psychogenic component of medical problems that have occurred during the course of your targeted conflict, and multiply this percentage times the premium increase imposed by your organization's insurer. Admittedly, this psychogenic component is difficult to ascertain, and you may not be privy to the insurance costs of your employer. So, enter a conservative figure based on your knowledge of these matters. A shortcut is to enter 10 percent of the number you have entered for Factor 6, "lowered job motivation," since the stress that results in reduced productivity is also related to our physical health.

What is the total cost?
Now add the figures in each of the eight cost factors to derive an estimated total cost of your targeted conflict. Remember, this accounts for the cost of just ONE conflict. How many others have occurred in your organization if you extrapolate your estimate over the period of a year?

How can costs be reduced?
There are two broad approaches to reducing the cost of organizational and team conflict: **Structural** interventions and **training**. These can be combined into a more comprehensive **systemic** approach.

Structural interventions entail the identification and removal of unnecessary sources of conflict that are inadvertently built into the formal structure of the organization. Some examples of structural features and illustrations of unnecessary sources of confict are:

1. Counterproductively competitive role relationships.
    Illustration: Sales teams who are rewarded for being the best producer, rather than meeting predetermined and independent sales goals
2. Undefined operating procedures.
    Illustration: An employee who was instructed by her previous supervisor to do her job in a particular way finds herself with a new supervisor whose instructions differ from those of the predecessor. No objective job description exists.
3. Antagonistic grievance resolution methods.
    Illustration: A grievance system fails to provide an early forum for discussion between disputants that is mediated by a trained employee relations specialist before a formal grievance is filed.
4. Disempowering performance appraisal processes.
    Illustration: A performance appraisal procedure fails to provide opportunity for employees to have a voice in setting their own performance standards or to provide upward feedback to the supervisor.
5. Inconsistent allocation of resources.
    Illustration: A manager allocates preferred office sites to personally favored employees, rather than by fair and objective means.

Training interventions provide behavioral skills, knowledge, and communication tools for effectively preventing, managing, and resolving team conflicts. Training topics might include:

1. Effective listening
2. Managing intra-team differences
3. Mediation methods for team leaders

4. Understanding team conflict
5. Bridging diversity on the team
6. Win-win problem-solving tools

A useful resource for redesign of grievance and other formal dispute resolution systems is Ury, *et al, Getting disputes resolved: Designing systems to cut the costs of conflict*, and is of primary interest to labor relations officers. A comprehensive systemic approach, intended as a guide for executives and senior human resource officers, is outlined by Dana in "Managing organizational conflict," a chapter in Golembiewski's *Handbook of organizational consultation*. A reprint of the chapter is available from the author.

How much can costs be reduced?
It is unrealistic to expect these costs to be entirely eliminated by even an excellent team conflict management strategy. However, by effective **resolution** and **prevention** of conflict, this cost can be reduced by 10 percent to 50 percent or more. Try multiplying this percentage times your extrapolated estimate for a yearly period. How much might strategic management of conflict in your organization save?

References

Dana, D. (Fall 1984). The costs of organizational conflict. *Organization Development Journal.*

Dana, D. (1990). Measuring the financial cost of conflict. In D. Dana, *Talk it out: Four steps to managing people problems in your organization.* Amherst, MA: HRD Press. Also a chapter in D. Dana (1989). *Managing differences: How to build better relationships at work and home.* Kansas City: MTI Publications.

Dana, D. (1991). Managing organizational conflict: A systemic approach. In R. T. Golembiewski (Ed.), *Handbook of organizational consultation.* New York: Marcel Dekker.

Thomas, K. W., and W. H. Schmidt (June 1966). A survey of managerial interests with respect to conflict. *Academy of Management Journal.*

Ury, W. L., J. M. Brett, and S. B. Goldberg (1988). *Getting disputes resolved: Designing systems to cut the costs of conflict.* San Francisco: Jossey-Bass.

About the Contributor

Dan Dana is a mediator, speaker, and educator whose 20-year career is dedicated to the development and practice of "user-friendly" noncoercive methods of resolving workplace conflict.

The originator of Managerial Mediation and Do-It-Yourself Mediation, Dan's licensable programs, "The Manager-as-Mediator Seminar" and "The Practical Communication Course," put the tools of the professional mediator in the hands of every employee for everday use.

Holding a Ph.D. in psychology, Dan has served as a professor of organizational behavior at the University of Hartford as well as other universities in New England and the Midwest. With his books published in five languages worldwide, he is a popular speaker at industry and professional conferences in the United States, Europe, and South Africa.

12

Continuum of Work Structures
Gayle Porter and Sue Easton

Objective
The continuum provides a comparison across a range of team structures. Use of the continuum is a process through which organizational members rate features and thereby develop their organization's profile. The profile identifies the organization's position relative to different team types. Participants are then able to consider a specific team implementation as a choice of the best structure for their current or desired state.

Participants
The group should consist of potential team members (the focal work groups), as well as supervisors, leaders, and managers who either interact with those employees or will be involved in the transition to a team structure. Any size group can participate in the overall assessment, although discussion is aided by use of smaller, break-out groups as reactions are consolidated.

Setting
The room should allow for small group interactions, as well as full group discussion; for example, movable chairs around tables. An overhead projector and screen are useful to display the instrument and record consolidated ratings.

Time
A short session can be done in as little as 40 minutes using steps 1 through 6 in the process description. If conditions support all process steps, allow at least 1 hour and 15 minutes.

Process
1. *Introduction.* Distribute a copy of Attachment 12-A, "Continuum of Work Structures," to each participant. Describe the objectives of the activity as an assessment of the organization's current state. Explain that you will be describing each feature shown down the left-hand side of

the matrix, and they will be rating each feature by circling the appropriate description reading across the continuum. In some cases a description is shown with an arrow continuing to the right. If that description is their choice, they are to encircle the words and the arrow. In this way they are indicating a range across the continuum that applies.

2. *Preliminary Information and Individual Ratings.* Present the features of the profile: work process, organizational factors, employee characteristics, and leadership characteristics. Explanations are provided in Article 21, "Selecting the Right Team Structure to Work in Your Organization," in section Part V (Practical Theory) of this Handbook. Allow a few minutes for them to finish the ratings after you have completed the descriptions. Allow a total of 10 to 15 minutes to establish individual perceptions of the organization's profile.

3. *Consolidation of Ratings.* For approximately 15 minutes, have small groups of five to seven people of the same work group discuss their individual ratings. Through comparison they can talk about differences and develop a consensus rating on each feature of the profile.

4. *Total Group Discussion.* Typically, 20 to 30 minutes is necessary to gather input from the small groups and establish the total pattern of ratings. If there is a high level of agreement, this may go faster. If there is substantial disparity, this may signal the need to shift the focus of the exercise and to talk about the basis of differing perceptions or development needs, rather than a decision on the best team structure. *Note:* This portion of the activity is valuable if everyone taking part is from the same work group. If participants represent several work groups, the conditions are likely to differ and this portion should be omitted.

5. *Reviewing Team Types and the Organization Profile Match.* The A through F designations on the continuum represent the following structures:
   A. Traditional structure—very directive with tight chain of command
   B. Quality Improvement Teams—voluntary members discuss improvements to save money or increase quality
   C. Input Task Teams—specific task with definite end; team makes recommendations
   D. Output Task Teams—specific task with definite end; team recommends action and works through implementation
   E. Leader Centered Teams—team involvement in natural work of the members; an external formal leader facilitates problem solving and coordination with others.
   F. Self-managed Teams—natural work of members; leader functions shared among team members.

The participants' ratings will indicate whether there is alignment under one particular structure and the nature of that structure. It is a good idea to discuss each structure briefly, so participants have a better understanding of what is being identified. See "Selecting the Right Team Structure to Work in Your Organization" in Part V, Practical Theory for more information on team types.

6. *Reactions to the Assessment.* Including the above descriptions, allow another 15 minutes to be sure people understand the different structures and have some opportunity to react to what they have discovered through this process. It is important to emphasize that no single team structure is the "best" answer for everyone. The strongest driving force should be the interdependence of the work process. Within the range of that initial rating, the other features will clarify the best use of teams at this time.

Variations
The continuum can be used for three related assessments:

1. To derive an organizational profile—the current state of the organization and its people—as an indicator of the type of team structure that fits that current state.
2. To identify developmental needs, when some factors indicate a particular structure could be used but others are lagging.
3. To generate discussion on differing perceptions about the factors.

In the process section, use of the instrument is described in terms of the first variation as the primary use. Adaptation for the other objectives is more a difference in how the information is used (discussions in steps 3 through 6) than in the initial administration of the instrument.

Continuum of Work Structures

Profile of the Organization	Appropriate Work Structure					
	A	B	C	D	E	F
Work Process						
• interdependence among group members	Members independent; need to be coordinated →				Interdependent	Highly Interdependent
Organizational Factors						
• responsibility/accountability	Held with Leader →			Team/Leader	Team/Leader	Team
• communication — information available/shared	Not readily available/shared →	Shared to some degree →		Shared on task only →	Shared with some reservation	Shared fully
— feedback on group performance	Not readily available/shared →	Shared some degree →		Shared on task only →	Shared with some reservation	Shared fully
Employee Characteristics						
• technical skills	Low →		Med →	High	High	High
• attitudes toward work (professionalism)	Low	Med		→	High	High
• trust in peers	Low	Med →		Med/High →	High	High
• trust in management	Low	Med →		Med/High →	High	High
Leadership Characteristics						
• need to control	High	Med →		Med/Low →		Low
• comfort with the unknown	Low →		Med →	Med/High →		High

Continuum of Work Structures

	Appropriate Work Structure					
Profile of the Organization	A	B	C	D	E	F
Work Process						
• interdependence among group members	Members independent; need to be coordinated →				Interdependent	Highly Interdependent
Organizational Factors						
• responsibility/accountability	Held with Leader →			Team/Leader	Team/Leader	Team
• communication						
— information available/shared	Not readily available/shared	Shared to some degree →		Shared on task only	Shared with some reservation	Shared fully
— feedback on group performance	Not readily available/shared	Shared to some degree →		Shared on task only	Shared with some reservation	Shared fully
Employee Characteristics						
• technical skills	Low →		Med →	High	High	High
• attitudes toward work (professionalism)	Low	Med →		Med/High	High	High
• trust in peers	Low →	Med		Med/High		High
• trust in management	Low	Med →		Med/High		High
Leadership Characteristics						
• need to control	High →	Med		Med/Low		Low
• comfort with the unknown	Low →	Med	Med	Med/High		High

©Easton & Porter 1995

About the Contributors

Gayle Porter is a member of the management faculty at Rutgers University, School of Business in Camden, New Jersey. Her industry experience includes technical work in the oil and gas industry, finance and accounting with a Fortune 500 company, and consulting on training programs and employee development. Gayle received her Ph.D. in Business Administration from The Ohio State University. At Rutgers she teaches courses in Organizational Behavior, Human Resource Management, Social Responsibility of Business, and Organization Change and Development. Her research interests center on employee development issues, particularly team interactions and personal factors that inhibit development efforts. Publications include articles in the *Journal of Social Issues*, *Journal of Occupational Health Psychology*, and *Journal of Business Ethics*.

Sue Easton is the president of Easton and Associates, Inc., a consulting firm that specializes in the design and implementation of high performance/high commitment work force and self-managing teams. Sue's expertise is recognized internationally in the area of employee involvement and participation. Sue's focus is on improving quality and productivity by empowering the human potential of each organization. Her guidance includes assessments and interventions that engender a realistic perspective of immediate and long-range issues that impact job performance. Her client base represents both small business concerns and Fortune 500 firms such as General Electric, Lockheed Martin, Price Waterhouse, and Walt Disney World.

13

The Team Competency Tool: A Team Development Instrument

B. J. Chakiris, Kenneth Chakiris, and Patricia Kay Felkins

Objectives
- To provide a process for team development.
- To assess six dimensions of team competency.
- To compare team rating on team's strengths and development areas.
- To agree on new action desired by members to improve team performance.

Participants
1. **An intact team** with members located close to each other (same region, country, city).
2. **A global team** with members located in various regions and countries of the world, and who regularly coordinate large projects and resources using communication via Internet; facsimiles; two or three team members meeting with a local resource group in a specific country; four to five times a year the total team coming together in the same room for performance feedback, professional development, and team development.

Time
1. Opening the session   10 minutes
2. Completion of Part I, Sections A, B, C   15 minutes
3. Completion of Part II   10 minutes
4. Processing the tool   10 minutes (*see* options)
5. Subgroup discussions   15 minutes
6. Reports of subgroups   10 minutes

7. Team action agreements	10 minutes (if voting)
8. Summary and close	5 minutes
Approximate Total Time	85 minutes

Process

1. The facilitator opens the session by providing an overview of the "Team Competency Tool," which explores six dimensions of team competency. A copy of Attachment 13-A is distributed to each team member. The facilitator asks members to complete Part I, Sections A, B, and C of the questionnaire. Background information in Part I can be used to compare various teams of one organization.

2. Upon completion of Part I, members register their scores on Part II of the instrument for each of the 26 statements: 1—very high competency; 2—high competency; 3—low competency; 4—very low competency; and 5—not applicable.

3. After completing Part II, members review the 26 statements and select *three* "low" or "very low" statements. For each statement selected, an action idea is suggested that would improve team performance. Comments should indicate whether the action suggested requires involvement of someone outside the team, e.g., the team's champion or sponsor, the team's customer.

4. There are three options for processing the instrument:

   A. The lead facilitator assigns subgroups (by two's or three's) to share their findings and consolidate action ideas for team development. A recorder charts the group's report.
   B. The lead facilitator collects the instrument from each member, placing it in a sealed envelope. Prior to the next session, the facilitator prepares a collective report. If this option is used, members may desire to duplicate the instrument prior to giving it to the facilitator.
   C. The lead facilitator, prior to a team meeting, mails or sends the instrument as prework by mail or electronically to all members who return it within 24 hours. The facilitator scores and prepares the feedback report for the next team session.

5. Team subgroup discussion follows. Following the option chosen (*see* 4 above), the lead facilitator assigns subgroups to share their findings. On a flipchart, each group records their very high and very low scores. The group looks for possible patterns, asking what impact these ratings have on the team's and the organization's performance. The group then discusses possible ideas for action and agrees on three. Each subgroup prepares to report their proposed action ideas to the total team.

6. Total group reports are presented. The facilitator calls for subgroup reports. This is followed by either:

    A. Establishing action priorities through voting, with each member given 30 votes to place on any combination of action items or placing all votes on one item. Allow sufficient time to share ideas, and to process agreement among the members on desired team action. The team also considers the roles and resources needed to take the action.
    B. Scheduling another meeting to complete the action planning portion of this session. The team may want to authorize one or two of its members to coordinate additional input relative to a specific action item.

Worksheet

PART I: TEAM COMPETENCY TOOL

A. Background Information

1. Identify the team you will analyze. _____

2. Why was the team formed? _____

    _____

3. How long in existence? _____ 4. What is the size? _____
5. How long a member? _____
6. Is the team dispersed or in one location? _____ Give location(s). _____

    _____

7. What clients or customers does the team serve?

    _____

    _____

    _____

8. Do you see new challenges emerging for the team's clients in the future?

    _____

    _____

    _____

B. How do you rate this team (see below) in its overall effectiveness in serving organizational goals?

Circle one.

1 = 90-100% highly effective	2 = 80-90% effective	3 = 70-80% somewhat effective	4 = below 70% needs to improve

PART I: THE TEAM COMPETENCY TOOL (concluded)

Circle one number for each competency

C. Please rate **your team's competency** on each of the following items.	Very High	High	Low	Very Low	Not Applicable
1. Appreciating cultural differences	1	2	3	4	5
2. Clarifying shared goals	1	2	3	4	5
3. Seeking ways to continuously improve team processes	1	2	3	4	5
4. Sharing influence so that members feel empowered	1	2	3	4	5
5. Optimism of team members toward achieving goals	1	2	3	4	5
6. Self-motivation of members to achieve team goals	1	2	3	4	5
7. Matching rewards with team performance goals	1	2	3	4	5
8. Communicating team performance objectives to members	1	2	3	4	5
9. Linking resources with goals	1	2	3	4	5
10. Getting agreement on team expectations	1	2	3	4	5
11. Involving customers early in team projects	1	2	3	4	5
12. Properly balancing team's focus on task and process	1	2	3	4	5
13. Openly and constructively talking about team issues	1	2	3	4	5
14. Using inquiry methods to validate premises/conclusions	1	2	3	4	5
15. Showing empathy toward members	1	2	3	4	5
16. Building trust and respect among team members	1	2	3	4	5
17. Developing best/worst consequence scenarios	1	2	3	4	5
18. Learning from team members' experience	1	2	3	4	5
19. Integrating member talent into dynamic group synergy	1	2	3	4	5
20. Members "self-managing" to stay on target	1	2	3	4	5
21. Keeping members informed in a timely manner	1	2	3	4	5
22. Team ownership of goals	1	2	3	4	5
23. Sense of connectedness among team members	1	2	3	4	5
24. Members accepting feedback to support new action	1	2	3	4	5
25. Opportunity for rotating the team facilitation role	1	2	3	4	5
26. Overall competency in change management	1	2	3	4	5

PART II: TEAM COMPETENCY TOOL

Tabulation and Analysis

1. Overall performance rating of the team _____% (See **Section B**).
2. Now record your scores from **Section C** for each of the 26 statements. Place your scores (VH=very high competency; H=high competency; L=low competency; VL=very low competency; NA=not applicable) next to the appropriate item code (1-26). After you have entered all scores, review very highs (VH) and very lows (VL).

COMMONALITY

Item	VH	H	L	VL	NA
2					
6					
10					
22					

DIVERSITY

Item	VH	H	L	VL	NA
1					
16					
19					
26					

COMMUNICATION

Item	VH	H	L	VL	NA
8					
13					
14					
21					

COORDINATION

Item	VH	H	L	VL	NA
9					
12					
17					
20					
24					

CONFIRMATION

Item	VH	H	L	VL	NA
4					
5					
7					
11					
23					

RENEWAL

Item	VH	H	L	VL	NA
3					
15					
18					
25					

PART II: THE TEAM COMPETENCY TOOL (concluded)

3. **Review the 26 statements and select *three* rated "low" or very low." For each statement selected, suggest an action idea to improve team performance.**

1. For Statement_____ I suggest this action idea:

_____

_____

_____

2. For Statement_____ I suggest this action idea:

_____

_____

_____

3. For Statement_____ I suggest this action idea:

_____

_____

_____

OTHER COMMENTS:

PART III: TEAM COMPETENCY TOOL

Group Discussion

Write three ideas for total group action.

1. _____

_____

_____

_____

2. _____

_____

_____

3. _____

_____

_____

OTHER COMMENTS:

TEAM COMPETENCY

Six Dimensions

The Team Competency Tool assesses six dimensions of team competency as shown in the model below and can be used for *action planning during a team development session.*

Team Competency Model

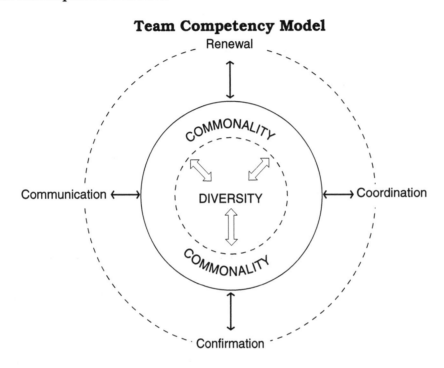

©1993 Copyright P.K. Felkins, B.J. Chakiris, K.N. Chakiris. *Change management: A model for effective organizational performance.* Chapter 7: Teamwork as a structure for change. New York, NY: Quality Resources. A Kraus Organization. Adapted and used with permission of authors.

COMMONALITY AND DIVERSITY—The challenge of teaming is often in striking a balance between commonality and diversity. Commonality assumes shared values, norms, and objectives in working together. Too often teams start by imposing commonality in task orientation rather than acknowledging individual differences, competencies, and values in creating shared objectives. Diversity broadens the team's perspective, helps them to be more innovative, and integrates each person's unique talents into a more dynamic group synergy.

COMMUNICATION AND COORDINATION—Successful teams are supported by effective communication and coordination that integrates directed and nondirected change in collective actions and daily work practices. Coordination is built on collaborative inquiry, negotiation, feedback, and agreement for reaching shared goals. Coordination encourages team learning and development rather than the building of barriers. Communication skills in contracting and clarifying roles, goals, and expectations can prevent misunderstandings later in the process.

CONFIRMATION AND RENEWAL—Confirmation comes from both the team members themselves and from the organization system in recognizing and affirming the values of the team and their contribution to organization performance. Renewal demands that the team regularly assess their work together, meet new challenges, confront difficult issues, and exchange resources with other teams to create partnerships or form new teams. A part of renewal is also looking at the continuing viability of the team. Both confirmation and renewal are important reality checks for the group in determining the future of the team in a changing organizational structure.

About the Contributors

B.J. Chakiris is CEO of BJ Chakiris Corporation, which serves Fortune 500 clients in organization development and executive education to include change management, consultation technology, simulations, and diagnostic action research teaming (ART) as a strategy for change. Clients are located throughout the United States, Europe, Southeast Asia, and Mexico. Leader positions include boards of International Professional Practice Area/ASTD, The Center for Ethics and Corporate Policy; Chairman of Lutheran Child and Family Services; adjunct position with Loyola University/Chicago; Registered Senior Associate of Organizational Renewal, Southeast Asia. B.J. holds the Walt Storey (of GE) Leadership and HRD International Practitioner Award (1994) and is coauthor of *Change management: A model for effective organizational performance.*

Kenneth N. Chakiris is designer of competency-based change management education with simulation and applications of teaming for change. Dr. Chakiris is Managing Director of BJ Chakiris Corporation and Metrex®. Change management instruments include organizational simulations, diagnostic instruments for looking at the Quality of Work Life, Human Resource/Organizational Effectiveness, Quality and Productivity, and Training/OD Needs Analysis for The Year 2000. As a former professor of mathematics at Harvard and the University of Iowa, Ken brings a unique background to improve organizational effectiveness performance. He is co-author of the new book *Change management: A model for effective organizational performance.*

Patricia Kay Felkins is Senior Consultant of BJ Chakiris Corporation specializing in education in areas of organization development, group process, and communications. Dr. Felkins is Associate Professor of organizational communications at Loyola University of Chicago/Rome and has co-authored *Teamwork: Involving people in quality and productivity improvement* with Charles A. Aubrey, II, and *Change management: A model for effective organizational performance* with B. J. Chakiris and Kenneth N. Chakiris.

14

The Team Realignment Tool: A Mature Team Assessment*
Deborah Harrington-Mackin

Objectives

- To measure a team's progress during the middle stages of team development
- To define areas of team strength and weakness
- To compare team member results and create a composite impression

Participants

Typically, the Team Alignment Tool is completed by an intact team with input from the coach, team champion, team customers, and others who are able to give feedback on the team's progress.

Time

1 - 2 hours based on how quickly the team desires to move through each topic area

Materials

1. A copy of Attachment 14-B for each participant. Copies of Attachments A and C.
2. Transparency of team alignment radar chart.
3. Overhead projector.

141

* This material is based on the author's forthcoming book, *Keeping the Team Going*, scheduled for Spring 1996 publication by AMACOM Books, a division of American Management Association. All rights reserved.

Process

1. Open the session by using Attachment A, the "Realignment Wheel" to demonstrate how an issue or problem develops that causes the team to recognize the need to assess its processes.

2. Distribute Attachment B, "Team Alignment Worksheet" to each team member. Team members may initially complete the instrument on their own or do it as a whole team with a skilled facilitator.

3. The team should review the 20 categories and weigh each category for a total weight of 100 points for all the categories. This allows the team to recognize that some categories are more important to them than others.

4. The facilitator opens the discussion on the first category by reviewing the "prompt" statements to get the ball rolling. Members discuss the category in detail and attempt to define the current state of the team relative to the category.

5. The team scores each item based on the following: 1 = not at all; 2 = somewhat; 3 = to a moderate extent; 4 = to a great extent; 5 = to a very great extent. Decimal scores (e.g. 1.5, 1.75) may also be used.

6. To score, multiply the category weight times the score for a team total. Then multiply the weight times the ideal score. Then divide the ideal score into the team score for a percentage total.

7. When the assessment is completed the team plots its results on a transparency of the Radar Chart, Attachment C, displayed on an overhead projector. *Option: plot individual assessments and then the team as a whole in a different color so members can see how their individual scores align with the team's score.*

8. When the Team Alignment Worksheet is completed, the team returns to The Realignment Wheel to complete **Step 7:** defining the problem as a group. The Team Alignment Worksheet will provide clear feedback for the team about what is and isn't working. At this point, the team drafts a problem statement, followed by a statement describing what the team would like to have happen.

9. Continue through the remainder of the steps on The Realignment Wheel culminating in an action plan.

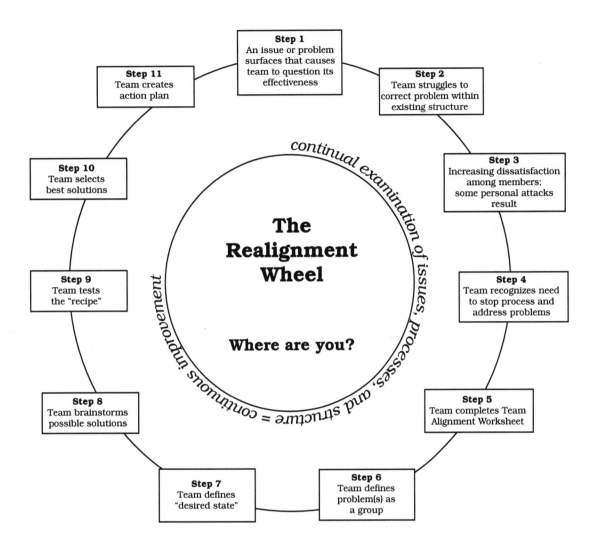

The
Realignment
Wheel

Where are you?

Step 1
An issue or problem surfaces that causes team to question its effectiveness

Step 2
Team struggles to correct problem within existing structure

Step 3
Increasing dissatisfaction among members; some personal attacks result

Step 4
Team recognizes need to stop process and address problems

Step 5
Team completes Team Alignment Worksheet

Step 6
Team defines problem(s) as a group

Step 7
Team defines "desired state"

Step 8
Team brainstorms possible solutions

Step 9
Team tests the "recipe"

Step 10
Team selects best solutions

Step 11
Team creates action plan

continual examination of issues, processes, and structure = continuous improvement

Team Alignment Worksheet

Directions: *There are a total of 20 categories. Assign a weight to each for a total of 100 points. Score each item based on the following: 1=not at all; 2=somewhat; 3=to a moderate extent; 4=to a great extent; 5=to a very great extent.*

1. Culture and Direction
                                               Wt. Score Total

- The team has written vision, values, mission, structure, roles, and goals.
- Empowerment plan exists and has been shared with the team.
- The charter is revisited periodically.
- The team approach still makes sense stategically for the organization and tactically for the department.
- Management still believes that the use of a team is the most effective way to proceed.
- The team is making a contribution to larger organizational goals.

5

%

2. Goal Clarity
                                               Wt. Score Total

- The team sets own specific, measurable goals.
- The goals are reasonable and current.
- The team has achieved the goals it originally set out to achieve.
- Goal attainment is regularly measured and results shared.
- Each member can clearly identify the vision, mission, goals, and values of the team.
- Team members have individual goals that are compatible with the team goals.

5

%

3. Leadership
                                               Wt. Score Total

- Leadership responsibilities are shared and rotated equally on the team.
- Describe the typical duties of the team leader.
- The team leader is functioning effectively and within the role assigned by the team.
- Authority delegation has been clear and consistent.
- The team takes a leadership role for a whole process.
- The team is empowered to share various leadership functions.

5

%

144

4. *Roles*

Wt. Score Total

- All team roles are defined and regularly rotated among team members.
- Duties are distributed fairly among team members.
- Both task and relationship (process observer) roles are used.
- Other significant roles have been identified.
- A team champion (coach) has been identified and interacts regularly with the team.

5

%

5. *Norms*

Wt. Score Total

- The team rules and procedures are defined in writing.
- Team rules address both task and relationship issues.
- An active help/hinder list is used to control behavior.
- The team regularly reviews compliance with its rules.
- The team assumes responsibility for disciplining members who violate team norms.

5

%

6. *Membership*

Wt. Score Total

- The appropriate people are on the team.
- The skills and abilities needed from the team members are available.
- Members understand what they are expected to contribute.
- Low turnover has occurred on the team.
- Replacement members have been brought up to speed.

5

%

7. *Team Participation*

Wt. Score Total

- There is high participation among all members.
- The level of participation expected has been made clear.
- Those members not participating at first are now participating regularly.
- Members are sensitive to encouraging full participation in all issues.

5

%

8. Team Meetings

Wt. Score Total

- An agenda is used at every meeting.
- Meetings start/end on time.
- Action plans are reviewed and revisited.
- Facilitators are skilled at helping the team reach decisions.
- Progress is made in meetings.
- All appropriate roles are performed at meetings.
- Team meetings improve the level of team functioning.
- Team meetings focus on problem solving and planning, not just information sharing.

5

%

9. Competency to Perform Tasks

Wt. Score Total

- Members are cross-trained in work and team tasks.
- Needed competencies have been identified.
- The competency of members has been identified.
- All team members are competent to perform all relevant tasks.
- A plan exists for the successful delegation of specific tasks.
- The plan is shared with the team.

5

%

10. Completion of Team Tasks

Wt. Score Total

- Tasks are assigned and completed on time.
- Team accepts responsibility and accountability for tasks.
- The team has a good history of taking on responsibility.
- Clear, measurable standards exist and are known to all members.
- The results of the team have been used and shared with others.
- The team regularly monitors and reviews process performance.
- The team workload is appropriate for the number of people and competency.

5

%

11. Interpersonal Skills

Wt. Score Total

- Team members are able to receive and give helpful feedback.
- Team members demonstrate good listening skills.
- Team members use gentle confrontation when dealing with a team issue.
- Team members understand the difference between acceptance and agreement.
- Team members uncover points of agreement during discussions by asking good questions.
- Members value diversity among members.

5

%

12. General Communication

Wt. Score Total

- Big-picture goals are being communicated regularly.
- Communication with others, including other teams, is adequate and effective.
- The team encourages feedback from others.
- Performance feedback is regularly given to the team.
- Communication systems, i.e. logs, memos, profs, are used to support team communication.

5

%

13. Atmosphere

Wt. Score Total

- The team's atmosphere is warm and accepting.
- The team has a high energy level.
- The team is open and direct with one another.
- The team readily shares thoughts and ideas.
- There is almost no fear demonstrated.
- Team members tolerate faults of other members according to guidelines.
- Members demonstrate that they trust each other.
- Commitment to the team's success is evident.

5

%

147

14. Team Decision Making

| | Wt. | Score | Total |

- The team checks its authority before entering the decision process.
- The team looks for mutually-supported alternatives when striving to achieve consensus.
- The team seeks advice from others outside the team during the decision-making process.
- The team is able to make effective consensus decisions.
- The team revisits and revises decisions when necessary.
- The team evaluates its decisions periodically.
- Members are willing to make all the necessary key decisions.
- Members are willing to be held accountable for their decisions.

5
%

15. Team Problem Solving

| | Wt. | Score | Total |

- The team is able to delay judgment and encourage the expression of new ideas.
- The team sticks to discussing one problem at a time and thoroughly explores the problem and causes of the problem before jumping to solutions.
- The team is using various TQM, team and reengineering tools for problem solving.
- The team gathers and uses all information needed to perform tasks.
- The team plans and organizes well.

5
%

16. Handling Conflicts

| | Wt. | Score | Total |

- Conflicts between different teams and departments are handled effectively.
- All team members are accepted on the team despite their differing opinions.
- The team has determined a protocol for how it will handle conflicts.
- Anger is handled constructively by the team.
- All team members are trained in conflict resolution and/or demonstrate the ability to achieve win/win resolutions.

5
%

148

17. Performance Management

	Wt.	Score	Total

- Management is visible and available to the team as a resource.
- Management shares the organization's vision, mission, goals, and values.
- Management gives regular feedback on the team's performance.
- Management communicates key information in a timely manner.
- Management encourages continuous improvement of methods and processes.
- Management assists in locating the necessary tools, information and resources for the team.
- Management helps the team stay focused on its mission, goals, measurements, and boundaries.
- Management familiarizes the team with company policies.

5

%

18. Work Tools and Training

	Wt.	Score	Total

- Team has received adequate team training.
- Training is ongoing and learner-directed.
- Adequate resources are available to the team.
- The team has received adequate on-the-job training.
- Members learn willingly.
- Members share their knowledge and skill with each other.
- Members are cross-trained in a variety of skills.
- The team is applying the training in the work area.

5

%

19. Inter-team Management

	Wt.	Score	Total

- The team develops and manages relationships with other teams, customers, etc.
- The team coordinates its work well with suppliers and customers (both internal and external).
- There is no duplication of effort among teams.
- Boundaries are flexible and varied.
- Problems with other teams are addressed promptly.
- Teams do not compete with each other.

5

%

149

20. Rewards/Incentives/Recognition

	Wt.	Score	Total

- Rewards have been identified and used.
- Team is regularly recognized for accomplishments.
- The type and frequency of recognition meets team's needs.
- The pay structure supports a team culture.
- The evaluation process recognizes both individual and team performance.

	Score	
	5	
	%	

Total weight = 100 points
Total score = _____

150

Team Alignment Radar Chart

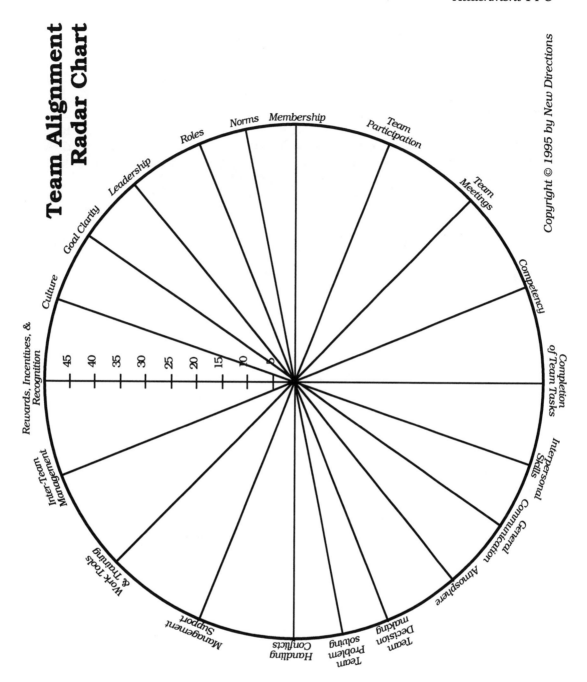

151

About the Contributor

Deborah Harrington-Mackin is the author of *The Team Building Tool Kit* and *Keeping the Team Going*, both published by AMACOM. She is a recognized presenter on teams, collaborative organizational planning, interpersonal skills, and conflict resolution. Deborah is the owner of New Directions Consulting, Inc. in North Bennington, Vermont and the mother of her own blended team of six children.

Part IV - Case Studies

15

Large-Scale Change at Amoco: Becoming Team-Based

J. Thomas Buck, Nancy J. Finley, Mary Rahaim, and Lynn Wilson

"Today's world is sharply different from yesterday's and will be equally unlike the world of tomorrow. We live in a time of change—rapid, radical, profound change. For many, this lack of stability is a threat. But for the bold, this is an exciting era of opportunity."
— Larry Fuller, Chairman of Amoco

Introduction

Today's business climate is rapidly changing. Processes that successfully worked in the past cannot keep up with today's fierce global competition. Companies are increasingly finding that to be successful, they must be open to opportunities, challenge perceived boundaries, and make change an acceptable part of their culture. Amoco Corporation is one company stepping up to that challenge.

For the past decade, Amoco Corporation has seen a changing marketplace. The global organization saw that the industry was steadily declining in the U.S. due to declining prices. Amoco projected that while its domestic production would decrease, costs would continue to increase with inflation. As a result, one of Amoco Corporation's business sectors, Amoco Exploration and Production Sector, looked for a dramatic plan to change the way it did business. Amoco Exploration and Production Sector's goal was $250 million in annual savings and revenue enhancements while cutting business costs.

Responding to the industry's climate, Amoco Exploration and Production Sector chose Business Process Reengineering (BPR) to radically redesign Amoco's organizational structure and business processes. Amoco first surveyed its employees on their needs. Amoco asked such questions as, *"What are your concerns? What should you be working on?"* Employees overwhelmingly responded that they wanted to see a move toward "true teams." Employees said they really did not

155

know how to work together—they needed the knowledge and tools and other resources in order to best work together. In response to this discovery, Amoco Exploration and Production Sector created their own team development process.

Amoco realized that it needed external expertise to make a project of this scope successful and partnered with Prism Performance Systems. For Amoco, it was crucial to choose a training and consulting firm that would truly partner with the organization and be completely flexible in meeting needs. Prism has been that partner to Amoco since 1993. Together, Amoco and Prism Performance Systems have designed, developed, and implemented the Team Development Process (TDP).

To date, 55 multidiscipline teams have been implemented in the U.S. using the TDP.

About the TDP Model

Originally, Amoco created the TDP specifically for a set of teams responsible for managing Amoco's field assets and properties (Joint Operations Management Teams). After many successful outcomes, the TDP Model was redeveloped to fit the needs of teams throughout the entire organization.

The TDP provides a sequential approach to establishing, developing, and maintaining high-performance teams. The Model is structured in the form of a process map that details actions in each of five phases: Structuring, Organizing, Applying, Achieving, and Excelling. The Model starts with a leadership vision and moves to team success and renewal. (Please see Attachment 15-A for a description of the model.)

The Model identifies key steps, skills, and knowledge needed in each phase of team development, and identifies specific team-related roles and responsibilities by key players in each phase of team development. While the responsibilities of all roles vary, they are all critical to team success.

A TDP Lifecycle Checklist is in place to support each phase of the Model so that teams may monitor their progress and ensure that each outcome or objective is met before moving onto the next phase. For instance, during the Organizing phase, a team develops its operating guidelines, establishes and identifies stakeholders and customers, and completes a team document. Upon completing these outcomes, the team is considered to be in the Applying phase of the Model.

How the Model Was Developed

Amoco studied internal and external teams in order to define how to develop high-performance teams. Amoco did this realizing the importance of understanding how teams develop, and to ensure that the new process was congruent to processes being used industry-wide. Amoco formed a Design Team of Amoco employees and consultants from Prism Performance Systems. The Design Team studied teams internal and external to Amoco, selected the best qualities of both, and melded them to form the best possible process. (See Attachment 15-B.)

In formulating the Team Development Process, the Design Team ensured that the TDP supported Amoco's existing initiatives, such as Progress (quality improvement tools), Career Management, and Performance Management. This provided critical alignment to the overall strategic renewal process and saved the company from duplicating any of its existing resources.

In addition, the draft Model was studied by internal and external gurus, and employees at all levels, to challenge, test, and validate the Model. During the pilot phase, the Model was continually enhanced through the review and documentation of lessons learned.

The Model's Supporting Resources

Supporting the Model are three major resources: the Core Curriculum, Subprocesses, and Resource Matrix.

The Core Curriculum provides a team quick-start and consists of six components that prepare leadership and multidiscipline team members to work together as a team to meet organizational, team, and individual goals. Its six components are conducted in the form of meetings and provide a menu-driven approach to efficiently getting teams performing effectively.

The Core Curriculum provides the learning to maximize the benefits of teams and offers local flexibility in its menu-driven approach. The menu-driven meetings call for specific outcomes, but allow for local flexibility and adaptability to the special needs of teams. For example, the Team Launch Meeting is designed to form, organize, and prepare the team for working together at a high-performance level. In addition, the team will focus on specific applications that will launch the team.

The Subprocesses provide more detailed, focused attention for important activities in the Model. While the Model illustrates what participants should do, the subprocesses give participants the specifics or the "how to" of many of the key steps on the Model. A subprocess can be used as an example to work through a step on the Model. A typical subprocess contains background information describing the importance of the subprocess, a graphic display illustrating the typical responsibilities of each role in the subprocesses' steps, a block diagram of subprocess steps, and a detailed discussion of each step. They have been designed as stand-alone materials or job aids, requiring no formal training to use.

The Resource Matrix Database supports each phase of the Model with targeted, proven training resources, both internal and external to Amoco, that link to specific "role" competencies in each phase. It consists of development programs; videos, books, and articles; structured experiences; assessments and inventories; cassette audio tapes; and job aids, available to employees on database and hard copy. The Resource Matrix serves as a detailed catalogue of information sources and specifies which role(s) and phase(s) of the TDP Model each resource supports. In addition, internal and/or external Amoco sources have evaluated each resource, ranking the level of quality of information and usefulness as it relates to Amoco.

In addition to the supporting resources, a TDP Checklist is in place to provide teams with a monitoring tool that allows them to determine how far they are the Team Development Process. The TDP Checklist also helps existing teams determine their entry point in the Team Development Process, depending on each team's maturity.

Marketing the Team Development Process

It's very important that an effort like this be communicated to the rest of the organization. Amoco did this in a number of ways.

To share general information, employees were involved in briefings and question/answer sessions. An information bulletin, easy-reference brochure, and case study were also developed and distributed to employees that provided such information as the TDP's history, the Model, the benefits, success stories, and comments from teams that went through the process.

The subprocess in the Organizing phase of the Model provides the Business/Service Unit vice president/manager, team sponsor, leader, and members with guidelines for defining and establishing a formal communication strategy. The purpose of the communication strategy is to inform and clarify the process to all key stakeholders. Together, the vice president/manager, team sponsor, leader, and members identify key stakeholders, communication sources, and objectives.

In addition to the communication strategy, a communication *process* is in place to guide teams. The communication strategy is more concerned with *who* the communication will be directed to, *why* the communication will take place, *what* type of information should be communicated, and *who* will prepare/transmit that information. In contrast, the communication process is concerned with *how* information will be communicated, i.e., the channel. Communication processes are chosen based on how optimal they are for both the sender and receiver. A typical communication process may include telephone conferences, meetings, newsletters, bulletin boards, faxes, regular mailings, etc. The communication process is measured to predict results and make improvements as necessary.

Lessons Learned

Gathering lessons learned is an important part of the TDP. Lessons learned are gathered at meetings that are conducted at the conclusion of each stage of the TDP. Each phase in the TDP's lifecycle ends with such a meeting where all lessons learned are surfaced and documented. During the meetings, the group moderator solicits events or results that *exceeded* expectations. The group moderator then solicits input regarding results or events that *fell short* of expectations. After processing the lessons learned, the group categorizes them according to how they relate to Amoco. The lessons learned are of value:

- to participants in this team only
- throughout the Business/Service Unit only
- throughout the company

After each meeting, lessons learned are distributed accordingly.

Following are lessons learned that were determined to be of value throughout Amoco, and to any organization that is considering implementing a team development process:

- Participants and managers were more interested in progressing toward team objectives than going to training. This required the TDP creators to redesign the training events into meeting events. Key team learning activities were restructured to become action-oriented events that accomplished a checklist item in the TDP lifecycle phase they were currently in. An example would be to write a mission statement for the team; instead of training the team to write mission statements, the new design shared characteristics of good mission statements and assigned them to write one for their team. Instead of training the team how to write ground rules for their team, the new design defined ground rules, then assigned the team to write their ground rules. Similar changes affected vision and goal development, role definition, interpersonal styles, conflict management, performance measure identification, and other topics/actions. This design change was implemented throughout the core curriculum supporting the TDP.

    The trade-off in this design change was the preparation of participants for future teams. The focus of activities on the current team certainly helped the current team move forward quickly. Did it prepare members, leaders, and sponsors for involvement with future teams? This question remains open.

- Ultimately, TDP was an organization redesign process. The steps in the TDP brought about concurrent redesign considerations and top-down consensus on a selected redesign alternative. This included the involvement of top management and middle management for each local unit. Typically the process began with the top management group working through alternatives and drafting a preferred design. Part of this process was called "pushing the frontier," an activity that allowed the group to create organizational designs that may be considered too radical for the present, but which could be considered for the future. The preferred design and the alternatives were then presented to middle management in a leadership awareness meeting. Ideas, input, questions and challenges were solicited as part of the meeting, and changes were made to refine the alternatives. A variation on this meeting was also designed in an orientation format for first-line supervisors. These steps tended to gain the

159

support of all levels of management for the new organization design and changed management roles.

- Set short-term performance challenges for newly formed multidiscipline teams. The sponsor should choose an issue from the business plan that would provide the team with a quick win. This allows the team to immediately focus on their teaming.

  The best example of the performance challenge came from one of the first Durango asset teams. The sponsor and team leader identified the "turning on" of seven new wells in a 60-day period as the team's initial performance challenge in their Applying phase. Normally it took as long as six to seven months to get newly drilled and constructed wells to be operational. Much of this challenge included the achievement of regulatory and company involvement of all functions represented on the team: technicians, administrators, accountants, supervisors, geologists, and engineers. This meets a performance challenge requirement of interdependence among the team members for this task. Again, the purpose of the task is to force team behavior.

  The team accomplished the "turn on" process in less than 60 days. In this particular example, achieving the challenge had a significant economic payoff; increased revenue. The value of turning these wells on "early" was estimated to bring in $380,000 in revenue over what was considered normal performance.

- Look at the organization's existing components as supporting resources. For example, Amoco found that it could use existing continuous improvement tools.

- Numerous possibilities for synergy are identified in the team's early activities. Many of these come from building collaboration in functions that previously had almost been organizational competitors. The turf identity had been functionally oriented prior to establishment of the redesigned structure. Finance people watched out for the finance function's objectives and engineering people watched out for the engineering function's objectives. The focus on the multidiscipline team's business process allowed turf to be sidestepped in favor of the team's business needs. Several examples of this surfaced in the early implementations. Billing errors that would go back and forth between finance and the local asset management office became resolved much faster and many business process steps were able to be re-evaluated and reduced or eliminated at the local level as a result of the collaboration between functions resulting from the redesign. See the next section on success stories for more on these examples.

- Be realistic—you won't get buy-in from all the teams right away. The team process starts off slowly, but after a few teams find success, the new process spreads to more teams.

- The best results from TDP implementation were always from teams with members ready to operate in a collaborative team style. While this seems obvious, some of the top management groups initially wanted to look at how they could use the team process to fix non-performing team members or group activities. Rarely are these non-performers immediately ready to offer their support to significant management or business process changes. They are struggling with stable processes in their current situation. Why make implementing the TDP that much harder by starting with people that will predictably fight it? The approach selected was to look for volunteer work groups, supervisors that willingly implement change, work groups that already display many characteristics of teamwork, etc. Then the TDP was building on success rather than fighting for it. Build some successes with successful initial teams, then take those successes to more reluctant areas and win them over.

Amoco Teams Share Their Success Stories
- Working together as a multidiscipline team, one group at a plant in Durango, Colorado, was able to identify and correct a billing error that had been occurring for the past four years. Correction of this billing error will result in approximately $100,000 per year in savings for Amoco.
- A team in New Mexico was able to eliminate three hours of overtime worked each day (at $25 per hour) by discontinuing an unnecessary practice in the company. Prior to the launch of the team, nobody had questioned the practice (the witnessing of each oil sale), which was assumed to be carried out in accordance to government regulation. At the first team meeting, a team member asked why the practice was implemented, which led to a discussion and an agreement to find out whether or not the practice was truly necessary. Research indicated that no such government regulation existed, and the team decided to discontinue the practice. The team leader estimates that his team will save $30,000 per year (one person's salary) as a result, and that $100,000 will be saved as other teams in New Mexico eliminate the witnessing of oil sales.
- Since the inception of one Durango, Colorado, team's multidiscipline approach to property management, the team has completed six wells in just one month, versus the six to seven months it used to take. As a result, the generation of gas revenues began five to six months faster, representing a net increase of $76,000 in revenues per month, or $380,000 annually.
- Within two months of its team launch, one Ft. Lupton, Colorado, multidiscipline team increased gas production, which in turn, increased revenue by $1,500 per day. The team was responsible

161

for the production of 808 gas wells and implemented the *best* practices from its highest producing wells as *standard* practices for all the team's 808 wells. The team projects that this new process will grow revenues an additional $3.8 million in 1995.

In addition to team success stories, team members have identified new strengths as a result of TDP:

- Heightened awareness of the "business"
- Improved communication across all disciplines
- Unlimited opportunities for increased revenues and cycle time reduction
- Enhanced teamwork by understanding how the individual team members' tasks fit into the "big picture"
- Significant involvement in the organization's day-to-day business operations by the team members
- Refocus by management from a tactical approach to providing strategic direction

Specifically, team members and leaders have made the following comments:

"Team members are working with their own budgets, etc. and this is really working well."

"There seems to be clearer, faster lines of communication due to having the resources on the team. . ."

"There is a heightened awareness of measures, objectives, and our vision, and these are now taken into consideration in team members' decision making. . ."

"Different disciplines are really starting to get together more— doing more up-front planning in order to lessen future problems and rework. . ."

"The team has seen a real advantage and realized gains as a result of the multidiscipline team approach. People are meeting with other teams. Not only is communication better, but there is good synergy and good gains being realized that probably wouldn't have happened under the old structure."

Amoco Moves Ahead

Amoco Exploration and Production Sector continues to take additional steps that will further enhance the new team structure.

- Amoco plans to operationalize the Team Development Process across the organization, which will include implementing teams on a worldwide level.
- Amoco may develop some of the Core Curriculum steps into self-study programs so that they can be completed prior to the core meetings.
- Amoco will keep the communication channels open with the teams from the initial launch to ensure that any additional skills and tools needed to move through the last phases of the Model are provided.

Team Lifecycles

Some recent heavy thinking about how permanent and semi-permanent teams grow and develop has helped us define five phases that teams grow through. These phases clarify the lifecycle of teams in a way that allows us to better help them mature into effective teams.

Karen Wallace of Svenson & Wallace, Inc., Mary Rahaim and Harry Higinbotham of Amoco Exploration & Production Sector, and Nancy Finley and Tom Buck of Prism Performance Systems defined these five phases. Our original assignment was to identify the steps each person in a team role (sponsor, leader, member, team consultant, etc.) should take to best develop an effective, ongoing team. One of the outgrowths of this work was a team lifecycle model that captures a root development path that most teams can follow.

This path has been present for most permanent teams, yet invisible. Many of our client organizations have thought of team building and team development as events that would get a team up and running. This thinking misses the long-term developmental view of the team lifecycle. How often is the "career path" of the team defined as a team is formed? How often are advanced team building or team effectiveness activities scheduled as a team is formed? Not very often?

The team lifecycle identifies five phases of growth for a team: Structuring, Organizing, Applying, Achieving, and Excelling. Each of these phases has unique characteristics and contributes to high-performing teams. These phases are different than the stages of group development defined in Tuckman's "orming" model (forming, storming, norming, and performing), or in Cogs Ladder (polite, why we're here, bid for power, constructive, and esprit). These group development stages describe how individuals behave in a group setting. (Please consider that teams are subsets of groups.) Groups may move up and down or over and back in the stages depending on membership and task characteristics. The lifecycle model is a sequential model with backward movement only when a team identifies a need for some make-up work or when it passes through Excelling and "celebration of mission achievement."

The Structuring phase occurs when an initial task is defined and identified as appropriate for the type of work structure we call a team. Essentially, the owners of the task have determined that a team can handle the task (management of a function, large project, or process) more effectively than an individual or a group. In structuring the task and the team, owners name those who should be on the team, decide what resources the team will be provided with, and explore the options for team leader selection. Structuring may also include completing any skill development needs individuals may have before joining the team. A final step in the Structuring phase would be to orient prospective team members to the task and to the thoughts of the initial task owners with respect to the team. The task owners will probably feel some tensions as they begin to actually put the team in place. This phase provides the initial architect drawing for the team and its work.

In the Organizing phase, the team and the task owners work together to better define the task, in part by developing a mission statement. Team roles are set and ground rules agreed upon. Team members learn about each other and how they will work together to accomplish the mission. The team leader starts to develop into a stronger role as he/she forces some initial decisions by the team. Goals are established and initial accountabilities may be determined. Performance challenges may be identified by the team or its sponsor as it begins to plan work. This phase will set the foundation for the ongoing work of the team.

It is during the Applying phase that the team goes to work. It takes its first steps toward completing the task. In this phase, the team will learn how to operate by the ground rules, or it will modify them. Tensions may come up, as they should, as the team members work to solve problems or are forced to creatively divide resources or meet a schedule requirement. Conflict should surface and be handled in a constructive way. Initial progress is made on the task. The team in this phase may appear to be "consciously competent" in familiar learning terminology. In keeping with our construction analogy, we see in this phase the rough outline of the structuring work start to become visible. The roof is on and the exterior walls are done.

The Achieving phase occurs when the team becomes "unconsciously competent" at performing as a team on the task. A team in this phase looks good at being a team. Teamwork is now coming naturally. Changes in the task or associated processes are handled effectively. Team member transitions are managed well. Member skill development may even be managed by the team. Interactions with the team's management link or sponsor become less frequent than at any other stage because things are usually going well, and when they are not, the team handles them well. Differences of opinion and conflict are seen as ways to get the best solution, not as painful or stressful situations to be avoided. The Achieving phase really puts the interior finishes on the designed structure and completes its livability.

The Excelling phase occurs when the team matures to the point that it challenges its boundaries. The team may very well come back to its management and ask to renegotiate its mission or charter. The team sees new opportunities that will offer new and enhanced value to the organization through a refocus of its effort. Not many teams get to this phase. When it happens, it's quite an event. Management will be challenged to offer additional authority or resources. New tensions will develop. This phase offers teams a way to get off the performance plateau. It is not the final stage of development, by the way. If a team "excels" it will probably move forward to new Structuring and Organizing phases. This may be a full remodeling of our building, such as adding a new room or moving to a new site.

Looking at teams in terms of where they are in their lifecycle provides guidance on how to support their efforts. Understanding the five phases also helps us determine how to prepare the team's managers to best motivate and guide the team since the team's needs will be different in each phase. This thinking offers the potential to dramatically improve the performance of individual teams and team-based organizations.

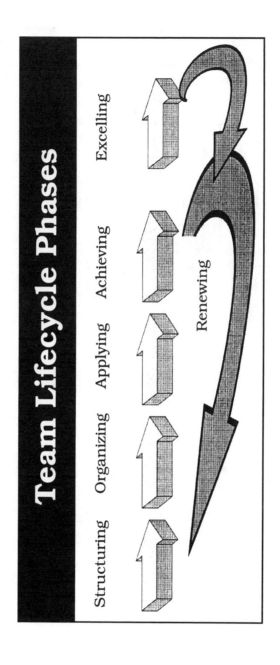

Amoco
Team Development Process Model

Structuring Phase: The team organization structure is identified and designed.

	BU/SU VP/ Manager	Sponsor	Team Leader	Team	Coach/Facilitator/ Consultant/Trainer

Develop and review business plan based on APC Strategic Plan.

Forecast & plan human resource, including discipline mix needed for the plan.

Determine if teams are the appropriate solution.

Identify team organization structure:
• Broad structure
• Substructure
• Transition states

Recommend appointment of managers.

Hold manager consulting meeting; define role.

Hold leadership planning meetings with manager and direct reports; custom design the detailed team organization structure/ process.

Communicate Business Unit/Service Unit vision, values & business plan. Support related. Reinforce desired organization culture.

Champion the Team Development Process and associated training.

Recommend and select team Sponsor.

Complete Sponsor preparation meeting.

Hold awareness meeting for all leadership.

Assess and recommend appointment of Team Leaders.

Definition of the team's scope of work:
• Mission Statement
• Team Results Framework
• Skill mix
• Budget

Establish Team Member selection criteria:
• Skills/knowledge
• Individual assessment
• Timing of need
• Number

Complete Team Leader preparation meeting.

Provide input.

Select Team Members.

Participate in development.

Although selection of Team Leaders and Team Members has not occurred, involvement from all levels of the organization is encouraged.

Orient stakeholders and members. All attend team development orientation meeting.

Document and review lessons learned.

Assess development needs of Coach/Facilitator/Consultant/Trainer.

Facilitate Structuring activities as needed.

◩ = Core Development

About the Contributors

Nancy J. Finley

Nancy J. Finley, vice president of project management systems for Prism Performance Systems, adds to Prism a specialization in team development, service quality, benchmarking studies, and organizational assessments.

Most recently, Finley served as project manager and senior consultant in a large-scale team development project at Amoco Production Company. The project involved the development of multidiscipline teams within several business units.

J. T. (Tom) Buck

J. T. (Tom) Buck is an expert on team development, innovation, and implementing total quality. He has worked with diverse organizations such as Amoco Production Company, the U.S. Postal Service, and Rubbermaid. He is co-founder and president of Prism Performance Systems.

Buck has served as a consultant on numerous large-scale change projects, including the implementation of self-directed work teams and the development of a team development process to support business process reengineering. He has recently been published in *Training and Development*, *Quality Digest*, and *Workforce Training News*.

Mary L. Rahaim

Mary Rahaim is an internal human resources representative for Amoco Power Resources Corporation, a start-up organization and business unit of Amoco Corporation. Rahaim manages the design of HR systems for the new organization, including designing a compensation system and managing a large-scale staffing project.

Prior to that as human resources consultant to Amoco Production Company (APC), Rahaim managed the design, development, and implementation of APC's Team Development Process.

Lynn Wilson

Lynn Wilson is an internal organizational capabilities consultant for Amoco Production Company. Currently, Wilson serves as lead consultant to APC's Environmental, Health and Safety Program. She also assesses the organization's training needs and manages the development of training courses to fulfill those needs.

Wilson also serves as Amoco's Career Management Director and conducts such training courses as Managing Personal Growth, Maximizing Career Choices, and Transition Management. Wilson played an instrumental role in Amoco's Team Development Process.

16

A Critical Examination of a Failed Attempt to Implement Self-Directed Work Teams: How a Success Turned into a Failure

Glenn Varney and Dan Diers

We must change and change dramatically! This is the message the president wanted to instill as employees filed in for the first in a marathon series of meetings to discuss the future of their struggling plant. The severity of the situation was such that it would not be enough to simply command compliance; this message needed to inspire commitment. This would later prove to be a challenge impossible to accomplish with a single speech, but would require continuous education and communication throughout the following months.

The employees consisted of approximately 100 union members and 35 salaried members of a manufacturing unit within a foreign-owned multinational company. This plant, located in a very rural area with relatively high unemployment, had employed many of the local residents for 15 to 20 years or more and represented the backbone of the local community's economy. Many of the statements these employees were about to hear had never been uttered before in this traditionally managed plant, which had suffered the effects of a long history of autocratic management and adversarial union relations.

As the first group of employees settled into the conference room, the president began his stirring remarks.

Good Morning!

As most of you know, I have worked for our company for nearly 23 years. During that period I have witnessed a great deal of change. While the need for change is virtually always present, there may never have been a period in this plant's history where change was as necessary as it is now. . ..

Our industry is a very difficult business. As evidence of this difficulty, we reduced our salaried work force by 18 percent in 1991. In 1992 we eliminated nearly 50 percent of all positions in the corporate headquarters. Last week, as you may know, we announced the decision to combine two divisions that will cause a further reduction in salaried employment. These actions were the result of an industry that suffers from too much capacity. In addition, the economies in Canada and the U.S. do not seem to be able to get back on their feet and we face extremely strong and very aggressive competition. This plant lost money in 1991. We have already lost (a considerable amount) in the first four months of this year; and we stand to lose substantially more in 1992 if current trends continue. It should be easy for all of us to predict what (the parent company) may decide to do. . .We must change and change dramatically.

Enormous change must occur if (this plant) is to again become a strong, competitive, and successful plant where employment security and increasing income levels are enjoyed by all. What needs to be done to achieve the magnitude of change required will be very difficult. I believe, however, that it can be accomplished if we all have the will and determination to make the necessary changes. As difficult as the changes may be, please remember two important points: the changes which I feel are required have already been accomplished by other companies; and whether we change and how much we change are decisions almost 100 percent within your control as employees. . .It is all too clear to me that management alone cannot successfully operate this plant. As a result, we have come here today to invite you, to urge you, the leadership of this union and all our employees, to become partners in this business. . ..

This plant has a long history, 26 years. That history includes a relationship between management and its employees that, at times, has been far short of what is required to make us a world-class manufacturer. That relationship has often been adversarial and confrontational, in large measure due to the company's historic management style. I understand that many employees describe that style as secretive, top down, non-participatory, political, oriented around fear, punitive, judgmental, etc. . .In the past, employees were basically employed only for their physical effort. Management reserved to itself the exclusive right to manage the business. Management made all the decisions, and employees were essentially excluded from making contributions to the business beyond simply applying physical effort. Given these conditions, it certainly is not surprising that the relationship between the management of the company and our employees is today far less than what is required to make this plant a more competitive, high commitment, high performance organization.

If management continues to think of employees principally as a variable cost, which can almost always be reduced, then we are most likely to emphasize changes or improvements in technology and work methods (resulting in less labor input) as the best way to contain or reduce costs and become more competitive. However, if management adopts the view that employees are both resources and collaborators in our business, the dynamics of our relationship can undergo incredible change. The challenge then becomes one of blending everyone's energy, experience, competence, and intelligence, and aligning them behind the common objectives of the business. Management's challenge shifts from how can we do it our way better or "how can we get them to work harder" to creating a work environment where all employees are committed to a common purpose. Your challenge is to lay aside the attitudes of yesterday and to actively participate in reversing the direction of this plant.

My strong opinion is that we must change our historic belief that the future rests principally on the development and application of even more sophisticated technology. We must instead seek and utilize technology which emphasizes a more central role for people in using and managing the production process and, frankly, all other processes in our business. The creative challenge for me, and for you, is to link employees and technology in ways which maximize both the best of our technology and most importantly, the best contributions of our employees. . ..

This plant has thus far survived despite all the conditions under which employees have had to work. However, survival does not mean the business is prospering nor does it mean the business will continue. What it means is that the plant has barely been getting by, and barely getting by often results in a slow but certain death. . .If we want to assure ourselves and our families of employment security and an improving standard of living then we cannot continue to operate "on the brink." We must change rapidly and dramatically, a change that I intend to lead, but a change that each and every one of you must support and actively participate in achieving. . ..

CIRCUMSTANCES DRIVING THE CHANGE PROCESS

Before going further, it is important to gain perspective by understanding some of the history of this plant that led top management to the decision of embarking on this change process and some of the circumstances shaping its initial path.

Difficult Business Conditions

During the decade of the 80's this company found itself faced with industry-wide overcapacity and severe competition from domestic and foreign producers resulting in financial difficulties. A number of attempts were made to improve performance and market share including layoffs, plant closures, product consolidations, new product lines, and changes in management. However, through all of these changes the basic management style of the company did not alter from the traditional, autocratic form. Despite temporary periods of performance improvement and positive financial results, the company as a whole continued to struggle. This plant, in particular, as the president remarked in his speech to employees, had lost between $1 and $2 million in 1991 and was on a similar track in '92. Hopes for an improving economy in the latter half of 1992 were to be dashed when a 25 percent shortage of business would force a layoff of both hourly and salaried employees. The plant's future was uncertain and depended largely on the outcome of the change process.

An Imposing Labor Relations Dilemma

The climate in this particular plant reflected a general mistrust of management and suspicion of the company's intentions. The company's labor relations official, dedicated to maintaining integrity and credibility with the local union, had done significant work in improving management's relationship with the union over the previous 15 years. However, the mistrust persisted for a number of reasons. Specifically, the difficult financial situation, described above, had resulted over the years in frequent layoffs, difficult bargaining sessions, periods of plant shutdown, several concessionary contracts, and occasional rumors about the possibility of a plant closure. The difficulty of this climate was undoubtedly amplified by the astounding degree of turnover in the plant manager's chair, numbering thirteen plant managers, or acting plant managers, in a 14-year period. This inconsistency in plant-level leadership understandably resulted in continual upheaval for the plant, abrupt changes in direction, and contradictory decisions between different plant managers, which caused employees to question and resist management's directions.

In early 1992, during preliminary discussions regarding the expiration of this plant's collective bargaining agreement, it had become clear to the labor relations officials in the company that a long and bitter work stoppage was very likely if normal contract negotiations were to take place. The key issue would undoubtedly be the company's employee health care policy, which held that all employees (in all locations) were to receive the same medical benefits and bear the same level of cost sharing. An increase in health care cost sharing in the last contract had adversely affected the already negative climate in this plant and remained a very sensitive issue. As some employees commented, the automatic health care deduction shown on each paycheck stood out as a bitter and continual reminder of the last negotiations. The company was convinced that the local union would insist (to the point of striking) on one of two health care benefit demands: the current health care plan must remain unchanged, or health care costs to employees must be reduced to the same level as in the years prior to the last agreement.

Neither of these would be acceptable for the company due to the fact that they would result in even greater differences in health care benefits between the union-represented employees in this plant and the balance of the company's employees, including the salaried employees in this same plant. This would almost certainly cause employee and labor relations problems in other locations within the company. Also, it was determined that if the company were to apply either of these anticipated demands on employee health care contributions to the entire organization, in order to avoid disparate treatment, the company would be faced with unbearable future financial consequences. It was the company's view that the advantages of a uniform health care plan far outweighed the disadvantages. Among the advantages was the view that the elimination of barriers and status symbols were some changes that must occur in creating the desired plant culture for true total quality management principles to take hold. A uniform health care plan was viewed as a step in the right direction toward this effort.

However, the company strongly believed that the unavoidable "test of wills" that would ensue over the health care issue would severely damage the plant's stability, and create additional animosity between the company and its employees regardless of whether a strike resulted, thus worsening the already unfit environment for total quality management. The company explored many alternatives to the situation and found them to be either unacceptable or not feasible, including: traditional negotiations that were likely to result in a strike or bargaining to the point of impasse; buying products from elsewhere in the organization or from competitors; shutting down the plant and moving to a new facility in another state; local-based HMO programs; independent benefit packages for each plant or division; offering a gainsharing or profit sharing package in return for the union agreeing to the company's health care package; and so forth.

A Proactive Solution to a Difficult Situation

The company's senior managers found a very difficult situation in this plant not only in terms of performance problems, but also due to this pressing labor relations dilemma. Of the apparent strategy options, only one seemed desirable and to have a strong chance for success. This approach carried the assumption that employees in this plant did not respect or trust management based on the historical adversarial relationship that had existed. This environment would almost certainly mean an inability to resolve the health care conflict, which was bound to have detrimental consequences for the plant. Also, it had been for similar reasons of lack of trust that management was unsuccessful in implementing its quality improvement process, which was damaging the plant's competitiveness. In fact the local union president commented, after the fact, that his international union had cautioned him to distrust any management programs that resembled quality circles.

Therefore, the appropriate solution seemed to be a radical proposal of redesigning and changing the way in which the plant operated, which would serve two purposes. First, it would be a proposal so different from past management practices that the union could not refuse to accept it and would agree to defer contract negotiations, which would allow more time to explore other health care alternatives and to develop a more collaborative relationship between the parties before dealing with this controversial issue. Second, and more important, it would create the change in culture, management systems, and operational processes necessary for improving the plant's long-term performance. Likewise, it would create the environment for total quality management principles to succeed by developing a plant full of high performance, high commitment employees dedicated to continuously improving plant performance.

If the local union were to view this proposal as a desired future worth deferring the upcoming contract negotiations, then the likelihood of success was viewed as being extremely high. The remaining obstacles would be largely up to management in the form of their own resistance to change, their ability to value the development and empowerment of employees without viewing themselves as losing control, and their depth of commitment to provide the necessary money, time, effort, and patience to ensure success.

Management chose to introduce and explain the need for the redesign process through a continuous series of meetings, described earlier, in which the company president, VP of Human Resources, Divisional HR manager, and a candidate consultant group met face to face with all employees in the plant. During these meetings management also proposed certain conditions for initiating and conducting the process. Some of these included the guarantee for employees of "a loud and very influential voice in the operation of the plant"; the open sharing of all business information; the formation of a joint "change team" (or planning team), including both production employees and management employees to take the lead in redesigning the operations of the plant (This change team would be included in the review of all candidates for employment and have veto power over these candidates.); and the union would be asked to participate in choosing a consultant to facilitate the process.

At the conclusion of his remarks the president also proposed to the local union these specific points in an attempt to relieve their predictable skepticism: the contract expiration date would be deferred for 18 months and when a new agreement was reached all economic improvements would be made retroactive to the current expiration date; in a spirit of fair play, all wage rates would be increased by $.35/hour upon agreement from the union to join in the change effort and extend the contract. Joint discussions would begin within two weeks concerning the initiation of the change process and formation of the change team. He then urged the union to move as quickly as possible in making a decision to accept or reject this proposal.

Eventually, the proposal was accepted as the union ratified the agreement to extend the contract and participate in the change process.

At that moment, the employees of this plant were posed to embark on a change process that would test their commitment, creativity, fear of change, and ability to let go of the past. Their goal was to start over and jointly redesign their plant with only a few expectations. Specifically, the plant would be a very different, more participative, and extremely open environment; all employees would be viewed as partners in the business; and the litmus test on the redesign would be its effect on plant performance. To be sure, there were many individual skeptics among the employees, and the mistrust did not subside overnight. In fact, there was a degree of mistrust on both sides; on the part of local management and the union toward one another. But, the union leaders were able to suspend their skepticism for the greater good of achieving the future that the company president had articulated for them. As the union president commented, "I was ecstatic about what they (management) were offering, it was what we have been waiting for all along (a chance to help manage the plant)."

LAUNCHING THE CHANGE PROCESS

In July 1992, management and union officials began their joint pursuit of a better future by agreeing upon a university-based consulting group to facilitate the change process. The vice president of Human Resources, Richard Deming, had worked with Glenn Varney, the director of the Institute for Organization Effectiveness (IOE), many times in the past. However, in the spirit of joint decision making, the choice for management was not to unilaterally hire the consultants, but instead to introduce them to the Union Executive Board as candidates. This would be a theme that management would have to try to repeat throughout the process, emphasizing openness and joint decision making over the use of management authority to gain trust and partnership with the union.

In a late July meeting, Varney addressed the Union Executive Board assuring them that he did not wish to be viewed principally as an agent of management, but that he viewed the union as a client as much as management, and for that reason wanted them to have a choice in the hiring of IOE. After some discussion about the consultants' experience and proposed roles in the change process, the executive board unanimously concurred with management's decision to hire the consultants. From the very beginning and throughout their relationship with this plant, the consultants made an effort to establish a true third-party stance, being careful not to take sides in this very adversarial environment, and instead emphasizing open communication, true participation, choice, and building consensus.

Forming a Change Team

On July 27, 1992, as promised in the president's speech to the plant earlier in the summer, joint discussions commenced between the union and management regarding the formation of a joint change team. A meeting was held to establish the number of people that would serve on the team, a process for selecting members, and a target date for the first change team meeting. It was decided by consensus that the team should consist of nine members with a majority represented by the union. It was also agreed that the union president and acting plant manager would be automatic selections, and that the first priority in selecting the remaining seven individuals would be to find the seven best qualified people. The selection process began with a letter to all plant employees, signed by the union president and plant manager, which asked for volunteers for the change team. The letter explained, "all volunteers will meet with our consultants in order to give each volunteer information about what is involved in being a member of the change team" and, "the Executive Board and management will then meet to review the names recommended by the consultants for the change team."

Within days of the distribution of this letter, the first of many hurdles was thrown in the path of the change process. This selection procedure, which had been so carefully planned by management and union leaders during consensus-based discussions, was being challenged by a largely supported union petition against the Executive Board having any responsibility for selecting the change team. The Executive Board handled this situation internally and rejected the petition. Having had experience with planning teams or design teams taking on too much control in the eyes of their co-workers, the consultants tried to address this hurdle by explaining from the outset that the change team would not be an exclusive or omnipotent decision-making body and that many more employees would have to play equally important roles throughout the change process. Also, the consultants would later build into the change structure an opportunity for increased numbers of employees to be directly involved in the design phase of the change process, with the change team eventually taking a reduced role.

The turmoil surrounding this petition eventually died down, but revealed some important information about the plant. It showed a substantial division within the rank and file. It clearly indicated the importance and attention that the employees of this plant were placing on the change process. The question of who would be on the change team and who would make the selections had attracted dramatic attention. Particularly, this event also showed that a great deal of thought, feeling, and opinion existed among the plant's employees regarding the change process. This energy somehow needed to be tapped and unleashed; hopefully through the course of open dialogue, rather than escalating into similar forms of political protest or worse, bitter apathy. This energy was indeed tapped and retained throughout the process through the use of an elaborate communication system, which will be described later.

This sweeping interest in the change process was further confirmed in that no less than 47 management and union employees volunteered for membership on the change team, nearly one-third of the plant. Each volunteer met with one of three consultants from IOE who explained the responsibilities and qualifications needed for change team members. The consultants ranked each volunteer using a point method based on his/her responses to interview questions involving availability, understanding, and commitment to the change process. Prior to the interviews, information was also gathered by asking the opinions of the Executive Board and local plant management on which volunteers would be competent and acceptable to them as change team members. To preserve objectivity, this information was not analyzed until after the interviews were completed, but it allowed the consultants to avoid making recommendations that might be unanimously unacceptable to the Executive Board or plant management.

Still, it was not easy for the Executive Board and management to come to a consensus on the makeup of the change team. The meeting lasted four hours with several different variations and back-up recommendations being considered before everyone could agree on the final team. The Executive Board took the task of selecting a change team very seriously, as they certainly tried to protect their own interests, being sure to exclude names who were viewed as "anti-union." But they also tried desperately to select people whom they felt could help the plant. As when one member commented emotionally with tears welling up in his eyes, "I hope you realize how important this is to all of us. I'm 47 years old and I don't want to have to look for another job. This has to work!"

Clearly, the atmosphere in this plant was emotionally charged with expressions of fear, distrust, anxiety, excitement, determination, and so on. With the long awaited announcement of who would serve on the change team, the leadership at the center of all of this attention and emotion fell upon the shoulders of the acting plant manager, the union president, the union chief steward, the inventory control specialist, a maintenance journeyman, the secretary/HR assistant, a technologist, and two machine operators.

The First Meeting of the Change Team

On September 3rd and 4th, the initial change team meeting was held at an off-site location. The team met with the IOE consultants along with Richard Deming and the Division Human Resources manager, Scott Janoch. The purpose of the meeting was to organize and agree on roles for the change process, and to help the group develop into a cohesive team.

At the start of the meeting the nine selected volunteers were clearly not yet a team. As some have expressed as they reflected back upon their first meeting, the group possessed a lack of understanding of one another, some false assumptions about one another, distrust of some members fueled by their adversarial history, uncertainty about one another's roles, etc. The meeting began with a discussion designed to increase understanding and communication within the group. Members openly answered questions about their values, how they felt about being on the change team, their concerns, and their hopes. This process revealed common ground within the group and opened up communication, breaking down many of the walls that had been constructed over the past 15 years. Some of the common feelings revealed about serving on the change team included: excitement, honor, challenge, a feeling of responsibility and accountability to co-workers, and optimism. For some their optimism was guarded due to their concerns about management's commitment, the union's commitment, the inability of people to accept change, and their own ability to make the right decisions. The group seemed to be united, however, in that they shared some common hopes for the change process, including job stability, a successful plant, quality of work life, and the elimination of the "us vs. them" mentality.

In a discussion of roles, both Deming and Janoch expressed a strong devotion to the change process and pledged to do everything in their power to help and support the change team. Deming explained that he would serve as a direct communication link between the change team and the president of the company. Janoch would serve as a consulting resource to the change team and would also serve as a communication link between the plant and the division. The consultants explained that their roles would be to provide the change team with information and resources, guidance in planning the process of change, and support and facilitation for day to day activities. The agreed-upon charter of the change team itself would be to study and learn about options for change, create a vision for the future, participate in the design of their new plant, communicate with all employees about the proposed changes, and participate in setting up an eventual implementation team. There was a sense of supreme responsibility among the change team members when discussing this role. They felt that the success of the change process, and the plant, was largely in their hands.

The change team also agreed to be involved in the recruitment and selection process for a new plant manager and HR manager. The plant had been without an HR manager for several months and was currently being led by an acting plant manager who was scheduled to return to his division level position. As the first step in this activity the change team drafted and distributed a questionnaire requesting feedback from plant employees on the qualities, experience, and skills they desired to see in plant manager and HR manager candidates. This information was later used by the change team to assemble key specifications for candidates that were forwarded to a search firm. It was also decided that the change team would be involved in the interview procedure once a candidate pool had been identified, and as management had promised earlier, no candidate would be hired of whom the change team did not approve.

In this first meeting, the change team began to understand and establish structure for the change process by agreeing upon the consultants' proposal of three phases of activity to be accomplished through the remainder of 1992 including an initial orientation and learning phase, a visioning phase, and a design phase. The learning phase would serve for the change team to build a knowledge base of information on high performance work systems and ideas for change options in their plant; the visioning phase would consist of the change team drawing from this knowledge base and feedback from their co-workers to shape a new vision for the plant; and the design phase would involve increasing numbers of employees in the creation of a detailed change plan based on the vision.

An essential component of all three phases would be the change team's system of communicating with the others in the plant. Everyone agreed that it would be absolutely critical to communicate well with those not directly involved in the change process in order to minimize the inevitable resistance to change. On repeated occasions during this meeting and thereafter, when change team members expressed concern about facing resistance from their co-workers, the consultants emphasized that the better they communicated throughout the process the less resistance they would ultimately face. With help from the consultants, the change team designed a thorough two-way communication system to be followed during their weekly cycle of activities. Each Monday written updates of the change team's activities and thoughts from the previous week would be posted and copies distributed to every plant employee by a change team representative (sample updates will be used to illustrate subsequent sections of this chapter). Sections of the plant were divided equally among change team members who volunteered to communicate directly with the employees in his or her section. Every Monday through Thursday, change team members would make themselves available to their sections to answer questions and listen to feedback from employees. On Friday, each change team member would share reactions and feedback from their sections, which would also be documented in the next week's update to close the feedback loop. This communication system was designed to encourage dialogue about the change process to keep all organizational members informed of the direction and progress of the change process, and to involve everyone as much as possible as participants in the process. As the next best alternative to having the entire organization in one room at the same time, this method would involve as many participants as possible in the early stages of the change process when it would be critical to generate support and momentum for change.

Consistent with this emphasis on involvement the change team ended their first weekly update to their co-workers by stating, "As a team of equals, we have pledged to make this change process work. However, we cannot do it alone; we need your help. Over the next few months we'll be asking you for a significant amount of input to assist us in meeting the challenges that lie ahead. We're in this together!"

LEARNING PHASE: 9/3 - 10/26

To achieve the kinds of changes described by the president in his speech to employees would require profound, systemic change in the operation of the plant—not just incremental or superficial tinkering with current systems. Change at this level meant letting go of old habits and ways of thinking and making a paradigm shift in the way one viewed organizations. This clearly required exposure to alternative ways of organizing and a great deal of learning before the real work of changing the plant could begin. In order to prepare the organization for change, it would be necessary to inform or educate not only the change team, but as many plant employees as possible to influence them in looking at the plant in a different way as well. The communication system described above would support this need. It was designed so that as the change team learned, the rest of the organization would learn along with them.

Acquiring Knowledge and Making Paradigm Shifts

Over the next six weeks the consultants supplied the change team with information on high performance plants and change process concepts in the form of articles, books, videotapes, guest speakers, and visits to other plants. The team spent many hours, some members on their own personal time, reading and studying options for change at the plant. Each Friday the change team met to interpret and discuss highlights from the week and to document what they had learned for use in educating the rest of the plant. They were building a knowledge base and a library of ideas related to employee empowerment, self-directed work teams, performance-based pay systems, and cooperative union management relations that could be used later in constructing a vision for change at the plant.

In the first few change process updates distributed to employees, the change team explained that they would not be making decisions at this point, rather they would be learning and studying options for change. The updates reported ideas and concepts that the change team had found interesting about what was occurring in other companies across the country, and requested feedback from employees in considering the feasibility of these ideas working in their plant. Initial reactions from the plant included pleasant surprise with being kept so closely informed by the updates, but also, a growing feeling of impatience in not seeing any tangible changes take place. Many employees incorrectly viewed this apparent lack of activity as a symbol of management's lack of commitment to the change process. Consequently, the change team, who by this time had gained a certain degree of credibility, spent a lot of time influencing their co-workers to set aside their skepticism and respect the fact that the change process was not a quick-fix program, but rather a long-term continuous process of change. Some of the anxiety about seeing nothing happen was generated, no doubt, by a fear of running out of time and the resulting consequences to the plant if it was not able to change and improve quickly enough.

Most of the displeasure and complaints centered on aspects of the plant that were important or nagging concerns for the individual, but were actually compartmentalized symptoms of larger, more systemic problems that needed to be carefully analyzed and understood. For example, there was a great deal of feedback from employees about the need to improve the production scheduling system in the plant, which stemmed from frequent confusion surrounding the weekly production schedule. Most of the feedback surfaced in the form of blaming those who seemed most responsible for the problems, the employees in production control, who naturally were threatened and took defensive postures in the face of all this blame. In reality, however, many of the problems surrounding the production schedule were resulting not from incompetence, but from unexpected machine breakdowns, needs for rework, production of the improper quantities, poor communication, etc. This just happened to be one of the most easily recognizable symptoms of a deeper problem that had to be understood more systemically before solutions could be prescribed and action taken.

The change team responded to the anxiety they had been sensing among their co-workers in the September 14th update, a portion of which is shown below:

"We know that many of you are anxious to begin seeing changes, so are we! But, as the change team, we cannot risk failure by making assumptions or jumping to conclusions and taking immediate action just to see something happen. After studying other plants, we have seen that making change can't be an overnight thing, it's a gradual process that first requires a lot of learning, analyzing and planning. . .We will be reading more articles, watching more tapes, and visiting other plants to further explore our options in the coming weeks. Our intent is that as we learn, you can learn with us. We would like to give everyone the opportunity to see one of the videotapes which we watched this past week examining three successful team-based companies. For those of you who are interested, we will be posting a schedule on the change process update board sometime this week. We will welcome your comments, suggestions, and questions."

Even though at this stage there were no tangible changes taking place that employees could point to, there was indeed significant learning and a cultural transformation underway. As they were being exposed to concepts and success stories from other companies in the areas of employee empowerment, self-directed work teams, performance-based pay systems and cooperative union/management relations, employees throughout the plant were making paradigm shifts. The traditional controls, policies, procedures, and relationships that had always been viewed as givens in the plant began to be questioned in light of these successful alternatives that the change team had been exposed to from other companies. The emphasis was slowly shifting from serving the boss or the established procedures for accomplishing tasks to serving the customer and the quality of the manufacturing process. A second shift also slowly began to take place in that people began choosing cooperation and partnership over adversarial relations and antagonism. This was apparent between salaried and union employees within the change team, as well as throughout the plant. Grievances dropped. Cooperation and teamwork between employees increased visibly. There was a heightened awareness about the need to cut costs and employees began making conscious efforts to avoid waste. And, there was a noticeable change in daily conversation topics that centered on the change process, the business, and how to improve the plant's performance. This was a slow process mind set; "it's difficult to let go of that mind set until you allow yourself to think of a new way of doing things."

Economic Difficulties

In late September the company announced a severe need to minimize costs for the remainder of the year. The ensuing economic slowdown consisted of approximately a 25 percent drop in production and a 25 percent layoff. Furthermore, there was some suspicion due to dwindling sales figures that a plant shutdown might have to occur for the last one and one-half months of the year. The layoff and impending shutdown presented more hurdles for the continued morale and enthusiasm surrounding the change process. Momentum for change would be difficult to maintain in the face of a production shutdown and management's credibility and commitment to the change process would again be thrown into question. Many questions surfaced regarding whether the need for cost cutting measures would impact the change process. Answers were provided in a meeting with Dick Deming and Scott Janoch as reported in this excerpt from a late September change process update:

"On Thursday, Dick Deming and Scott Janoch explained the causes and implications of the current economic situation. We were told that the change process cannot and will not be deterred or slowed due to our economic situation. We have been encouraged not to give up. We cannot ignore these events and their impact, but we cannot allow them to stop progress of the change process either. Now we are more determined than ever to help improve the performance and quality of work life in this plant and plan to begin meeting more often each week. And so, with your help we will forge ahead."

Also, in an effort to re-establish management's commitment to the change process and dispel any rumors surrounding the cost reduction activities in the company, the president visited the plant to meet with the change team and talk with employees. In answer to the change team's questions about the economic situation, the president assured the change team that the process would not be shorted in stating: "We're tightening our belts but we cannot stop the change process. If it means cutting something that I'm doing to give you the necessary funds, I'll do it. But we need to respect the need to use discretion in our spending."

Thus, a decision was made to stick very close to the original plan for the change process including provisions for the change team to take trips to visit other plants to complete the learning phase. Barring a production shutdown, the change team planned to draft and gain commitment to a finalized change vision by mid November, and to then begin the design phase of the change process.

Fortunately, feedback from employees was generally positive with the common sentiment that the change process must continue and the change team should not start cutting corners. In fact, many employees who were laid off requested that the change process updates be mailed to them at home so they could continue to stay informed. Employee devotion to the change process was never more apparent than when one employee, in his last week of work before being laid off indefinitely, confronted the president on the manufacturing floor and virtually demanded that he follow through on the change process and devote the necessary resources to make it work.

During the change team's meeting with the company president, one member articulated the team's motivation to continue the process this way: "We as the change team are also motivated. . .The layoff has slowed us down some, but comments from employees affected by the reduction were that (1) we should and must continue the process, so they will have a chance to return to work as quickly as business allows and (2) the motivation and commitment of people who have lost their jobs, should be used to inspire, and move the process forward for the betterment of (the company), the union and all employees." In a show of true dedication, some change team members and other employees close to the process expressed a willingness to volunteer their own time in the event of a production shutdown to continue working on the change process. Ultimately, the plant was able to avoid a complete production shutdown with the exception of the last two weeks in December, and momentum was sustained as employees had the fortitude to look beyond the short-term pain of the layoff and keep focusing on the long-term survival and success of the plant.

VISIONING PHASE: 10/30 - 11/15

With the learning phase completed the change team shifted its focus to creating a vision for change. The consultants emphasized strongly that this vision would have to be a truly shared vision in order to generate the commitment, energy, and understanding needed to accomplish real change. Far too often, in efforts to create intended common visions organizations hire a consultant to take top management on a two-day retreat to undergo team building activities and assemble a vision statement that sounds terrific with many references to teamwork, valuing employees, putting the customer first, world class quality, etc. The intent is sincere, but predictably results in a vision statement that lacks ownership, except by top management, and is inevitably difficult to implement. The best that can be hoped for is employee compliance minus the energy and determination that true commitment would bring. Other organizations make the mistake of chartering a steering committee or design team made up of a diagonal slice of the organization to draft a vision statement and detailed change design, and then roll them out through extensive communication and training. The mistake in this case is the assumption that the diverse, representative membership of the team will ensure buy-in throughout the organization. In these scenarios, design teams can come to be seen as elite groups much like top management and ultimately fail to inspire organizational commitment to a common vision. These were mistakes that the change team was fully aware of and determined to avoid.

Establishing a Common Vision

The change team set about the task of creating a draft vision statement during a two-day off-site meeting. Referencing the catalogue of ideas and concepts they had compiled over the past two months and the input and feedback gathered from their fellow employees, the team followed a collaborative process in assembling the draft vision. Change team members worked in pairs, one union member partnered with one salaried member, in writing the initial rough drafts of each section which were then critiqued and edited by the entire team. After a great deal of writing and rewriting and countless sheets of flipchart paper, the team reached agreement on a vision they all felt strongly about. Their work was not yet complete, however; the vision still needed to be held up for examination by the remainder of the plant's employees.

The change team had done an admirable job to this point in communicating closely with employees, listening to their feedback, and keeping them involved in the process as much as possible. This had undoubtedly "greased the wheels" to minimize potential resistance to the vision. However, they knew instinctively, after two months in the change process, that they could not simply announce, sell, or impose the vision on their co-workers. The flaw with this traditional leadership thinking is that a vision created by a select few for the rest of the organization to endorse and live out cannot lead to individual ownership and commitment. Therefore, the change team chose appropriately to "propose" the vision as a first draft to all employees in the plant and allow them to make informed individual choices about whether or not this was indeed their vision. The process used was to hold small group meetings with employees to present the vision with the expressed purpose of allowing employees to examine and understand the vision before providing feedback at subsequent meetings. During the first series of clarification meetings, the change team explained the vision, shared learning experiences which led to the vision's content, and answered questions. A common question from employees regarded how specific issues would be decided and by whom (i.e., will there be team leaders and who will select them?). The change team answered by explaining that they did not view it to be their role to dictate specifics and assured employees that many of the specifics would be further defined by design teams in the next phase of the change process, such as whether or not team leaders would be needed. They also emphasized that the work teams themselves would have to make decisions on issues directly affecting them, such as who the team leader would be and whether that position is rotating or permanent, etc. Questionnaires were also distributed at the conclusion of the meeting asking employees to take the next week to further examine the vision and indicate their reaction.

During the second series of meetings, questionnaire results were fed back to employees and suggestions for altering the vision were recorded and discussed. It was the change team's intention with the second series of meetings to answer the question, "Is this our vision, and if not, what needs to be added or changed?" In response to the questionnaires, 75 percent of the respondents indicated that they felt it was "a good vision for the future," while 25 percent said that it was "ok and they could support it." No one expressed total opposition. However, there were numerous suggestions offered for changes to the vision. These were aired and discussed with all employees during the feedback meetings and many were incorporated into the final vision. This method appeared to be the next best thing to having all 150 organizational members in the same room to agree on and wordsmith their collective vision. To be certain, there were undoubtedly individuals at this stage who were apathetic to the vision and probably a few who were privately opposed, but for the majority who used their opportunity to contribute and participate, this vision was their vision and they were committed to it.

Our Vision for Colusa, California Plant

OUR VISION for the Colusa, California plant of Pirelli is to produce the highest quality cables and to be the most competitive and highly regarded manufacturer in the industry. We will have a culture, supported by the Union and Management, that allows and encourages all employees to participate, develop, and become empowered through education and training in a climate of mutual trust and respect. We will be an adaptive, innovative organization committed to meeting and exceeding customer expectations and continuously improving our people, methods, technology, and products. We will be recognized by our customers, suppliers, and community as a safe, cooperative, team-based organization where employees are proud to work and where they continuously strive for improvement. We will be a profitable operation in which employees share in the success of the plant and enjoy job stability. MANAGEMENT APPROACH We will use a participative approach to managing the Colusa plant which includes: 1) Placing decision making at the appropriate team level; 2) Seeking counsel and advice from the appropriate teams throughout the plant; 3) Establishing standing and special committees to focus on areas such as safety, quality, rewards, etc.; and 4) Annually reviewing the Colusa Vision and making any recommendations to the entire plant.
ORGANIZATION STRUCTURE We will have a team-based organization structure with fewer levels that encourages utilization of all available resources.
GOALS We will encourage employees to participate in setting short- and long-term organizational and operational goals.
POLICIES We will have policies which support our vision and which recognize and value our employees, environment, community, and company.

INFORMATION AND COMMUNICATION We will use open communication systems that keep employees informed of all needed business information and encourage employee input.

TASKS AND JOBS We will be an adaptive organization using a team-based approach. We will provide training and education opportunities for all employees. These will include joint Union/Management education, cross training, and other training programs that will enhance our ability to achieve this Vision.

PERFORMANCE MEASURES We will provide financial, quality, and other appropriate indicators to enable employees and teams to assess their own performance and continuous improvement. Total plant performance is the sum of all individual and team performance.

WORK FLOW AND PRODUCTIVITY We will utilize an efficient, team-based work flow system designed to support continuous improvement. Staff support will be readily available to all teams. There will be strong internal customer/supplier communication. Work teams will have standard operating procedures, manufacturing process control, timely scheduling, and inventory control to achieve production efficiency which will contribute to cost effectiveness and profitability.

QUALITY We will be an organization renowned for its world class quality. All employees will be responsible for the quality of their work. Quality will be defined by manufacturing process control standards and documentation based on customer and industry specifications. We will consistently deliver products on time that meet or exceed customer requirements.

LAYOUT We will have an environment where employees have influence on, and input into, the decisions which affect the physical layout of their work areas, and where barriers are minimized.

SHARING THE GAINS We will have a financial reward system based on continuous improvement in the plant for all employees. In addition, we will have other recognition and reward systems designed to enhance quality of work life.

CUSTOMERS We will be a world class supplier with a culture in which employees are encouraged to have direct contact with internal and external users of our products and services. There will be partnerships with our customers which will be continuously improved by involving employees in customer visits to our plant and in visiting customer locations where our products are used. To improve our customer focus, Colusa employees will be part of joint efforts with sales, marketing, and engineering personnel to develop initiatives which will enhance sales and profitability.

SUPPLIERS To achieve our objectives of making Colusa a world class supplier, we must have suppliers who are also world class.

To accomplish this, employees will maintain partnership with internal and external suppliers which will ensure quality, cost competitiveness, and timely delivery.

DESIGN PHASE: 11/16 - 3/15

The next step in the change process would be to develop specific change plans that would help the plant achieve this common vision. This would require months of analysis and planning and would require the direct involvement of increased numbers of organizational members. The change team explained the transition into the next phase of the process with this November 16th change process update:

"We believe that after only two months of work something tremendous has been achieved in the plant. Together, we have established a vision for the future that has received the input, agreement, and support of virtually every employee. . .this common vision can and should be used to guide us through the many decisions that must be made over the next year and beyond. . .Together we have agreed upon our destination; now we must determine the best way to get there.

"Thus far, 34 employees have asked to be considered far participation on the design teams. . .On Thursday this week, the change team will meet to determine which employees are needed to accomplish the implementation design. Due to the abundance of talent and excitement in the plant, we're confident these decisions will be difficult. If you do volunteer and are not selected, don't be surprised if at some point you get asked to help with the tremendous amount of work that needs to be done.

"There will be four design teams consisting of approximately 5 to 6 members each. . .Each design team will be charged with the task of developing an implementation plan which will be presented to both division management and plant employees. The plans should include a description of the current state; description of proposed changes; and resource requirements."

Forming the Design Teams

The first task of the change team was to select the right individuals from among the 34 volunteers to serve on four design teams. Each change team member nominated those volunteers whom he or she felt would best fit on the respective design teams. Through a process of consensus decision making, the change team then formulated the makeup of each design team on the basis of needed knowledge and skills. This process was not without controversy as one union member staunchly protested the initiative of the rest of the team to include a manager who had acquired an anti-union reputation over the years. The rest of the team contended that this individual had knowledge and skills that the design teams could not do without and did not feel that he posed a threat to the union. After a great deal of discussion the opposing union member eventually reconciled that he could go along with the decision so long as he did not have to serve on the same design team. Clearly the distrust and animosity between management and the union was

189

persisting, but the manager was appointed and after a few days of complaints from some of the more senior union members the turmoil dissipated as the manager proved to be a key ingredient in the design phase.

The first meeting of the design teams was held in early December. The stated purpose of the two-day meeting was to organize the four design teams for their work and to give the members an opportunity to share expectations and begin developing into cohesive teams. At the beginning of the meeting there was a great deal of open discussion regarding team members' expectations, concerns, and hopes for the future. This resulted in an inspiring discussion as individuals stood up and proclaimed their commitment and motivation for the work that lay ahead. Here is a sampling of what was said: "People need to forget about the past, there is too much 'us and them' between union and management." "We need to break down the barriers between union and management, employee and supervisor, hourly and salaried, etc." "Look at the opportunity we've been given to help manage this plant! Look at the people in this room and the people back at the plant! We have the ability and the experience to do this if we just work together."

The agreed-upon role of the design teams was to prepare a detailed change plan to be proposed to both plant employees and division management. In accomplishing this, the teams would hold weekly meetings, share technical expertise, conduct detailed studies regarding feasibility of changes, collect needed data, contact outside and inside resources for help as needed, and continue the plant communication process that had been started by the change team. It had been decided that each design team would be assigned two to three different points from the vision for which specific change plans would be developed. It was also decided that the change team would remain in operation to ensure coordination and communication among the design teams and throughout the plant by continuing to publish the weekly change process updates.

Analyzing the Current State and Planning the Future

In mid-December the design teams began meeting weekly with a first priority of analyzing and understanding the current systems in the plant and identifying problems and opportunities for improvement. Their ultimate focus would be to analyze the current conditions in the plant, compare those with the vision to identify any gaps, and design changes intended to close those gaps. Over the next three months each team worked diligently on these activities while maintaining close communication with the remainder of the plant. Again, as with the development of the vision statement, it would be critical to manage resistance to change by keeping all employees informed of the design teams' progress and to provide opportunities for feedback and input.

Early on in the design phase, uninvolved employees became increasingly anxious and dissatisfied that they weren't seeing anything happen, wondering why it was taking so many meetings and so much time to implement changes. The change team again tried to address this sentiment by explaining that a common mistake made by many companies undergoing change is to rush ahead, which often results in chaos, disorganization, and confusion. The change team emphasized that the design teams intended to avoid that mistake by taking the time necessary to carefully analyze the current conditions in the plant and plan the appropriate changes.

In partial response to this situation, actions were taken to involve more employees in order to increase their understanding of the change process. For example, the design teams and change team began holding open door meetings during which anyone could observe the discussions and have access to real time information about the process. Many design team members who were taking criticisms from some co-workers personally invited those co-workers to attend upcoming meetings, which typically helped the situation. Also, several design teams provided involvement opportunities by soliciting feedback and information from co-workers through informal interviews and questionnaires, and by requesting the help of experts within the plant to aid in the design process.

An additional example of increased involvement resulted in response to the growing impatience of many production employees with the production scheduling system, mentioned earlier in this chapter. In dealing with this impatience, the technical design team chose to ask one outspoken production worker to spend a few weeks in production control in order to understand the scheduling system and collaborate with production control employees and the design team in understanding the problem. After a few weeks of perception sharing and communication on mutual problems, this individual had completely changed his opinion about the source of the scheduling problems. He, along with the production control supervisor, was able to provide the design team with valuable feedback on the feasibility of various redesign options. This also helped ease the tension and blame of production control as this employee shared his newfound understandings with fellow employees, many of whom became less quick to judge production control and considered instead how their own actions contributed to problems with the production schedule. The barriers separating the two functions had clearly prohibited this understanding in the past and added to the problem

Gaining Support for the Design Proposal

By late February, each of the four design teams had completed their analysis and planning and had written a rough draft outlining the plant's current state in relation to the vision and specific proposals for change, including the implementation of self-managed work teams, a gainsharing system, technical system changes, and increased employee involvement with customers and suppliers. They decided to meet first with one another to review and integrate their respective proposals and to critique each proposal before communicating them with the rest of the plant. The meeting consisted of each design team presenting their proposal to the other three teams allowing time for questions and feedback. After some discussion and agreeing to make a few adjustments, each design team received 100 percent support for their proposals.

It was decided to communicate the final proposal to the rest of the plant by distributing copies to every employee to pre-read. Next, department meetings were held during which a representative from each design team and a consultant were present to discuss the change proposal, answer questions, and record feedback. Also, a questionnaire was administered at each meeting to determine the level of support for the change proposal. It was explained that the designs contained in the proposal were not intended as an ending point, but that they should serve as a starting point for continuous learning and improvement. It was further emphasized that making changes would involve a learning process during which the plant would test new ways of doing things and discover which designs worked and which did not, and that if problems arose these designs may need to be adjusted. Based on feedback gathered at these departmental meetings several minor changes were made to the proposal. However, the questionnaire resulted in an astounding 95 percent response of support.

A Change in Management and the End of the Change Process

After nearly eight months of preparatory work, the plant was poised to begin implementing the changes that the company president had spoken so strongly about in his speech to employees when the change process was introduced. Plans were underway for a pilot implementation phase to begin upon the acceptance of the proposal by division management. Ultimately, no implementation was to take place due to a dramatic change in the management of the company and division. Prior to implementation, the European-based parent company assigned a new division general manager and the company CEO resigned. The new leadership of the division could not and would not support the change initiatives underway in this plant because of a philosophical disagreement about what was needed to correct the company's slumping financial performance. Unable to see the value of the change process, they opted instead for the traditional autocratic management approach with which they were more familiar; while emphasizing cost reduction, technical improvements, improved market strategies, and aggressive labor relations as keys to the success of the business.

Despite the disappointing fact that few tangible changes resulted, a clear success was achieved in terms of effective change management principles. That success is reflected by the overwhelming level of commitment among the plant's employees to achieving their vision of becoming a high performance plant. These employees were not simply following or adhering to a management initiative. This vision was their own and they were dedicated to achieving it.

Companies and organizations who venture into major changes of the scope discussed here need to pose a very important question before embarking on such a project. Although it is repeatedly mentioned as critical to successful change, the question of top management commitment and understanding about the consequences of changes needs to be tested. Executives lose direct control when they empower teams to manage themselves. This means the leader no longer knows all the details of how the business is operating. If they have had close contact with the operation of their business, they are likely to feel that they have lost control. When this happens they take control back by canceling projects or by reducing the level of empowerment.

About the Contributors

Glenn Varney

Glenn is the President of Management Advisory Associates, Incorporated, a Professor of Management, Associate Graduate Coordinator of the Master in Organization Development, and Director of the Institute for Organization Effectiveness (IOE) at Bowling Green State University. He is also the founder of the Self-Directed Work Team Resource Center (SDWT). Glenn is nationally recognized in the field of Organization Development and Change as an author, educator, and consultant.

His accomplishments include over fifty articles published in professional journals and he is the author of *Goal Driven Management* (1988), *Building Productive Teams* (1989), *Productivity Improvement* (1992), and *Skilled Change* (1992). He is also the author of *Self-Directed Work Teams: a Concise Guide to Understanding and Implementing Self-Directed Work Teams.*

Glenn consults internationally with major U.S. and foreign companies and is a frequent speaker at professional organizations and societies. His areas of specialization include building productive teams; designing organizational change strategies; designing and retrofitting "world class" organizations; organization analysis and problem diagnosis; "visioning" for future organizations; assessing and developing management competencies, and implementation of self-directed work teams.

Daniel Diers

Dan is currently working as an Organizational Effectiveness Facilitator helping to implement High Performance Work Systems in a division of Rockwell International. Dan has also worked for Bowling Green State University's Institute for Organization Effectiveness as an external OD consultant. He is a graduate of Bowling Green's Master of Organization Development program.

17

The Performance Appraisal Team: A Peer Appraisal Case Study

Lee Royal

The Industry

The Information Technology industry consists of organizations that design, assemble, and operate a combination of hardware and software that processes information in support of client operational missions. Components of such systems may be centralized or distributed. Organizations in the industry are having to acquire numerous new technical skills because of technology improvements.

The Company

FMC Corporate Information Resources, more commonly known as the Dallas Data Center (DDC), was a information technology organization of just over 100 people that managed centralized mainframe and midrange data processing 24 hours a day, seven days a week, for FMC Corporation, a Fortune 120 company manufacturing a wide variety of products in the defense, chemical, mining, oil field equipment, food processing machinery, and heavy machinery industries.

Corporate FMC decided that the DDC should compete with outside business organizations to support FMC organizations. In response to this strategic change, the DDC implemented a drastic culture change, known within the organization as the conversion to "HPO," or the high performing organization. In short, the DDC implemented a team-based structure, radically restructured the role of middle managers, eliminating the many middle manager and supervisory positions. Additionally, the DDC began to peruse and acquire customers outside FMC. As a part of this transition, DDC management began to emphasize MRAs, an FMC wide document for clarifying individual responsibilities, performance objectives, and actual performance. This document became the basis for an attempt at participative performance feedback. By 1990, a peer performance system had been developed. The system has evolved, but it has become a cultural artifact that exemplifies the interdependance of all people within the DDC.

The Organization and Team Structure

The DDC currently employs about 100 people, about 80 percent of whom are salaried. There are two levels of managers, and a total of four levels of leadership (see Figure 1). The top level consists of one (1) site director. The next level consists of managers, some of whom are also directors, depending on their level of contribution. Before the organization was purchased (see Epilogue), though there were some individual contributors at the director level, there were eight people to whom teams reported. This is about half the managers in comparable organizations elsewhere. The third level consisted of technical and administrative project leaders. Anyone in the DDC could be called on to lead a project. It was considered a part-time job, and though a few people coordinated multiple projects, they usually were technical contributors in other people's projects at the same time. The fourth level was everyone else, any person in the organization could be asked to serve in a leadership function, such as a team representative to the Employee Leadership Board, or a cross-DDC problem-solving team.

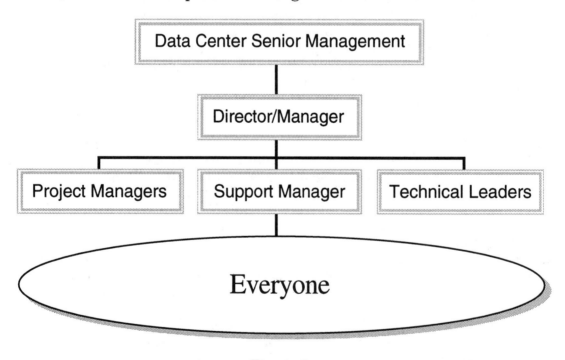

Figure 1

Below the manager level, there were three types of structures; work teams, work groups, and individual contributors. Work teams are interdependent teams of people with clearly defined group objectives. Work groups are groups of individual contributors who work in a related area. They collaborate on up to 30 percent of their work, but their collaboration is usually centered around three areas: (a) creating common standards for delivery of their products and services, (b) sharing best practices, and (c) group administration. Their technical expertise is usually highly specialized, and cross training is not practical. Their missions are mostly individual, though some group missions are needed in the three areas described earlier. These groups are not designed to become work teams. Individual contributors are technical specialists whose contribution is so broad that grouping them with others would be counterproductive. They interact with many teams, groups, and individuals, and report to a manager.

- Information is free, and it is appropriate for anyone to seek any information that a team, group, or person believes is needed to do the job.
- Teams may be established by anyone and include anyone who can be convinced of the potential team's mission. Teams like this are set up, do their work, and disband, often with no manager or even project leader involvement.

This flexible way of operating requires a clear understanding of who a person/team's suppliers and customers are, and these relationships change frequently. The structure creates unusual appraisal criteria.

To meet the challenge, the DDC's performance appraisal system has evolved uniquely.

The Performance Appraisal (PA) System

Forming the PA Team
Work teams: The appraisal team is simply the team of which they are a member, though a customer may be included.
Work group: For work groups (see definitions) the appraised member selects three to five members that have the most direct knowledge of the appraised member's (AM) performance. Internal or external customers may be included. The individual's manager must approve the membership of the team. The manager facilitates the team, as long as the organization requires that the final document contain his/her signature.

Meeting Preparation (the responsibility of the appraised member)
- The AM completes the "Actions Completed" area of their MRAs (last column), and sends a copy to PA team members one week prior to scheduled meeting.
- A meeting time is set up and all participants are informed ensuring attendance.

197

The Meeting - The PA team meeting has 3 parts; Present Accomplishments, Planning Feedback, and Present Feedback.

1. Present Accomplishments
    a. The appraised member presents his/her accomplishments of their goals.
    b. Questions from team members during this phase are limited to clarification and summarization of what the AM is presenting.
    c. Notes are taken by team members on the Feedback Form (Attachment C).
    d. Upon completion of his/her presentation, the AM writes down on a 3 × 5 card the rating he/she believes is deserved, and places it face down on the table as he/she leaves the room.

2. Planning Feedback
    After the AM leaves, the facilitator will host a discussion about the AM's performance. When all team members are prepared to give feedback, it includes:
    a. AM's job performance in accordance with their MRAs.
    b. Team skills performance.
    c. Individual development activities.
    d. Activities not on the original MRAs.
    e. Group consensus for a rating.
    f. Review the rating offered by the AM.
    g. Decide how to give feedback.

3. Presenting Feedback
    a. When the AM returns, *each team member* will provide feedback as planned.
    b. The AM asks questions to clarify the feedback.
    c. The team members provide the completed Feedback Form (Attachment C) to the AM to use in writing their PA at year-end.
    d. Ratings are not given during this period. It is critical to the success of this process that ratings are kept confidential.

Writing the PA. Feedback provided will be incorporated in the PA. This action occurs only during the year-end review. The written PA is not required for mid-year.

Organizational Processing. The BU manager, a member of the PA team, will determine a final rating for the AM. After the ratings have been approved at DDC level, the BUM meets with each member of their unit in the final step of the PA process.

BU Manager/AM Final Performance Feedback

1. Preparation: The AM creates the final draft of the PA, incorporating all feedback from the PA meeting (year-end only). The only blank is the rating. The form is then given to the BU manager prior to the individual performance feedback meeting.
2. Individual Performance Feedback Meeting: During the meeting, the manager verifies that the PA form accurately reflects the feedback given previously (year-end only). The manager then tells the AM what the team rated him/her, and what the final rating was. If there are differences between the team's rating and the final rating, the manager explains with a performance reason.
3. Collective Performance Feedback: Once all the individual performance feedback meetings have been held, the BU manager holds a BU-wide meeting, in which he/she addresses, as a minimum, the following:

   A summary of the final ratings of team members without assigning names to them.
   The BUM's assessment of how the PA process went:

   1. Timeliness
   2. How the team feedback planning went
   3. How the team feedback went
   4. Areas that need improvement next time
   5. Things that went well.

The Learnings

Jail-house Lawyer Archetypes. In every organization, there are those who learn to work the system. Below are a few examples, and how the organization adapted. Those who work the system are often very creative, which is another reason the PA process is an evolutionary process.

The Cheerleading Section. Early in the process, the appraised individual selected his own team members, and managers selected one member. This enabled the appraised member to "stack" the appraisal team selectively, omitting projects where they didn't perform especially well. This essentially created an appraisal team that was a cheerleading section, and the facilitator had to really pull hard to get anything but laudatory comments.

This problem was addressed by changing the Performance Appraisal guidelines so that the manager validates the entire membership of the appraisal team. The appraised member then has to make a case for each member. This made it more difficult for the appraised member to "stack" the team. The key to this success of the validation of team members, however, is the skill of the manager. In interdependent teams, especially as they mature, I find that peers seldom let a team member get away with stacking their appraisal team.

The Payback Panel. Occasionally, an individual that has a secret grudge will become an appraisal team member. The team member may never have given feedback to the appraised member about his/her performance, except to exchange pleasantries. When the appraisal team meets, however, they use the process to "pay back" the appraised member by giving devastating feedback that the appraised member has never heard before the appraisal team meeting. To address this issue, as well as others, the Employee Leadership Board (an issue/communication oriented cross-Data Center team) developed a set of behavior standards for all people who are a part of the DDC. One of the standards is "I have a responsibility to give timely feedback to individuals not adhering to these principles." Behaving in accordance with the Standards of Conduct is a performance objective, so by giving delayed feedback, a team member with a grudge is not adhering to the principles themselves.

The "This is too hard" Panel. There was once a work team that decided they did not want to appraise each other, so they abdicated their responsibility by giving everyone on the team the highest possible rating. The performance of the team throughout the year had been marginal. This required an intervention by management, and the manager gave the ratings for that team.

An Organization Development assessment and intervention was required. This abdication of responsibility was really a symbol of resistance. The team had developed norms counter to organizational objectives. When these counter-culture norms were made explicit for the team, and the inevitable ends to such behavior identified, they put a plan into action to develop some new norms. Some interventions between individuals were required, and venting some frustration over a previous organization change helped the team move forward. The team members were ready to give feedback the next time the appraisal teams were formed.

The Hostile Witness. A few people, especially in the early stages, avoided serving as appraisal team members by asking others on their teams to do it. When it became apparent that a person was avoiding responsibility, the team members would sometimes decline to stand in for them. Rarely, a person would serve but behave as a "hostile witness," constantly complaining about how uncomfortable he/she was, and contributing little feedback of value.

This changed over time. As serving on appraisal teams became commonplace, people became more and more comfortable with the concept and the behavior. Though some people still do not enjoy the activity, fewer and fewer become the "hostile witnesses."

Conclusion

Though the system is time consuming, it has been a key activity in our transition. People who initially refused to believe that team feedback had real impact have learned that when they ignore their peers and customers, no matter how high the technical quality of their work, their performance rating is affected. People then become less focused on managers, and more focused on their customers and teammates.

Epilogue

FMC Corporate Information Resources Dallas Data Center was purchased by SHL, a Canadian-based information technology company in May of 1995. Now called The Dallas Outsourcing Center, the performance appraisal system discussed above is being integrated with SHL's guidelines. To date, it appears that only minor modifications will have to be made to the appraisal process.

About the Contributor

Lee Royal is an Organizational Development Specialist at SHL Systemhouse, an information technology company. Lee works with the Dallas Outsourcing Center. He has done organization development work with FMC Corporation and is a former member of the Center for the Study of Work Teams at the University of North Texas. He is a former Army officer, and has served as a co-author, presenter, discussant, panel chair, or panel member at the International Conference on Work Teams, Symposium on Knowledge Worker Teams, and the Annual Convention of the Society of Industrial and Organizational Psychologists.

18

A Model for GlobalWork Teams: Maxus Energy and Holderband

Sylvia Odenwald

Forming productive cross-cultural teams is a complex process. To accomplish project goals through GlobalWork teams, the work group must progress from being a collection of individuals with cultural differences to an effective working unit—from collision to coexistence in the team's formative stage, to individuals operating as a collaborative GlobalWork team.

Team Member Progression

Figure 1 illustrates this four phase progression.

	Team Formations		Team Operation	
	Phase I	*Phase 2*	*Phase 3*	*Phase 4*
Primary Orientation	Self-centered	Awareness Shared	Team Contributor	Team/Company Shared
Technology	Proprietary	Selectively Shared	Team Shared	Collaboratively Shared
Influence on Company	Small	Small + Open	Larger	Largest
	COLLISION—COEXISTENCE		**—COLLABORATION**	

Figure 1. Team Member Progression

Phase 1

All teams members bring to the team their own cultural perspectives. Early in the formation of the team, members must begin to understand their own cultures, values, and workstyles before they can work effectively with others.

Phase 2

After self-awareness, members must gain awareness and an understanding of the cultural perspectives of others. Corporations should provide cultural awareness and multicultural training to increase trust, communication, and cooperation among team members to get work done. In this way, individuals begin to see how their work preferences are similar to or different from other team members. This allows them to work alongside other team members as they move toward greater understanding and cooperation.

Phase 3

At this stage, cooperation takes on increasing importance. As trust builds, team members are more willing to share their knowledge and technology with each other. The team's focus shifts from themselves to accomplishing team goals.

Phase 4

Cross-cultural dynamics influence the team as it is now transformed into a collaborative working unit. It incorporates the company's vision and strategy into its kinetic team culture and contributes to organizational goals. As new members become part of the unit, the work group must reconfigure its work process to incorporate new perspectives.

How does a corporation get work done amid the collisions of cultural differences in the formation and operations of teams? Corporations have met these challenges with a number of different strategies. Maxus Energy and Holderbank are examples of global corporations who have creatively met the challenge.

Maxus Energy

Maxus Energy is an example of a company that has risen to the challenge of bringing teams from collision to collaboration. It is an oil and gas exploration and production company based in Dallas, Texas. The company is an operator of a Production Sharing Contract for Pertamina, the Indonesian government's oil company, in the development of the vast oil resources of the country. Maxus is the second largest producer of oil in Indonesia.

Typically, oil production declines rapidly after the first few years of production. In 1985 production over the next several years was expected to decline by a total of 14 percent. The company, working with Bob Sneider, a consultant on teams in the oil patch, initiated a multidisciplinary team approach to attempt to reduce the severe production decline. As a result of implementing the teams, the company's production from old fields was virtually flattened over the next 10 years and significant amounts of reserves were added. (Steve Ginsburgh, 1995 interview.)

Numerous issues had to be addressed in the development of the teams, which represent many cultures as well as technical disciplines. With 17,508 islands (6,000 of which are inhabited), Indonesia is the world's largest archipelago. The geographical separation of the people promotes varied subcultures in addition to the national culture. Some are mild-natured and others are more aggressive. Additional cultural influences come from significant numbers of Asian people of varied national origins in the population as well as the presence of Dutch, Australian, English, Canadian, and U.S. expatriates.

Other key cultural differences at issue are:

- The view of the individual and the community. American individualism is in sharp contrast with the general Indonesian group mentality.
- The view of class and leadership. The American view of equal opportunity and earned leadership is very different from the Indonesian culture based on age and seniority.
- The style and method of communication. Americans are more direct, formal, and confrontational than Indonesians who tend to be more subtle and indirect, respectful, and accommodating. The Indonesian style is the result of hundreds of years of rule by colonial influences and Pancasila, which is the national ideology. The five inseparable and mutually qualifying fundamental principles of this ideology are:

  1. Belief in the one supreme God.
  2. A just and civilized humanity.
  3. The unity of Indonesia.
  4. Democracy led by the wisdom of deliberations among representatives.
  5. Social justice for all the people of Indonesia.

- The view of work and the company. Americans are task-oriented and have a single loyalty to the company, while Indonesians tend to be relationship-driven with multiple loyalties to the company and the government.

In setting up a culturally relevant team structure, Maxus established the following guidelines:

- Promote representation of varied functions and cultures.
- Define the role of the multidisciplinary teams. (Maxus refers to these teams as Asset Management Teams or AMTs.) The roles of the teams, the team leaders, and the team managers were identified and guidelines were developed.
- Establish clear guidelines for team function and operation including goals and objectives, specific times for required meetings, and deadlines for reports.

- Monitor the team's progress through quarterly updates, annual reports, and electronic databases to monitor progress and communicate areas of concern.
- Be hesitant to make changes to team decisions, and do so only after very careful examination and team input.
- Provide support as follows:

    - *Technical support.* Tools to get the job done, expertise to minimize wasted effort, and computer databases and communication software to expedite processes and improve communication.
    - *Verbal support.* Talk about the teams. Recognize the efforts being made at every opportunity and celebrate the accomplishments.
    - *Monetary support.* (This area is currently being addressed. Provide individual as well as team rewards and a bonus system to recognize teamwork and effort.)
    - *Decision making.* Give as many decisions to the team as practical and operationally possible. If management decides to change a decision, respect the team by giving the members an opportunity to discuss and defend their decision.

Maxus's team approach has been very successful. In 1992 the company evaluated their team guidelines for the year to determine what they had or had not done well. On the plus side, they had set up teams with at least one technical expert in each discipline in every AMT. They had given clear objectives for AMTs, limited the size of teams to 10 members, and had given leaders the responsibility to experiment with structure and format.

They also found some activities on the minus side, which they corrected:

- They had assigned people to more than one AMT and found that was not effective.
- They had formed too many AMTs with limited scope, so in 1992 they decreased the number of AMTs and enlarged the boundaries based on geographical areas/geological setting versus fields. This allowed an AMT to have several fields and assign responsibilities within the AMT. The number of AMTs was based on the number of experts available, production, the number of wells, and geological setting.
- They had not required AMTs to meet on a regular basis and changed this so that they now meet at least once a week.
- They had located offices in the building based on functional groups and not by AMTs. This was to be corrected.

The company has identified additional issues that will require improvement such as the need to focus on key issues, establish meeting agendas and eliminate time wasters, and move people around less to maintain continuity.

The following are charts showing the guidelines developed for teams, leaders, and managers.

ASSET MANAGEMENT TEAMS

Objective: Efficiently and effectively optimize production and reserves from producing areas and serve as a training vehicle for technical as well as leadership skills.

The primary responsibility of each AMT is to optimize results by applying multidisciplinary expertise to all technical evaluations in the given geographical area of responsibility.

The AMT is:

- A multidisciplinary team. All disciplines needed to perform the required task are represented.
- Self-directed. Leader and manager serve a support function.
- Optimally sized (8-15).

- Focused by clear self-generated goals and objectives that had management's input and agreement.

The AMT does:

- Set aggressive goals and objectives with input and agreement from management.
- Meet regularly to discuss progress and jointly work out problems.
- Promote cross-functional solutions and input from all members (synergy).

- Seek technical audit from functional groups (i.e., chief geophysicist).
- Recommend expenditures for projects based on team decisions.

The AMT is not:

- Competing disciplines working the same area.
- Managed/directed by one person.
- Too large (difficult to focus). Too small (lacking functional representation).
- Working on multiple conflicting agendas from functional departments.

The AMT does not:

- Receive goals to achieve without input (top down).
- Only meet to solve major problems.
- Restrict participation to individual's discipline and expertise (for example, geologist—geology; product engineer—workovers).
- Recommend projects without the scrutiny of a competent technical audit.
- Approve expenditures without approval from appropriate functional managers.

207

AMT LEADER ROLE

Objective: Coordinate the team's efforts to accomplish goals and objectives.

The AMT leader's chief responsibility is to coordinate and facilitate the activity of the team to ensure team focus and input from all disciplines.

The Leader is:

- A coordinator/facilitator.
- An engineer/geoscientist who spends less than 15 percent of his/her time on administrative tasks dealing with the team.
- Focusing the majority of his/her effort on technical work to accomplish team goals and objectives.

The Leader does:

- Coordinate the goal-setting process with the team and management.
- Call, chair, and document all formal team meetings and arrange for informal work sessions when appropriate.
- Actively seek input from all appropriate members and disciplines.
- Encourage new ideas and innovation from all disciplines.
- Strive to create an atmosphere of unity and cooperation.
- Arrange meetings and work sessions to maximize efficiency.
- Search out ideas from all members, especially new and young members.
- Lead effort to formalize team goals and objectives seeking input from ALL team members and from management.

The Leader is not:

- A boss.
- A full-time AMT manager/leader.
- Allowing administrative tasks of the team to overshadow his/her technical responsibilities.

The Leader does not:

- Determine the team's goals and objectives.
- Allow too many idle discussions, intradisciplinary discussions, and wasted time in meetings.
- Look only for the obvious singular discipline input.
- Criticize or allow negative criticism to dominate discussions or reviews.
- Allow trivial arguments to continue.
- Expect attendance from all members at every meeting.
- Allow a few strong personalities to dominate the team.
- Wait for management deadline to gather team goals.

208

AMT "RESPONSIBLE MANAGER" ROLE

Objective: Support the AMT leader and facilitate communication with management.

The Responsible Manager's chief responsibility is to support and develop the team leader to accomplish the team's goals and objectives. He/she is also to act as a liaison between the AMT and the management team.

The AMT Manager is:

- A coach/communicator.
- A functional manager who spends less than 20 percent of his/her time on team administrative tasks.
- Mainly behind the scene in the AMT.

The AMT Manager is not:

- A boss.
- A full-time AMT manager.

- Focal point of team.

The AMT Manager does:

- Support and mentor the leader; provide guidance and opinion when needed.
- Give input on goals and objectives that are consistent with company/division objectives.
- Ensure that the proper mix of talent is maintained for the required job.
- Communicate personnel issues to functional managers (including input for salary administration and evaluations).
- Seek functional manager's input when needed.
- Is present at the majority of team meetings, especially when major decisions are being made.
- Communicate on a regular basis. (Leader notes database, memos, informal meetings).

The AMT Manager does not:

- Manage or direct the team or the leader.
- Determine the team's goals and objectives.
- Enlist help from other AMTs on a regular basis.
- Deal with the personnel issues directly.
- Assume technical audit role for all disciplines.
- Let AMT struggle with decisions unproductively.
- Meet only once a week to discuss major items.

209

- Promote new ideas and unique solutions.

- Hold members accountable for work product and timing.

- Conduct post operations reviews (i.e., post drill review, etc.).

- Allocate team members to only one team.

- Look for cookie-cutter solutions and procedures rather than being over-critical (negative) of new ideas.

- Conduct regular follow-up on work plans.

- Look back.

- Allow multiple team membership.

FUNCTIONAL MANAGER ROLE

Objective: Responsible for technical quality of the final product in the functional area and functional operational support for all teams.

The functional manager's chief responsibility is to set technical standards and procedures to assure the high technical quality of projects performed by the teams. He/she is also responsible for administrative and operational activities required by his/her discipline to fully support the efforts of the teams.

The Functional Manager is:

- An auditor/trainer/staff developer.

- Primarily responsible for functional administrative, operational, and personnel matters.

- Mainly behind the scenes at the team level.

The Functional Manager does:

- Support and mentor the leader, provide guidance and opinion when needed.

- Give input on goals and objectives that are consistent with company/division objectives.

- Ensure that the proper mix of talent is maintained for the required job.

The Functional Manager is not:

- A one-person show.

- A full-time AMT manager.

- Focal point of the team.

The Functional Manager does not:

- Manage or direct the team or the leader.

- Determine the team's goals and objectives.

- Enlist help from other AMTs on a regular basis.

- Receive input on personnel issues from the AMT manager.
- Have a separate staff outside the AMTs to cover administrative and operational functions.

- Coordinate department goals with AMT goals and objectives.

- Deal with personnel issues independently.
- Require AMT members to spend large amounts of time on administrative functions not dealing directly with the AMT's goals.
- Have a separate agenda for AMT members.

(John Girgis, paper presented at the 1995 Indonesian Petroleum Association Meeting.)

Holderbank

Holderbank is another corporate example of successful transnational teamwork. It is a Swiss conglomerate composed of companies in 34 countries. The company produces and distributes ready-mixed concrete, cement, aggregates, and concrete chemicals. A variety of teams work throughout the organization including: executive and working teams and productivity, quality, and energy circles. Each is organized within the same function area but is also cross-functional. Many of the executive and working teams consist of members from different cultures.

The potential for collision occurs because of their cultural differences such as team members' attitude toward work, accountability, religion, and customs (e.g., not looking into the eyes of the person to whom one is speaking, which is a behavior resulting from inferiority structured by cultural experience in India and Vietnam). Holderbank addresses cultural differences through training and education. Numerous training programs for its multinational project teams and managers have been developed. These programs consist of workshops in productivity and project circles, team moderation, team dynamics, and team development coaching. The company's Team Dynamics courses and workshops have clearly designed program elements that focus on cross-cultural exercises. These exercises help participants understand the cultural uniqueness of their team members' behavior. The exercises are structured so that members of one culture explain their customs and traditions to the group. This is followed by honest discussions about how other team members' cultures are different.

Holderbank has had many successful experiences using this approach but has also had failures. Dr. Willi Walser, vice president of corporate human resources, states, "Mobilizing teams from various countries and motivating them to achieve high performance and successful results requires my total commitment and sensitivity for the various cultures and persons involved." (Walser, 1995 interview.)

211

Cultural Synergy

Synergy results when team members collaborate—when they listen to each other and enter into the private worlds of their teammates. As Philip R. Harris and Robert T. Moran say, "[Synergy] can occur when diverse or disparate groups of people work together. The objective is to increase effectiveness by sharing perceptions, insights, and knowledge. The complexity and shrinking of today's world literally forces people to capitalize on their differences." (Moran, *World Executive's Digest*, January 1993.)

Team members have two choices:

- They can either try to impose *their way* upon the other team members, often to the mutual detriment of the team, or
- They can work together to form a kinetic team process culture.

The team's resources can be strengthened when intercultural differences are used for synergy rather than allowing them to become a cause for divisiveness. The differences of perception that arise from different cultural factors and national parameters, education and training backgrounds, and work experiences can enrich the GlobalWork team's ability to solve problems and accomplish project tasks. This synergy helps establish a strong team culture that enhances team communication and stimulates growth and collaboration. Collaboration should be evident not only within each GlobalWork team but also in the interaction between company teams within the corporation.

A GlobalWork Team Motto

Bibliography

Harris, P. R., and R. T. Moran. *Managing cultural differences.* Houston, TX: Gulf, 1993.

About the Contributor

This chapter is taken from *Global Solutions for Teams: Moving from Collision to Collaboration* (Irwin, 1996) by Sylvia B. Odenwald.

The author is president of The Odenwald Connection, Inc., a Dallas-based international consulting firm of 500 representatives located throughout the United States and 50 countries worldwide. They specialize in performance-based skill development and interventions for multinational and virtual teams. Odenwald is an active member of the Society for Human Resource Management and American Society for Training and Development (ASTD) and previously served on ASTD's Board of Directors. In 1993, she received the Gordon M. Bliss Award, ASTD's highest award. She is the author of *Global Training: How to Design a Program for the Multinational Corporation* (Irwin, 1993) and coauthor of *Desktop Presentations* (AMACOM, 1990).

19

Success with Pay-for-Knowledge Compensation: The Evolution of a Program Shaped by Operators

Gerald D. Klein

This paper reports on the creation and development over three years of a pay-for-knowledge compensation system in a production department of a manufacturing organization. The pay-for-knowledge system was introduced at the same time the department was reorganized into self-managed teams. While guided by management, the program has largely been shaped by the ideas of the operators affected. The pay-for-knowledge system was installed in an operation having a conventional compensation system and is working very well. The policies and procedures that operators have evolved have eliminated the tension and conflict that can arise under pay-for-knowledge that undercuts teamwork. This company's experience, then, is especially valuable for organizations contemplating the use of this approach.

Pay-for-Knowledge Compensation

With pay-for-knowledge compensation, workers are offered monetary incentives for the mastery of additional tasks. By cross-training workers in several jobs, the organization gains flexibility in the assignment of personnel, a work force able to cover for one another during absences from work, and whatever improvements occur in production as a result of improved worker attitudes. For most workers, acquiring additional skills fulfills needs for challenge and variety at work and can increase feelings of job security, responsibility, and most certainly self-esteem. Pay-for-knowledge is often used in conjunction with the development of self-managed work teams. There are a number of issues involved in establishing a pay-for-knowledge compensation system. Many of the important ones will be addressed here as the experience of the company is described. While this case involves a manufacturing firm, service organizations have also successfully used pay-for-knowledge (see Fenn, 1993, for an example).

The Company, the Initial Seminar, and First Steps

The site of the pay-for-knowledge experiment is a U.S. manufacturing firm whose operations are situated in one location. The company is primarily a supplier to a major domestic industry, employs under 5,000 workers, is organized by business group, and is not unionized. Because the company has been the site of a number of innovations derived from the behaviorial sciences, such as survey feedback, gainsharing, and a participative/democratic approach to new policy development, and holds optimistic beliefs about people and their capabilities, the climate of the company could be said to have been favorable to the development of self-managed teams and a pay-for-knowledge compensation system.

Promising applications of sociotechnical systems (STS) theory in other organizations led to thirty-five senior company managers receiving a three-day orientation to STS theory from an outside consultant. As a result of this conference, a decision was made by managers in one of the business groups to work with the consultant to explore the application of STS theory to the business group's operations. The next step required detailed analysis by a selection of business group employees of the work performed in the three production departments of the business group. An Analysis Team was assembled, its management and non-management members drawn from the three production departments that comprised the business group. Each department produced different products.

Eventually, a provisional design was created which would, it was hoped, ultimately alter work arrangements in all business group production departments. The design had these key features:

- Rigid individual job descriptions and the permanent assignment of workers to specific tasks on a production line would be eliminated. Workers would be expected to assume primary responsibility for production and, as individuals and teams (i.e., shifts), do whatever was necessary to accomplish team goals.

- Each worker would become skilled in several tasks and would rotate among them, depending on work priorities and needs. A pay-for-knowledge compensation system would be developed to encourage the development of multiple skills, and to achieve the additional benefits described above.

216

- Quality control technicians would be eliminated and their functions assumed by production line operators.

- Operators would engage in a variety of activities and contacts formerly the responsibility of others. They would do preventative maintenance on equipment, trouble-shoot equipment problems, and complete maintenance work requests and purchase requisitions.

- To underscore the versatility expected of operators on the production floor, and because workers would not have an assigned permanent job, all operators were to be given the title of *Production Technician.* To emphasize the responsibility of the production supervisor for the development of individuals and teams, his or her title would now be *Team Development Manager.*

- Product "champions" among *Production Technicians* were envisioned. A technician possessing all the skills necessary to produce a particular product and who knew the product well would become a liaison to the customer. The technician would accompany members of management and others on trips to customer facilities and brief his/her team afterwards.

- To encourage team autonomy, the three shifts in each department would be overseen by only a single *Team Development Manager.*

- Aspects of the system would be subject to change and evolution on the basis of working experience.

Subsequently, operators in one department in the business group, Communication Products (a pseudonym), agreed to go forward to try to implement the provisional design.

The Communication Products Department and Pay-for-Knowledge Start-Up

With twenty-five operators arranged unequally over three shifts, the Communication Products Department is a small and relatively young group in the company, though it is staffed with experienced, older operators. The Department manufactures products for the information display industry, a young and developing market. While production lines in the company's traditional businesses produce identical or similar products in great numbers, the work in Communication Products is characterized by the production of small volumes, prototypes and samples, one time runs and changes within a run required by the customer. It is a low volume but high margin business. Since not all of the twenty-one separate processes along the production line are required every day, it would be costly to have a full-time operator assigned to each

217

process. Considerable benefits can be realized by having a flexible, multiskilled, self-directed, and responsible work force on this particular line.

The successful development of the pay-for-knowledge system was seen as crucial to the success of the new work arrangements that were envisioned. A task force was established in Communication Products to develop specific policies and procedures for implementing the pay-for-knowledge compensation system.

The knowledge, skills, and productivity required to function successfully in a position or process was labeled a "skill block." In other words, a skill block for a particular position specified what a worker needed to know, what he/she must be able to do, and indicated the volume, quality level, etc. that would have to be achieved. Teams of workers, with each team experienced in a different process, met on their own and often without a supervisor present to create the skill blocks for the twenty-one processes in the Department. The following were decided by the Department and approved by management:

- When an employee mastered a skill block a pay increase of $.20 an hour would be granted. All processes in the Department were considered important and awarding the same pay increase for each mastered eliminated the problem of technicians competing to train on "high return" work stations. This decision also enabled the program to get off to a rapid start.

- The only exception to this was employee mastery of a basic skills block, requiring knowledge of the Department's products, equipment, forms, codes, records and safety, quality control, and other procedures. Mastery of this block would lead to a $.30 an hour increase.

- There was no upper limit proposed for the compensation plan. Pay would be based on the number of processes mastered.

- As the work of the Department changed skill blocks could be added and eliminated.

- The elimination of a skill block, reflecting the elimination of a process no longer needed, would result in a reduction in pay of $.20 an hour for all those who were certified in that skill block.

- The addition or elimination of skill blocks would be a Department decision.

To minimize subjectivity in the evaluation of employee skills, a source of problems in early pay-for-knowledge programs, written guides were prepared for each process, describing the specific knowledge, skills, and proficiency to be achieved. These were available to all technicians and were considered a training tool as well as an evaluation device. Department members skilled in a process were expected to use the guides in evaluating technicians attempting to become skilled. The following procedures were also established:

- Technicians assigned to a new operation would be trained by a skilled operator.

- When the technician believed that he or she had acquired the knowledge, skills, and proficiency necessary in the position he/she would initiate a request for a certification session.

- A group of approximately five others would be assembled, including the Team Development Manager, the employee's trainer, other team members certified in the skill, and a team member from a following operation who had worked with the product produced by the candidate for certification.

- The knowledge, skills, and proficiency were rated by each member of the group individually, on scales numbered from "0" to "5"; ratings were then discussed. A "0" represented "no knowledge or skills," while a "4" represented "fully qualified - meets all skill and knowledge requirements." A score of "5", the highest rating, indicated that the technician was capable of teaching others.

- All scores would be averaged. A pay increase would be granted if a technician earned at least a "4" in each of the items constituting the skill block. (In some pay-for-knowledge systems only an employee's trainer need certify the employee as skilled in a process.)

- Pay increments, if awarded, would be retroactive to the date of the request for certification.

Compensation System Transition and the Decision to Assign a Technician a Permanent Position

Because of the extra responsibilities of the technicians under the STS design, entry level pay was set at $9.81 an hour, a grade (Group 8) and rate higher than entry pay in the company at large. When the pay-for-knowledge plan was implemented a number of technicians in the Department were making Group 9, Group 10, or Group 11 level pay. Before implementation, it was agreed that no one would lose pay through the implementation of the pay-for-knowledge system. For reasons of equity, if a technician's pay was above entry level pay it would be frozen until they became certified as skilled and proficient in enough processes to justify or "earn" their current pay.

Employees in the Department at the system's introduction had the option to be in the system or not, although employees joining the Department after the development of pay-for-knowledge had to participate in it. Of all the technicians in the Department, only one on second shift indicated that he did not want to work under the new conditions, although he did want to stay in the Department. Because he possessed a crucial skill (which will be given the pseudonym, "framing"), one that would be difficult to replace in the short term, he was permitted to remain in his position. He was required to train others in framing. Also, while not formally part of STS, he was required to learn a few other processes and, on many fewer occasions than most, fill in for others when needed. Because of the especially strenuous nature of framing and the relatively harsher working conditions, his pay was set at the Group 12 level.

Implementing Pay-for-Knowledge

Initially, Department members were anxious about having their knowledge, skills, and proficiency appraised by peers and anxious about judging other technicians. Gradually, however, fears of unfair and negative evaluations and evaluating colleagues eased as norms evolved and experience was acquired. Raters had to back up a negative rating or assertion with information; more generally, an appraiser had to be able to defend his/her ratings, positive or negative. Also functional in reducing fear was the practice of developing action plans identifying what needed to be done or mastered by individuals who did not receive certification.

Experience began to suggest that most processes in the Department could be learned in 240 hours, about 30 working days or approximately a month and a half of accumulated work-time in an operation. To make more likely the development of sufficient skill and proficiency and to minimize negative evaluations, the Department decided that technicians had to log a minimum of 240 hours on an operation before they could request a certification session. Some pay-for-knowledge systems do not require a minimum number of hours in a position; an employee can request certification when he/she feels ready.

For the better part of a year, many hours were spent by the department in certifying technicians, mainly in tasks they had performed prior to STS. Since the Team Development Manager tried to take part in most of these early sessions, much of his time in that year was consumed by the certification process. Initially, the 240 hours requirement was waived in certifying operators in tasks they had been doing for a long time.

Additional Experiences under Pay-for-Knowledge

As the Department's customer base and business have expanded, new skill blocks have been added. A few skill blocks have been eliminated and hourly earnings reduced accordingly. These decisions, and the actual content of new blocks, have been matters for Department discussion and decision making. Also, three years after the project's beginning, the Department contains a few operators who have not become certified in enough skills so as to "justify" their current level of pay. Their pay is at the level it was when the transition was made to the pay-for-knowledge system. The Team Development Manager and the Department are working to resolve this issue.

An experience on one portion of the line raised the issue of whether awarding the *same* pay increase for the mastery of each Department task was fair. This is an issue that must be dealt with in all pay-for-knowledge systems. While thirty days was sufficient time to learn most processes, the framing job took considerably longer to master. Because of the difficult working conditions on this job and the time required to learn framing (a technician could learn several skills in the time it took to learn this one) technicians avoided the framing process. The framing responsibility on first shift came to be shared by two technicians. When one of the framers on first shift left the Department for a promotion, the team decided to hire a permanent framer rather than provide a larger cash incentive for becoming skilled in framing. An individual was hired into this position at the Group 12 level, the same rate being paid to the framer on second shift. Because this created an inequity between the two framers on the first shift — one was at a Group 8 rate, the other a Group 12 — the Department, believing it likely that there would always be a permanent framer on first and second shift, subsequently decided to permanently split the framing skill block in two. There would be a basic skill block in framing. Technicians mastering this block would be capable of relieving and assisting a permanent framer. There would also be an advanced skill block. Technicians mastering this block would be capable of achieving the proficiency and would have the knowledge of the permanent framer. A technician who mastered framing would now receive certification in two skill blocks, not one.[1]

RECENT ISSUES

Is There the Need to Train Everyone in Every Skill?

The intention in many pay-for-knowledge systems and the intention in this one as well is to provide technicians with unlimited opportunities to learn additional skills and to pay them for each skill mastered. The goal under which the Department has been operating is to continue training until everyone is trained in everything and everyone is making top pay. The Department is now questioning the wisdom of this commitment.

A primary purpose of cross-training was to enable workers to cover for one another during illnesses and other absences from work. This is already working well in the Department, and the Department is far from training everyone to do everything. The Department sees a point being reached in the future when continued training adversely affects the Department's productivity and margins. Clearly, training workers in skills that aren't absolutely vital to the daily and weekly success of a department can hurt productivity and margins in two ways. During training a certain amount of production is lost because of the low proficiency of the trainee, the reduced productivity of the trainer, and because a larger than normal number of defective units are produced. Acquiring skills under a pay-for-knowledge compensation system also inflates a department's payroll (and reduces margins) once certification is achieved. The Team Development Manager favors reducing the opportunities for training and refocusing the experiment on the number of other advantages of membership in the Department besides the potentially unlimited opportunity to learn new skills and increase one's pay — e.g., growth in earnings more rapid than in comparable positions elsewhere in the company and the opportunity to learn new jobs.

A Tendency to Put Training ahead of Department Needs

In the Team Development Manager's view, the reduction of training opportunities and the refocusing of the experiment might also lead to the reduction of a particular employee behavior of which he has become aware: For some team members, the quest to increase their pay by acquiring additional skills is occasionally placed ahead of the Department's work priorities. Tasks lower in priority are assumed and performed by technicians because these are the ones in which they are not certified.

A change has been suggested by technicians to deal with this problem and a Department payroll that can soon become too high in relation to competitive realities. This change involves rewarding skill acquisition using *group levels* instead of the $.20 per hour pay increments. Successful mastery of three or four skill blocks would result in an employee moving up an entire group level, e.g., from a Group 8 to a Group 9. As envisioned, advancement by group levels would result in an overall per hour pay increase that would be smaller than would be received by workers on a per skill basis. While this approach would reduce the immediacy and the size of the reward for learning new skills, it nevertheless still rewards skill acquisition. In the short term, until the current system is changed, it seems necessary for the team to amend daily staffing policy to require that technicians assume and complete the highest priority tasks first, before lower priority tasks can be undertaken.

An Unaddressed Issue

The changes being contemplated by the Department do not address the issue of how training opportunities are to be distributed among the technicians. Training in the recent past has been on a "catch-as-catch-can" basis; it has been based on where the Department needed someone and who they could get there the fastest. Well-defined procedures for assuring *equity* in the assignment of training opportunities are extremely important in a pay-for-knowledge program but do not currently exist in the Department. Since pay increases will probably continue to be associated with skill development, in order to minimize interpersonal conflict it would appear to be important to remedy this deficiency in the future.

ACHIEVEMENTS AND LEARNINGS

Organizational Achievements

Emphasizing continuous learning and multiskilled workers, a pay-for-knowledge compensation system has many benefits for organizations and employees. Characteristics of the system described here that represent its chief strengths include:

- thoroughness in the delineation and description of the knowledge, skills, and proficiency required in each of the department's positions or processes

- the widespread dissemination of these standards in written form

- maintenance of high standards and fairness in the assessment of candidates seeking certification

- the requirement that a certain minimum number of hours be logged in a process before a technician can request a formal assessment of his or her skills

- the development of action plans for individuals seeking but not receiving certification

As the nature of the department's business has changed, requiring new employee skills, the department has also been able to develop new skill blocks, and to expand the pay-for-knowledge system to reward technicians for acquiring these new skills. Even more surprising, the department has been willing to identify technician skills that are no longer required because of changes in the business, and to reduce technician pay accordingly. Its method of handling the transition from a conventional compensation system to one rewarding workers on the basis of the skills they acquire provides at least one model for others to consider in thinking through this transition, or to try.

Major Learnings

This case indicates the value and importance of thoroughness in planning when introducing novel approaches to compensation. The inability of plans and planners to foresee everything in advance—the

223

certainty of the unexpected—is another learning, as is the desirability of remaining flexible and modifying plans and procedures on the basis of experience.

Ironically and surprisingly, the continued material gains of the project are threatened by one of the project's original, and seemingly laudable, goals: to train all operators in every task. As was seen, the wisdom of attempting to train all technicians in the department in every skill is currently being questioned. It is likely that this goal will be altered in the future.

That technicians would on occasion compromise departmental performance by seeking out and performing lower priority tasks for the sake of certification and the corresponding increase in pay was not foreseen. It is also likely that some action will be taken in relation to this activity in the future, as well.

Footnote

1. The decision to permanently assign an operator to a work station in the Department was made twice in the three-year period. The permanent assignment of workers to tasks violated at least two fundamental premises of the experimental project, namely, that workers would become skilled in multiple tasks and would rotate among them. Generally, decisions made in the course of a work redesign experiment that violate fundamental premises of the experiment weaken it, whereas decisions that are consistent with the premises strengthen it (Walton, 1975, 15-16; 1982, 264-65). There were strategies available for handling these situations which would not have required deviation from the basic plan for the system. The Department could have required that everyone learn and rotate through the more noxious but nevertheless crucial Departmental tasks, and have created a plan to make this expectation operational. It could have increased the incentive for mastering such tasks. Finally, it could have made the tasks avoided by technicians priority ones for Departmental brainstorming. It may be possible to change framing and similar tasks so conditions are less noxious, task performance is less strenuous, the learning time is less and so on.

Bibliography

Fenn, D. (1993). "Skill-based pay takes off." *CFO*, January, pp. 57-60.

Walton, R. E. (1975). "The diffusion of new work structures: Explaining why success didn't take." *Organizational Dynamics*, Winter, pp. 3-25.

Walton, R. E. (1982). "The topeka work system: optimistic visions, pessimistic hypotheses, and reality." In *The innovative organization: Productivity programs in action*, edited by Robert Zager and Michael P. Rosow, pp. 260-87. New York: Pergamon.

About the Contributor

Dr. Gerald D. Klein is Associate Professor of Organizational Behavior and Management at Rider University. He has a long-standing interest in self-managed work teams, has taught about them virtually since their inception in this country in the early seventies, and has researched and written about these and other forms of employee empowerment. Dr. Klein is a regular and invited presenter at the International Conference on Self-Managed Work Teams and has organized and chaired panels at this conference on the supervisor's role under team self-management and self-managed teams in services. His articles have appeared in such journals as *National Productivity Review, Personnel, California Management Review,* and *Journal of Management Education.*

Part V - Practical Theory

20

Teams in the Age of Systems
Peter R. Scholtes

We trained hard—but it seemed that every time we were beginning to form up into teams, we would be reorganized. I was to learn later in life we tend to meet any new situation by reorganizing, and a wonderful method it can be for creating the illusion of progress while producing confusion, inefficiency and demoralization.

– Petronius Arbiter
Satyricon, 66 A.D.

This delightful observation from Petronius Arbiter tells us a number of things:

- Teams aren't new. They have been around for a long time.
- It takes a while for a group of individuals to "form up into teams."
- From time immemorial, teams have been undone by managerial decisions that disregard how the workers in the workplace will be affected.
- For a long time we have learned to settle for the "illusion of progress."

I would add to Petronius' observations a few of my own:

- Many managers mistakenly believe that "adopting a new philosophy" (Deming's Point #2) involves establishing a proliferation of teams. "Teams" and "Quality" are NOT synonymous. Too many teams or the wrong kind of teams will interfere with "adopting a quality philosophy" and give teams a bad name. Teams can themselves become "an illusion of progress."
- In addition to the problem of too many teams, I observe the disconnectedness of teams. I see teams in isolation from each other, working on things that individually may be worthwhile but collectively their efforts lead nowhere. Sometimes they even work at cross purposes.

229

This paper was first published in the December, 1995 issue of *Quality Progress*.

One cheese company was having a problem with consistently producing top grade commercial cheese. When the cheese was below grade it had to be sold to the makers of animal feed. This company ended up with two teams. The Production-based team was seeking to remove the causes of below-grade cheese. Meanwhile a team begun by the Marketing Department was seeking new markets for below-grade cheese. My fear was that both would succeed.

This article will be in two parts. Part I will explore some new concepts that should lead us to rethink our approach to teams. These concepts include "systems," "customer-in," "Gemba," "the team as a system," and "a system of teams." Part II will look at some of the current popular applications of teams and reconsider them in light of the concepts presented in Part I. Part II will include such icons as "high performance work teams," "self-directed teams," "management teams," "business teams," and "quality circles." Part II will ask the question, "When do you need a team and when do you not?"

PART I. REVIEWING SOME CONCEPTS THAT HELP US RETHINK TEAMS

In this part of the paper, we will look at the new prism or set of lenses through which we can examine teams. The new era of management requires that we "adopt a new philosophy." The new point of view is the managerial equivalent of shifting from flat-earth thinking to spherical-earth thinking.

The focus of this article is this: We have changed from a managerial era focused on individuals, hierarchy, and control to an era focused on customers, systems, and improvement. The challenge to teams, therefore, is how to function in a way that supports customers, systems, and improvement. Teams, remember, have existed in both eras. A second major theme is that teams must not only support the system, as part of their individual missions, teams themselves must *be* a system.

Just as the net value of a team should exceed the sum of its individual members (this is called *synergy*), on a larger scale, the net value of all the teams in an organization should exceed the sum of all the individual teams. Synergy and interdependence should exist not only within teams but across teams. There needs to be a *system* of teams, an interacting network of efforts that operate in synch toward common purposes. This requires a different mode of leadership.

The Basics of an Organization

Every organization—whether it is your business organization or your Friday-night poker group—consists of three basic elements (see Figure 1). Every organization consists of an aggregate of *people* pursuing some common purpose using some *systems, processes, or methods.*

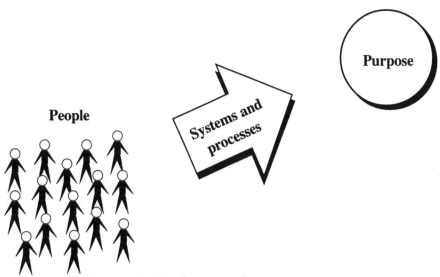

Figure 1. The basics of an organization

Conventional management has focused on the people, believing that if you wish to successfully pursue your purpose, you must introduce some interventions into the people. Managers must "motivate" the people, reorganize the people, put them into teams, hold people accountable, empower them, or offer them promises of rewards or threats of punishment. This has been the prevailing approach to running a business since the mid-1800s.

The Quality Movement, begun in Japan in 1950, represents a shift in focus from the *people* to the *systems*, *processes*, and *methods*. The philosophy of management taught by Deming, Ishikawa, and Juran emphasized that virtually all of our problems are caused by inadequacies in our systems. Therefore all of the motivated, teamed-up, empowered, accountable, self-directed, "incentivized" people in an organization cannot compensate for its dysfunctional systems and processes. And unless we let go of our obsession with people as the cause and the cure of poor quality, we will never discover what quality is all about.

The shift in management paradigms that began in 1950 was not a shift from hierarchical, individual focus to team focus. The shift was from hierarchical individual focus to *systems* focus (see Figure 2).

The paradigm shift in management philosophy

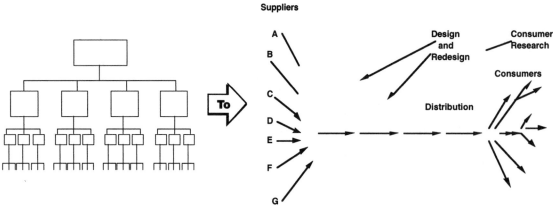

Figure 2. The old paradigm and the new paradigm

Let's look at some differences between the two.

Hierarchical approach to management	Systems approach to management
• Origin: The Prussian army. First used in business in the rail industry in 1840	• Origin: Deming and early systems thinkers. First used in business in Japan in 1950
• Focus on management	• Focus on the customer
• Quality is achieved by each one doing his job	• Quality is achieved by creating and maintaining systems that produce quality
• Improve the output by improving the people	• Improve the output by improving the system

In the hierarchical paradigm, teams were seen as an extension of management, used to assist and support the needs of management. In a systems paradigm, teams are participants in and stewards of the system, serving the needs of customers.

Teams in the Age of Systems

The new perspective on teams is shaped by two concepts inseparably linked to each other. One concept is that of "customer-in," a frame of mind fixed on delighting the customer and having an awareness of the customer dominate our thinking, values, planning, and decision making. The other concept is "Gemba," the flow of work within our organization that directly contributes to the products and services which go to our customers. Teams must be shaped by *customer-in* thinking and *Gemba* thinking. First let us explore the notion of "customer-in."

Customer-in Thinking

This is more than an intellectual exercise. "Customer-in" embraces a set of values and priorities that are then translated into routines and everyday behaviors. The notion of "customer-in," adapted here from the ideas of Ishikawa and Kano, is best understood when contrasted with its opposite, a "product-out" mentality.

Product-out mentality	Customer-in mentality
• Our company defines what a "good job" is.	• Our customers define what a good job is.
• We design products or services that please us and then convince the customer of its value.	• We learn from the customers what they value and design products and services to meet and exceed those expectations.
• Marketing consists mostly of sales promotion. "How can we get more customers to buy this?"	• Marketing consists mostly of customer research: "What do they need that they are not getting? What are they getting that they do not need?"

Some attitudes of a "product-out" mentality	Some attitudes of a "customer-in" mentality
• Arrogance: "We are the experts. We know better than others."	• Humility: "We must learn continuously from our customers."
• A "not-invented-here" reaction. "If an idea is worthwhile, we have already thought of it. If we didn't think of it, it isn't worthwhile."	• Altruism and flexibility: "The customers will help us identify ideas that are good for them. We must be nimble in our response, wherever the idea originated."
• Self-absorption, complaisant isolation— win-lose.	• Thoughtfulness, empathy responsiveness, modesty— win-win.

233

While there are probably shades of incremental difference between these two ends of a continuum, the tendency in this country—especially after World War II—was to be "product-out" in our thinking. The undoing of the U.S. position in the world economy can be largely attributed to decades of a "product-out" mentality.

A "customer-in" mentality should affect how teams work, how they define a good job, how their priorities are identified, how they measure progress, and much more.

The Gemba

Along with the notion of "customer-in," the concept of "Gemba" is an important part of the new context for teams. *Gemba is the assembly of critical resources and the flow of work that contribute directly to those efforts that add value to the customer.* Some comments on "Gemba":

- Gemba is a Japanese expression that has no equivalent English word. It is formed from two Chinese symbols GEM: "important work" and BA: "a place of action."
- Everyone does not work in the Gemba, only those who are part of the value-adding flow as it heads toward the customer. The organization consists of the *Gemba* and *those who support the Gemba* (see Figure 3).

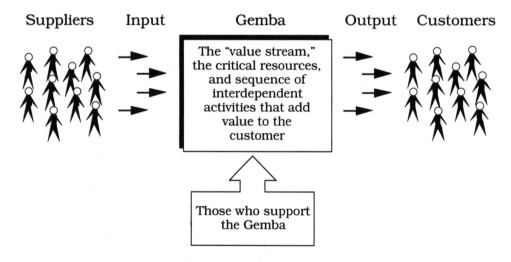

Figure 3. The Gemba

Note: Your organization consists of many systems and numerous "work flows." Not all of them are "Gemba." Only those systems directly related to a flow of work that adds value to the customer is "Gemba."

- Gemba is the part of your organization that does the work about which your customers care the most.

These are the Gemba	**These are not Gemba but provide services to the Gemba**
• Product or service design	• Most management services
• Product development activities	• Customer research
• Service development activities	• System or process design
• Potential customer contact and sales	• Human Resources
• Delivering products	• Plant or facilities repair and internal maintenance
• Delivering services	• Payroll and other financial services: accounts payable and accounts receivable
• Instructional and other after-delivery services for the customer	• Purchasing
• Routine customer maintenance services	• Administrative services
	• Training
	• Budgeting
	• Management information services

The Gemba's measure of success is customer delight. The success of the rest of the organization should depend on how well it serves the Gemba.

The purpose of this distinction between Gemba and non-Gemba is not to establish yet a new hierarchy of importance among the people, a new internal pecking order. The purpose is to define the organization's systems and identify which functions should systemically serve others.

Teams and the Gemba

The Gemba's teams are groups that collaborate—within and between each other—for the smooth functioning of Gemba's systems and processes and for the delight of the outside customers. All other teams interact with the Gemba and serve the needs of the Gemba. The Gemba should be seen as the customer of every other team in the organization.

The commissioning of any team should describe its purpose and mission and how the work of this team is relevant to the needs of the Gemba and the outside customers. The needs of the Gemba should shape the focus of the teams, not vice versa.

Systems and Teamwork

The notions of customer-in and Gemba give a different and important new context for specific teams. It is important also to look at *teams* (that is, small groups) and *teamwork* (an environment of collaboration) in a

235

larger context. When speaking of the micro sense of "teams" or the macro sense of "teamwork," we can learn to look at them systemically.

As depicted in Figure 4, there is an interdependence between purpose, systems, and teams.

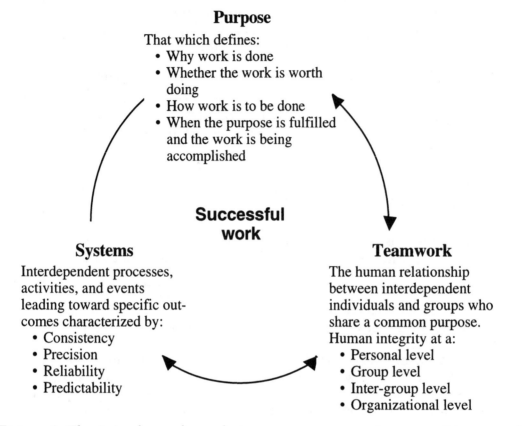

Purpose

That which defines:
- Why work is done
- Whether the work is worth doing
- How work is to be done
- When the purpose is fulfilled and the work is being accomplished

Successful work

Systems

Interdependent processes, activities, and events leading toward specific outcomes characterized by:
- Consistency
- Precision
- Reliability
- Predictability

Teamwork

The human relationship between interdependent individuals and groups who share a common purpose. Human integrity at a:
- Personal level
- Group level
- Inter-group level
- Organizational level

Figure 4. The interdependence between purpose, systems, and teamwork

1. PURPOSE IS NECESSARY TO CREATE A SYSTEM.
   If you are asked to clean off a table, without knowing the purpose you won't know the appropriate method or process or system. The appropriate approach for cleaning the table for the purpose of eating is different from cleaning it off for the purpose of performing surgery. As Dr. Deming taught, without a purpose, there *is no* system.

2. PURPOSE IS NECESSARY TO CREATE A TEAM.
   In the same way, purpose gives definition, focus, and direction to a team. The purpose will help you decide if a small group (team) is necessary and, if so, which capabilities or resources need to be represented on the team. Without a purpose all you have is a room full of people trying to figure out why they are there. That team won't last very long. Sometimes it is possible to observe what a team does and how it spends its time and infer from that what the team's purpose is. Using this approach one would conclude, for instance, that the purpose of a major league baseball team is to argue over money.

3. SYSTEMS AND TEAMS REQUIRE EACH OTHER.
   A team with a purpose and no method will flounder and fail for the lack of a means to achieve its end. But having a system, process, or method available for doing work is insufficient if there are no working relationships between those who are pursuing the purpose.

A small group of people—a team—with its purpose, methods, and team relationship exists within a larger context. The organization in turn has its purpose, systems, and processes and the environment of teamwork. At the organization level, there are the same or equivalent interacting and interdependent dynamics. These are shown in Figure 5, along with a third level of system. The small group exists within an organization which, in turn, exists within a larger context still, the world around it.

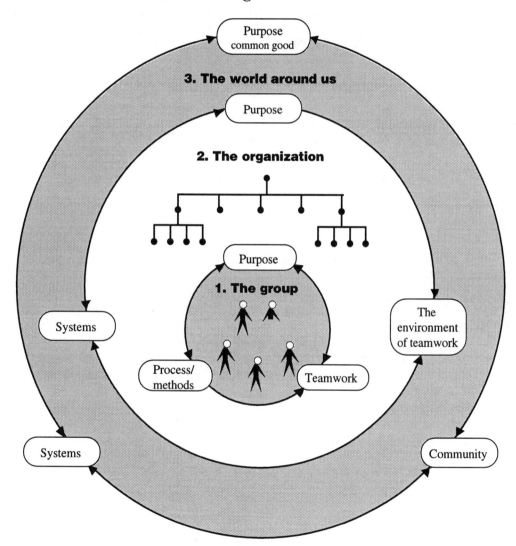

Figure 5. Teams and systems

Some comments on teams and systems:

- As proposed earlier, the small group (team) should have as its purpose the needs of the outside customers, the work of the Gemba, or the task supporting the Gemba. That is the larger context for the team's work.
- When the larger organization lacks a sense of purpose, customer, system, and Gemba, it will make the work of the small group enormously more difficult. There should be consistency and alignment between the small group's sense of purpose, systems, and teamwork and the larger organization's sense of those dynamics.
- The organization, however, exists in a community or a society, a nation or a planet. Misalignments of purpose, systems, and a sense of community between these larger systems and the organization will create dissonance and disequilibrium. One of the emerging studies in systems-thinking is how organizations can start living with the planet and stop fighting the planet, not seeking to control it.

The point of this brief planetary excursion is to help us see the complexity of systems and interdependent interactions. The challenge of a team is to succeed in the midst of many contrary dynamics. The challenge to leaders is to lead *systems* not simply to proliferate teams.

Conclusion to Part I

So far, we have explored a few concepts that should lead us to rethink our approach to teams:

- Teams should be an expression of and vehicle for a systems-view of the organization.
- Teams should adopt a "customer-in" point of view.
- Teams should be seen as either "doing Gemba work" or "supporting Gemba work."
- Teams are mini-systems within macro-systems. A team will benefit from or suffer from the degree of consistency and alignment between its area of limited focus and the larger systems surrounding it and interacting with it. No team acts in isolation.
- The starting point for all teams is, "What is this team's purpose?" If the purpose is inconstant or unclear, there will be no team.
- Leaders must lead systems, not merely proliferate teams.

Part II will attempt to examine the current world of teams through the prism of these concepts.

PART II. TAKING A SYSTEMS VIEW OF CURRENT, POPULAR TEAMS

Part I of this article looked at several concepts that affect how we approach the establishing of teams. The concepts include these:

- Teams should be an expression of and vehicle for a systems-view of the organization.
- Teams should adopt a "customer-in" point of view.
- Teams should be seen as either "doing Gemba work" or "supporting Gemba work."
- Teams are mini-systems within macro-systems. A team will benefit from or suffer from the degree of consistency and alignment between its area of limited focus and the larger systems surrounding it and interacting with it. No team acts in isolation.
- The starting point for all teams is, "What is this team's purpose?" If the purpose is inconstant or unclear, there will be no team.
- Leaders must lead systems, not merely proliferate teams.

Here we will examine some of the currently popular approaches to teams and look at them using some of the concepts explored in Part I.

Self-Directed Teams

Leadership can be viewed as a role in which one person performs several functions, or it can be seen as a system of functions that can be shared by several people. There is no necessary advantage to being self-directed. Self-directed teams are just as capable of genius or stupidity as other-directed teams.

What is the purpose of being "self-directed" or "leaderless"? This question should be resolved before dubbing any team "self-directed." How does this team—and its leadership mode—fit into the larger systems of the organization? This is another important question.

It is hoped that self-directed teams will have a higher level of ownership, pro-activity, creativity, and mutual challenge and support. Self-directed teams may also result in reduced supervisor head-count costs (which, frankly, seems to be the primary reason why self-directed teams are established). Self-direction should come from a carefully thought-through purpose and strategy, not simply copying the current fad.

Self-direction is not an *either-you-have-it-or-you-don't* situation. It is always a matter of *how much self-direction* do you have? This is shown in Figure 6.

239

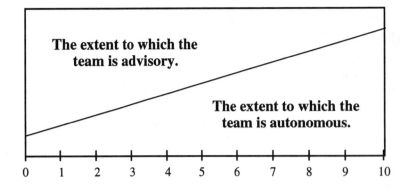

Figure 6. The continuum of self-direction.
Note: No team is entirely autonomous. No team is entirely advisory.

If you are thinking of converting to a "leaderless" team, start out on a small scale. Experiment with one team and learn from it, using the Plan-Do-Check-Act cycle. Figure 7 shows how to plan for self-direction.

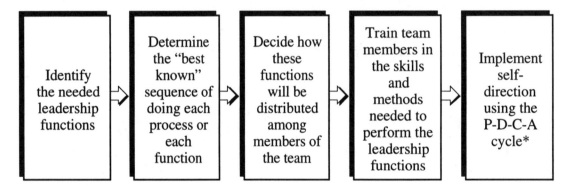

Figure 7. Planning for self-direction

Do you need a team or can this work be effectively accomplished by an individual?

To determine whether or not to use a team involves an examination of the nature and purpose of the work to be undertaken. You don't need a team to add paper to the copy machine. As with architecture, form should follow function. The use of a team is a choice of "form" and as such use should be determined by the "function" or work to be done.

---

*PDCA is an acronym for Plan-Do-Check-Act, a cycle of improvement and learning. Deming taught this cycle to the Japanese in 1950 and called it the "Shewhart cycle" after his mentor, Walter Shewhart. Deming preferred the work "study" to "check." Thus you will hear some refer to the "PDSA" cycle. The word "check" and PDCA is the common usage. (Cf. Scholtes, Peter R. *The Team Handbook*. Madison, WI: Joiner Associates Incorporated, 1988, pages 5-31 and 5-46 ff.)

1. IS THE ISSUE SIMPLE OR EXTREMELY COMPLEX?
    Generally the more complex the issue is, the more it must be broken
    down into its component parts, each possibly needing an individual
    or sub-group to do the work.

2. DOES THE ISSUE REQUIRE NO SPECIAL EXPERTISE OR MULTIPLE EXPERTS
    FROM MULTIPLE DISCIPLINES?
    While not all areas of expertise need to be represented on a team
    (some may be occasional consultants to the effort) there is a similar
    correlation here to that described above regarding complexity.

3. CAN THE ISSUE BE DEALT WITH QUICKLY (DAYS) OR WILL IT TAKE A LONG
    TIME (MONTHS)?
    With a prolonged effort there are more likely to be transitions and
    turnovers. More members can help reduce disruption and assure
    continuity.

4. DOES THE WORK OF THE TEAM INVOLVE ISSUES THAT ARE SINGLE-
    FUNCTION ORIENTED OR DOES IT CUT ACROSS FUNCTIONS?
    Cross-functional work usually needs a cross-functional team.

5. IS THE ISSUE UNCONTROVERSIAL OR IT IS EXTREMELY CONTROVERSIAL?
    Generally it is better to put some dissenters on the team helping to
    develop the work, rather than have them snipe at the work after it is
    completed. Besides, their dissent may well be based on legitimate
    considerations.

6. WILL IMPLEMENTING THE PROJECT'S RECOMMENDATIONS BE EASY OR VERY
    COMPLEX?
    Those who are needed to implement a solution will understand it
    better and commit themselves more to the solution if they helped
    develop it.

Types of Teams

I decided to collect a "catalogue" of teams and spent several months
asking various people from various organizations, "What kind of teams
do you have?" I combined this with a search of various current books
and articles on teams. The result is the list on pages 243 through 246

One answer I often heard was, "We are using high-performance
teams!" I kept searching for what was unique about these H-P-Ts and
could determine only one difference: High-performance teams are called
that, other teams are not called that. I fear we have uncovered another
fad phrase.

On the following pages, I have listed seven different types of teams.
For each I have described what it is and whether or not it is—or could
be—a "Gemba" team. (See Part I of this article for an explanation of
"Gemba.") I have also tried to state its ideal purpose and when it is most

useful. The strengths and vulnerabilities of each are described. One column of information attempts to describe the likely methodology of its work: the strategies and tools it might employ. These are described in more detail in many of the books referred to at the end of this article.

Types of Teams

Type of team	Description	Purpose	When to use it	Strengths	Vulnera- bilities	Strategies/ methods/ tools	Comments
1. Natural work group (whether self-directed or other-directed). • This may be a "Gemba team."	• People who work together every- day: same office, same machine, same location, same process. • These sometimes are developed into "quality circles."	• To study and improve the process, to receive and/or communicate vital information, to participate in planning. • To establish and maintain the current standardized methods.	• When the issues need a "local" perspective. • When the focus is limited to this group's process, customers, and everyday work- life. • These should be constant and in every organization.	• Can create routine monitoring, feedback, study, and quick response systems. • Creates local ownership and pride. • Improves awareness and attentiveness.	• Overemphas- izing their part of the system to the detriment of the whole system. • Tampering with the system. • Chasing after symptoms of deeper systemic causes.	• Key process indicators. • Feedback loops from internal and external customers. • Standardization. • P-D-C-A. • Communications links with line management.	• Leaderless groups will need to identify the functions of leadership and the methods by which these functions will be carried out without a designated leader. These functions, too, should be standardized, best-known methods.
2. Business team (leaderless or leaderful). • Ordinarily these are "Gemba teams."	• Usually a cross- functional team that oversees a specific product line or customer segment. • Depending on the business it "owns," it may include such functions as sales, production, marketing, customer service, etc.	• To maintain and improve an entire coordi- nated system of customer- focused activities from start (marketing, orders) to finish (delivery, installation, service). • To rapidly adjust to chang- ing customer needs.	• These should exist in every organization, at least as a vehicle for periodic review of the organization's performance regarding particular customers, products, and services.	• Can create a systems-based flow and inter- action within a conventional, hierarchical organization. • Can create more rapid and nimble responsiveness to market changes.	• Can stretch people too thin (a small marketing staff may be required to be part of too many business teams). • Conventional managers (e.g., a plant manager) may resist having authority diminished. • Must not lose sight of larger systems.	• Market and customer research. • Quality function deployment. • Production/ service planning. • Key process indicators. • Monitoring of ongoing customer satisfaction.	• A major challenge will be for business teams to successfully shift from an autonomous- function mentality to an interdependent systems mentality. It requires that each member adapt a team mentality and the whole group create an environment of teamwork.

243

Types of Teams (continued)

Type of team	Description	Purpose	When to use it	Strengths	Vulnerabilities	Strategies/methods/tools	Comments
3. Management teams: Executive team. • This team should support the Gemba but is not a Gemba team.	• A group of managers who are peers and the person to whom they commonly report. • The managing director, CEO, president, etc. and his/her reports.	• To lead that part of the organization over which they have control. • To give direction and focus to the organization.	• This group should be a constant presence, with regular meetings.	• Can build consensus and common purpose at the top. • Can create support for each other.	• Group think: An unquestioned acceptance of the correctness of its beliefs. • Managerial fads and "viruses." • Arrogance, the "not invented here" syndrome. • Short-term thinking. • Conflict and risk avoidance.	• Skills in gathering and analyzing data. • Inquiry and review. • An obsession with pleasing the customer. • Systems and statistical thinking. • The seven management tools.	• All management and business teams need "profound knowledge."* • People in leadership roles need a clear sense of purpose, values, mission, and priority and be masters at communicating these. • Too often what is called a management team is a collection of independents who listen to each other's pronouncements. • These groups need planned and facilitated meetings; the managers need to learn group skills. • These hierarchically-based teams must develop processes of coordination with systems-based teams.
4. Management teams: "Linch-pin" teams. • These are not Gemba teams, but they support the Gemba (comments here apply to any middle-mgmt team).	• Linch-pin teams are a cascading network of teams, starting with the executive team, in which each manager is a member of a team led by his or her boss and leads a team consisting of his or her direct reports.	• To create a leadership network so that constancy and consistency is maintained throughout the organization. • To deploy information and collect input rapidly.	• These should probably be constants, meeting regularly. The frequency of "regularly" will be shaped by the work and needs of the organization, but the *minimum frequency* would ordinarily be monthly.	• Maintaining ready avenues for communication throughout the organization. • Helps to maintain constancy of purpose. • Useful in planning cycles for communicating emerging priorities and eliciting input.	• Being not a team, but an aggregate of independent functionally autonomous leaders; "a council of sovereigns." • Not working collectively for the good of the whole system. • Insufficient planning for, and management of, the meeting process.	• The methodology of improvement. • Change strategies and methods. • Stability, strategies, and methods. • Consensus building group processes.	

*"Profound knowledge" is Deming's final legacy. See *The New Economics*, Cambridge, MA: MIT, 1994.

Types of Teams *(continued)*

Type of team	Description	Purpose	When to use it	Strengths	Vulnera-bilities	Strategies/methods/tools	Comments
5. New product/service design teams ("skunk-works" or conventional). • These are usually Gemba teams.	• Usually a cross functional group assigned to redesign all or part of a product or service. • "Conventional" means the team works within the ordinary context and environment of the organization. • "Skunk works" means a radical departure from how and where such work is ordinarily done.	To develop: • New markets • New products • New services • New applications or capabilities to be offered to customers. • To create and maintain a market edge.	• As one innovation is being introduced, another one or more should be be planned.	• Can maintain the vitality and continued well-being of the organization.	• Group-think. • Innovations that please the innovators while disregarding the needs of the customers.	• Market research. • Continuous closeness to the customer. • Quality function deployment. • Understanding the processes and methods of creativity. • Understanding the processes and methods of data based studies of important characteristics and indicators. • P-D-C-A is a reflex and a constant.	• Customers generally can't tell you directly what innovations to create. But a close understanding of the customers or users and their experiences, concerns, frustrations, etc. can identify needs that the innovators can then seek to satisfy.

Types of Teams *(concluded)*

Type of team	Description	Purpose	When to use it	Strengths	Vulnera-bilities	Strategies/methods/tools	Comments
6. Process redesign or systems re-engineering. • These may be Gemba teams.	• Similar to new product/new service teams, but dealing with the internal operations which create and deliver the product or service.	• New methods, processes, or systems for design, develop-ment, delivery, and/or service.	• Continuously but selectively used as part of a larger strategy (probably an annual strategy) to pursue carefully selected organizational priorities. • Don't overdo these.	• Can result in dramatic reductions in cycle-times, waste, staffing needs. • Allow the organization to do more with higher quality and at less expense.	• Tampering: not basing changes on data, but on guesswork. • Disregarding the needs of the outside customers and the inside workers.	• P-D-C-A. • Standardization. • Systems analysis. • Statistical thinking. • Measurement systems. • Participative methods.	• Redesigners must keep in close contact with those who will bear the brunt of their innovations.
7. Improvement project. • These projects ordinarily provide a service to the Gemba.	• A natural work group or cross-functional team whose responsibility is to achieve some needed improvement on an existing process; an ad-hoc assignment.	• To improve an existing system or process for the design and delivery of a product or service. These projects are usually more specific and have a narrower focus.	• These projects can be combined and integrated into a system of efforts aimed at achieving needed improvements. When successful, these projects eliminate the causes of problems. Problems don't recur.	• To successfully undertake these efforts requires considerable support from the entire organization.	• Overkill: using overly complicated methods. • Underkill: cutting corners without an understanding of what is lost. • Not applying the specific, proven hard-nosed methods; reverting to old-time problem-solving methods.	• Improvement methodology in general. • Standardization. • 7 Step Method. • Methods for communicating with, educating, and involving others who work with the process under study.	• Much of the quality improvement literature has been written with this approach in mind (see *The Team Handbook*). • Don't create a proliferation of these projects and teams. These are easily started but hard to sustain.

Systems of Teams, Networks of Efforts

In Part I of this article, I stated that too often there are teams that individually may do worthwhile work but collectively go nowhere. This is usually indicative of the absence of those internal strategies and systems that would link teams and their individual missions into a larger collaborative purpose.

Figure 8 shows a Tree Diagram, one of the seven management tools. For me the Tree Diagram is as much a way of thinking as it is a tool.

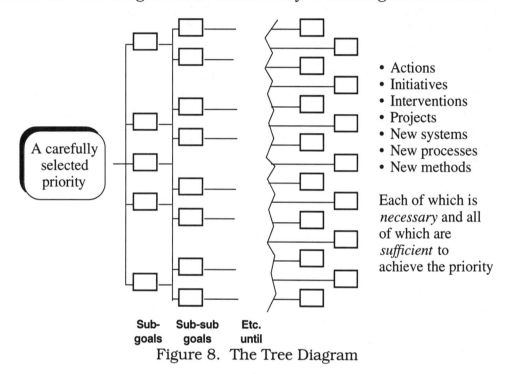

- Actions
- Initiatives
- Interventions
- Projects
- New systems
- New processes
- New methods

Each of which is *necessary* and all of which are *sufficient* to achieve the priority

Sub-goals   **Sub-sub goals**   **Etc. until**

Figure 8. The Tree Diagram

The great Japanese teacher of Quality, Dr. Noriaki Kano of Tokyo Science University, urges us to go "an inch wide and a mile deep" rather than "an inch deep and a mile wide." Rather than many priorities worked on superficially (too many teams working in diverse directions), we should coordinate our efforts around fewer priorities.

Beginning with a carefully selected priority—one that benefits customers and the long-term survival and growth of the organization—we ask, "What will it take to successfully accomplish that priority?" The first round of answers is likely to be a list of subordinate goals. For each we repeat the "what will it take" questions, perhaps continuing through further sequences of subordinate goals, until we start listing actions.

Some items on the list of necessary and sufficient actions may be undertaken by one person with a simple stroke of the pen. Many items will probably involve complicated projects that will require either an assignment to an already existing, ongoing team or the commissioning of a special ad-hoc team. Some comments on tree-diagram planning:

- THIS GOES BEYOND MBO. Management by objectives consists of goals (usually too many) with no method. MBO is not leadership. It is the abdication of leadership.

- NOT ALL EFFORTS MUST BE UNDERTAKEN BY A TEAM. The architectural adage "form follows function" applies here. Determine first the purpose of the work and the nature of the task. Then choose the appropriate structural needs, such as "team or no team."

- The work of each individual or group is linked to all the other efforts in a network of collaboration. Everyone is doing his or her share, each pulling in the same direction.

- This system of work should be overseen by managers or specially selected teams of managers who offer support and challenge, provide linkage to line management and key internal resources, and who periodically review the separate efforts. These leaders conduct the "check" step of the Plan-Do-Check-Act cycle and lead by asking good questions.

Conclusion

We should develop a healthy skepticism about teams. Teams should not continue to exist if their usefulness and necessity can't be demonstrated. Teams should be part of a coordinated effort—a system of teams—pursuing some high priority need. Teams should be able to describe how they either contribute directly to the outside customers or contribute to the "Gemba," those who are in the work flow that leads directly to the outside customers.

It is not hard to establish a lot of teams, just as it is not hard to plant a lot of seeds in a garden. The hard work of gardening and setting up teams is tending to them, nurturing them, supporting them, and preparing to process what they produce. Such direction, focus, challenge, support, and caretaking must come from leaders. It is part of the leader's new job.

Some Readings on Systems, Teams, or Topics Related to Teamwork

Ackoff, Russell L. (1994). *The democratic corporation.* New York: Oxford University Press. Almost anything by Ackoff is a gold mine of useful insight. On pages 18-35 of this volume, Ackoff discusses systems.

Brassard, Michael (1994). *The memory jogger II.* Methuen, MA: GOAL/QPC.

Brassard, Michael (1989). *The memory jogger plus+: Featuring the seven management and planning tools.* Methuen, MA: GOAL/QPC.

Chang, Richard, and Matthew Niedzwiecki (1993). *Continuous improvement tools* (vols. 1 and 2). Irvine, CA: Richard Chang Associates.

Deming, W. Edwards (1994). *The new economics* (2nd Edition). Cambridge, MA: MIT. Dr. Deming's last book. In chapter three he discusses systems.

Dyer, William G. (1987). *Team building* (2nd Edition). Reading, MA: Addison Wesley. Part of Addison Wesley's Organization Development series, Dyer's book is considered a classic in the field.

Fisher, Rayner, Belgard, et al. (1995). *Tips for teams.* New York: McGraw Hill. Some useful approaches for dealing with common group problems.

Gitlow, Howard, Shelly Gitlow, Alan Oppenheim, and Rosa Oppenheim (1989). *Tools and methods for the improvement of quality.* Homewood, IL: Irwin.

Ishikawa, Kaoru (1982). *Guide to quality control.* Tokyo: Asian Productivity Organization.

Kume, Hitoshi (1985). *Statistical methods for quality improvement.* Tokyo: The Association for Overseas Technical Scholarship.

McGregor, Douglas (1985). *The human side of enterprise* (Anniversary Edition). New York: McGraw Hill. The environment of teamwork by a giant in the field and his definitive work. Chapter 16 discusses "The Managerial Team."

Mizuno, Shigeru (Ed.) (1988). *Management for quality improvement:* The 7 new QC tools. Cambridge, MA: Productivity Press.

Neave, Henry R. (1990). *The Deming dimension.* Knoxville, TN: SPC Press. Dr. Neave provides a good and readable presentation of W. Edwards Deming's philosophy. Chapter eight is entitled "Processes and Systems."

Parker, Glenn M. (1994). *Cross-functional teams.* San Francisco: Jossey Bass. Some useful guidelines for perhaps the most challenging type of team. I disagree with what Parker says about performance appraisal, however.

Scholtes, Peter, et al. (1988). *The team handbook.* Madison, WI: Joiner Associates Incorporated. A manual intended to be useful for teams working on improvement projects.

Total quality transformation: Improvement tools (1993). Dayton, OH: QIP Inc. and PQ Systems Inc. (Available by calling [800] 777-3020. Note: this is an excellent manual. But it is very expensive. There is an alternative edition for education [K-12], which is also very expensive.)

Tregoe, Benjamin B. and Charles H. Kepner (1981). *The new rational manager.* Princeton, NJ: Princeton Research Press.

Weisbord, Marvin R. (1991). *Productive workplaces.* San Francisco: Jossey Bass. A book full of insights and practical approaches to a collaborative environment.

Wellins, Schaaf and Shomo (1994). *Succeeding with teams.* Minneapolis, MN: Lakewood Books. A little book with lots of short tips.

Wheeler, Donald and David Chambers (1992). *Understanding statistical process control* (2nd edition). Knoxville, TN: SPC Press.

Wilson and George (1994). *Team leader's survival guide.* Pittsburgh, PA: Development Dimensions International. A manual with a model and methods for team development.

About the Contributor

Peter R. Sholtes is an internationally known author, lecturer, and consultant. From 1987 through 1993, he was an instructor sharing the platform with Dr. W. Edwards Deming. Mr. Sholtes' post-graduate education and early professional experience was in Organizational Development. He was one of the first to combine this discipline with the teachings of Dr. Deming.

Mr. Scholtes has consulted with more than twenty companies during the past twelve years, helping managers to apply the principles and methods of Quality, looking at work with the perspective of systems, statistical thinking, and teamwork.

Mr. Scholtes is the author of *The Team Handbook*, which has sold nearly 700,000 copies. He has written award-winning articles on several Quality related topics, especially with Dr. Deming's encouragement, on the controversial topic of performance appraisal: What's wrong with it and what to do instead. He is featured on over twelve videotaped presentations, and has been a keynote speaker at many international conferences in such places as London, Sidney, Moscow, and Rio de Janeiro. In March of 1995, *Quality Digest* recognized Mr. Scholtes as one of the 50 Quality leaders of this decade.

21

Selecting the Right Team Structure to Work in Your Organization

Sue Easton and Gayle Porter

Everyone seems to be restructuring, reorganizing, or re-engineering, and many companies have shifted to team structures as a part of the change. Unfortunately, there is no guarantee that use of teams will lead to success. Why do some companies report that initiating a team structure transformed the organization into a more productive and more satisfying workplace, while others have abandoned similar efforts in frustration? One reason may be a tendency to over-simplify the original decision. It is more complex than a *Yes* or *No* choice about using teams. If you are considering teams, you must give some thought to how they will best serve your needs. Decision making then turns toward determining which team structure you need, based on a realistic profile of your organization.

Developing an Organization Profile

Use of teams is a choice of structure. Teams can dramatically affect business performance through bottom-line improvements. Benefits may include increased productivity, improved quality, reduced costs, and more adaptability. Positive results might also take the form of increased customer satisfaction, getting to market faster, or increased innovation. Discussion of the appropriate structure for your organization must begin with a focus on strategic business objectives and specified outcomes to support those objectives. Only after there is clear agreement on desired outcomes, are you in a position to begin considering the best structure for achieving them. Keeping those objectives in the forefront of all discussions will eliminate the tendency to become distracted by implementation issues. Too often people get so wrapped up in the

253

process of teams they lose sight of their initial goal. Performance is the end to be achieved; teams are one means to that end.

To be effective, structure must be suited to the work itself. Therefore, the first consideration is the worker interdependence required to do the job. Interdependence is a mutual reliance required to accomplish the work. Overall, if the work process involves interdependence among the workers, teams definitely should be considered. At this point, it is also important to understand that there are different types of teams from which to choose. Judging which type fits your organization's current situation depends on three additional considerations:

1. Context: organizational factors that must support the teams
2. Employee characteristics: team members' skills and attitudes
3. Leadership characteristics: readiness of those who will directly lead and support the teams

To facilitate a diagnostic process, these factors have been placed in a matrix with different team structures. We refer to this as a "Continuum of Work Structures." This format has been a helpful tool in many ways: as an assessment of the current situation, as an indication of specific development needs, and as a check on the alignment of a work group's experience and perceptions. For each use, the process begins with an appraisal of the work itself and the situation surrounding that work. The following describes, in more detail, the four considerations for building this profile of the organization.

Work Process—The Interdependence among Work Group Members

Traditional structure was built up around the concept of division of labor. Historically, when we moved from craftsman to mass production, each worker became extremely specialized in one task. The job classifications of supervisor and manager were roles created to coordinate the disconnected tasks. Only this one person—the leader—needed to know how it all fit together. Current streamlining of organizations involves removing many of these coordinating roles. To replace them, the involved workers must take over responsibility for awareness of the total process and interact with each other in new ways.

The extent to which this is desirable depends on the nature of the work. If one person does not show up, can the others simply work around that function, or does someone have to fill in for the work to continue? The latter implies interdependence. Some tasks are collectively important to an overall outcome, but the individual workers do not need high interaction. Members produce their best work independently with someone coordinating their output, somewhat like taxi cab drivers working for one dispatcher. In other task situations, such as a construction crew, workers are more directly interdependent. In still others, like a soccer team, they may have very high interdependence. In cases of high interdependence, an additional person in a coordinating role would be more of a burden than a help.

254

Organizational Factors

There are several important organizational factors involved in the consideration of team structures.

1. *Responsibility and Accountability.* Closely related to interdependence is the issue of accountability. In a traditional structure, only the leader (supervisor or manager) has an overview of individual workers' tasks and how they must fit together. Therefore, the leader is the only one who can be held responsible for the final outcome. So the leader's job is to push or persuade workers to a level of performance that will support higher management's goals. While some workers may respond well to this situation, others perform at less than their full capability because they have limited personal responsibility.

Responsibility and accountability may rest with the leader of the work group, may be shared by the leader and team members, or may be held entirely by members of the team. This aspect of empowerment sometimes occurs as a gradual transition. The important thing is to recognize where the organization is at this point in time, in order to compare this with other related factors.

2. *Communication: Available Information.* We often speak of empowerment as moving decision making down the organizational hierarchy. Too much focus on downward direction can lead us to think the lower the better, which may not be the case. It is important to put decision making at the level in the organization that matches the body of knowledge needed to make the decisions. We can locate the body of knowledge and go to those people for decisions, or provide training and the necessary information to the people we want to be able to make those decisions. Traditional organization structure requires that information flow up and down the chain of command. At each level, someone is making judgments on the "need to know" of workers below. The advantage of this is the clarity of a single point of contact and avoidance of information overload. The disadvantage is slower communications and redundant costs of information dissemination.

Informal information networks will develop to supplement the formal structure, but the quality of these "grapevines" can vary greatly. Shared information includes both formal and informal exchanges—moving official information through the structure and maintaining enough openness in informal networks to eliminate inaccuracies. Access to computerized data now allows us to disseminate information to every level of the organization in a key stroke, which contradicts the traditional hierarchical flow of information. The concern is whether the correct information is efficiently provided to the people who need it. In some team situations, task information may be available, while more general information is not readily shared. Some organizations share a greater range of information but do so cautiously—they clearly have reservations. Finally, there are organizations who make extensive information available.

3. *Communication: Feedback on Group Performance.* Performance feedback is a very specific type of communication. Similar to other information, communication on performance may be unavailable, shared to some degree, shared on task only, shared with some reservation, or shared fully. It is critical to determine what really exists in an organization, so a structure can be chosen that is consistent with that degree of communication.

Many organizations have often fallen into a pattern of annual performance reviews, where discussion is separated from the actual time of most events. On a day-to-day basis, supervisors and managers may focus on problems only. When problems are pointed out, there may not be accompanying information on how to improve. These tendencies, in whatever structure, interfere with the positive potential of performance feedback. Creating teams will not eliminate the problem. On the other hand, lack of adequate feedback can certainly sabotage efforts to implement teams. The type and extent of feedback varies for different types of teams, but low communication on performance does not support any team structure.

Employee Characteristics

It would be difficult to overemphasize the importance of the organizational factors in considering team structures, because these characteristics are the context within which teams must operate. Success is possible only when the environment supports the effort. Of course, the organization exists through its people, so characteristics of the personnel are also critical to structure considerations.

1. *Technical Skills.* From its origin, the traditional hierarchical structure was an effort to break down tasks into the lowest skill level possible, with the coordinating leaders responsible for bringing together the components as necessary. Any variation from the traditional structure begins to include workers in problem identification and formulation of new approaches to the work. In order to offer intelligent and meaningful input, a team structure requires higher levels of proficiency. Competency is the first requirement. Following competency, workers need to gain experience that will build confidence in their skills. The final step is empowering workers to apply those skills fully in day-to-day work activity. It is a mistake to empower people who have not been allowed to first develop both competence and confidence.

Too often organizations empower everyone simultaneously, with no consideration to the degree of readiness among various work groups. With appropriate training and opportunity to practice new skills, empowerment progresses in a logical fashion. Because different team structures entail different levels of empowerment (more information, more accountability, and less control by management), the team members' technical competence must be appropriate to the choice of structure.

2. *Attitudes toward Work.* Typically, the traditional organization does not require a broad skill base from individual workers and does not hold them accountable for more than a narrow task responsibility. Thus, it may limit elements that build toward an attitude of professionalism among employees. Professionalism can be thought of as an individual's desire to apply his/her personally held high standards to the job. Work, then, is an expression of an individual's own views on quality and expertise. Empowered workers are free to apply these standards directly; their personal standards guide their conduct.

With use of teams, we often see an increase in professionalism, as the scope of workers' involvement increases. However, determining the existing attitude is important for determining how well employees are prepared to work in various types of teams. At least a moderate level of professionalism is required for any team structure to succeed. For greater levels of responsibility to be considered, team members need a high level of professionalism in their attitude toward work. Jumping to a high team responsibility structure, when there is little current attitude of professionalism, is likely to cause resentment. It can be viewed as a burden, rather than an opportunity.

3. *Trust in Peers.* The more interdependence the task requires, the greater the need for cooperation among workers rather than competition. Trust among co-workers sometimes develops from personal relationships, regardless of the structure in which they work. With teams, it becomes increasingly important that members have confidence in each others' motives to pursue a cooperative organizational goal, and confidence in others' ability to perform the job well. If the level of trust in peers is not adequate for such cooperation, the team structure will not succeed. It is a mistake to think that simply shifting to team performance rewards will, in itself, cause people to pull together toward a goal. If the trust has not developed, time and energy will be spent on tracking who is or is not doing their share, rather than on the task itself.

4. *Trust in Management.* Trust in management most frequently correlates with information sharing and performance feedback. Although more communication will not automatically translate to higher trust in management, a good match between amount of information provided and the amount needed to do the job is likely to set the stage. Trust also builds from consistent and reliable displays of good judgments. Perceptions about management have built up over time and are not going to change instantly because a new team structure is implemented.

As mentioned earlier, shifting away from a traditional structure involves increased worker accountability. The extent to which work group members will view this as a positive change is partly determined by their trust in the motives of management. With a base of trust, employees are more likely to interpret changes as a move toward efficiency that benefits everyone. If mistrust prevails, they can interpret the same new responsibilities as exploitation. You may hear reactions like, "If we're taking over the supervisor's work, why don't we get the supervisor's pay?"

Leadership Characteristics

The influence of leadership plays a critical part in determining the successful team structure. Here we discuss leaders as people who interact directly with the workers but have a different formal status. This role varies across structures. At one extreme is the traditional role with a formal title of supervisor or foreman. This person's job is often defined in terms of directing and controlling. Moving away from that traditional role, the leader in a team environment does less directing but is still involved in coordinating activities within the team. At the other extreme, the leader may still handle some coordination between the team and others in the organization, but internal coordination primarily is a responsibility shared among team members.

1. *Need to Control.* Individuals have different levels of need to be in control and have different interpretations about what being in control means. Some people are comfortable simply being informed about what is going on, while others want to be integrally involved at each step along the way. Leaders with a very high need for control will be least effective in shifting responsibility to teams. Those who can delegate more easily are suited to situations involving highly interdependent work processes.

2. *Comfort with the Unknown.* In a traditional structure, the leadership role is a position of control and, therefore, dealing with the unknown is minimized. Leaders who are only comfortable with familiar approaches and regimentation have been able to experience a fair amount of success in hierarchical organizations. There are fewer opportunities for this formula in today's organizations. The rate of change continues to accelerate and familiar approaches just aren't working. Success with team structures may depend on how well the leaders have been able to establish their own comfort with trying new methods.

Comfort with the unknown can also be described as tolerance for ambiguity and risk-taking. In considering a team structure, one risk involves the leaders' willingness to trust the workers. The leaders will be more able to work with limited knowledge of every detail, when they have confidence in workers' skills. This confidence includes belief in workers' technical skills on task, their decision-making and problem-solving skills, and their demonstrated judgment in knowing when they need help and how to obtain it.

Structures to Match the Profile of the Organization

Examination of these factors requires considering a range of possibilities for each. This is the reason a decision about use of teams is not a yes or no question. As shown on a "Continuum of Work Structures" (see Attachment 21-A), different team structures correspond to varying combinations of the factors. One use of the continuum is to develop a profile of the organization by having organizational members rate each factor. By omitting or concealing the structure identifications, it is possible to elicit ratings of the organization, without any bias toward a structure people think they want or need. As a pattern emerges, the position of the ratings will identify the type of structure most fitting for that organization in its current state. See Article 12, Continuum of Work Structures, in Part III, Team Instruments.

It is important to remember that this continuum does not represent bad to good nor old to new. The change across the continuum is a progression through increasingly complex team structures, but *greater complexity does not necessarily mean better.* Each structure has benefits. The hope is to avoid pursuing a structure that is not matched to needs and conditions: the interdependence of the work process, organizational factors, employee characteristics, and leader characteristics. It is a good structure when it is the best way to meet strategic business objectives.

Quality Improvement Teams

Under this structure, a group of employees voluntarily meets to identify and analyze any problems that affect either production or product quality. Quality improvement teams, originally referred to as quality circles, make suggestions to management for improvements to either save money or improve quality. Members of the quality team have independent natural jobs. That is, they work in related areas and come together for their regular meetings, but their day-to-day work activities are not interdependent.

Because quality improvement teams only make recommendations, the accountability for results still rests with the manager or supervisor of the work. The group needs a certain amount of information to guide their efforts and some feedback relating to use of their ideas. Although the members typically need some training in group process techniques, the formation of a quality improvement team does not require a higher level of technical skills. The natural work of the members has not changed, so their technical skills are adequate. The interactions within the quality team, as well as between the team and management, require at least a moderate level of professionalism, moderate trust in peers, and moderate trust in management. The leaders must be willing to give up some control, because the workers are meeting to discuss problems they have not previously been expected to address. However, because quality improvement teams only make recommendations, this structure can operate in an environment where leaders have low comfort with the unknown.

Input Task Teams

When employees join with others to give input on a specific, predetermined task, they are an input task team. The issue might involve quality, but the task could also relate to areas of safety, communication, and other organizational concerns. These groups meet on a regularly scheduled basis to develop a proposed plan of action, but their suggestions require management approval prior to implementation. The amount of interdependence, accountability, and communication is parallel to the situation supporting quality circles. A moderate level of professionalism and trust in peers and management is still adequate, but technical skills must be slightly higher when the task involves either solving a specific problem or finding a more innovative approach.

Because the group forms to address a specific task, the organizational leaders have made a commitment to the issue by forming the team, but cannot foresee the direction the team's recommendations may take. Leaders are giving up some control and must be even more comfortable with the unknown.

Output Task Teams

While input task teams only make recommendations, an output task team also implements the plan. To enable this extended involvement, there must be more communication to the team, although it need only be task-related information and feedback. The team activity is a special involvement, which is outside the members' natural jobs. These teams often function without a formal leader, or the leader takes a role of sponsor and resource person rather than coordinating team activities. Because the team is acting as well as recommending, these leaders have less control of activities than with input task teams or quality improvement teams; they must have a lower need to control and higher comfort with the unknown.

The implementation aspect also requires that technical skills be high. Moderate professionalism is adequate, but trust in peers and trust in management must be slightly higher than the level required of input task teams and quality improvement teams. These employee characteristics and the decrease in the leader's need to control combine so that the accountability and responsibility are shared between the team and the leader.

Leader Centered Teams

When workers are involved in interdependent tasks as their natural jobs, rather than some special assignment, teams are a beneficial structure. We distinguish such teams, in terms of their degree of autonomy, as either leader centered or self-managed. The designation of a leader centered team means there is an external formal leader, who facilitates problem solving within the group and communicates with others in the work system. The team is sharing responsibility with the leader, which requires a high degree of professionalism.

Leader centered teams need more communication and should receive general information and feedback in addition to task related communication. In many cases this information may be provided with some reservation, but the level must be greater than with either task teams or quality improvement teams.

Self-Managed Teams

In a self-managed team, the leader functions are handled as responsibilities shared among the team members. An external person may be involved but serves only as a resource to the team, someone who may occasionally provide some direction but does not interfere with team functioning. This structure is appropriate when the work process requires high interdependence among team members to meet their goals. There must be a full sharing of information and feedback on group performance, because the team takes over full responsibility and accountability. Technical skills and professionalism must be high to assume this level of accountability.

The self-managed team cannot succeed unless there is a high level of trust among peers and high trust in management. The leaders who work with the teams must have a low need to control and a high degree of comfort with the unknown. Trying to implement self-managed teams without organizational supports would be a frustrating experience for all concerned. If the leaders or group members do not have the necessary attitudes, the effort will fail. If the work process is not interdependent, there is no need.

The types of teams used here as examples provide a continuum of structures. The movement from quality improvement teams to self-managed teams, in the sequence described here, can be seen as a steady progression away from traditional organization structure. Yet each structure, including the traditional hierarchy, may be effective for business objectives. Each has certain differences in terms of how process, organizational factors, and employee and leader characteristics must combine for effective operation. A careful and honest examination of these aspects will allow an organization to determine their best structure. The "Continuum of Work Structures" aids this examination and creates an awareness of the variety of options available.

Other Uses for the Continuum of Work Structures

When the ratings of a particular factor do not align with others, this highlights areas in which development is needed. For example, an organization might be attempting to utilize output task teams. Information on task is being shared. The leader, who is reasonably comfortable with the unknown and has a medium to low need to control, has been sharing accountability with team members. These are all

261

indications that an output task team is appropriate. Ratings indicate, however, that team member technical skills are low to medium. In order for the teams to succeed, technical skill training is needed.

In another case, employee and organizational factors might be in sync, but the leaders demonstrate a high need to control. Then leader development is needed, so they do not sabotage the effort. The most difficult developmental needs to address are the organizational factors, or the contextual support for each structure. These are not simply training issues. If one or more organizational factors lag the other ratings (appear further to the left on the worksheet), extensive top management involvement may be required to bring about a necessary shift in these systems.

It is also possible that one factor could be leading the others (appear more to the right on the continuum). If it is interdependence that is further to the right, a multifaceted development program should be considered to bring employee, leader, and organizational factors in line with the work process. If another factor stands out by being further to the right, the correct structural choice is probably the one indicated by the majority of ratings. However, some change may still be needed to bring the factors into alignment. The unique factor could indicate expectations that will not be realistic within the chosen structure, and unmet expectations lead to frustration.

The ratings of various factors may not align under a particular structure for a number of reasons. As described above, there may be real differences among factors. These differences indicate either a need for development or possibly a reduction of certain practices. Another possibility is that different people or groups of people have different perceptions of the situation. People working in the same organization often do not share the same experience. Non-alignment of ratings within factors may signal problems in communication or areas of conflict in the organization. These issues may require resolution before ratings across factors can be effectively used to select a structure.

Multiple Answers to a Complex Question

Any organization considering use of teams can use the continuum of structures in a variety of ways:

1. to help decide which team structure could be used most effectively to meet strategic business objectives
2. to determine needed development before undertaking a new team structure
3. to identify differences in how workers perceive the organization

Regarding the best type of team, several different structures may be the answer. An organization may have individual contributors in one area and self-managing teams in another, in addition to task teams who deal with special issues and then disband when the task is complete. "The Continuum of Work Structures" allows a view of all these considerations.

Continuum of Work Structures

Profile of the Organization	Appropriate Work Structure					
	Traditional Structure: very directive with tight chain of command	Quality Improvement Teams	Task Teams: Input	Task Teams: Output	Leader Centered Teams	Self-managed Teams
Work Process						
• interdependence among group members	Members independent; need to be coordinated	→		Team/Leader	Interdependent	Highly Interdependent
Organizational Factors						
• responsibility/accountability	Held with Leader	→		Team/Leader	Team/Leader	Team
• communication — information available/shared	Not readily available/shared	Shared to some degree →		Shared on task only	Shared with some reservation	Shared fully
— feedback on group performance	Not readily available/shared	Shared to some degree →		Shared on task only	Shared with some reservation	Shared fully
Employee Characteristics						
• technical skills	Low	Med →		High	High	High
• attitudes toward work (professionalism)	Low	Med →			High	High
• trust in peers	Low	Med →	Med/High			High
• trust in management	Low	Med →	Med/High			High
Leadership Characteristics						
• need to control	High	Med →	Med/Low			Low
• comfort with the unknown	Low	Med →	Med/High			High

©Easton & Porter 1995

263

Continuum of Work Structures

Profile of the Organization	Appropriate Work Structure				
Work Process					
• interdependence among group members	Members independent; need to be coordinated →		Interdependent		Highly Interdependent
Organizational Factors					
• responsibility/accountability	Held with Leader →	Team/Leader	Team/Leader		Team
• communication — information available/shared	Not readily available/shared	Shared to some degree	Shared on task only	Shared with some reservation	Shared fully
— feedback on group performance	Not readily available/shared	Shared to some degree	Shared on task only	Shared with some reservation	Shared fully
Employee Characteristics					
• technical skills	Low	Med	High	High	High
• attitudes toward work (professionalism)	Low	Med		High	High
• trust in peers	Low	Med	Med/High	High	High
• trust in management	Low	Med	Med/High	High	High
Leadership Characteristics					
• need to control	High	Med	Med/Low	Low	Low
• comfort with the unknown	Low	Med	Med/High	High	High

264

About the Contributors

Gayle Porter is a member of the management faculty at Rutgers University, School of Business in Camden, New Jersey. Her industry experience includes technical work in the oil and gas industry, finance and accounting with a Fortune 500 company, and consulting on training programs and employee development. Gayle received her Ph.D. in Business Administration from The Ohio State University. At Rutgers she teaches courses in Organizational Behavior, Human Resource Management, Social Responsibility of Business, and Organization Change and Development. Her research interests center on employee development issues, particularly team interactions and personal factors that inhibit development efforts. Publications include articles in the *Journal of Social Issues, Journal of Occupational Health Psychology,* and *Journal of Business Ethics.*

Sue Easton is the president of Easton and Associates, Inc., a consulting firm that specializes in the design and implementation of high performance/high commitment work forces and self-managing teams. Sue's expertise is recognized internationally in the area of employee involvement and participation. Sue's focus is on improving quality and productivity by empowering the human potential of each organization. Her guidance includes assessments and interventions that engender a realistic perspective of immediate and long-range issues that impact job performance. Her client base represents both small business concerns and Fortune 500 firms such as General Electric, Lockheed Martin, Price Waterhouse, and Walt Disney World, Co.

22

Trust: The Great Teamwork Enabler
Larry Meeker

What is trust, and why is it such an important component of teamwork?

"Trust is a supremely important element in relationships between people. To trust someone makes a statement of faith about the other human being. It means you believe in the person, that you are willing to rely on his/her integrity, strength, ability and surety. It rings of confidence. Relationships strong in trust have a feeling and sense of security and strength" (Meeker, 1994).

For teams, trust is one of the great enablers. It is not a skill that is learned by intellectual study. It is learned, or more appropriately "built," as more of an emotion, based on our experiences. For teams, it is vital to have effective relationships among team members—relationships that are based on trust. When this exists, the team finds success in areas such as communication, timely decision making, successful problem solving, and cooperation between team members. Success in these areas enables progress toward business goals.

Absence of trust has an extremely negative impact on groups. Such a lack can be far more serious than simply a lack of confidence between people. It can have much deeper consequences, and even result in loss of progress toward business objectives. When trust is absent, negative emotions and actions, such as suspicion and placing of blame, can detract from a team's productive energy, and undermine and bankrupt the positive work the team should be attending to.

Trust and Empowerment

Empowerment is a major goal of many team based organizations. Empowerment means vesting people with the responsibility for action, action that will help serve the customer, and make the business successful. The process of increasing empowerment, whether to an individual or a team, occurs over time. It is definitely not an instantaneous change. The change involves two parties, the person or team receiving increased empowerment and responsibility, and the party giving up some of their responsibility or authority. At the heart of this giving and receiving of empowerment is trust. It requires trust on the part of the one doing the empowering, and trustworthiness on the part of those receiving the increased scope of work and responsibility. It requires both time, and experience, for this trust to evolve.

The scope of the team may be increased in small ways at first. When these are handled successfully, an increasing level of action and authority may be transitioned to the team. It is important for both parties to understand the dynamics of this, so that they will know what is at stake in their activities as empowerment is increased. Knowledge of this will accelerate the process, because everyone will be expecting an outcome that moves the process forward.

The best way to teach everyone involved about the process of building trust, through demonstration of trustworthiness, is by using experiential training processes. With experiential learning processes, people get to experience first hand the impact of trust. They experience that trust is essential to successfully accomplishing the training activities. The impact and importance are usually quite vivid. The experience in the activity then provides a safe and comfortable platform for discussing the issues related to trust in the workplace.

Covey's "Emotional Bank Account" Metaphor

Stephen Covey, in his famous book, *The 7 Habits of Highly Effective People* (Covey, 1989), refers to an emotional bank account that we all have with each other. Our actions toward each other either make deposits, or withdrawals, to and from these accounts. Covey states beautifully that if we make deposits, through courtesy, kindness, honesty, and keeping commitments, trust levels increase. The opposite effect occurs if we are not courteous, if we are disrespectful, dishonest, etc. When this is how we treat people, these emotional withdrawals reduce or eliminate levels of trust.

These important lessons can be woven into the processing that accompanies experiential exercises. Again, it is a safe arena for the group to hold such a discussion. The focus is on what just occurred in the activity, but the lessons stick, as they pertain to the team's workplace.

Trust cannot be taught. As we stated above, trust is not a skill that can be acquired intellectually. You cannot gather all of your team members into a classroom one day, and say, "Folks, today we are going to learn to trust each other." It simply does not work that way.

Trust develops over time. Based on our experience with each other, we know it takes time, but this important process should not be left to chance. There is too much at stake to not proactively try to create team relationships that are strong and based on trust. Remember, if trust is absent, the result will likely not be neutral, the result will probably be negative.

Experiential learning processes can accelerate the development of trust. It is **the most powerful way** to proactively educate and stimulate the building of trust within a team.

Many, many excellent experiential learning activities exist that can help groups experience the issues related to trust. Some example activities include (Meeker, 1994):

1. "Willow in the Wind"
2. "Trust Walk"
3. "Trust Fall"
4. "Spider Web"
5. "Human Knot"
6. "Minefield"
7. "Toxic Waste"

One of the newer activities that emphasizes trust is called the "Trust Gauntlet." It will be described in detail, to illustrate how such an activity is facilitated.

TRUST GAUNTLET

Purpose
Through this powerful activity, team members get to "feel" the trust involved in successfully undertaking a physically demanding activity. Trusting each other in a physical manner provides a great platform for discussing the issues of trust as they apply in the workplace. Expect some interesting and vital points to surface in the discussion following the activity.

Time
Allow 15 to 30 minutes for this event. The number of team members will be the controlling factor regarding the length of the initiative. Allow time for plenty of discussion after everyone has had a chance to run the gauntlet.

Setup
This event works well with larger teams and groups. Groups of 25-30 are optimum. Members stand shoulder to shoulder, forming two lines. The two lines face each other, with enough space between the lines for a person to pass. As you have the group form the two lines, you, as the facilitator, can be walking between the two lines. This will gauge the space that they are allowing for the runner. Set up in an area where

there is sufficient room for the runners to begin about 15-20 feet prior to the end of the lines, and where you have this much distance or more at the finishing end, to allow for deceleration. Members of each line extend their arms out in front of them. The arms are interwoven in a zipper pattern; i.e. every other arm is someone else's. Individuals then run the gauntlet, one at a time. As the person runs, the extended arms are quickly raised, just in time to allow the member to pass, and then just as quickly brought back down behind the team member. For the runner, this creates a sensation that can be quite startling. Some runners will slow. Some will duck down. Most will have looks of astonishment cross their faces as they proceed between the lines.

Once the lines are set at the right distance, lead the members in practicing lifting their arms rapidly. As you do this, you can explain what they are to do as the runner enters the line.

As the facilitator, you should be the first one to run the gauntlet. If there is a problem with timing on the first attempt, it will not impact a team member who is running. As the facilitator, you will be ready to react if their timing is off slightly for this first attempt. By going first, you also have an opportunity to demonstrate the commands:

—"Are you ready?" (by the runner)   —"Ready." (by the team)

—"Running." (by the runner)   —"Run." (by the team)

These commands are important. They alert the team that a member is preparing to go. They also alert the team to the pace at which the member will move through the line, e.g., running, sprinting, walking, jogging, are all possibilities.

Safety and spotting
This event should be "challenge by choice," with no one being forced to run the gauntlet.

As always, it is the facilitator's job to carefully observe the total process, and not allow any procedures or actions that might compromise safety. Watch for attentiveness by the team. Look for feet that might be extended too far forward, creating tripping hazards.

Once again, as the facilitator, you should be the first to run. This demonstrates the process and commands, and allows the group to calibrate the rapid movement of their arms relative to the runner.

Lessons
The most important goal of this event is to teach team members to have trust and confidence in their teammates. Quite often in most work settings, if our performance as a team is going to be optimum, we must trust the information, instructions, analysis, data, etc. provided by those around us. If not, we will spend an awful lot of time and energy validating inputs and performing redundant activities.

When team members find that they can trust their peers for safety in a physically demanding challenge, it often becomes much easier to have faith in them in many other settings. Then, over time, the evolution of trust, trustworthiness, and confidence in each other can fully develop. Providing for this development can propel a team rapidly forward in their ability to efficiently interact on a daily basis.

Sample Summary Questions

1. How did you become able to rely on each other to succeed in this event?
2. What are some aspects of your job for which you need to depend on each other?
3. Do you wish you had more confidence in those around you for certain aspects of your job? Explain.
4. Are there any cases in your workplace where you do redundant work, because you do not feel you can rely on others? Explain.
5. How does trust develop?
6. What are the consequences if trust is violated?

High levels of trust between team members is a clear advantage. There is much to be gained by investing in these powerful learning processes to help your teams understand and build their levels of trust. It is the key to effective relationships, which, in turn, results in effective teamwork.

Bibliography

Covey, Stephen (1989). *The 7 habits of highly effective people.* New York: Simon & Schuster Inc. pp. 188-203.

Meeker, Larry (1994). *High performance teamwork.* Amherst, MA: HRD Press. pp. 8-11.

Meeker, Larry (1994). *Experiential activities for high performance teamwork.* Amherst, MA: HRD Press. Section 1.

About the Contributor

Larry Meeker is the President of Advanced Team Concepts, a training company based in Plano, Texas that specializes in organizational and leadership development. Larry has been in industry for 26 years. The last 14 years of his career have been in management at Texas Instruments. At TI, Larry was one of the pioneers in developing innovative human resource and organizational concepts such as empowered, or self-managed, teams. Through the application of these, and many other processes under TI's "Total Quality" umbrella, his organization made significant contributions to the company's businesses.

Larry is a frequent speaker and workshop presenter at national and international conferences on training and teaming. Two of his books published last year were *Experiential Activities for High Performance Teamwork* (1994), and *High Performance Teamwork* (1994), published by HRD Press.

23

Handling Conflicts in Teams
Lois B. Hart, Ed.D.

After forming, teams eventually run into conflicts. They occur when high hopes and initial expectations come up against the reality of how the team members interrelate and how well they are accomplishing its tasks. Individual members may not be getting what they need or want out of the team experience.

Following are some more examples of conflicts in teams generated by the people who:

- Really don't want to be on a team but were told to be a member
- Have hidden agendas and won't reveal their real motive
- Contribute ideas that are ignored so they withdraw from participation
- Have so much work to do that they resent the time needed in team meetings
- Always tell the team why suggestions won't work
- Gloss over conflicts and hope they will just go away

As a leader or facilitator of a team, you will need to improve interpersonal relationships by helping team members resolve their conflicts. Unresolved conflicts will negatively affect the productivity of the group and the team members' relationships. Most people do not like conflict and will want to avoid the uncomfortable feelings associated with it. Therefore, you need to be confident in helping them to face these conflicts.

The Conflict Cycle

The Conflict Cycle provides you with a graphic representation of the phases that most conflicts go through. (See Attachment 23-A.)

The first phase, **Anticipation**, is the starting point. Humans, like the turtle, need a protective shield to survive. However, people know they have to stick out their necks in order to function in this world. They anticipate and expect to deal with conflict because it is a normal part of human existence. No one relishes facing conflict, but everyone knows it will occur.

The Conflict Cycle

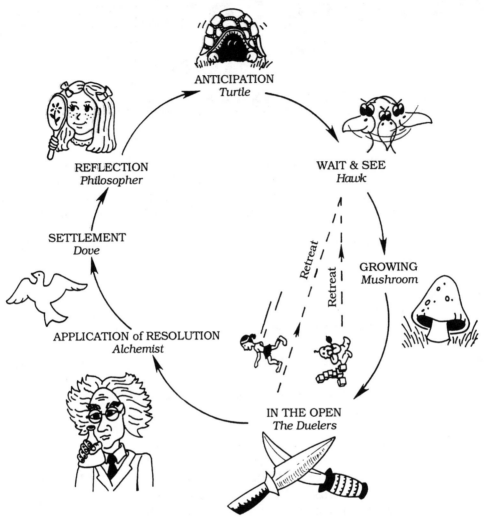

Conflicts go through a cycle of seven phases as shown here.

Once a conflict emerges, it moves to the second phase, **Wait and See.** Like the hawk who can fly over his territory surveying what is there, individuals take time in this phase to look over the situation, assess what is happening, and determine how serious it is.

Sometimes, you can resolve the conflict at this point, but if it isn't solved, it will mushroom into the **Growing** phase. Often, conflicts mushroom very slowly; other times they can quickly erupt into a full-scale problem. What might have been avoided cannot be ignored any longer.

Now the conflict is **In the Open** phase where there is no denying the existence of the conflict. At this point, some people will retreat from dealing with the conflict because they are avoiders or because they want more time to assess the situation.

Once the conflict is out in the open and named, **Resolution** can be sought. As an alchemist was once able to miraculously change a thing into something even better, today we can also experiment, trying out various resolution techniques until the right one is successfully applied.

The conflict moves from an **Application of Resolution** to a **Settlement** phase. The conflict is resolved when all those involved in the conflict are satisfied. This dissipates stress and energy is redirected to other activities. Like cooing doves, the people in the conflict are ready to recapture the good feelings they previously had for one another.

The last part of the *Conflict Cycle* is critical although often neglected. The **Reflection** phase requires that the team members reflect upon the conflict they have resolved and analyze what happened so they can learn from the conflict. They ask:

- "What was the cause of this conflict and have we eliminated it so another conflict won't emerge?"
- "How did we each behave when it was obvious we had a conflict? How can we reduce our resistance to conflict?"
- "What did we do to resolve the conflict? Was it an effective method?"

Turning Theory into Practice

Before a conflict arises within your team, take time to review the *Conflict Cycle* with them. Choose as an example a conflict that was resolved in the past. Walk through the seven phases of the cycle using your conflict story. This helps them to learn what generally happens at each phase.

Then the next time there is a conflict, everyone will have a common vocabulary to describe which phase they are in. Refer to the *Conflict Cycle* until they can easily recognize the phases.

Causes of Conflicts

Conflicts can be caused by one of eight reasons or a combination of them. Teams need to recognize the causes of their conflicts because then

275

they can work on them and thus prevent future conflicts from arising. Also, identification of causes is the first step to resolving a conflict successfully. Following are the eight primary causes:

1. Unmet Needs and Wants
The first cause may be within individuals and their unmet needs and wants. Conflicts happen when people are physically unwell—tired, hungry, and overstressed. They happen when people's basic need for recognition, affection, and affiliation are not met in the team or work environment.

2. Values
Second, explore if the conflict comes from a difference in team members' values. Values are those beliefs that we hold dearly and that drive all of our behavior. You will find that members' values may differ about time, money, work, health, relationships, and politics.

3. Perceptions
The third source of conflict may be differing perceptions. We filter what we see and hear around us and select what has meaning for us. For example, one person may perceive that the agenda item the team is working on is critical, whereas another may consider it as unimportant and want to move on. Each person's perception is valid, but because they are different, there is a conflict.

4. Knowledge
One team member has information she obtained from the team sponsor but neglects to tell the rest of the team. This fourth cause of conflict, knowledge, can be easily corrected when team members initially identify what resources they bring to the team in the form of education, training and work experience. They should regularly share what they know so that everyone is "on the same page."

5. Assumptions
Based on what we know, we make assumptions. For instance, one team member is one hour late and the team assumes he doesn't value the team's time. Assumptions should be checked out for accuracy or they will cause conflicts. In this example, he was late because his son's school had called him with a serious problem.

6. Expectations
The sixth cause of conflict occurs when team members do not know each others' expectations. Conflicts occur when expectations are not initially clarified and not reviewed when they change. If shared, members can try to meet each others' expectations better.

7. Different Backgrounds
A seventh cause of conflict is complex since conflicts will occur because we come from different backgrounds. This cause can include the results of growing up in a particular racial, ethnic, or religious group or because

of our gender. Each of these gave us specific messages about how to deal with others and with conflicts. For instance, girls were taught to be the peacemakers and boys were encouraged to fight out problems.

8. Willingness and Ability to Deal with Conflicts

An underlying cause that keeps people from resolving conflicts is their *willingness* and *ability* to deal with conflicts. We can all learn how to deal with conflicts through reading, training, and coaching but resistance to dealing with conflicts makes it difficult to find resolutions. Here are some reasons why people avoid conflict:

- Our childhood experiences with conflict set the pattern for the way we deal with conflict as adults.
- Dysfunctional family life results in an avoidance of conflict later on.
- Conflict has a negative connotation.
- There are too few models in our lives of people who successfully deal with conflict.
- If we are not successful dealing with conflict in our personal lives, we will not be successful at work.
- There aren't enough workshops or opportunities to learn about how to deal with conflict.

TURNING THEORY INTO PRACTICE: LOOK FOR CAUSES OF CONFLICTS

Your team members need to learn how to quickly recognize the causes of conflicts because this naming of the causes facilitates moving into resolution. Review the eight causes outlined above with your team and discuss examples for each cause.

The following is a scenario in an office that exemplifies many causes of conflicts. Make copies and ask team members to identify as many causes as they can for each of the conflicts in the story. Even better, assign each of the characters to a team member and have them read the script while the others listen. Then give copies to everyone to identify the causes of the conflicts.

Characters:
Lois—Narrator
Bill—Boss
Warren—Manager of Marketing
Jill—Supervisor of Research Team
Andy—Supervisor of Design Team

LOIS: *Imagine the following scene. We are listening in on a conflict that occurred in a marketing office. Here's Warren, the Manager of Marketing. It's Friday at 4:00. He's reflecting on a tough week. Let's listen in to what he's thinking.*

277

WARREN: "Boy, working in this department stinks! I can't get any cooperation from my boss! If he wants results, he's got to cooperate and keep me informed. I haven't got a crystal ball.

"And why is it so hard for my staff to do their jobs right? If they want me to go to bat for them, they must keep me posted and give me more cooperation. I can't do this alone.

"I'm ready to look for a new job. Thank God it's Friday!"

LOIS: *Let's look back at Warren's week. It's Monday morning and Warren is looking over his progress reports.*

WARREN: "Look at this report! It says that Jill's team was supposed to finish their marketing research by today but they still aren't done."

LOIS: *Warren picks up phone and says to Jill:*

WARREN: "Jill, I'm pretty upset that you didn't finish that report by today. What's with you anyway?"

JILL: "Well, while you were at your doctor's appointment last Friday afternoon, your boss stopped in and ordered me to do a rush job ahead of what you asked me to do. When I explained that I had to finish this report for you by today, he yelled at me and said, 'You take orders from me! I can't have every Tom, Dick and Jill coming in here and lousing up my schedule!'"

LOIS: *The next scene is a chance meeting in the hallway with Warren and his boss, Bill.*

WARREN: "Bill, Jill, and I ran into a conflict when I discovered that she hadn't finished a job on time today because you asked her to do something else."

BILL: "Warren, the job had to get done and you weren't around. I can't talk any more than that now, I'm late for a meeting. Just see that the work gets done."

WARREN says to himself as he walks away: "How in heaven's name can I run my department with attitudes like that?"

LOIS: *Our scene changes to Tuesday. Warren is looking over his messages. Listen to his comments on one of them.*

WARREN: "Boy here's a complaint from the boss. He stopped in early this morning and says that Andy's design team left their area in a real mess."

LOIS: *Warren picks up his phone and calls Andy, the supervisor of that team.*

WARREN: "Hey, Andy, we've gotten a complaint from the boss about how messy your area looked after you left last night. I think he's upset because he has a new client visiting soon."

ANDY: "You're right, boss, we were so busy finishing that new marketing campaign that I'm afraid we ran out of time to clean up. We'll leave enough time today to do it right."

WARREN: "I want you do that right now! I don't want to hear any more complaints from the boss."

LOIS: *It's now Wednesday morning and Warren checks his messages and there are no complaints from his boss about his department but Andy's report showed no progress on the new marketing campaign so Warren calls Andy again.*

WARREN: "Hey Andy, what did you do yesterday. . .have a party? Your report shows very little was done on that campaign!"

ANDY—defensively and angrily: "Well Warren, you wanted us to clean up the area so that's what we did. Now you're complaining again."

WARREN: "Just get the job done right!" (**Warren hangs up the phone with a bang.**)

LOIS: *It's now Thursday morning and Warren is checking his messages. After reading the top one he yells out loud:*

WARREN: "He's got to be kidding! This is impossible!!!"

LOIS: *Warren calls Andy again.*

WARREN: "Hey Andy old buddy, I've got some good news and some bad news and I need your help.

ANDY: "What's the problem now?"

WARREN: "The bad news is that the boss just let me know that we need to finish the design of the job sooner that we thought. . .in fact by tomorrow and not Monday! Your people will need to work overtime but the good news is that he'll bring in pizza."

ANDY: "They aren't going to like this at all."

WARREN: "Sure, I know that, but we have no choice."

LOIS: *About 3:00, Warren stops in to check on the work's progress. Andy takes him aside and says:*

279

ANDY: "The team is working hard but they won't stop grumbling. Sue is going to miss her son's play at school. Tom had to find someone to pick up his kids from day care. Sally was miffed to have to cancel a hot date she had for tonight. And Sam had to tell his wife she'd have to do the grocery shopping, make dinner, and go to the 6:30 PTA meeting alone.

"Gee Warren, couldn't you ask the boss to re-consider that deadline?"

WARREN: "Look, I'm tired of all this griping. Just tell them to get the work done and I'll bring in donuts every morning next week."

LOIS: *Warren thinks to himself as he walks away:*

WARREN: "They just don't get it. We have to do what the boss tells us to do. Why are they being so unreasonable?"

AVOID CONFLICTS WITH THESE BASICS

Many conflicts could be avoided if teams would take the time at the beginning when they first form to establish their team guidelines and discuss their expectations. Here are specifics on how to do that:

Setting Team Guidelines

When the team first meets, the members need to establish some guidelines on how they will work together. Before that meeting, look over the following suggested guidelines in Attachment 23-B.

Next, explain why teams must agree on some guidelines. Agreement is a signal that everyone is committed to the team's efforts. The existence of written guidelines keeps some conflicts from ever developing and they help to resolve problems that do emerge because team members can refer back to these guidelines.

Distribute these guidelines shown in Attachment 23-B and discuss each one until there is consensus. Write up a final list of guidelines and have each team member sign the agreement. Periodically review the guidelines, add to the list, and modify them as needed.

CLARIFY EXPECTATIONS

Each of us has expectations and these affect our attitudes and behaviors in teams. A core cause of conflicts occurs when we do not clarify our expectations with those we are working with at any particular point in time. A second cause of conflict occurs when our expectations change and we don't tell others about this shift.

Start out your team on the right foot! Ask everyone, individually, to write out their expectations for this team. Each person then shares them with the team.

Make a list and provide a copy for everyone. Periodically, refer back to it to assess if the direction the team is going is meeting team members' expectations.

What ELSE Can Team Leaders and Facilitators Do to Help Their Teams?

- Believe in the value of learning from the conflicts that emerge in your team and remain committed to your belief. Do not avoid dealing with conflicts. They will only get worse if you do.
- Model how you want them to deal with conflict (with your words and behavior). Disclose your own experiences with conflict and the times you have successfully dealt with conflict.
- Use other skills you have learned such as listening, negotiation, and mediation. Review these skills with your teams as they are needed.
- Be persistent and patient. It takes time to confidently deal with conflicts, but it is worth it! You will build better relationships in the team, reduce people's stress, and improve their productivity.
- Track your progress. Celebrate successes when your team deals with conflicts. Review how they handled their conflict so they will continuously learn from them.

Attachment 23-B

- We will be as open as possible but honor the right of privacy.
- Unless we agree otherwise, what is discussed in our group will remain confidential.
- We will respect differences of opinion. We won't discount others' ideas.
- We will be supportive rather than judgmental.
- We will give feedback directly and openly, it will be given in a timely fashion, and we will provide information that is specific and focuses on the task and process and not on personalities.
- Since we all have resources to offer (our experiences, educations, and training), we will tell others what we can offer and will contribute freely.
- We are each responsible for what we get from this team experience. We will ask for what we need from our sponsor, our facilitator, team leader, and the other team members.
- We will try to get better acquainted with each other so we can identify ways we can work better together and develop professionally.
- We will use our time well, starting on time, returning from breaks and ending our meetings promptly.
- When members miss a meeting, we will share the responsibility to fill them in.
- We will keep our focus on our goals, avoid sidetracking, personality conflicts, and hidden agendas. We will acknowledge problems and deal with them.
- We will not make phone calls or let others interrupt the group with messages.

TEAM SIGNATURES

_____   _____

_____   _____

_____   _____

_____   _____

About the Contributor

Dr. Lois B. Hart has over 25 years of training, organization development, coaching, and public education experience. Lois has worked with many professionals who want to be effective facilitators and trainers. Through Leadership Dynamics, Lois offer programs on facilitation, leadership, team development, conflict, and train-the-trainer skills.

Dr. Hart earned a B.S. from the University of Rochester, a M.S. from Syracuse University, and Ed.D. from the University of Massachusetts. Her studies included organizational behavior and leadership development with Dr. Ken Blanchard, co-author of *The One Minute Manager*.

She has written 20 books for trainers and group leaders including:

LEARNING FROM CONFLICT
CONNECTIONS: FIVE POINTS OF CONTACT WITH PARTICIPANTS
THE SEXES AT WORK INSTRUCTOR'S MANUAL
50 ACTIVITIES TO DEVELOP LEADERS
FAULTLESS FACILITATION—A RESOURCE GUIDE
FAULTLESS FACILITATION—INSTRUCTOR'S MANUAL
TRAINING METHODS THAT WORK
SAYING HELLO: GETTING YOUR GROUP STARTED
SAYING GOOD-BYE: ENDING A GROUP EXPERIENCE
A CONFERENCE AND WORKSHOP PLANNER'S MANUAL

24

Every Player Contributes to the Process
Maureen O'Brien

Your team meeting has two major focal points that require your attention: content and process. Content is what your team is working on; process is how your team members are working together. If I asked you to tell me how your last meeting went and you said, "We discussed the consolidation project, put together a plan for year–end closing, and decided to set up a meeting with the Quality Team to discuss error rates," you would have reported on the *content* of your meeting. Content sounds like those items you would summarize in your meeting minutes.

If your response was, "Discussion became very heated and members stopped listening to one another; the energy level was very low, and a lot of time was wasted talking about unrelated topics," you would have described your team's *process.* In other words, process is a description of how members behaved during the meeting. Another word used interchangeably with process is *dynamics.*

There may be times during a team meeting when you feel you can't participate because you're not conversant with the topic being discussed. Just because you can't contribute to the content doesn't mean you can't contribute at all. You are in a perfect position to observe and facilitate the team's process—and that's where teams need the most help. Teams generally do fine with content; they usually have the right items on the agenda and enough contributing experts. Ineffective meetings are usually the result of dysfunctional team dynamics or process. The entire team is responsible for the success of your meeting so *all members should play an active role in facilitating healthy dynamics.* But when you are not engrossed in the content of the meeting, you have the advantage of perspective; you can concentrate solely on process.

This paper has been excerpted from the author's recent book, *Who's Got The Ball? (AND OTHER NAGGING QUESTIONS ABOUT TEAM LIFE),* Jossey Bass, 1995.

How do you know whether a team's process is functional or dysfunctional? If the team strikes a balance between satisfying both its task and relationship needs, it has a healthy, functional process underway. Members behave in ways that facilitate getting the job done and at the same time make members feel valued, respected, included, and energized. Members leave the meeting saying, "We were very productive and I sure do like being a member of this team." When there is an imbalance between task and relationship need satisfaction, or not enough attention paid to either, the team's process is dysfunctional. If you hear members saying, "We got a lot of things accomplished, but I can't stand the way members treat each other," it's a sure sign that the team hasn't paid enough attention to its relationship needs. And if you hear, "We are so cohesive; just like a family. But we sure didn't get much done," the team has slipped on the task side. And if ever you should hear, "Another waste of two hours—nothing accomplished. Why can't people at least be civil to each other?" you know there is much work to be done on both the task and relationship sides of the equation.

Learning how to observe your team's process and intervene appropriately takes time and practice. If you randomly try to watch everything, you'll see nothing. *The key is to train your eyes and ears so that you can focus your observations.* A good way to start focusing is to become acquainted with a few specific team facilitation roles, also known as intervention behaviors. Then look for the appropriate situations during your meeting to apply them. In other words, first learn what the helping behaviors are, and why and how they help. Then you will more easily see places where you can be helpful.

SOFI HAGE: Team Facilitation Roles

Over dinner in the course of a team coaching session about eight years ago, I was determined to create a mnemonic device that would help teams remember the task and relationship facilitation roles that contribute to team effectiveness. The terms themselves have been in widespread use for some time, but no source I consulted had organized them in an easily memorable way. Two glasses of Chardonnay later, I came up with an acronym in the form of a woman's name: **SOFI HAGE.** I know it's obscure, but I had to use the letters available to me. So now I tell teams, "Don't forget to take **SOFI HAGE** to your meeting. Put her to work and I guarantee she will make a significant contribution to your team's progress and success."

The exhibit "Team Facilitation Roles" introduces and explains **SOFI HAGE.** The name comes from the first letter of each of the task and relationship roles.

TEAM FACILITATION ROLES

TASK	RELATIONSHIP
Summarizer	**H**armonizer
Orienter	**A**nalyzer
Fact Seeker	**G**atekeeper
Initiator	**E**ncourager

It's important that all team members understand and employ each of the four task and relationship roles listed in the exhibit. Let's spend a few minutes examining each of them.

Task Roles

The *Summarizer* urges the group to acknowledge consensus and reach a decision. When team members are wound up like the Energizer Bunny, the Summarizer breaks in with, "It seems like we're all in agreement with the various aspects of the program that need to be changed; can we move off that topic and discuss specific changes to be proposed?" By asking for verbal agreement with the summary, the Summarizer helps the team get past one decision and onto the next decision point.

The *Orienter* prevents the team from wandering too far from the topic at hand; he or she brings them back and focuses them again when they do stray. This redirecting should not be done abruptly as in, "Hey, we're way off here; let's get back on track," or "David, you just took us off topic again," because you don't want to introduce a negative effect into the relationship side of the equation. A useful and neutral way to intervene is with the question, "Are we off topic right now?"

The *Fact Seeker* tests reality to make sure the decision the team is about to make is doable. This team member always wants more information and is quick to point out the difference between a fact and an opinion. The *Fact Seeker* is also very helpful in pointing out when a team does not have all the information it needs to make a good decision. The *Fact Seeker* will suggest that the team get more data before proceeding. He or she is also good at checking the decision–making boundaries of the team, asking, "Do we have the authority to make this decision?"

The *Initiator* gets the team started on the right foot by always beginning discussions with the question, "How should we approach this task?" Getting agreement on a game plan before starting to work on the task itself is the guaranteed remedy for the "ready, fire, aim" team disorder and is the distinguishing characteristic of the *Initiator*.

As you can see, when you play the *Summarizer*, *Orienter*, *Fact Seeker*, and *Initiator* roles, you contribute to your team's productivity by moving the task along to completion.

Relationship Roles

Play the following relationship roles to ensure that team members feel valued and respected and you will make a major contribution to your team's cohesiveness.

The *Harmonizer* realizes that conflict is inevitable and that if left unresolved, it is the biggest barrier to a team's achieving health and success. The *Harmonizer* calls the team's attention to a conflict (especially if team members haven't wanted to acknowledge it), by saying something like, "Let's be honest: we've got some strong conflicting feelings about this issue. What steps can we take to resolve our differences?" The *Harmonizer* is also able to focus discussion on satisfying the conflicting member's *needs* versus their *wants* as a way of mediating conflict.

The *Analyzer* watches for changes in the vital signs of the team and brings these changes to the attention of the team. The *Analyzer* is the team member most likely to ask, "How is everyone feeling about how we're working together?" or "It seems we've lost our energy; what is happening?"

The *Gatekeeper* is concerned primarily with team communication and participation. This member makes sure all team members are actively listening to each other and understand each other's messages. The *Gatekeeper* paraphrases messages to make sure that everyone is on the same wavelength by ensuring that every idea is understood by the group before being discredited or discarded. The *Gatekeeper* invites quieter members to participate and makes sure that more active members don't dominate.

The *Encourager* builds and sustains team energy by showing support for people's efforts, ideas, and achievements. If the *Gatekeeper* focuses on making sure the content of team members' ideas is clearly understood by all, the *Encourager* emphasizes members' participation by giving verbal approval: "Good point—that's a great idea." This is another role that helps people to feel valued.

It is extremely important that every member be ready and able to intervene as a facilitator. If you were an eight–member team and each person had a delegated responsibility to wear one of the **SOFI HAGE** hats and intervene appropriately, you would see a significant increase in your effectiveness. But you can do better than that by having each member wear all the hats and thus provide maximum facilitation coverage.

Learning the eight different roles may, at first, seem like an overwhelming challenge to you and your teammates, but you'll probably be surprised to find that some team members are natural at orienting or encouraging, or that some easily assume the role of *summarizers* and *gatekeepers*. To have all eight roles covered may just be a matter of learning a few more facilitation behaviors. It *can* be done and the team will be glad they did so.

Learning Team Facilitation Roles

There is a fun way for the whole team to learn how to function in these facilitation roles. Try it out for ten meetings and before you know it, every member will be able to wear all the **SOFI HAGE** hats.

1. Post the **SOFI HAGE** roles on a flipchart in your meeting room so they are visible to all the members.
2. Discuss the roles as a team to make sure that everyone understands each role and knows when to apply it. For example, if the team is off topic, play the *Orienter* role.
3. Start your meeting with the understanding that whenever any member sees a situation that lends itself to one of the facilitation roles, that member should play the role. In addition, any time a member notices a teammate applying a role, the member should name the role and offer positive reinforcement by calling out "great orienting." Each time a member plays a role or notices one being played, he/she is awarded a point.
4. The two members with the highest number of points at the end of the meeting receive a traveling "Great Facilitating" trophy, which they keep until the next meeting.

About the Contributor

Coach Maureen O'Brien, author of *Who's Got The Ball?* *(AND OTHER NAGGING QUESTIONS ABOUT TEAM LIFE)*, has specialized in team development for the past fifteen years. Her extensive involvement in athletics, both as a touring professional basketball player with the Harlem Globetrotters and as a coach for various team sports, serves as the foundation for her unique Scrimmage Training approach to coaching work teams.

O'Brien is president of OB Management Consultants in Myrtle Beach, SC. Before starting her consulting business, she was Manager of human resource development at Branson Ultrasonics Corporation, a division of Emerson, and Dean of Students at the University of Connecticut, Waterbury.

25

The Elements of Team Empowerment

Kenneth W. Thomas, Ph.D. and Walter G. Tymon, Jr., Ph.D.

Top managers seem to be clear about what they want from empowered teams: they want teams to become more self-managing and to take active responsibility for the quality of their work.

Where we find most confusion is among the managers, trainers, or consultants who must help those teams *become* responsible for their own work tasks—without a clear notion of what that involves.

Some Learnings about Empowerment

In our work on empowerment, we have learned the following:

1. Empowerment is not something that managers and facilitators **do to** a team. Team empowerment is about a growth process that must occur **within the team itself**. It is a kind of maturation that others can only help nurture.

2. Empowerment is not simply a skill-building activity. It involves fundamental changes in the **psychology** of how the team experiences its work. To manage empowerment, you have to know something about the nature of work tasks and the **satisfactions** that teams can get from them.

3. Work tasks, in turn, are not just **activities** that must be performed. Work tasks are activities directed toward accomplishing **purposes**. Many of the satisfactions of empowerment come from pursuing worthwhile purposes.

The Elements of Empowerment

The grid below builds upon these insights to identify four main psychological elements of empowerment: choice, competence, meaningfulness, and progress. As shown in the grid, these psychological elements involve both the task **activities** that team members perform and the task **purposes** they are trying to achieve. The task activities provide a vehicle for a sense of **choice** and a sense of **competence**. The

291

task purpose provides a vehicle for a sense of **meaningfulness** and a sense of **progress**. Feelings of competence and of progress are the two rewarding elements of task **accomplishment** or performance—how well team members are performing activities and accomplishing the task purpose, respectively. Feelings of choice and meaningfulness, in contrast, are rewarding elements of task **opportunity**—being able to use one's own judgment and to pursue a worthwhile purpose, respectively.

EMPOWERMENT GRID*

	OPPORTUNITY ELEMENTS	ACCOMPLISHMENT ELEMENTS
TASK ACTIVITIES	Sense of CHOICE	Sense of COMPETENCE
TASK PURPOSE	Sense of MEANINGFULNESS	Sense of PROGRESS

The four elements are described as follows:

CHOICE is the felt *opportunity* to select task activities that make sense to team members and to perform them in ways that seem appropriate. It is the freedom to choose and to do what one believes is right.

COMPETENCE is the sense of *accomplishment* from skillfully performing task activities. It is the feeling that good, quality work is being done.

MEANINGFULNESS is the felt *opportunity* to pursue a worthy task purpose—one that is worth the team's time and energy. It is the sense that one is on a valuable mission, that the purpose matters in the larger scheme of things.

PROGRESS is the sense of *accomplishment* in achieving the task purpose. It is the feeling that the task is really moving forward, that the team's activities are really accomplishing something.

These four elements identify the essential characteristics of a responsible, self-managing team: exercising its best judgment (choice), performing capably (competence), pursuing goals to which it is committed (meaningfulness), and keeping track of how well it is achieving those goals (progress). Thus, the four elements provide a detailed way of recognizing what empowered teams look like, and for measuring how well the team is doing in terms of those characteristics.
    Equally important, these four elements capture the psychological **rewards** (satisfactions) that team members can get from managing their

*Source: Adapted from Thomas and Tymon, *Empowerment Inventory* (NY: XICOM, 1993). © XICOM. Inc. (914) 351-4762.

team's operations. Feelings of choice, competence, meaningfulness, and progress are intrinsically rewarding and **energizing**—providing the team with the excitement it needs to keep growing. Thus, the four elements also provide a way of assessing the motivational foundation for empowerment, and for diagnosing any motivational problems that block empowerment.

Practical Applications

The four elements of empowerment can be used to help teams examine their overall level of empowerment, or to examine their empowerment on any particular task (e.g., planning or process improvements). Team empowerment itself can be viewed as a task—so that the four elements can even be applied to the team's own growth and development. (Is the team excited about its own development?)

Elsewhere, we have provided a framework for team members to use to help them contribute to their own empowerment (Thomas and Tymon, 1993). Here, we will focus on some guidelines for managers and facilitators.

Choice. The point here is to help the team recognize that it has many options and that it is safe and possible to trust their own judgment in choosing among them. Dialogue is required to agree on any boundaries around the teams' discretion, which can be gradually extended. Within that boundary, it must be clear that the choices are the team's. Rigorous consistency is required not to delegate responsibility and then take it back whenever the team stumbles. The team also needs enough honest information to make sound decisions, as well as reassurance that team members will not be punished for honest mistakes while learning.

Competence. Here, the manager or facilitator needs to adopt the role of a coach (Evered and Selman, 1989), who is there to provide help to the group, but without taking over the task. It will usually be helpful to provide some training on group development/ empowerment/conflict management. However, the most effective training occurs at the "teachable moment," when the group realizes that it needs this training, and chooses it itself. It is therefore desirable for the manager or facilitator to help the group diagnose what its own training needs are. Given the inevitable setbacks along the learning curve, it is also important to help the group recognize what it is doing well.

Meaningfulness. The point here is to help the team "reinvent and own" its purpose, in ways that tap into team members' passions. Some teams will find clear meaningfulness in helping customers. Where there is little initial enthusiasm for team empowerment, it may be necesary to help members see how empowerment may be an opportunity to "control their own destiny," "do things right," "get rid of the b.s.," "be treated like adults," or whatever else taps their feelings. In helping the team articulate what it cares about and would really like to achieve, the team can begin to create a shared, meaningful vision for itself (Block, 1987). It may also begin to eliminate meaningless, busywork tasks that contribute little value.

Progress. As a team begins to care about its shared purpose, it will usually *want* to know how much progress it is making. Here, the team may need help developing measures or otherwise tracking the progress it has made. Progress can be a tremendous sense of pride for the team. Our experience is that it is well worth the time to stop for celebrations of important task milestones. Likewise, the manager or facilitator can help a team look back to track and appreciate its own development.

Bibliography

Block, P. (1987). *The empowered manager: Positive political skills at work.* San Francisco: Jossey-Bass.

Evered, R. D., and J. C. Selman. (1989). Coaching and the art of management. *Organizational Dynamics, 18* (2), 16-32.

Thomas, K. W., and W. G. Tymon, Jr. (1993). *Empowerment inventory.* Tuxedo, NY: Xicom, Inc.

Thomas, K. W., and B. A. Velthouse. (1990). Cognitive elements of empowerment: An "interpretive" model of intrinsic task motivation. *Academy of Management Review, 15,* 666-681.

About the Contributors

Kenneth W. Thomas is professor of Systems Management at the Naval Postgraduate School in Monterey, CA. He was formerly on the faculties at UCLA, Temple University, and the University of Pittsburgh. He received his Ph.D. in Administrative Sciences from Purdue University in 1971. Dr. Thomas has published extensively on conflict management, empowerment, and the applied relevance of behavioral science research. He has also developed various training instruments, including the *Thomas-Kilmann Conflict Mode Instrument*, the *Empowerment Inventory*, and the *Stress Resiliency Profile*, published by Xicom.

Walter G. Tymon, Jr., is an assistant professor of management in the College of Commerce and Finance at Villanova University. He was previously on the faculty of Rutgers University. He received his Ph.D. in Business Administration from Temple University in 1988. Dr. Tymon has published articles in such publications as the *Academy of Management Review*, *Journal of Management Systems*, and *R & D Management*. In addition to empowerment, his research involves work on stress management, intrinsic work motivation, and the management of research and development. He is also co-developer of the *Empowerment Inventory* and the *Stress Resiliency Profile*.

Part VI - Organizational Issues

26

Aligning the Organization for a Team-Based Strategy
David W. Jamieson, Ph.D.

In the past decade, the use of teams has mushroomed throughout all types of organizations. No doubt this shift in structural form is spawned not only by real needs but also by cogent arguments and a proliferation of supportive literature (e.g., Katzenbach and Smith, 1993; Orsburn, et al., 1990; Parker, 1990; Shonk, 1992). Yet, the promise and potential of using teams often goes unrealized. Sometimes a team is not the appropriate structure for the work. If work is best performed individually with little interdependence to other's work, then a team structure is an artificial overlay, not useful in the management or productivity of the work. In other cases teams may be formed purely to meet administrative or social needs, with no task basis. In these cases, there is little teamwork required and such a structure is an administrative convenience (departmentation, supervision, etc.) or created as a shell for inclusion, belonging, support, or other social/interpersonal needs.

Even when teams are appropriate, the problems in realizing the advantage of teams stem more often from not aligning the rest of the organization to support the strategy and team-based structure. As more organizations attempt significant strategic change, it is becoming increasingly clear that key components of an organization need to be aligned for change to really occur.[1] In earlier work, Old (1992) identified key components of an organization system that needed to be redesigned and lined up with each other, in relation to a new strategy. Her key design components included structure; culture; systems and processes; and policies, procedures, and practices. She further highlighted the critical leverage points for change as the strategy, structure, culture, reward, information and decision systems. More recently, Old (1995) has defined these components and their relationships as level two (systemic) in talking about the need for change to occur on three levels (transactional, systemic, and deep structure) in order to really transform the whole organizational system.

299

---

[1]This idea has been discussed by others in various forms, e.g., Nadler and Tushman, 1977, 1988; Galbraith, 1977, 1994; and Tichy, 1983.

The alignment model depicted below uses the same basic components and their relationships identified by Old (1992) in a slightly different form, based on my work. This article applies the alignment thinking to the design of an organization for a team-based strategy.

THE ALIGNMENT MODEL

Figure 1 depicts the basic Alignment Model. This model identifies five major components that need to be in alignment for the "system" (the organization) to operate as desired. They either work together to reinforce and support intended behavior or, when not aligned, can work at cross-purposes, undermining the change goals. Consider, for example, a structure with many layers (for decision making) not supporting a strategy involving speed and responsiveness. Or, a culture valuing individualism and competition working against the need for collaboration within and between teams. Or, a desire to move more decisions to the front line with a misaligned information system that stops at middle management. These and other examples highlight how lack of organizational alignment creates mixed messages, confusion, conflict, and resistance, and seriously undermines real change. Conversely, when an organization works to align its structures, culture, systems, and

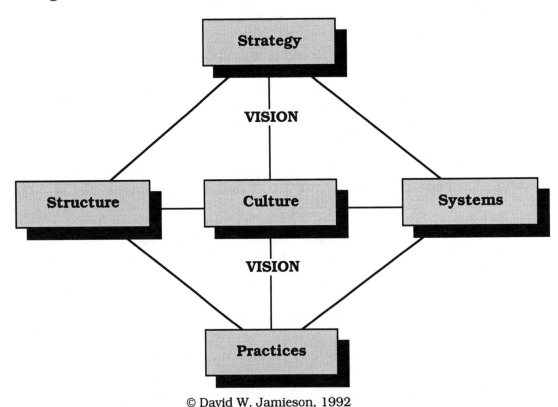

© David W. Jamieson, 1992

Figure 1. Alignment for Strategic Change

practices with its strategy, the messages are clear, there is mutual reinforcement, and the necessary "critical mass" is reached for change to occur and stabilize in a new state.

In the Alignment Model:

- **Strategy** refers to *what the organization intends to do* and includes whatever the organization calls mission, purpose, goals, objectives, plans, and priorities.

- **Structure** is *how work, technology, and people are put together* and includes the design of jobs, roles, work systems, teams, departmentation, and all forms of structuring the organization.

- **Culture** is the *values in operation* and includes what's right, wrong, expected, encouraged, and what is really valued in how the organization and its members operate.

- **Systems** refers to *the ongoing operating policies, procedures, and processes* and includes all of an organization's routine functions such as planning, decision making, budgeting, performance evaluation, reward systems, pay, benefits, procurement, and many more.

- **Practices** means the *day-to-day behaviors, interactions, and styles of working* and is most evident in what managers do, how people work with one another, the types of interactions that occur regularly, and the skills that are used.

- **Vision** is the *word picture of how the organization operates in its desired future state*—in its most aligned, effective performance.

It is important to remember the lines connecting the various components for they signify the interdependence and how they all have influence on each other. Some interrelationships are stronger than others, but all potentially have multiple impacts. Ideally, the strategy should drive the rest of the organizational components. The middle three (structures, culture, and systems) are popularly referred to as the organization's design. The practices should be developed to work in the chosen organization design and to support the strategy. The vision helps people to see and understand the desired end state. It often serves as "the north star," guiding the organization toward a new way of being and providing motivation to people working through the changes.

With this basic overview of what's involved in alignment, it is now possible to use this concept in understanding how an organization must change to support and operate effectively with a team-based strategy.

PRE-TEAM ERA

Historically, organizations have not been designed or aligned for the use of teams. Even where teams have been used, the preponderance of structures, systems, and practices were still geared to individuals (pay, evaluation, incentives, promotions, etc.). In addition, most of the organization's values (its culture) encourage or reinforce individual action (getting ahead, competing with peers, making decisions, etc.).

Since the early days of scientific management (Taylor, 1915) work has been designed into its smallest task units for individuals to perform. Not withstanding attempts to improve these earlier designs (job enrichment, job enlargement, job rotation, socio-technical systems), it was not until teams became more popular and people moved beyond functional thinking, that it became evident how organizations had been designed and managed for individuals. The advent of team-based organizations has created competing structures, systems, cultures, and practices and continues to surface numerous alignment issues.

ALIGNING THE ORGANIZATION FOR TEAMS

Strategy

First, there needs to be a compelling business strategy driving the use of teams. Generally, this would include something to do with competitive advantage, quality, customer service, innovation, cycle time, or cost, where the nature of the work will benefit from team interaction or teams are known to be superior to individual efforts. For example, where the work requires a lot of specialized information from different perspectives and/or tasks require a lot of coordination, teams make the most sense. When all the parts of a complete process can be teamed together, the group can see the bigger picture and is better able to re-engineer, streamline steps, or reduce cycle time or costs. Also, research has generally confirmed that creativity, innovation, and decision quality can be enhanced through teams, *when they work effectively*.

Many well-known companies have successfully used teams in pursuing their business strategies. 3M is well-known for their use of teams in accomplishing their strategic goal of continuous innovation. There are many examples from the auto industry where survival was dependent on improving productivity, reducing costs, enhancing quality, and accelerating the new product development schedules. The Ford Taurus project, Saturn plant, and NUMMI joint venture are representative, as well as Volvo's replacement of the assembly line with self-managed work teams. Motorola, GE, and Xerox have consistently been noted in the business press for their success with teams, particularly in manufacturing areas. Boeing's recent 777 success in meeting customer needs was a product of using teams to accomplish a business need. Today, there are endless examples throughout the world of business strategy driving the appropriate use of teams.

Structure

Teams are basically a *structural* alternative in which the team, not the individual, becomes the primary unit of organization. From a management perspective, one "manages" teams not individuals. As teams naturally take on more self-management when the organization conditions are aligned and supportive, there is less and less "management."

Self-Management

The value of teams (in terms of productivity, quality, cost, etc.) is limited if they are only a structural change without also moving toward self-management. The real advantage comes from the *combination* of people working together on core work because of their task interdependence and their taking on increasing responsibility for "managing" tasks (e.g., planning, scheduling, problem solving, decision making, evaluation, etc.). It is through this combination that team members are able to see the larger picture, feel empowered, become committed, and take on accountability. Accountability is one of the critical issues in team-based performance (Katzenbach and Smith, 1993). Yet, it is difficult, at best, for people to feel accountable or for the organization to hold people accountable when they don't manage critical variables that impact work performance and output. A team-based strategy, therefore, needs to incorporate both the appropriate structuring of people into teams around interdependent work processes and movement toward greater self-management within and between those teams. Greater self-management occurs when a team can manage not only what goes on *within* the team, but also the processes and interactions coming *into* the team (with their "suppliers"), and the processes and interactions going *out* of the team (with their "customers"). Lawler's (1986) work on high involvement is helpful in this context. He identifies four conditions necessary for involvement (i.e., self-managing teams) to work effectively: *power* over their sphere of work; *knowledge* and *skills* to do the core work and management tasks; relevant *information* to make decisions and evaluate results; and meaningful *rewards* tied to their performance.

The Strategy-Structure Relationship

Teams require much more than structural thinking (as discussed below), but it's important to first get clear about the significance of the structural change and the alignment of all necessary structures. It's also important to stay customized in thinking about the strategy-structure relationships throughout the organization. At each level, within each function, and across various parts of the organization the use of teams needs to be driven by the "strategy" or framing of the mission for that level, part, or slice of the organization. A driven team-based choice will probably affect most of the organization, but it does not have to be universal. Some

303

work may not benefit from team structure. Some parts of the organization may perform more effectively as individual contributors. In other words, either/or thinking is not needed in designing and aligning the organization. The old adage of "form follows function" (Chandler, 1962) is most relevant: first at the level of the complete organization's strategy and then within divisions or functions, across business processes, or for specific organizational units. For example, teams may be highly appropriate to perform a complete business process that cuts across functions, but may not be appropriate in some sales functions or some research units.

In considering the structure component one must keep in mind that it involves the process by which work, people, and technology are put together. Generally, teams are first implemented in the organization's core work (main manufacturing process or primary service flow, etc.). It's also important to look at support functions and management levels to also see where teams would be appropriate and help to support and reinforce desired behavior.

Teaming at the Top

Another structural element that needs to be looked at is the degree of team character (structure and processes) at the top. If senior managers operate independently and only from their functional perspectives, they may impact the work teams with confusion, mixed-messages, or conflicting purposes. A lack of team-based behavior (decision making, coordination, integration, etc.) at the top sends a very different message than the one all of the teams are trying to follow. It is also difficult for a team that is functioning well and managing its complete set of tasks to interface with a variety of support functions that lack teamwork, are fragmented, and often work at cross-purposes to the team structure, philosophy, and style.

Use of Technology

Another aspect of structure is technology. Technology can also support individuals or teams. Increasingly, teams may need to be technologically linked either because of geography, shifts, or even trans-organizational relationships. In addition, with teams, there's a greater need to share more information, develop common data bases, and bring what is known into accessibility for all team members. This will often raise questions about who gets certain information, how to provide greater access, and how to simultaneously share. This requires a shift from a more traditional control-oriented mind-set that would use information as power, e.g., keeping it secret, giving it out selectively, etc. Therefore, technology needs to be structured for team use, accessibility, and support.

SYSTEMS

Information

The above discussion of technology for teams leads directly into thinking about systems and processes to support teams vs. individuals. The information system is one of those needs. What is relevant information and how it's assembled and distributed are critical to the support of teams. Key information has often flowed only to higher and middle levels, which works against building the knowledge and skills of teams to perform their work, and is disempowering in that it reduces the team's capacity to act with accuracy and confidence. Information systems will also need to report more team data and organize operating and financial information for use by teams.

Rewards

In a team-based organization, everything that has to do with salary, rewards, and recognition needs to be reviewed. Most of those systems have been designed around the individual as the basic organizational unit. Now the organization needs to consider how people get paid both for their individual skills and contribution *and* as part of a team. The concept that needs to be further developed is how to pay teams for their specific performance and their contribution to the overall strategy. Other forms of reward and recognition also need to be developed for teams. It's important to build rewards around what you want people to do (Kerr, 1995). Individual reward and recognition are still important, but get subsumed within the team or get wider visibility at the team's initiative.

Performance Evaluation

Evaluation is another process that is often misaligned with a team structure. A supervisor evaluates an individual. If you want teams to work, be responsible, and be effective, some different process needs to be used. First, teams as a unit need to be evaluated—by themselves, by those they serve, by those that serve them, and by those who manage a number of teams from a higher level. Second, team members need to be involved in feedback/evaluation with those whom they work most closely so that an individual's appraisal is based more on the person's team and others who work closely with them than on one person with only a hierarchial relationship.

Planning/Budgeting

Planning and budgeting are organizational systems traditionally seen as the responsibility of managers. If teams are to realize their potential and provide the strategic advantage desired, they have to become accountable for their work. That means they are given the opportunities to develop needed knowledge and skills (capacity) and the authority to decide and act on issues within their sphere of work. Planning and budgeting are critical parts of establishing a work system, realizing a mission, setting performance goals, developing commitment, designing measurements, and becoming accountable. Teams need to be a part of planning and budgeting. They need to be chartered with appropriate boundaries around their sphere of work. Teams need to be setting standards for their work, finding ways to improve their work system, managing costs, and identifying their resource needs.

Training

Training and development has also been traditionally focused on individuals. However, with teams, it is more effective to be trained together in some knowledge/skill areas. Also, teams might more accurately identify needs for individual development and might even be best qualified to conduct some training for themselves. This would create a very different system than training department led by needs assessments, catalog offerings, one-size-fits-all training, and other common systems in place. In essence, the customers (teams) might determine more of their needs and participate together, with more grounding in the reality of their work.

Decision Making

How decisions get made is another important area of consideration. First, all the important decisions can't be made outside of the team or the team loses viability as a functioning unit. This will involve chartering with appropriate boundaries and authority, holding teams accountable when conditions and alignment support that, providing needed information and facilitative help. Over time, the organization needs to get clear about what decisions are the team's, which teams and at what levels, and what individuals at different levels are expected to decide and act on.

Other Systems

Other potential systems and processes that can be influenced by a team strategy and might deserve consideration in alignment include: how people are selected and promoted; the types of careers and paths in the organization; job assignments, transfers, rotations and movement; and any disciplinary processes that may be needed.

Practices

New practices will be needed in a team-based organization. Different behaviors (and the skills that support them) are needed among team members for the team to operate effectively. Different behaviors are also needed throughout the organization to create day-to-day interactions and an operating style that supports teamwork. In general, the use of teams will require people in the organization to:

- Communicate more (creating the need for skills in communicating and listening)
- Make decisions jointly (creating the need for skills in data generation, analysis, decision methods, and collaboration)
- Resolve differences (creating the need for skills in conflict management, negotiation, and compromise)
- Participate more (creating the need for skills in inclusion, cooperation, sharing, and assertiveness)
- Conduct meetings (creating the need for skills in meeting design and management, group process, and facilitation)
- Plan (creating the need for skills in using planning tools, goal setting, visioning, and budgeting)
- Evaluate results (creating the need for skills in performance and financial analysis, evaluation tools, measurement, and feedback)

The above kinds of practices are called for more often and by more people when teams are used extensively than when most people work singularly performing their individual job. Developing these practices will require a great deal of training, cross-training, on-the-job coaching, modeling, and reinforcement. A critical mass of people will need these competencies for teams to function well. In their absence, old practices, (more command and control behaviors; individual, independent, decision making; primarily individual-to-individual interaction, etc.), that have become routine, will operate and undermine the intent of teams.

With teams there will be team-building issues. They will have to develop ways of operating and the necessary skills for working together. There will be needs to define their purpose, clarify their roles, establish norms and processes for working together, resolve interpersonal issues and optimally utilize their resources. Ongoing team building needs to become part of their practices.

Culture

The culture is at the heart of the organization and in many ways is the most pervasive component. The culture or values in operation pervades all parts of the organization. It operates visibly and invisibly to guide and shape behavior. The culture manifests itself in many ways — through language, symbols, rituals, and stories, through the norms of behavior, and through the systems and practices of the organization. The operating values become embedded in what is taught, rewarded, and promoted; in what is considered "successful"; in the procedures that get designed and policies that get defined; and in the accepted and expected ways people work with each other.

307

In a culture that has long encouraged, reinforced, and rewarded individual action, competitive behavior, secrecy, one-on-one interaction, and similar values, moving to a team-based structure will immediately create misalignment and tension between the values needed to support teamwork and the old culture. Even issues of equality, status, diversity, and hierarchy can continue to guide behavior that had become the norm, when what's really needed is more level playing fields, involvement based on expertise, less use of hierarchy for communicating or decision making, more inclusion of differences, and valuing of collaborator/ negotiator/facilitator over the power-wielding, quick-draw, independent decision-maker telling someone what to do.

In a culture to support a team-based strategy some different values would need to be more prominently operating and embedded throughout the organization's structures, systems, and practices. For example:

- Being "in it" together (we vs. I thinking)
- Success comes in joint, collaborative action
- Participation is needed and expected
- Different perspectives produce quality work
- Everyone is a useful resource
- Supporting or teaching others helps my career
- Sharing expertise and information helps our performance
- Facilitating the work of our group is valuable
- Learning more skills and jobs makes me more valuable to the company

The culture change is often the most difficult because the existing culture is so ingrained. However, if the culture isn't aligned with the new strategy and philosophy, all the structural, systems and practice changes won't really take hold to bring about the full alignment that's needed.

Vision

Visioning is a way for people to see a desired future and to better understand, and even get motivated by, how the organization would work differently. Visions are also a way to provide the entire organization with a bigger picture of where they are going. From this picture, individuals, teams, and other units can develop their role and how they need to fit in. For a team-based organization, visions could be developed at both the organization and team levels depicting how the various parts work together in producing the desired results. Involving people throughout the organization will help to develop more meaningful visions, greater understanding, and more ownership by more people who want to make it work.

CHANGING TO A TEAM-BASED ORGANIZATION

Ideally, it would be best if an organization could plan for and design all of the components, with alignment, before implementing the team-based strategy. Realistically, this rarely occurs. More often, teams will be structured first and then struggle for some time, due, in part, to the numerous misalignments that will exist. In this case, changing other aspects of the organization to support teams is playing "catch up." You can utilize the alignment thinking to focus on creating shifts in the culture and new systems and practices that reinforce, support, and work in concert with the team structure.

Whether you're thinking about becoming team-based, are currently designing for teams, or have already restructured into teams, the questions in Figure 2 can serve as a guide. You can use them in more fully developing the organization to realize your strategy or to identify and diagnose problems in functioning as a team-based organization (often forms of misalignment). In any of these situations your goal will be to manage changes that will provide mutual reinforcement and embed team-based values into structures, operating systems, and day-to-day practices.

FULFILLING THE PROMISE OF TEAMS

Whatever team-based strategy one is pursuing, the components of the organization (system) will need to be aligned if that strategy is to be fully realized. It is most critical that the organization first think through, clarify, and integrate its strategy. It may include something to do with quality or speed to market or innovation or new product development or customer responsiveness or all of these. But whatever the strategy is, it will have implications for the organization as a system and the appropriateness of a team-based structure.

The use of teams is one structure that is being widely used to support numerous strategies. It is proliferating with changing environments and the increased understanding that teams are often superior in productivity, quality, speed, and economy. However, all too often people are organized into teams, but little else in the organization changes. A team-based organization cannot operate effectively unless key components of the organization are aligned with the team-based strategy. When parts of the system are not aligned, mixed messages are rampant, confusion and frustration occur, and the impact that the new structure could have on the organization's effectiveness is undermined. In time, the old, more deeply-rooted ways will prevail. By considering the five components in the Alignment Model, an organization can be created that works as intended, is less frustrating to work in, and produces desired results. Only when the organization becomes an aligned system around its team-based structure will it be capable of fulfilling the promise of teams.

STRATEGY

- What is the strategy?
- Does the strategy require teams?
- Why are teams required?

STRUCTURE

- Are teams formed with the right boundaries around interdependent tasks?
- Where does the work require team structure?
- Can teams be formed at various levels? In core and support work?
- Is the technology integrated to support team functioning?

CULTURE

- Are the values in operation supporting team or individual behaviors? How?
- Does the culture encourage:
  - ☞ Equality
  - ☞ Empowerment
  - ☞ Inclusion
  - ☞ Collaboration
  - ☞ Participation
  - ☞ Group Decision Making
  - ☞ We thinking
  - ☞ Working together
  - ☞ Sharing
  - ☞ Facilitating
  - ☞ Multiple skills
  - ☞ Diversity

SYSTEMS

- Do policies and procedures support team functioning? How?
- Are the systems and processes designed for teams or individuals:
  - ☞ Information
  - ☞ Rewards
  - ☞ Pay
  - ☞ Evaluation
  - ☞ Planning/ Budgeting
  - ☞ Training
  - ☞ Decision Making
  - ☞ Selection
  - ☞ Careers
  - ☞ Assignments
  - ☞ Discipline

PRACTICES

- Do the day-to-day interactions manifest teamwork behaviors?
- What skills are being used? Needed?
- Are people:
  - ☞ Team Building
  - ☞ Facilitative
  - ☞ Jointly Deciding
  - ☞ Cooperative
  - ☞ Inclusive
  - ☞ Sharing Information
  - ☞ Communicating
  - ☞ Listening
  - ☞ Providing Feedback
  - ☞ Working through Differences
  - ☞ Involving
  - ☞ Communicating More
  - ☞ Making Decisions Jointly
  - ☞ Resolving Differences
  - ☞ Participating More
  - ☞ Running Meetings
  - ☞ Planning
  - ☞ Evaluating Results

Figure 2. Aligning the Organization for Teams

Bibliography

Chandler, A.D. (1962). *Strategy and structure*. Cambridge, MA: MIT Press.

Galbraith, J. (1977). *Organization design*. Reading, MA: Addison-Wesley.

Galbraith, J. (1994). *Competing with flexible lateral organization (2nd Ed.)*. Reading, MA: Addison-Wesley.

Katzenbach, J.R., and D.K. Smith. (1993). *The wisdom of teams*. Boston: Harvard Business School Press.

Kerr, S. (1995). "On the Folly of Rewarding A, While Hoping for B." *Academy of management executive*, 9, (1), 7-14.

Lawler, E.E. (1986). *High - involvement management*. San Francisco: Jossey-Bass.

Nadler, D., and M. Tushman. (1988). *Strategic organization design*. Glenview, IL: Scott, Foresman & Co.

Nadler, D., and M. Tushman. (1977). "A Diagnostic Model for Organization Behavior" in *Perspectives on behavior in organizations*. (Eds.) J. Hackman, E. Lawler, and L. Porter, eds. New York: McGraw - Hill.

Old, D.R. (1995). "Consulting for Real Transformation, Sustainability, and Organic Form." *Journal of organizational change management*, 8 (3), 6-17.

Old, D. R. (1992). Personal Communication and Unpublished Material.

Orsburn, J.D., L. Moran, E. Mussellwhite, and J. Zenger (1990). *Self - directed work teams*. Homewood, IL: Business One Irwin.

Parker, G.M. (1990). *Team players and teamwork*. San Francisco: Jossey-Bass.

Shonk, J.H. (1992). *Team-based organizations*. Homewood, IL: Business One Irwin

Taylor, F.W. (1915). *The principles of scientific management*. New York: Harper and Row.

Tichy, N. (1983). *Managing strategic change*. New York: Wiley.

About the Contributor

Dr. Jamieson is President of the Jamieson Consulting Group and Adjunct Professor of Management, Pepperdine University. He has 25 years of experience consulting to organizations on change, strategy, design, and human resource issues. He is a Past National President of the American Society for Training and Development and the 1995 - 96 Chair, Managerial Consultation Division of the Academy of Management. He also serves on the Editorial Board for the *Journal of Organization Change Management.* Dave is co-author of *Managing Workforce 2000: Gaining the Diversity Advantage* (Jossey-Bass, 1991) and author of "Start-up: Successfully Engaging with the Client" in Rothwell, et.al *Practicing Organization Development* (Pfeiffer and Co., 1995).

27

Update Your Tool Box for Teams
Steven L. Phillips, Ph. D.

Teams are everywhere. There is no longer a question about whether teams in the workplace are effective. Numerous recent studies have confirmed the facts that we all suspected. Teams, when properly prepared and trained, consistently outperform traditionally structured work groups. The question is: Do you have the tools to make your organization's teams successful?

Before you begin to assess your tools, you need a strong understanding about the different types of teams and what tools each of those teams need to function successfully. The place to start your analysis is with a model. Models provide definition for team diagnosis and development. The Team Strategies Model describes five different types of teams based upon the intersection of two continuums, depth of participation and time, resources, energy, and training.

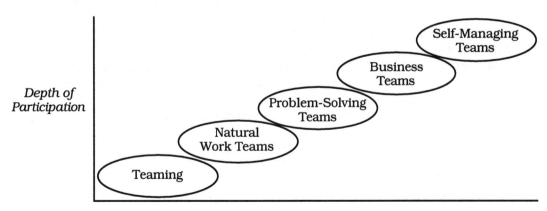

This model helps organizations focus on the right type or level of training.

As with all models, this representation is not comprehensive. There are numerous other team types, but for the simple purpose of identifying the major categories of teaming and their development needs, this model works very well.

MAJOR CATEGORIES OF TEAMS

Teaming

The first type of team, "teaming," is not really a formal team at all. Teaming here represents when people from different functions come together to achieve some end result. That end result can be as simple as creating better working relationships, or as complex as reducing the cycle time of a large cross-functional process.

In one catalog sales consumer-product organization the people in the purchasing, marketing, and merchandising functions had never sat down and spoken with each other. For the most part the people in each function just did their jobs as best as they could without really knowing if what they were producing truly served the needs of those next in line in the work process. This often left the employees in the dark about the quality of their work, how to deal effectively with crises and emergencies, and ignorant about the total work process. Moreover, without any contact with the people in neighboring functions, building effective one-on-one working relationships was never encouraged or facilitated.

Teaming in this situation was as simple as setting aside time for a four-hour facilitated meeting for each function to introduce itself, describe how it perceived the other functions, and to get feedback on what it was doing that was working well and what it needed to do differently from the other functions' point of view. This process not only expanded the employee's awareness of the work processes but also helped to build positive long-term working relationships geared toward productivity improvement.

In a more targeted teaming approach a convenience food company had specified its core development process for a cycle time reduction intervention. This company wanted to reduce the total number of days it took to find and buy a piece of land, build a free standing restaurant, and then open that restaurant successfully. The teaming effort they used was to bring regional real estate, construction, and operations employees together for a series of facilitated meetings. In the first meeting they performed very similar exercises as the purchasing, marketing, and merchandising functions of the catalog sales consumer-product organization. The people from each function introduced themselves, described how they perceived the other functions, and gave and received feedback on what they were doing that was working well and what they needed to do differently from the viewpoint of the other functions.

In the second and subsequent meetings, after the working relationships had improved, the regional groups flow charted the development process in order to reduce unnecessary steps, targeted and acted upon high leverage improvement opportunities, shared best practices, and ended up with a significant reduction (about 40 percent) in the overall cycle time of the core development process.

Natural Work Groups

Natural work groups are intact work groups that are usually composed of a supervisor or manager and that person's direct reports. These groups have been the traditional mainstay of the command and control organization. In the majority of cases, natural work groups are not organized around a "whole" piece of work, but rather, are structured as a control mechanism within a given function. Nevertheless, the people in these groups often want to think of themselves as a team, and consequently use the team metaphor for improved work performance.

To best understand (and consequently help) the members of a natural work group who want to think of themselves as a team, the first step is often to have them consider the nature of their work and the level of interdependence needed to effectively complete their prescribed tasks. We use a simple, yet powerful, sports analogy to help natural work groups clarify what sort of a team they would like to be. For example, a group of individual contributors who act in isolation of each other but all report to the same boss may be compared to a tennis or golf team. If, to complete the work of the group the members have some level of interdependence, or need to work with some but not everyone else in the group, then this may be considered analogous to a baseball team. Moving up the interdependency scale even further, the members of a work group may be compared to a football team when the nature of their work requires subteams to tackle day-to-day tasks. Just as a football team has an offensive team, a defensive team, and a number of special teams, natural work groups may also have subteams all hopefully aligned to a strong vision or strategy. Finally, work groups that are relatively small, fluid, and fully interdependent may be considered similar to a basketball team where managing the process of the team takes on paramount importance.

Natural work groups like the ones described above often need help establishing the right framework from which to improve (golf, tennis, baseball, football, or basketball). After they decide on the framework that best suits their needs, they often need help in developing or clarifying one or more of their key elements to effective team performance: roles; goals; relationships; processes and procedures; and leadership.

Project and Problem-Solving Teams

Project and problem-solving teams are usually cross-functional teams that come together to work a particular issue or solve a specific problem. These teams range in size from about five to twelve members and have a definite beginning and ending point. Problem-solving teams may go after cost or cycle time reductions, or they may target improvements in quality or customer service. Different than the quality circles of the past, these teams are empowered to act. They are often sponsored by a senior manager with the purpose of results, not recommendations.

315

In one newspaper plant, a team of employees were put together for eight weeks to reduce costs. Their net result of reduction in newsprint waste ended up saving the company over $500,000 a year. In an oil refinery a cost reduction team re-negotiated electricity and power bills resulting in a hard dollar savings of over $200,000 a month or 2.4 million dollars a year. Gains such as these are not all that unusual. In a security and investigations firm, teams were put in place to improve customer service and overall quality of their performance. These teams not only increased overall customer satisfaction ratings (which led to an increase in customer retention) but also partnered with their local clients to come up with enough quality improvements to offer reductions in customer fees year after year.

Business Teams

Business teams take the next step deeper into employee involvement. In essence, business teams run their own business unit. They not only run the day-to-day operations of their unit, but they also have control over their schedule, budget, quality, and goals. Business teams create and manage their own business plans, set quality and productivity improvement initiatives, develop and manage a workable budget, set and adjust their own schedules, ensure the training and development of their members, and make sure their direction is in alignment with the overall goals and objectives of the company.

Business teams take many forms. A business team can be created using multifunctional players brought together around a whole piece of work. In an aerospace manufacturing arena, multifunctional teams were given full responsibility for different parts of the airplane. For example, there were teams created for the tail, wings, wing joint, nose, and fuselage. In a software development company, business teams were formed to create, design, market, and produce new software products. Business teams can also be created from a single function. For example, in a waste water treatment plant, business teams were formed from existing shift crews. In a financial institution, the human resource function became a business team. When an organization chooses to structure with business teams and/or self-directed work teams it must also consider creating or shifting to an employee involvement culture.

Self-Managing Teams

Self-managing teams are similar to business teams because they too have full responsibility for successfully operating their designated business unit. What makes a self-managing work team different is the added responsibility of human resource planning and administration. Whereas a business team may have human resources support, a self-managing team also has the responsibility of hiring, firing, performance appraisal, and discipline. Self-managing teams are a more extreme version of a business team and must be considered carefully. Successful self-managing teams can be found in many industries including manufacturing, finance, hospitality, convenience foods, retail, consumer products, and health care. More often than not, the successful self-managing teams have either been created in a greenfield site, or have been put in place after a massive corporate culture change. Both business teams and self-managing teams require a high employee involvement culture, including alignment of the corporate resources, strategic initiatives, management practices, organizational policies, information systems, and if applicable, labor management practices.

DEFINING THE DEVELOPMENT NEEDS OF EACH TEAM

Teaming

Although effective teaming does not include a formal team, the people involved in teaming nevertheless have developmental needs. They must, at a minimum, consider three important questions:

1. How would we describe the other functions?
2. What do we think is most important to them?
3. What feedback do we want to give them about their performance?

After each group has responded to each question, facilitate a discussion that allows for open and candid feedback from each group to every other group.

The rules for the feedback are simple. Each group presents its list (the feedback is usually put on a flipchart) to another group. The group receiving the feedback must stay quiet while the information is being presented even if some members disagree or do not understand what is being said. When the presenting group has finished, only then are the recipients allowed to speak, and then, only to ask for clarification. If any defensiveness or explanations start to occur, the facilitator must put a stop to them immediately. This session is not about who is right or wrong, it's about hearing the other group's perspective and perception of their reality.

This feedback discussion will usually include humor and that helps to break the tension. More times than not there are several misunderstandings and inappropriate assumptions made about each other. There will be plenty of time for that to come out later. So each group in turn presents to each other group and answers clarifying questions and then receives feedback about itself.

The next step is to have a general discussion with all participants about what was learned during this feedback session. This should be facilitated so people speak about themselves with "I" statements (I never realized that. . .) versus using "you" statements (you never told me that. . .). In these discussions, the facilitator should try to capture any significant issues that have been put on the table. Many issues are simply

317

perception differences, but some real issues (usually no more than five to seven) do surface. These issues should be captured on an issue list and put aside for future problem solving.

Following this discussion, the participants should form back into their groups to complete the final feedback for the other groups. They should respond to the following two statements for each other's group:

1. Start doing or do more of. . .
2. Stop doing or do less of. . .

These flipcharts are also presented. Groups can ask clarifying questions and then the receiving group must take all of its feedback and respond. Give them some time to absorb and discuss their feedback and then have each group present its final action steps to all other groups. This feedback loop is very powerful and often changes small aspects of behavior which, in turn, create important perceptional changes in others.

Finally, with the list of serious problems that has been set aside, you can form small task forces to work on those items and report back by a certain date or at the next meeting. At times, it is appropriate not to form smaller task forces to work out the issues, but to save the issues for another all-hands meeting. Either way works, just make sure the larger group buys into the methodology that is chosen.

Further, if the desired outcomes for the teaming intervention do go beyond building better working relationships and start to address the more serious operational issues, then deeper levels of development are likely to be important. In the example cited earlier where the teaming intervention was used to reduce cycle time, people had to be trained in process flow analysis, creative thinking, and benchmarking.

Natural Work Teams

The basis for development of a natural work team is an assessment based upon team leadership, roles, goals, relationships, and processes and procedures (see Team Effectiveness Model).

This assessment will allow either a facilitator or team leader to establish team strengths and weaknesses and to work with the team to chart a plan of action accordingly.

Moreover, if customized team building is too time and labor intensive, you may want to consider a team leadership course for your supervisors. Whereas customized team development works specifically with an intact group, a team leadership course is designed to teach already existing team leaders (supervisors and managers) how to effectively assess and develop their own team. The most effective team leadership course should be designed for supervisors, managers, and team leaders offering the participants specific tools and techniques to use in the development of their team.

TEAM EFFECTIVENESS MODEL

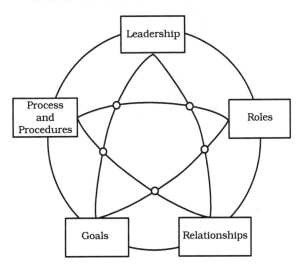

Although a team leadership course should be customized to meet your specific needs, we have included a sample outline:

Team Leader Training Course

Objectives / Outcomes
- To help team leaders start up and run effective teams
- To clarify team leader roles and accountabilities
- To offer team leaders effective tools to help with their new positions

Agenda

I.   Introduction
    A. Objectives
    B. Agenda
    C. Expectations and concerns

II. Introduction to High Performance Teams
    A. Benefits / characteristics / downsides
    B. Teamwork continuum
    C. Types of teams
    D. Team effectiveness model

III. The New Role of the Team Leader
    A. New job requirements
    B. Issues and pressures
    C. Dealing with change

IV. Building a Team Purpose
    A. Definition
    B. Constructing a rough draft
    C. Team participation

V.   Team Meetings
    A. Common meeting problems
    B. When to conduct a meeting
    C. Meeting tools

VI.   Managing Team Performance
    A. Process diagram of work
    B. Customer / supplier management
    C. Success factors
    D. Business information

VII. Team Motivation
    A. Social motives
    B. Team member assessment
    C. Team motive profile

VIII. Coaching Team Members
    A. Model and process
    B. Skill practice and tools
    C. Follow up and discussion

IX.   Managing in a Team Environment
    A. Framework
    B. Context and assessment
    C. Action plans

X.   Learning Styles
    A. Modes of learning
    B. Styles of learning
    C. Implications and application

XI.   Teaming Tools
    A. Team assessment
    B. Role clarification
    C. Giving feedback
    D. Etc. . .

Project and Problem-Solving Teams

If your company has project or problem-solving teams, then you will need a solid course in the process, tools, and techniques of team problem solving as well as trained facilitators to help the team through the process. The problem-solving course should be based on a short-term (six to ten weeks) success probability and entail tools, techniques, and procedures for the team members to identify opportunities for improvement, select a goal, prepare a plan, initiate action, review weekly progress, measure results, assess learning, and present their outcomes. This course should be heavily outcome oriented and go into extensive detail regarding data collection and analysis techniques.

We recommend that all problem-solving teams be sponsored by a senior manager. This sponsorship helps the team remove obstacles and barriers to success. It also ensures the team a sufficient budget to incur appropriate and needed expenses.

The problem-solving training the team encounters is more facilitated than taught. Each team should have an appointed team leader and team facilitator who have either had previous problem-solving team experience or who have been trained in team leader and/or facilitator roles. In essence, the team leader's responsibilities are to:

a. Select team in conjunction with facilitator, project leader(s), and steering committee
b. Contribute to goal setting and work plan creation as would any other team member
c. Schedule and manage team meetings
d. Keep team focused and organized
e. Monitor action plan and progress against goal
f. Help team members accomplish difficult tasks
g. Work with management to gain necessary support
h. Communicate with facilitator, project leader(s), and steering committee

The team facilitator's responsibilities are to:

a. Act as problem-solving team process expert
b. Lead team through kickoff meetings with support of team leader
c. Assist team leader with creating meeting agendas and weekly work plans
d. Help team establish baseline at an early stage
e. Coach team leader and individual members on problem-solving; assist as necessary
f. Make sure everyone communicates and participates fully
g. Help team leader run meetings; urge team to reach closure on one issue before moving to the next
h. Communicate with key people as necessary to clear obstacles
i. Assist team with preparation of management and final reviews

The format of the training usually occurs in two-hour sessions once a week. These sessions help the team members define the current process, identify problem areas, determine root causes for problems, set goals, write improvement action plans, improve the process, evaluate status and success, celebrate success, and develop a plan to sustain and build upon success accordingly. In between facilitated sessions, team members spend four to ten hours a week collecting, and analyzing data as well as implementing and adjusting plans.

The two-hour a week sessions serve as planning and learning sessions where the team learns the process, learns new techniques, solves problems, and makes decisions. It's the time spent outside of these sessions where the real work gets done.

Business Teams

Business teams are organized around a business unit of the organization. If you are developing business teams you will need training tools founded in three fundamentals: interpersonal and group dynamics; quality and productivity improvement techniques; and business planning and operations. Business teams are responsible to work together to run their unit. To that end they will need skill and practice in a variety of interpersonal and group techniques including topics such as meeting management, conflict management, and decision making. They will need to know how to assess and improve their quality and productivity, consequently requiring training in such topics as process analysis, productivity improvement techniques, and customer service. Finally, to run their "business" they will need to do such things as clarify their purpose, create and implement business plans, and set and manage realistic budgets.

The approach to developing business and self-managing teams influences the quality of the work the team does and the longevity of the team. If team development is seen as a one-shot training event, the effort is not likely to contribute much to a long-term involvement strategy. If, on the other hand, the team strategy is viewed as an ongoing, complex learning process, the result can increase the chances of long-term success.

Developing the team can be compared to learning to play golf. Anyone who has attempted the game knows that golf cannot be learned in a week nor can one get beyond the fundamentals by reading a book or watching one of Jack Nicklaus' videos. Rather, one learns golf by acquiring the fundamentals (stance, grip, swing, what club does what) and going to the driving range or course to practice. It is the actual "hitting of the ball" (and the score) that tells the golfer whether or not he or she is learning. And, since the game of golf requires complex eye-hand-body coordination (to say nothing of what is required of the mind), it is not likely that one will become proficient at golf right away. Instead, one learns, practices, gets feedback (*#@% slice!), and returns to learn. With enough teaching/coaching, time, practice, and most of all, patience, some day the game may all come together. Breaking a 100 (with honest score-keeping) is typically a milestone for the golfer. Then the target is 90, and so forth. Golfers keep moving the goal and doing what they can to improve toward that goal. (Nobody ever lost a dime underestimating the gullibility of golfers to buy any new tool that has the possibility of shaving a stroke off their game.)

If we extend the analogy to the development of the team, the approach to teaching and learning is different than if team development is compared to teaching someone to add numbers (2+2=4) or install spark plugs in a car. Teaching addition might be done in one or two sessions after which participants have the skill to add the numbers every time they encounter them. The task of installing spark plugs requires a certain basic set of knowledge and skills; beyond that only the context

322

changes. This is not the case with team development. Learning and development is a continuous process characterized by increasing complexity.

Self-Managing Work Teams

If you have self-managing or self-directed work teams then you will need all of the tools for a business team plus the tools and techniques to create a semiautonomous unit. The philosophy for this training stays the same as the one described above for business teams. The difference is that self-managing work teams will need the additional skills to deal with personnel management (staffing), team performance assessment, and rewards and recognition. In addition to specific team development, it is also important to consider the new developmental needs of your general management and supervision. Managing in an organization with teams is not the same as traditional management. Teams require a new set of skills and competencies often not included in traditional management development curriculums.

DEFINING THE DEVELOPMENTAL NEEDS OF YOUR MANAGEMENT AND SUPERVISION TO SUPPORT YOUR TEAM-BASED ORGANIZATION

Supervisory Training: The Supervisor as Trainer, Coach, and Leader

For business teams and self-managing work teams you will need a new kind of supervisory training. The control model of supervision found underlying the majority of the existing training on the market was built to create supervisory competence in a traditional hierarchical organization. The training mostly centers on the traditional functions of supervision including planning, organizing, controlling, motivating, and coordinating. In an organization with business or self-managing teams, the model of supervision must transform away from control and toward commitment. Consequently, the role of the supervisor shifts to one of training, coaching, and leading. Your supervisory training must reflect this new role and its associated values. Many existing supervisory programs are the same old materials repackaged into an updated form. Be sure to check yours closely for its foundational assumptions about work and team performance.

Although any new supervisory program should be custom tailored to fit your specific needs and culture, the following is a sample outline that we have used with our clients in the past:

323

Group Leader/Team Leader Training:
The Supervisor as Trainer, Coach, and Leader*

Overall Objectives:

- Prepare participants for a new way of doing business
- Clarifying new job requirements
- Developing new thinking and associated competency

Agenda   Session 1

    I. Introductions and expectations

    II. The business case for change

    III. The new role of supervision/management

    IV. Leading in turbulent times

    V. Leadership, culture, and climate

    VI. What leaders really do

    VII. Aligning and enabling

    VIII. Management feedback and development planning

    IX. Personal reflections

    X. Summary/close

Session 2

    I. Introductions and expectations

    II. Building a learning organization

    III. Continuous improvement

    IV. What drives performance

    V. The art and science of enabling others to act

    VI. In-depth coaching

    VII. Developing others

    VIII. Managing resources in the new environment

    IX. Business planning and operations

    X. Summary/close

* These outlines are based on the original work of Pattie Grimm.

Session 3

    I. Introduction and expectations
   II. Understanding teams
  III. Team member operating styles
  IV. Team development exercises
   V. Team project work
  VI. Communication and information systems
 VII. Managing your boss
VIII. Managing your career
  IX. Feedback to the senior team
   X. Summary/close

Session 4

    I. Introduction and expectations
   II. The game of business
  III. How to read financials
  IV. Business simulation
   V. Company specific numbers
  VI. Key indicators
 VII. Impacting key indicators
VIII. Business simulation
  IX. Open book management
   X. Summary/close

Management Development Curriculum: The New Role Of Management

Whereas the traditional role of management centers on creating successful individual and functional area performance, the new model of management focuses on creating an environment for high performance teams. This new perspective re-engineers the manager job into:

1. Creating an organizational context that supports and reinforces competent task work via reward, educational, and informational systems.
2. Creating the design of teams that prompts and facilitates competent work via structure of the task, composition of the team, and team norms about performance processes.

325

3. Offering coaching and facilitation to assist the team in reducing process losses and creating synergistic gains.
4. Ensuring the sufficiency of material resources to accomplish the desired tasks at hand.

Creating an Organizational Context

In essence, it is the manager's job to ensure that the reward system is aligned with the desired team outcome. Too often, reward systems encourage individual objectives and leave out any incentives to be a good organizational team player or to reward outstanding team accomplishment. Additionally, many organizations do not put enough emphasis and/or spend too little on training. This mistake is especially critical when teams are put in place. Employees, although they may be competent in their area of expertise, often need development and education when it comes to participating on an effective team. Finally, it is the manager's duty to make sure the team gets the information it needs to plan, assess, and improve its performance. When teams are put in place, management often takes for granted that the informational needs of the team will be the same as they always have been for individuals. This is simply not true. Teams often not only need new information that has never been collected in the past, but will often need existing information reformatted for the team as the unit of analysis (versus the division or entire business unit). It is the manager's job to make sure team members do not get bogged down into data collection but rather have data provided to them to analyze, plan, and improve performance.

Creating the Design of Teams

Managers must also be cognizant of the design of teams. They must look at work differently than in the past. Work should be considered in the context of a "whole" piece of work that a team can accomplish. Traditionally, work has been logically broken down into small bite-size components that individuals can easily do, often on a repetitive basis. When designing work now, a manager must consider the true task appropriate for six to twenty-five multiskilled individuals who, when complete, will feel a group sense of accomplishment. It's the difference between building an entire car and just mounting engine after engine. Along with the design of work is also the design of the team. There is no magic formula for prescribing personality types for a team, but most people would agree that team members should possess all of the requisite skills needed to do the task. This often means putting together a cross-functional, multiskilled, heterogeneous team versus the traditional, functional, same skilled, homogenous groups we have seen in the past. Finally, managers must encourage high standards and performance norms that are clear, challenging, and outcome oriented.

Offering Coaching and Facilitation

Managers must be great coaches. It's not enough to be a good coach. The new role of management calls for very skilled and informed coaching. These coaches have to know when and how to intervene on the team. The latest research is very clear on when teams are open to coaches and when they are in a momentum phase and not open to outside help. The new coach has to think about team synergy and when process losses may occur. For example, teams are very open to their environment at the beginning and in the middle of any given task. Coaches should step in right at the start to make sure the team starts off strong. But, during the next several weeks of team momentum, the coach, unless called upon, should stay out of the way. Likewise, when the team needs help and calls upon the manager, the expert coach must know how to help the team assess its efforts and redirect them without squashing motivation or taking away ownership for the task. These are not simple skills and although most experienced managers will say they have them, they most often need some help.

Ensuring the Sufficiency of Material Resources

Finally, managers usually have more resources than their teams. If not more, at least more access to those resources. Part of their new role is understanding how to marshall those resources in support of their team's efforts. If, for example, one of their teams wants to purchase $15,000 worth of equipment for a two-year return on investment, it's the manager's job to either approve the expenditure or help the team make the case to get the funds. Too often, teams are stifled by their inability to acquire funding to support their good ideas. Besides cash outlays there are other resources the new manager may have to consider. Issues such as co-location, overtime, job sharing, off-site work, four-day work weeks, access to senior executives and other company officials may all be resources that a team looks to its manager to provide.

Needless to say, to train managers in their new role, you must take an entirely different look at the tools in your management development tool box. You may even want to consider a completely different format for this education than what is traditional. In many places we form management teams, lay out the new role, are courageous in format design, and have the team members take turns on a once a month to once a quarter basis, taking responsibility for a given topic. They decide how and when to train the others. Do not be afraid to break the tradition of classroom learning in a typical training format. Be creative!

Checklist for Assessing Your Tool Box

• Do you have team training that looks at the team (vs. the individual)?

- Do you have a team development process for each of your different types of teams? Teaming? Natural work teams? Problem-solving teams? Business teams? Self-managing work teams?

- Do you have a team leadership course for team leaders and/or supervisors?

- Does your management development process include redefining the new role of management?

- Do you have a management development process that emphasizes managing in a team environment?

- Has your organizational reward system been revamped or originally designed to support teams?

- Does your information system give the teams the information they need at the appropriate level and in the right format?

- Do your teams get the education they need to be effective over the long run?

- Do your managers know how, when, where to give and get resources to support their teams' initiatives?

- Have you created an integrated development plan for the successes of your teams, management, and overall company?

Summary and Next Steps

In summary, teams are everywhere. Now is the time for you to step back and examine your toolbox to determine if you have the necessary tools for helping these teams reach their maximum performance potential. Have you stepped up to offer your organization the tools and techniques it needs to make your teams successful? Whether it's a team assessment inventory and customized team building; a team leadership course; breakthrough problem-solving techniques for project teams; business team or self-managing work team training; an advanced course in the new role of the supervisor or an updated version of your management development curriculum, it is now time to assess your current team development needs and step up to the challenge by designing your toolbox and stocking it with the tools that enable your teams to push the boundaries of maximum team performance.

Bibliography

Argyris, C., and D. A. Schon. (1978). *Organizational learning: A theory of action perspective.* Reading, MA: Addison-Wesley Publishing Company.

Belasco, J. A. (1990). *Teaching the elephant to dance; Empowering change in your organization.* New York, NY: Crown Publishers, Inc.

Brocka, B., and M. S. Brocka (1992). *Quality management: Implementing the best ideas of the masters.* Homewood, IL: Richard D. Irwin, Inc.

Davis, K. (1957). *Human relations in business.* New York, NY: McGraw-Hill Book Company.

Deming, W. E. (1986). Out of the crisis. *Journal of Organizational Behavior Management, 2* (10), 205-13.

Harshman, C. L., and S. L. Phillips. (1994). *Teaming up: Achieving organizational transformation.* San Diego, CA: Pfeiffer & Company.

Johnson, D. W., and F. P. Johnson. (1987). *Joining Together.* Needham Heights, MA: Allyn & Bacon Paramount Publishing Group.

Kuhn, Thomas. (1984). *The structure of scientific revolutions.* Chicago, IL: University of Chicago.

Lee, Clyde E. (1992). *The handbook of structure experiences for human resource training* (vol. 6). San Diego: Pfeiffer and Company.

Parker, G. M. (1990). *Team players and teamwork: The new competitive business strategy.* San Francisco, CA: Jossey-Bass, Inc.

Peters, Tom (1988). *Thriving on chaos: Handbook for a management revolution.* New York, NY: Harper and Row.

Rosow, J. M., R. Zager, and J. Casner-Lotto. (1991). *New roles for managers series: The manager as trainer, coach, and leader.* Scarsdale, NY: Work in America Institute, Inc.

Schrage, M. (1990). Managers' journal. *Wall Street Journal, 3* (19).

Senge, P. M. (1990). *The fifth discipline: The art and practice of the learning organization.* New York, NY: Doubleday/Currency, a division of Bantam Doubleday Dell Publishing Group, Inc.

About the Contributor

Dr. Phillips has extensive experience as an organization development professional. He has worked with a variety of public and private organizations as both an internal and external consultant. As an internal consultant, Dr. Phillips worked for the City of San Diego, assisting in several city improvement projects, and for Douglas Aircraft Company where he helped implement an extensive company-wide cultural change effort.

Dr. Phillips' best-selling books, *The Team-Building Source Book*, *Teaming Up: Achieving Organizational Transformation*, and his newest release, *Team-Building for the Future: Beyond the Basics* are used in corporations throughout the world. His fourth book, on self-directed work teams, will soon be released by McGraw-Hill.

28

The Truth from the Trenches: Team Members Speak Out
A new survey reveals what employees really think about participating on teams

Amy J. Katz, Ph.D.,
Darlene Russ-Eft, Ph.D.,
Linda Moran, and
Lilanthi Ravishankar

In their struggle to boost quality, increase customer satisfaction, and enhance their overall market position, North American companies have embraced the team philosophy with an evangelical fervor. And why not? Collaboration is a powerful tool, and teams typically can outperform any individual acting alone, especially when the task at hand requires multiple skills, judgment, and experience.

Yet the culture of business and society at large has traditionally valued individual achievement over group accomplishment. Working together is fairly new for most of us, and teamwork doesn't happen naturally or without significant effort. For this reason, managers must put considerable thought into the team development and implementation process. To do that well, they must seek input from team members themselves.

Surprisingly, however, few surveys on team success have taken into account the participants' viewpoint. In fact, few organizations have collected data on the team member perspective; far greater emphasis has been placed on management preferences and/or hunches.

What is the team experience really like? What are teams best at achieving? Where do problems arise? What contributes to these problems? And what impact do organizational changes such as downsizing have on team members?

In seeking the answers to these questions, Zenger Miller (ZM), the international consulting, training, and education firm, which specializes in leadership, employee involvement, customer focus, and process management, commissioned a survey of teams. They did so in conjunction with the Association for Quality and Participation (AQP), a 10,000-member nonprofit association dedicated to promoting the principles and practices of quality and participation in the workplace.

This survey, "Team Members Speak Out," is one of the first to go inside the teams in an effort to learn how employees feel about working in a team environment. It is one of the few studies to review team success in both U.S. and Canadian companies.

Key Findings

The majority of team members surveyed believe teams are very successful in achieving the objectives of improved quality, greater customer satisfaction, improved productivity, and employee skill development. This success, however, is contingent upon several factors, including a strong commitment to teams on the part of top management.

In achieving their goals, team members struggle with a host of problems. Inefficient meetings top the list, followed by inadequate resources and performance problems among team members.

Although 90 percent of team members reported they have received training in how to work on teams, a third of them claimed the training has been inadequate. Not surprisingly, those team members who have received adequate training are significantly more successful in achieving their objectives than those who have not received adequate training.

Teams in service industries and small companies are more likely to experience problems than are teams in large companies and industrial settings. This difference probably results from several factors. For one, the prevalence of team-based Total Quality Management (TQM) initiatives has made teams a part of the organizational structure in large manufacturing firms for a longer period of time; thus, these teams are more experienced. Additionally, measuring the output of manufacturing teams and organizing these teams around output is typically easier. In contrast, service industry businesses and smaller organizations usually have fewer resources and more interruptions than manufacturing organizations.

Organizational changes such as downsizing and the increased use of temporary and contract workers do affect teams, but not always in a negative way. In the view of some respondents, for example, downsizing has actually increased the efficiency of team members, and the presence of temporary and contract workers on teams has enhanced productivity and team success.

Teams in which participation is voluntary achieve significantly greater overall success than those teams where participation is required. Yet more than half of those team members surveyed (57 percent) are required by management to participate on teams.

With few exceptions, there was little difference between the experiences of team members in Canada and the United States.

One telling part of the survey came in the form of responses to the open-ended question, "What one thing has surprised you most about working on a team?" Responses ranged across the board, from the positive aspects of achieving new heights in productivity, creativity, and performance through a team approach, to the more negative issues of lack of trust among team members and the peril of hidden agendas.

Study Methodology

"Team Members Speak Out," with research conducted independently by the American Institutes for Research, Inc., was distributed to 2,000 team members in the United States and Canada. Fifty-eight percent of the respondents work in service industries, and the remainder work in non-service, product-based industries. All participants are current members of working teams.

Altogether, 480 questionnaire packets were mailed to the survey population of AQP members (240 in the United States and 240 in Canada). These individuals were asked to complete one survey, and then to distribute copies of the survey to two randomly selected team members in different departments or functions in their organization. All respondents were asked to focus their comments around one team of which they were currently a member, with a "team" being defined as having three or more participating members.

Other AQP members from the sample were contacted by telephone prior to being sent the same questionnaires. A second follow-up mailing was carried out to non-responding organizations. Overall, the study garnered a favorable 22 percent response rate. (Detailed information regarding survey methodology, respondent demographics, response, and analysis is available upon request.)

What Do Teams Look Like?

The most "common" team in North America has eight to ten members who represent many different departments or organizations and who have been brought together for the purpose of quality and process improvement. Most team members (57 percent) are required by management to participate on these teams.

Some Specifics

Size: Team size ranges from three to fifty-two people, with eight members being the most common and ten members being the average. While nearly one-half (47 percent) of team members think their team is the right size, nearly one-third (31 percent) feel there aren't enough members.

Makeup: Nearly two-thirds (64 percent) of teams have members from different departments or different organizations. Service industries are more likely to have multi-departmental teams than are non-service industries.

Length of service: Although some teams are expected to have a finite life (such as project teams), other teams exist indefinitely. In this survey, the average team member reported being on his or her team for 25 months, with the overall length of service ranging from one month to nine years. Over half the respondents have been with their teams for less than two years, and only 10 percent of team members have been with their teams for five or more years.

Full time/part time: Nearly half (45 percent) of team members work full time on teams, and teams at smaller work sites have more full-time members than those at larger work sites. Furthermore, nonmanagers are more likely to work full time on teams than managers. This may signify that the more highly coordinated an individual's work is, the more likely it is to require full-time participation on the team.

The Makeup of Teams

Type of team	Prevalence	Average Size
Quality/process improvement (team designed to improve quality or processes)	40%	9 members
Self-directed (ongoing team fully responsible for finishing a well-defined segment of work)	33%	11 members
Project(temporary team set up for a specific project)	17%	9 members
Union/management	1%	13 members
Other	9%	Varies from 9 to 11 members

Focusing on the Customer

Three-quarters (75 percent) of team members reported that their team tries to determine outside customer expectations. This is accomplished in four ways: talking with customers (94 percent), surveying customers (83 percent), reviewing customer expectation data (82 percent), and reading written customer requests (72 percent).

Fewer teams (58 percent) try to measure customer satisfaction than try to determine customer expectations. Those who do measure satisfaction look at data on customer satisfaction (87 percent), talk with customers (86 percent), survey customers (84 percent), and review the number of orders taken (54 percent).

Performance Measurement and Compensation

More than half (60 percent) of team members reported they are measured on both individual and team performance, slightly more than a quarter (26 percent) are evaluated on individual performance alone, and only 14 percent of team members are evaluated solely on team performance. Regardless of how they are evaluated, however, nearly all team members are satisfied with how their performance is measured. In fact, the average score is 5.0 on a scale of one to seven (1 = not at all satisfied and 7 = very satisfied).

The way team members are compensated corresponds loosely to the way they are evaluated. Almost half (48 percent) of team members are compensated based on individual and team achievement, 42 percent of full-time team members are compensated based on individual achievements alone, and only 10 percent are compensated based solely on team performance. Since team compensation systems often are not established early in the development of many teams, these findings may relate to a large number of relatively new teams in the response population.

Where Are Teams Most Successful?

Team members were asked to rate the success of their team in accomplishing sixteen specific goals. The chart on the following page indicates where teams in the study were most and least successful.

Where Teams Are Most Successful	**Where Teams Are Least Successful**
1. Improving quality	1. Dealing with domestic competition
2. Improving productivity	2. Reducing employee turnover
3. Improving employee skills	3. Dealing with global competition
4. Improving customer satisfaction	4. Improving ethics and values
5. Increasing employee participation	5. Strengthening management

Interestingly, the top five team successes noted above were also reported as areas of success by quality and human resource directors in a separate study conducted by the American Institutes for Research conducted on behalf of Zenger Miller in 1994, titled "Winning Competitive Advantage: A Blended Strategy Works Best."

The indication that teams in manufacturing companies are much more successful in reaching their objectives than teams in service industries is probably not a startling observation. After all, the team movement took shape in the manufacturing environment, where goals have been more concrete and measurable. A related finding shows that teams also have been successful at larger work sites, especially in improving quality. The reason could be that managers at these sites have a larger pool of employees from which to select team members with specialized skills.

Teams in smaller companies and service industries are not as yet showing the same quality results as teams in larger manufacturing companies, and these less successful team members report significantly less progress in improving both productivity and employee skills. This lack of success is not necessarily due to inexperience. Instead, team members believe that inadequate training and the lack of time for meetings hinder their potential the most.

What Factors Contribute to Team Success?

Top management support. A strong correlation was found between top management commitment and the overall success of teams. Managers and white-collar workers reported less support from top management than nonmanagers and blue-collar workers.

Training. A consistent, underlying theme throughout the survey was team members' strong belief in training as the key to team success. In fact, team members who have received training rated their team's performance (on a variety of measures) significantly higher than those whose teams had not received training.

Voluntary participation. The overall success of teams is significantly higher in teams where members participate of their own free will. Voluntary groups are more motivated and, as would be expected, perform at higher levels. Since many organizations are moving to a team-based structure, this finding suggests that differences between voluntary and mandatory participation on teams need to be minimized or eliminated in internal communication activities, compensation, and other areas.

In one sense, the survey findings about team success may not be all that surprising, since any major change initiative will require management support, training, and the willingness of employees to participate. Rather, these results confirm what we already know to be important. What may be critical information for corporate executives and human resource managers is the specific ways they can support teams on the way to achieving success.

What Hinders Team Success?

Problems Facing Teams	Percentage Who Agree
1. Inadequate resources	49%
2. Inadequate time for meetings	46%
3. Lack of coordinated work schedules	46%
4. No/low reward systems	42%
5. Lack of decision-making authority	41%

The problems most frequently cited by respondents include inadequate resources (e.g., human and financial), lack of time for meetings, and lack of coordinated work schedules. Generally speaking, these hindrances pose a greater problem for teams in service companies than in product-based companies.

The lack of time for meetings is especially a problem in service companies (63 percent versus 36 percent in nonservice organizations). Small work sites contend the most with a lack of decision-making authority. This struggle may imply that authority is more centralized at the top in small organizations and that there is resistance to sharing this power, or it may suggest that corporate offices control the decision making and the sites do not have the authority to transfer decision making to the teams.

Teams with members from different plants or sites have unique problems as well. Chief among them are the difficulty of communicating on a regular basis (61 percent), the inability to coordinate schedules (58 percent), and the expense of meeting face to face (51 percent).

Lack of upper-management commitment also causes team members to struggle a great deal, especially white-collar workers and managers who participate on teams. Overall, blue-collar team members perceive their organizations' top management as being more committed than their white-collar counterparts. Team members indicating a lack of top

337

management support reported that their management appears reluctant to offer teams any decision-making authority (61 percent), provides few, if any, rewards (57 percent), provides inadequate resources (53 percent), won't participate (50 percent), doesn't trust the team's ability (47 percent), and provides no recognition (46 percent).

The Stress of Meetings

Stress seems to be a major consequence of working in the team environment, with team meetings as the major cause, according to more than half the respondents (53 percent). Although the majority of team members claimed there is not enough time for meetings — which in itself is stressful — once the teams do meet, they have a host of other problems to contend with. Staying focused, having difficulty in reaching consensus, having to spend an inordinate amount of time in meetings, and leading meetings are the most troublesome issues. Working with different types of people is not a significant problem.

The Impact of Organizational Change

The Impact of Downsizing

Factors	Percentage Who Agree
1. I work harder.	73%
2. I am confused about direction due to mixed messages	71%
3. It is hard to aim for long-term solutions	65%
4. I have too many clerical/administrative duties.	49%
5. I have new opportunities for growth.	43%
6. I have become more efficient.	43%
7. I have no time to learn new skills.	43%
8. I have greater decision-making authority.	37%

Downsizing

What has euphemistically been called "organizational restructuring" has become a fact of life for many North American companies. In fact, more than one-third of respondents (36 percent) reported their companies are currently going through efforts to downsize. Large companies and white-collar teams are feeling the impact of downsizing the most.

As one might anticipate, the impact of downsizing on teams is mostly negative, with a majority of respondents claiming that they work harder (73 percent), are confused about company direction (71 percent), and have difficulty aiming for long-term solutions (65 percent). Once again, teams in service industries are having the toughest time, with nearly three-quarters (72 percent) of service team members reporting that a lack of time to learn new skills is a major consequence of downsizing. Only 27 percent of non-service teams reported this problem.

The impacts of downsizing are not all negative, however. Positive effects include new opportunities for growth (43 percent), being more efficient (43 percent), and having greater decision-making authority (37 percent). Respondents from white-collar teams in particular have acquired greater decision-making authority as a result of downsizing. Downsizing can also have a positive impact on teams as a whole, with 35 to 40 percent of teams reporting improved skills in setting priorities, increasing collaboration, and improving team communication.

The Role of Temporary and Contract Workers

As any manager who has survived a downsizing will agree, the number of employees may decrease, but the amount of work seldom does. In the struggle to get business done with fewer employees, North American companies are using an ever-increasing number of contract and temporary workers, and these workers are finding their way onto teams. Temporary or contract workers have a place on 20 percent of the teams represented in this survey.

Teams that use temporary or contract workers tend to be more successful than those that don't, even though respondents agreed it is sometimes difficult for temporary workers to buy into the organization's vision. Almost 70 percent of team members believe contract workers meet immediate work needs, and 52 percent believe these workers bring new ideas to the team.

The Impact of Temporary and Contract Workers

Factor	Percentage Who Agree
1. They meet immediate work needs.	70%
2. It is hard for them to buy into the organization's vision.	57%
3. They bring new ideas to the team.	52%
4. They bring energy and enthusiasm to the team.	42%
5. Permanent employees fear being replaced by them.	20%

What Is Surprising about Working on Teams?

In an attempt to go beyond the numbers to learn how team members really feel about working in the team environment, the authors of this study included one open-ended question: "What one thing has surprised you most about working on a team and why?" The response to this question was considerable, with the majority of survey participants taking the time to share their personal perspectives.

The most frequently mentioned positives about working on a team were the abundant cooperation and communication among team members and each individual's willingness to contribute to common goals. Respondents seemed especially impressed by the synergy that develops among team members, as well as by the positive, supportive environment that teams provide.

The next most-common response had to do with productivity. Comments included: "project objectives were accomplished more quickly and efficiently," "the group dynamic induced energy and enthusiasm," and "the strengths of the whole team overrode the weaknesses of the individual." Additional surprises had to do with the creativity of the team and with better understanding and communication among departments.

Not all surprises about working on teams, however, were pleasant ones. Nearly one-third of the comments dealt with the negative aspects of working on a team that arose due to personal politics or conflicting agendas. Respondents also were surprised by "deep-rooted authoritarian thinking," team members who are "back-stabbing and resistant to team efforts or change," and the extreme difficulty in reaching agreement or consensus.

Some respondents went beyond comments about the surprises inherent in working on teams and offered their insight into what makes teams more effective. Several of them conveyed the importance of having a good team leader. Many cited communication skills as essential for their further development, including training in meeting leadership and meeting participation, decision making, presenting ideas, process management, and basic interpersonal skills.

Teams Are Here to Stay

The widespread acceptance of teams, combined with their tremendous ability to achieve strategic goals related to quality and customer satisfaction, clearly indicates that teams and teamwork are here to stay. As the Association for Quality and Participation/Zenger Miller study reveals, however, helping employees adapt to the team environment is not necessarily easy.

Interestingly, the research revealed that many marketplace and demographic factors presumed to be major impediments to team success were being overcome through the considerable flexibility of team members. This can be viewed as a real plus. However, the study does suggest some important conclusions for executives and human resource practitioners.

First, teams should be allowed more time for learning and for meetings, even when productivity suffers initially. This kind of support can be one strong indicator of true management commitment to the teams. Second, organizations need to minimize the differences between voluntary and mandatory participation on teams and between what is "regular work" versus "teamwork."

Third, due to the considerable stress that results from inappropriate and/or ineffective meetings, team leaders need to intervene quickly when problems arise. Fourth, to address the uneven distribution of work and to enhance team creativity, companies should consider using more temporary and contract workers.

Fifth, while downsizing is in itself a major harbinger of stress, there are positives to be gained. Team members can benefit from the opportunities to learn new skills, to increase collaboration among team members and other colleagues, and to improve communication both within and beyond the team.

Finally, as the study shows, teams throughout North America are feeling the heat from a perceived lack of resources. Insufficient resources ultimately can impede a team's continued development and success. Therefore, it is imperative that organizations identify the types of human and financial resources teams need and provide them to the teams on a timely basis.

As the late quality expert W. Edwards Deming once said, "No one person knows as much as a team." The encouraging findings from the AQP/ZM research indicate that team members generally know what they need in order to be effective, and they ardently want to make a difference. Organizations that truly capitalize on team member brainpower and commitment can find teams a most helpful tool in mastering the challenges of today's marketplace, and finding new and creative ways to deal with organizational and societal issues.

Team Surveys: Final Observations

Teams in the United States survey their customers more frequently than Canadian teams (86 percent versus 68 percent).

More Canadian team members feel their teams are successful in dealing with domestic and global competition than do members of teams in the United States. Canadians are less likely than Americans to receive training in how to work on teams. Nearly all U.S. team members in the study (92 percent) received training, whereas 71 percent of Canadian team members received training. Possibly as a result of this, Canadian team members are more likely to deal with a problematic member by simply removing him or her from the team.

Significantly more Canadian teams report inadequate resources as a problem than do U.S. teams (66 percent versus 47 percent). Significantly more Canadian team members feel contract workers bring new ideas to the team than do U.S. teams (92 percent versus 49 percent).

341

About the Contributors

Amy J. Katz, Ph.D.

Amy J. Katz, Ph.D. is a social psychologist and Director of Educational Services and Research at the Cincinnati, Ohio-based Association for Quality and Participation (AQP). Prior to joining AQP, she consulted for organizations in the public and private sectors and served for seven years as an internal consultant on employee involvement and organization change with GE Aircraft Engines. She has also had five years of experience as a medical social worker at the University of Cincinnati Medical Center.

Darlene Russ-Eft, Ph.D.

Darlene Russ-Eft, Ph.D. is Director of Research Services in the San Jose, California corporate office of Zenger Miller. She has responsibility for directing the company's work with clients in the areas of research, needs assessment, and evaluation. She also has responsibility for all corporate market and product research activities. Her 20-year career includes positions as Senior Research Scientist with the American Institutes for Research, and Research Fellow with the Human Performance Center and the Center for Research on Learning and Teaching at the University of Michigan.

Linda Moran

Linda Moran is an Executive Consultant with Zenger Miller. Based in Simsbury, Connecticut, her area of specialty is work team strategy and implementation. She is a co-author of the best selling business book *Self-Directed Work Teams: The New American Challenge* (Irwin Professional Publishing, 1990). This book has become a widely popular "how-to" guide for organizations implementing self-directed work team initiatives.

Lilanthi Ravishankar

Lilanthi Ravishankar is Market Research Manager with Zenger Miller, based in San Jose, California. She has primary responsibility for the management of market research projects and data analysis and reporting. Prior to joining Zenger Miller, she attended the Master's Program in Sociology and Demography at the University of Texas at Austin.

29

Implementation Myopia to Implementation Mania: Five Ways to Make the Transition

Dominick Volini, Ph.D.

"Our redesign for the manufacturing line was spectacular, our teamwork was the best I've ever experienced, and maybe sometime next year one of our ideas may even make it to the shop floor," a design team member reminisced and lamented. What went wrong? Why is the redesign of manufacturing still in a three-ring binder and not contributing to organization prosperity? Because the team did everything very well regarding the design specifications but they neglected the equally important set of success criteria—transition specifications.

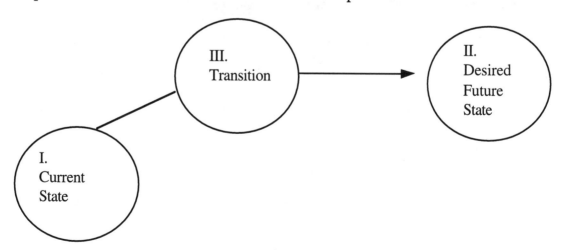

If we reflect on the three arenas for design team energy, usually the arenas that get the most attention are the current state (I) and desired future state (II). Transition (III) is left to happen essentially by good will. Teams exhaust themselves by making sure the current state is thoroughly analyzed and the new design, the desired future state, is cutting edge and marketable upstairs. The transition state gets lost by neglect.

But here is the good news. If the team thinks and acts *transition* from the very inception of the project, more redesigns can see the light of day, and implementation myopia can turn to implementation mania. Here are five techniques drawn from over a decade of design teams' experience that help people realize the true goal of any redesign effort: implementation.

1. Focus on the future, beyond report-out.

Teams often fall into a myopic drive to complete the task of designing a new organization. Teams want their ideas to be accepted and they become concerned that they will be perceived as being too radical on the one hand or not creative enough on the other. This concern compels teams to limit their horizons to just developing their "baby" and they lose the real goal of implementing change.

A major technique to allow a team to look beyond the design phase is to create a Program Evaluation and Review Technique (PERT) chart that includes a time frame for implementation. Then assign team members accountability to plan the transition and include these transitions plans in the design report-out. The "deliverable" becomes expanded from design only to design and implementation together.

A contact-lens manufacturing redesign team projected over a 3-year period, using a timeline chart, a major redesign effort for soft lenses. They went beyond implementation of this design and began thinking of continous change, due to continuous change in the technology.

2. Over-communicate about the new design options.

Rather than spring a completed, fully thought-out plan on the target population for fear of criticism, accept the reality that there may be some great observations out there that will not only enhance the design itself but may ease the transition.

To get these great enhancements, the design team needs to communicate widely about what they are considering. These communications can be multimedia—written, verbal, video, or audio. The most simple way to communicate and get feedback is for each team member to have an established constituency they are responsible for informing on a routine basis. They can then call their constituency together and hold quick meetings, meet informally, send out written material, or use all three approaches.

Another strategy is to hold periodic update meetings or send out newsletters on a regular interval to the entire work force. Some teams video an update report and distribute cassettes for broader audiences.

344

The value of these sessions is twofold. First, the design team can receive valuable feedback for design and transition improvements. Second, the rest of the work force can start mental preparation for the inevitable turmoil that change brings.

In a gas and oil supply company a design team held "town hall" meetings once a month with display booths showing their progress and then held general question/answer sessions toward the end. Pizza and soft drinks were offered to entice people to come.

3. Broaden the circle.

The team members do not possess all the knowledge required to both design and implement a major organizational change since there are often social issues and politics that need to be considered in a smooth transition. Even if we allow that the technical issues can be adequately solved by the team members (which may be a precarious assumption) the broader population can be included in clever ways during the whole process of design and transition planning to ensure implementation.

One method used by teams to expand their circle is to maintain an "empty" chair during meetings. This chair is filled by either inviting people to sit in on the meeting and comment as appropriate, or providing a method for people to self-select if they wish to comment on the proceedings. This can have a temporary downside of making meeting management messy but the longer term benefit to the ultimate team product, the team process, and the credibility in the work force can be of greater value.

Another way to broaden the team is to conduct "focus groups" of the work force on the team products. These marketing meetings provide access to a wide range of information while also keeping the team current on the organization and the impact of their task.

A paper producer had all design teams conduct "sunshine sessions" in public areas, such as the cafeteria. Co-workers were encouraged to sit in and just listen or make comments during periodic input breaks designed for just such interaction.

4. Experiment, pilot, and demonstrate some features of the new design early in the process. Get feedback even before all the parts are put together.

Partial implementation also allows the workplace to adjust while giving valuable information not only about the design itself, but the possible transition issues that may arise.

The partial trials can be within one department or across the whole organization. Two critical factors make these tests work best. First, frame the pilot, set the boundaries, measurements, and time frame very explicitly. What often sinks pilot programs is lack of understanding about when the program starts and stops, who will measure it, and how it fits with the whole change. Rather than evaluating critical elements of the future design, feedback gets lost.

345

The second critical factor in creating a demonstration program is to choose a credible manager. Feedback is only as good as the evaluator. The team needs to set up a strategic alliance with the manager to test their product. They do not need compliance or hostility. They need professional assessment that will contribute to both the design and transition plans as well as the spirit of change in the organization. The work force puts more faith in *who* says something about a design feature than about the design feature itself.

The primary emphasis here is to use the pilot project as both an opportunity to try out design ideas and to test reactions to change. One successful pilot at a tag and label manufacturer actually set up a trial line using new designs and then rotated people through. Many important improvements were made based on the feedback, and the subsequent implementation went very smoothly.

5. Face your fears.

What keeps teams from becoming creative and following through to full implementation is their own ambivalence about their task and their fears about task accomplishment. This calls for team building in order for the team to understand their own potential dysfunctional differences, as well as frank and frequent dialogue among the team, the sponsoring management, and the work force about the real and imaginary problems arising from the new design. This type of dialogue not only benefits the design and transition, but it sets a standard for organization discussion of issues beyond the present scope of the team.

Team building sessions and dialogue sessions need to be periodically set up throughout the PERT chart. Even when people complain, as they inevitably will, that "we don't have time for this team discussion, we need to get the job done!" hold firm and face your fears. This, too, may be avoidance.

Several design teams have put aside one half-day meeting every few weeks to explore their own team dynamics or the interaction of themselves with others. Sometimes they use paper and pencil instruments with discussion, sometimes modified "ropes courses" and sometimes classical survey/feedback/action-planning methods.

These five ideas to get design teams to include implementation in their task will only help if the rest of the conditions for success are also fulfilled, such as, accurate determination of new requirements, innovative new processes, and a non-adversarial work environment. One guarantee is made, however. The use of one or more of these techniques will transform the design team from implementation myopia to implementation mania.

About the Contributor

Dominick Volini is a partner in Block Petrella Weisbord, Inc. He focuses on achieving organizational results by working with clients to determine their organizational goals and the consultation services needed to reach them. Of primary importance in goal clarification is their relationship to customers, their commitment to quality services and products, their standards for productivity, cost containment, and employee involvement. Most often his consultation involves a strategic design to align the change effort with the organization's mission and the way people in the organization prefer to work.

Dominick works with industrial, professional, and not-for-profit organizations. He has held management and line positions in various work settings. He earned a B.A. (UCLA), M.A. (New School for Social Research), and Ph.D. in Clinical Psychology (University of Windsor, Canada).

He is a registered Psychologist in the State of New York, and belongs to the American Psychological Association, the National Organization Development Network, and is the Executive Director, The International Society for the Psychoanalytic Study of Organizations.

30

How to Measure the Results of Work Teams
Jack Zigon

Introduction

Many U.S. businesses are using self-directed and cross-functional work teams as a way of improving their competitiveness in customer satisfaction, cost reduction, product quality, and new product development cycle time. For the most part, measurement of these teams has focused on either organizational result measures or team process measures, neither of which gives the precision needed to fine-tune the team's efforts. And a team that can't measure itself can never become a truely self-managed work team.

This article will present a process that self-directed and cross-functional work teams can use to develop measures for themselves. The process integrates five existing models and describes the steps a team can use to create both team objectives and objectives for individual team members that directly support the team's results. Examples of ongoing applications in U.S. companies will also be presented.

Types of Teams

Lawler and Cohen (1992) define three general categories for teams and describe just how pervasive teams have become in America.

- Nearly 87 percent of all Fortune 1000 companies are using *parallel teams*, groups of individuals working in parallel to the existing organizational structure to improve quality. Examples are quality circles and other temporary problem-solving teams.
- Nearly 100 percent of all companies are using *project teams*, usually cross-functional teams brought together to complete a clearly defined task lasting several months to several years. After the project is completed, the team disbands. Examples include product development teams or a team to open a new plant.
- 47 percent of all Fortune 1000 companies are experimenting with *permanent work teams* as the way of getting work done. These teams are not outside the organizational structure, they *are* the

349

organizational structure. For example, Kansas City-based Hallmark Cards is using cross-functional teams made of designers, marketers, and production and distribution employees to handle the creation and launch of new greeting cards for a particular holiday (Hammer and Champy, 1993).

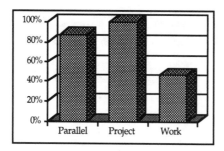

Figure 1. Percent of Fortune 1000 companies using three types of teams (adapted from Lawler and Cohen, 1992)

The process presented in this article is most worthwhile when used with project and permanent work teams, especially with cross-functional ones. The transient and part-time nature of parallel teams results in a situation where the cost of developing and maintaining a measurement system usually exceeds the value of the system to the organization.

Five Measurement Models

The team measurement process this article describes grew out of the integration of five separate performance measurement models:

- Balanced scorecard (Kaplan and Norton, 1992; 1993)
- Performance Pyramid (Lynch and Cross, 1991)
- Process re-engineering (Hammer and Champy, 1993)
- Accomplishment identification (Gilbert, 1978)
- White-collar employee performance measurement (Zigon, 1992; 1993)

Kaplan and Norton (1992, 1993) called for a balanced corporate scorecard that goes beyond the typical financial measures to track the four key elements of a company's strategy (customer, financial, internal business, and innovation and learning). Cross' model (Lynch and Cross, 1991) expands this idea and makes more explicit connections to corporate strategy, business processes, and department-level work. Hammer (Hammer and Champy, 1993) describes a model for defining and improving key, cross-functional business processes. Teams eligible for measurement are either assigned to improve processes or are made up of individuals who make the process work.

MBO-type measurement systems can fail to improve performance because they can allow people to measure activity rather than results. Gilbert's performance engineering model (1978) builds on this finding and emphasizes measurement based on accomplishments rather than activity. Zigon (1992, 1993) describes the specific steps needed to address the hard-to-measure, *qualitative* aspects of work.

Each model will now be explained in more detail and then organized into a seven-step process for creating team and individual performance objectives.

Organization Measures Provide a Context for Team Measures

Teams do not exist in a vacuum. They are part of an organization with business units, work processes, and departments. A team's goals should be based on and supportive of the goals of the organization above and around it. Cross' Performance Pyramid (Lynch and Cross, 1991) suggests a way of identifying performance measures at four levels within an organization.

1. *Organization* — The organization's measures are defined by the corporate strategy and business unit objectives. Key business operating systems are identified and the teams responsible for them are defined.
2. *Business process* — The key business operating systems are flow-charted or mapped to identify the results, hand-offs, and opportunities for measurement.
3. *Team* — Team results are defined and individual results that support the team process are identified. Measures are created for both quantitative and qualitative aspects of these results.
4. *Individual* — Individual measures are defined as a combination of team and individual accomplishments.

Figure 2 illustrates potential general measures at each level of the organization.

At the highest levels of an organization, corporate strategy is key. Measures that allow the success of the strategy to be measured need to be created early in the process.

A business unit (division, etc.) is interested in two general kinds of measures, financial and market. While financial measures (profit, cash flow, balance sheet and income statement type numbers) are very common, too often there seems to be a lack of marketing measures at the business unit level. Measures such as market share, position in market, etc. are often missing from executives' incentive compensation objectives to give a real-world check on the always present financial measures.

Moving down the pyramid, the work has to get done inside the business units. And it usually involves a business operating system, or sequence of process steps that cuts *across* the organization's hierarchical structure. A sequence of steps that starts with the receipt of a customer order, moves through production and distribution, and ends up with a satisfied customer is an example of a business operating system. Other

351

examples of business operating systems are the process an oil company uses to locate new reserves or the production process used to print greeting cards.

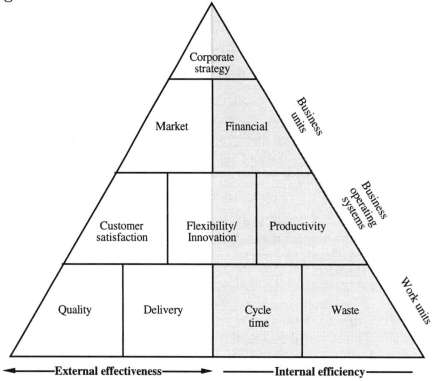

Figure 2. Cross' Performance Pyramid (adapted from Lynch and Cross, 1991)

More detailed measures are needed at this level of the pyramid, as profit and market share are too gross to be useful. To achieve the financial and market goals, the business operating system must improve performance in the areas of customer satisfaction, flexibility/innovation, and productivity. How to use a map of the operating system to create relevant performance measures will be discussed later.

At the department or work unit level, customer satisfaction is supported by quality and delivery measures: are you meeting the customer's quality requirements and do you deliver when you say you will? Flexibility is supported by delivery and cycle time. If you can complete the process in less time you have a better chance of meeting the delivery schedule or changing the process to meet new customer requirements.

As Kaplan and Norton's (1992, 1993) balanced scorecard concept recommends, the pyramid provides a balanced set of performance measures. The left half of the pyramid represents external, customer-oriented measures, while the right side measures internal, company-oriented measures. The left side provides a "real-world" check on the right side's measures.

Re-engineering and Process Maps Identify Measures

Hammer's business process re-engineering model (Hammer and Champy, 1993) is the next source of guidance for developing team performance measures. Hammer has said that incremental changes in quality as a result of continuous improvements are sometimes not enough to remain competitive. What is often required is a complete re-engineering of the business processes that the customer is interested in.

The mapping (and re-engineering) of the business operating system work flow identifies customer contact points and the process used to service the customer at each of those points (See Figure 3). The final product the customer receives is also identified during this mapping and re-engineering process. The work flow diagram for a team can identify three places for measurement: the final product, hand-offs, and the process steps in the work flow.

The final product the customer receives can be evaluated in terms of customer satisfaction and flexibility/innovation and the entire work flow can be evaluated in terms of flexibility/innovation and productivity.

At the department level, the hand-offs between departments can be evaluated based on delivery and quality. The boxes or process steps can be evaluated using waste and cycle time measures.

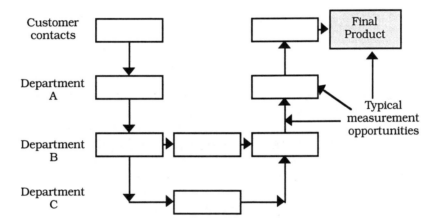

Figure 3. Schematic of business process flow with team measurement opportunities identified

Team and Individual Measures Flow from the Process Map

Up to this point, the models have given guidance only on how to create *team* measures. But most employees on a team want to know what the team's goals are *and* what their role is in helping the team be successful. And a combination of team and individual objectives allows the team leader to more effectively manage the team and its individual players. The process map can be used to create a role-result matrix which will help us identify individual objectives which directly support the team's objectives.

353

A role-result matrix is a table with a simplified version of the business operating system work flow along the top, and the team members listed down the left side (See Figure 4). The team members could be either individuals, functions, or departments. Most role matrices of this type list responsibilities or tasks in each cell. But Gilbert's work in performance engineering (1978) suggests a better content.

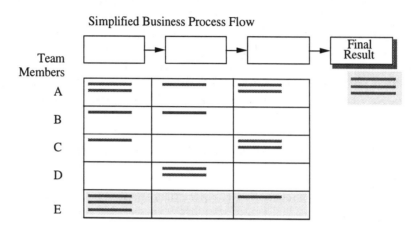

Figure 4. Schematic of role-result matrix

Gilbert found that better employee performance could be obtained by focusing measurement efforts on the valuable *accomplishments* of the best performers, rather than on the behaviors (tasks or responsibilities) they used to produce these accomplishments. It's cheaper to evaluate an accomplishment because you don't have to be there to watch the activity that produced the accomplishment. And measuring accomplishments fosters employee freedom to be creative in producing the accomplishment rather than stifling their creativity by demanding conformance to an arbitrary behavioral standard. This produced a leaner measurement system that cost less to maintain and reinforced employee creativity. Accomplishments are the end results of a business process that a customer needs. They are always defined from the *customer's* perspective.

Sometimes the best definition of an accomplishment is only subtly different from the obvious result. For example, an internal training function might be held accountable for conducting training sessions. This would lead to measures such as the number of classes held, number of students taught, cost/class, etc. But line management isn't interested in classes, they want *competent employees!* Changing the definition of the accomplishment to competent employees leads to measures such as percent of learning objectives met, number of employees using what they learned on the job, or changes in job performance after training. These are far different measures than the training sessions measures.

Using this idea, we answer the following question for each cell of the role-result matrix, "What accomplishments does this team member have to produce to support this step of the work flow?" The question is re-peated for each member and each step in the work flow.

The results in any given column describe how the team must work together to support that step in the work flow. The results for any given row are the results that an individual must produce to support the team's results (see Figure 5).

To summarize, measures for the entire team will flow from three points in the team's work flow (final result, hand-offs, and process steps) and the measures for any member of the team will flow from the accomplishments the member has to contribute to support each step in the work flow.

This combination of team and individual measures can be used to make performance appraisal systems more "team-friendly." Any individual's performance objectives will be a combination of team measures, individual measures that support the team, and other non-team related measures.

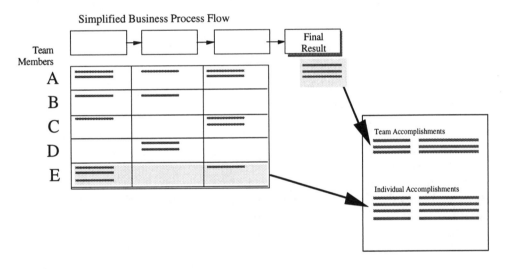

Figure 5. Each team member's objectives include team and individual measures

How to Create Performance Measures and Standards

The models up to this point have identified what should be measured, but not the details of *how* to write performance standards for either the team or the individual members. Some teams contain research scientists, customer service reps, graphic artists, and design engineers and as such are usually much more difficult to create standards for because of the qualitative nature of this creative work.

Zigon's work in measuring this white-collar employee work is the final model needed to measure team performance (Zigon, 1992; Zigon,

1993; Philips, 1994). Developing performance standards for a difficult-to-measure position such as a graphic artist starts with a clear definition of the customers of the position and what accomplishments these customers need from the position. Measures for each accomplishment are first developed at a general level (quantity, quality, cost or timeliness) and then at a more specific level. Finally standards are set that represent meeting or exceeding expectations.

Zigon found that the key to developing useful standards for these positions is not trying to measure everything with numbers. The accomplishments of some work can't be meaningfully measured with numbers, but *can* be *described* using words. The key is verifiability—can we verify that the performance standard has been met or exceeded? If so, the standard will be useful. Numeric measures are easy to verify, but there are other equally valid measures. Verifiable *descriptive* performance standards have three components: a judge, what the judge looks for, and a verifiable description of what would represent meeting expectations.

Seven-Step Process for Writing Team and Individual Performance Objectives

Models, while useful, fall short in practicality unless they can translate into specific techniques that can be applied in real-life situations. These models form the underpinning for a seven-step process for creating team and individual performance objectives.

1. Review and revise organizational and business unit measures.
2. Review and revise business operating system measures.
3. Map the business process.
4. Identify team measurement points.
5. Identify individual accomplishments that support the team's process.
6. Develop team and individual performance measures.
7. Develop team and individual performance standards.

The following is an explanation of each step along with examples drawn from various organizations' applications of the techniques. A quick-reference summary of the steps appears at the end of the article. (See Attachment 30-A.)

Steps 1 and 2. The first two steps suggest that a *review and revision of organization, business unit, and business operating system measures* is in order. Questions such as, "Do the business unit measures flow from and support the corporate strategy? If only financial measures are being used, why? Are there measures to evaluate both strategic success and market results? Are there measures for customer satisfaction? Flexibility or innovation? Productivity?" A cross-functional team responsible for a Valentine's Day greeting card line might have a performance pyramid similar to Figure 6.

Pyramid Level	Generic Measure	Specific Measure
Strategy		• $ sales from new channels • # new outlets opened
Business Unit	Market	• % market share growth • % market share over nearest competitor
	Financial	• % ROI • $ sales/Division • $ stock value
Business Operating System	Customer satisfaction	• Focus group opinion • Value exceeds price
	Innovation/ Flexibility	• # new products • Product cycle time reduced to 11 months
	Productivity	• Cost reduction per stock-keeping-unit
Department and Work Unit	Quality	• # complaints from production
	Delivery	• % development milestones met
	Cycle Time	• % reduction in artwork development time
	Waste	• # production delays due to incomplete or wrong hand-offs

Figure 6. Example performance pyramid for greeting card cross-functional team

Executives responsible for the team define a strategy and two global measures. The corporate strategy was to break out of a limited distribution channel made up primarily of company-owned greeting card stores and distributing its cards through every retail outlet customers might expect to find greeting cards (department stores, drug stores, etc.). The global measures (dollar sales from new channels and number of new outlets opened) will be used to evaluate how well the strategy is working.

At the business unit level, two market share and three financial measures are set by the executives. The expansion into new distribution channels should result in market share growth both on an absolute level and compared to their nearest competitor. Financially they want to make these investments keeping an eye on return on investment, total dollar sales and the effect on the stock price over the long term.

Step 3. Map the business process says to identify the team's customers, the products/services the customers need, and identify all the major process steps and hand-offs that lead to the final product the customer receives. Change the process to simplify it and increase the value to the customer. This leads to the next step.

Step 4. Identify the team measurement points. The final products of the team are always worth measuring, as are selected hand-offs (arrows) or work processes (boxes) on the diagram.

357

A cross-functional exploration and exploitation team at American Exploration Co., a Houston-based oil company, defined their business process with the flow in Figure 7.

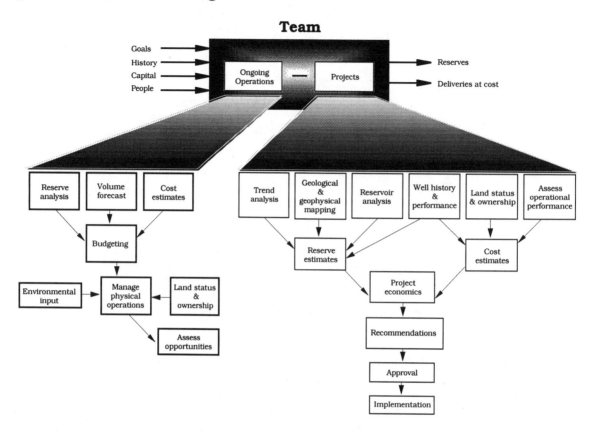

Figure 7. Example work flow for cross-functional oil exploration team

They were able to use the diagram to create team measures for total oil reserves and oil deliveries made at a given cost plus one surprise measure. Getting projects approved and implemented on a timely basis is one key to profitability for an oil company. The diagram made it obvious that flow time through all of the boxes on the right side of the diagram was a measure that was critical to the overall success of the team, but one which had never been measured before.

Step 5. Identify individual accomplishments that support the team's process. This is where the role-result matrix is built. The team members are listed down the left side and the work process goes across the top, with accomplishments needed to support each process step inside the cells. Figure 8 shows part of the role-result matrix for three tasks and five functions of the oil exploration team.

Work processs→ ↓Team members	1. Geological mapping	2. Reservoir analysis	3. Well history and performance
Exploitation Geologist	• Subsurface interpretation	• Log analysis • Volumetric maps	• Log correlation • Zone identification
Geophysicist	• Seismic interpretation • New exploitation and exploration prospects • Subsurface interpretation	• Amplitude and attribute studies • Volumetric maps	
Exploration Geologist	• New trends • New exploration prospects	• Recognition of depositional environment • Log analysis • Volumetric maps	• Log correlation • Zone identification
Reservoir Engineer	• Reservoir parameters that affect mapping	• Reservoir characterization • Material balance evaluation	• Production and performance anomalies • Volume forecasts • Analogies identified
Production Engineer			• Descriptions of well mechanics • Production and performance anomalies • Volume forecasts • Analogies identified

Figure 8. Example role-result matrix for cross-functional oil exploration team

A variation on the role-result matrix was used at Kentucky Fried Chicken. A new product development team used the team's *project milestones* as the basis for the top row of their role-result matrix (See Figure 9). This seemed to be a more manageable technique because the work process flow they mapped out had over 450 steps!

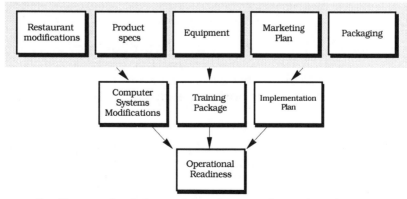

Figure 9. Example deliverables for product development team

Figure 10 is part of the role-result matrix based on these milestones.

Deliverables→ ↓ Functions	Restaurant modifications	Product Specs	Equipment
Marketing	• Customers' favorable response to restaurant modifications	• Customer promise • Product design	• Equipment criteria (from customer's view) • Evaluation of equipment vs. customer's viewpoint
Training	• Status of restaurant modifications		• Evaluation of equipment from operator perspective
Operations	• Operational impact of modifications • Store scoping (criteria, form, actual scoping) • Timetables and plan for doing the modifications • Qualified vendors • Risk management criteria • Modified restaurants • Costs and installation within schedules and budget estimate	• Operational fit of the product • Customer serving procedures • Operations shakedown testing • Market roll out • Product up to specs for use in consumer research and market test	• Equipment criteria from Ops perspective • Evaluation of equipment vs. Ops criteria • Operations shakedown testing • Changes to procedures • Suggestions for equipment optimization • Roundtable feedback information • Final equipment approval
R&D	• Location of equipment (with variations) • Variations on locations • Equipment designs and specs	• Product formulation and MRD testing • Draft of product procedures • Product nutritional information • QA program design • FP&L standards for product	• R&D criteria • Equipment concept • Evaluation of equipment vs. all criteria • Equipment spec. • Evaluation of equipment vs. all spec. • Final approval of equipment

Figure 10. Example role-result matrix for product development team

The last two steps in the process describe how to develop measures and performance standards for both the team and the individual members.

Step 6. Develop team and individual performance standards. For each accomplishment, select the general measures that are important (quantity, quality, cost and/or timeliness). For each general measure, answer the question, "How could I measure the (quantity, quality, cost or timeliness)?" If you can measure the accomplishment with numbers, record the units you would count or track the percentage of. If you can only describe the performance, list who will judge the work and what factors they will look for.

Step 7. Develop team and individual performance standards. If the measure is numeric, ask, "For this measure, how many would represent 'meeting expectations'?" Establish a range of performance above which special recognition is warranted and below which a performance problem exists.

If the measure is descriptive, ask, "For each factor the judge will look at, what would this person *see* that means a good job has been done?" List the judge, factors, and what constitutes a good job for each factor. Ask, "If this description equals 'meeting expectations,' what would 'exceeding' look like?" Write what the judge would see happening if these expectations were exceeded.

For example, a graphic designer produces logos for the marketing department at R.L. Polk & Co., a Detroit-based publishing and direct marketing firm. Figure 11 shows the measures and performance standards that were created with these steps. These standards will allow us to verify that the logos meet or exceed expectations. The first two standards are descriptive and the last three are numeric.

Accomplishment	General Measures	Performance Measures & Standards

Product logos developed	Quality	1. Supervisor is satisfied that the logo:
		  a. Reproduces well in various sizes and in three dimensions.
		  b. Can be used as one color, line art, and half-tone versions.
		  c. Conveys the function of the product.
		  d. Has a strong identity and reads well.
		  e. Uses type in a unique manner.
		  f. Has high-quality art.
		2. Client is satisfied that the:
		  a. Image conveyed to the public is the image the client wants to convey.
		  b. Message is clear.
		  c. Logo is easily recognizable.
		  d. Typeface matches the personality of product/program.

	Cost	3. Vendor costs are within the agreed-upon budget. 4. Designer's hours are within ±10 percent of the agreed upon budget.
	Timeliness	5. All agreed-upon deadlines are met.

Figure 11. Example descriptive and numeric performance standards for a graphic artist

Example Set of Team and Individual Performance Standards

A complete set of performance standards for a team is usually several pages long. It includes a list of the team's common standards as well as performance standards for each member of the team. The length of the listing is governed by two competing values: completeness and practicality. The list should be long enough to cover all the important facets of the team's performance, but not be so long that the time required to collect the data exceeds its value to the team or the organization.

The following represent a partial listing of the team and individual objectives from a Kentucky Fried Chicken product development team (see Figures 12 and 13).

Team Category	Example Team Performance Objectives
Customer	• 90 percent to 95 percent of customers say they are "likely" or "very likely" to purchase the product. • 50 percent to 75 percent of customers say they are "likely" or "very likely" to repurchase. • 10 percent to 15 percent sales increase, first 90 days.
Operations	• No negative impact on customer satisfaction scores. • Restaurant managers are satisfied that: The labor standards are accurate. They had enough storage capacity and the product was easy to store. The complexity of the procedure didn't prevent them from selling within required service and hold times. They were able to handle all customer questions about the product. All needed supplies were received on time and to spec. The procedure is simple enough to allow the food to be prepared consistently.
Financial	• 45 percent to 70 percent internal rate of return on investment.
Project management	• $5K to $10K national average capital/store. • Test completed by 9/92. • No more than $26.7 MM capital project investment.

Figure 12. Example of team performance objectives

Team Member	Example of Individual Performance Objectives

Operations person in charge of restaurant modifications	• 90 percent to 95 percent restaurant managers say they are satisfied that:
	    Utility hookups are in right location.
	    Utility service level meets equipment's needs.
	    No negative effect on restaurant operations.
	    Modification scheduling was coordinated with the restaurant's schedule.
	• VP Operations is satisfied that the modifications support the project's goals.
	• Modifications are completed by agreed-upon deadlines.
	• Installation is no more than 10 percent above estimate.

Marketing person in charge of product design	• Customer wants to buy the product based on multiple market research test data. • Store manager says that the product is doable in the restaurant environment during the single store test and multiple-store market test. • Design meets or falls below product cost targets.
Procurement person in charge of equipment	• Restaurant services and R&D sign off on equipment specs. • Specs and prototype are created by agreed-upon deadlines. • Equipment costs are ≤ 10 percent above budget for capital cost/store. • Installation is completed by agreed-upon deadlines. • Equipment has 99.5 percent to 99.8 percent uptime. • No retrofits are required. • 90 percent to 95 percent of service calls are responded to within 24 hours or the service contract terms. • 88 percent to 92 percent of repairs are completed correctly the first visit.

Information systems person	• Restaurant managers are satisfied that cash register changes have:
	    Minimized the keystrokes.
	    Keyboard overlay that matches data.
	• Download to cash registers occurs in time for training or the night before product roll out.

Training representative	• Procedure produces a consistent product.
	• Restaurant managers are satisfied that the training package:
	    Clearly communicated the procedures.
	    Is complete (job aids, procedures, etc.).
	    Fits restaurant environment.
	• Package arrives two weeks prior to product roll out date.

Figure 13. Example of individual performance objectives

Benefits of Measuring Work Team Performance

This process for measuring work team performance has the following positive results:

- *Reduces the time needed to create team measures.* The author was called upon to review the results of a Fortune 500 company's two-year team measurement effort. While the resulting measurement system was excellent, the process couldn't be replicated easily with the company's 100 other teams because of the resources and time required. The process described in this paper can produce a first draft of a measurement system in three to four weeks—a considerable reduction in cycle time!

- *Fosters team cohesiveness.* Helping a team develop its own measures can help a group of individuals become a team in less time. The process provides the team with a results-oriented development exercise that fosters team cohesiveness and defines its purpose in measurable terms.

- *Combines individual and team measures.* In the United States, most employees want measures of both their team's results and their individual contributions to the team. The process identifies both individual and team measures that promote cooperation while allowing individuals to be rewarded for their unique contributions to the team's overall results.

- *Builds on previous process re-engineering efforts.* Many companies are involved in process re-engineering. This team measurement model builds on the results from these analyses if they've been done, or demands a partial process analysis if one doesn't exist.

- *Allows performance appraisal of teams.* Most companies' appraisal processes are oriented toward individuals only. This usually results in performance objectives that create conflict between the individual and the team. This process provides the measurement data that allows performance appraisal systems to be expanded to include teams.

- *Supports team pay for performance.* Companies can't pay for performance unless they can first measure the performance. This process provides the data to pay individuals based on a combination of team and individual results.

- *Defines the hard-to-measure jobs.* Most measurement systems work well if you are measuring widget making or sales. Positions such as R&D scientist, graphic artist, customer service representative, design engineer, etc., are not easily measured with numbers. This process explains how to create verifiable performance standards for these kind of positions.

Summary

Developing team measures is a straightforward process if you keep in mind the following points:

- *Use different measures for different levels of the organization.* Don't try to automatically use the same measures at all levels of the organization. Look for the measures that make sense as you move down from organization to business unit, process and work unit or departments.

- *Start with customers and work flow.* When you get to the team level you'll save time by identifying the customer of the team and then defining the team's work process.
- *Re-engineer to get the right measures.* Measuring an ineffective process might improve its efficiency but you'll end up measuring the wrong things. Take the opportunity to re-engineer the process and identify the process steps and hand-offs that are worth spending resources to measure.
- *Measure accomplishments whenever possible.* Measuring behaviors is more expensive and tends to stifle creativity when compared to measuring results. You'll also save time when you use an accomplishment as your starting point for measurement.
- *Verifiability is the key.* Don't try to measure everything with numbers. If your goal is to verify that a result was done well or not, a good descriptive measure will sometimes work much better than a poor numeric measure.
- *Employee objectives = team + individual.* Rather than choosing between team and individual objectives, try measuring a combination of both. You'll have the common objectives that bond the team together and the individual data to recognize your stars and work with your lower performers.

Job Aid: How to Develop Team Measures

1. Review and revise organizational and business unit measures.

Do the business unit measures flow from and support the corporate strategy? If only financial measures are being used, ask why. Identify measures to evaluate both strategic success and market results.

2. Review and revise business operating system measures.

Are there measures for customer satisfaction? Flexibility or innovation? Productivity?

3. Map the business process.

Identify the team's customers and the products/services the customers need. Identify all major process steps (boxes) and hand-offs (arrows) that lead to the final product. Change the process to simplify it and increase value to the customer.

4. Identify team measurement points.

Always measure the final product. Decide which process steps and hand-offs are worth measuring. Measure processes using measures of waste and cycle time. Measure hand-offs using measures of delivery and quality.

5. Identify individual accomplishments that support the team's process.

Build a role result matrix with team members down the left side, key process steps across the top, and accomplishments needed to support each process step inside each cell.

6. Develop team and individual performance measures.

For each accomplishment, select the general measures that are important (quantity, quality, cost and/or timeliness).

For each general measure, answer the question, "How could I measure the (quantity, quality, cost or timeliness)?" If you can measure the accomplishment with numbers, record the units you would count or track the percentage of. If you can only describe the performance, list who will judge the work and what factors they will look for.

7. Develop team and individual performance standards.

The goal is verifiability. If the measure is numeric, ask, "For this measure, how many would represent 'meeting expectations' ?" Establish a range of performance above which special recognition is warranted and below which a performance problem exists.

If the measure is descriptive, ask, "For each factor the judge will look at, what would this person *see* that means a good job has been done?" List the judge, factors, and what constitutes a good job for each factor. Ask, "If this description equals 'meeting expectations,' what would 'exceeding' look like?" Write what the judge would see happening if these expectations were exceeded.

Bibliography

Gilbert, Tom. (1978). *Human competence: Engineering worthy performance.* New York: McGraw Hill.

Hammer and Champy. (1993). *Reengineering the corporation: A manifesto for business.* New York: Harper Business.

Kaplan, Robert S. and David P. Norton. (1992). The balanced scorecard—measures that drive performance. *Harvard business review*, January-February.

Kaplan, Robert S. and David P. Norton. (1993). Putting the balanced scorecard to work. *Harvard business review*, September-October.

Lawler, Edward E. and Susan G. Cohen. (1992). Designing pay systems for teams. *American compensation association journal, 1* (1) 6-18.

Lynch, Richard and Kelvin Cross. (1991). *Measure up! Yardsticks for continuous improvement,* Cambridge, MA: Blackwell Business.

Zigon, Jack. (1992). Performance appraisal lessons from thirteen years in the trenches. *1992 National Society for Performance and Instruction Conference Proceedings.* Washington, DC: National Society for Performance and Instruction.

Zigon, Jack. (1993) How to measure white-collar employee performance. *1993 National Society for Performance and Instruction Conference Proceedings.* Washington, DC: National Society for Performance and Instruction.

Philips, Jack (ed.). (in press, 1994). How a new appraisal system saved Yellow Freight System $20.8 million, In *Return on investment in human resource development: cases on the economic benefits of HRD,* Alexandria, VA: American Society for Training and Development.

About the Contributor

Jack Zigon is president of Zigon Performance Group, a management consulting firm specializing in the design and installation of custom performance management and performance appraisal systems. His latest work has resulted in a state-of-the-art model for measuring the performance of self-managed and cross-functional work teams. He has developed eleven performance appraisal systems for companies such as Hallmark Cards; General Dynamics/Lockheed; Yellow Freight System; United Telephone; Air Products and Chemicals; Kentucky Fried Chicken; Consumers Water; and R.L. Polk and Company. His projects have won four national awards and he is a frequent speaker at National Society for Performance and Instruction, American Society for Training and Development, Society for Human Resource Management, and American Compensation Association conferences.

31

Team Design of a Group Incentive Plan Brief Overview of the Model of Reinforcement
Jerry McAdams

STRATEGIC OBJECTIVES AND DESIRED CULTURE

Performance improvement through people is reinforced and accelerated by reward systems. All forms of reward plans in the system should be aligned with the strategic objectives and desired culture of the organization. One of the most basic of these objectives is to be able to attract and retain the most appropriate type of employees as an objective directly aligned with the base pay plan. Other objectives, along with their associated critical success factors, include profit; return to shareholders; financial ratios; productivity; market penetration; customer satisfaction or value; responsibility to the community; EPA standards, etc. Any objective that can be directly or indirectly influenced by the majority of the employee population should be supported by some portion of the reward system.

Culture can be shaped by the nature of the reward plans. A desired culture of teamwork is most effectively supported by at least one meaningful group incentive plan—one of personal growth and competency by a developmental pay plan.

A lack of alignment with either the organization's objectives or desired culture sends a contradictory message to employees. Alignment provides the opportunity for employees to affect those measures of an organization's success and allows the organization to maximize its investment in its employee asset.

TOTAL EARNING OPPORTUNITY

The total earning opportunity includes compensation (base pay, adjustments to base, benefits, capability pay) and reward and recognition plans (group incentive, employee involvement and recognition plans). It should be made clear that a reward system is not the only way to improve organizational performance. Far from it. Organizational development; TQM; new processes and products or services; re-engineering; proper hiring and orientation practices; succession planning and career development; training; communications; and involvement all are significant interventions. These processes are often thought of as *leading* interventions, however, only to be *followed* and *supported* by the reward system. Today, reward systems can *lead* by setting the tone, focus, and speed of a change process.

COMPENSATION

Compensation has been too broadly defined as anything that rewards people, while its real role is to attract and retain employees, improve individual performance, and develop employees' skills and competencies. Compensation represents from 95 to 99 percent of money spent on employees.

The fulfillment of the employee-employer contract (negotiated or implied) represents the bulk of the employee's earnings — base pay and benefits. They are, by definition, entitlements. It is unfortunate that the common adjustments to base pay—cost of living adjustments, merit increases in a performance management program, and bonuses given solely based on a manager's discretion—have also become entitlements, based on the market or subjective criteria. Entitlements are the essence of the primary objective of compensation—to attract and retain people. Entitlements and the objective of performance improvement, however, are at cross-purposes. The contingent relationship between performance and reward is critical for improvement. The only thing contingent in entitlements is showing up for work and following the rules. The challenge is to continue to refine the base compensation package to make it more flexible and responsive to an organization's needs and as a foundation for other reward plans.

Compensation is generally the cost of doing business and is critical to a business' day-to-day operations. There is little relationship between compensation plans and business success. Therefore, you cannot attribute success to the compensation plan.

Capabilities can restructure or adjust base pay in a more objective way—the acquisition of skills or competencies important to the organization. These skills and competencies can be taught, tested, and certified. Capabilities, particularly through the use of competency systems, are farther to the right in the continuum than compensation. There is a greater likelihood of results being attributed to the capability plan.

Either way—compensation or capabilities—the focus is on the individual, affecting performance from the bottom-up.

REWARD AND RECOGNITION PLANS

Reward and recognition plans have been too narrowly defined, as "after the fact" recognition of individual jobs well done. They are much broader, dynamic, and underutilized, for their objective is to improve business performance through people. The plans break into three types—recognition plans, group incentives, and employee involvement. Recognition plans celebrate events, recognize extraordinary people in the organization, reward activities and the accomplishment of projects, and provide small spot awards based on fellow workers' or management's opinion. Recognition plans keep the focus, interest, and activity on what an organization needs to do. They are slightly to the right of capability plans on the attribution continuum in that slightly more specific results can be attributed to the plan.

In group incentive plans, the strategic objectives of the organizational unit (anything from the whole corporation down to a work group) are translated into measures. Performance improvements reflected in these measures create rewards for generally all employees in the organization unit. The ever present question is one of financial rationale and attribution. How much was the gain and what is it worth? How much of it was due to the plan and the people? These issues are addressed in plan design, implementation, and reassessment. In any case, the business results are far more attributable to a group incentive plan than compensation, capabilities, and recognition.

Employee involvement plans come as team idea plans, continuous quality improvement teams, and ad hoc problem-solving or project teams. Their contributions are generally in the cost reduction, process improvement, and customer satisfaction arenas. A value is put, subjectively or objectively, on the contributions of employee involvement teams and team members are rewarded appropriately. In employee involvement plans in which the contribution is valued and rewarded, there is little question of attribution — the performance would not have improved without the employee involvement plan. Clearly the contribution came from those who suggested, developed, and implemented the change.

Reward and recognition plans are not "just a nice thing to do." They are the primary tools we have to improve business performance through our people, in a cost efficient way.

SUMMARY

Organizational success can be accelerated by investing in its people and expecting a return on that investment. The total earning opportunity must be a balance between compensation and reward and recognition plans to properly capitalize on our human assets.

Reinforcement Model

```
┌─────────────────────────────────────────────┐
│  Strategic Objectives and Desired Culture     │
└─────────────────────────────────────────────┘
                      │
                      ▼
┌─────────────────────────────────────────────┐
│           Total Earning Opportunity           │
└─────────────────────────────────────────────┘
```

| **Compensation**
Individual Focus
Bottom-up Performance | **Reward and Recognition**
Improve Business Performance
Top-down and Bottom-up Performance |

| **Compensation**
Attract, Retain, Improve Individual Performance | **Capability**
Develop Individuals | **Recognition**
Reinforcing the Process | **Group Incentive**
Improve Organizational Performance | **Employee Involvement**
Enabling Involvement; Rewarding Contribution |

Cost of Doing Business ──────────→ **Performance Improvement Results**

Performance and Attribution Continuum

Enhanced by performance management, assessment, education, communications, feedback, reassessment, and some fun

DESIGNING A GROUP INCENTIVE PLAN

Group incentive plans cover a wide range of reward plans aligning organizational objectives and employees. All the popular names (gain sharing, goal sharing, success sharing, etc.) are variations on the same theme:

- they focus on an organizational unit,
- define its measures of success, and
- reward all or some of the employees for improved performance based on all or some of the measurements.

Group incentives are the most powerful of all reward plans in aligning employees with organizational objectives.

Group Incentive Plan Definitions

Group – Any organizational unit; any group of people seen as a "set" when viewed from the top down. These can be the whole organization, a business unit, facility (location), department, or work group.

Incentive – Any type of award (cash or non-cash) made contingent on some measure of performance. It is not made based on largess or any other non-performance based criteria (that's a bonus).

Criteria That Define Group Incentive Plans

Group incentive plans have a pre-announced reward formula. People are told before the plan starts what they can earn based on each group performance measure. The formula also tells people *when* and *how* the plan will pay out.

Once the award is earned as a group, everyone in the group earns unless they are on probation. Group incentive plans do not limit awards to a few "winners" chosen by their supervisors. Programs that use management discretion to determine who is rewarded undermine team performance improvement. They rely on objective, measurable results. The only exception is when an employee is on probation, which may knock him out. Differentiation among employees is the purpose and responsibility of compensation, not group incentive plans.

The Development of a Group Incentive Plan – Overview

The macro view of the development is straightforward.
1. Top management decides on their "desired culture." They determine their primary objectives that can be influenced by the majority of the employees. They weight the objectives. They appoint a design committee.

2. The design committee lives up to its name — it designs the plan. The steps are:

    *   Assess the current plans and culture. (This may be done in conjunction with Step 1, giving top management more information to properly identify their desired culture and primary objectives.)
    *   Determine the measures for each objective.
    *   Determine the appropriate organizational units to be covered by each measure based on what's possible and reasonable.
    *   Set baselines and goals for each measure.
    *   Decide what amount of reward is necessary to motivate employees to reach the goal in each measure.
    *   Agree on who should be covered in the plan.
    *   With the help of appropriate financial departments, place a dollar value on the performance gain at goal for each measure. For those measures for which a dollar value of the gain cannot be determined, the goal achievement is expressed in terms of the measure itself.
    *   Calculate the return on payout (return on investment) at goal. If the return is not acceptable and reasonable, adjust the plan elements accordingly.
    *   Create the reward (payout) structure.

3. Agree with top management that the plan is justified to become a business strategy and worthy of their commitment and support.

THE DESIGN TEAM

Most plans are designed by a team of managers, usually numbering six to eight from the middle ranks. Teams with management and non-management members are also common. Members are generally appointed to the project. It takes about 45 working days over a fifteen-week time span to create a group incentive plan proposal for top management. The time invested and the span is shorter for service industries and longer for manufacturing. When nonmanagement employees are a part of the team, the number of working days doubles and time span increases slightly.

Some Rules for Getting the Job Done

"How to run effective team processes" is another one of those subjects extensively covered elsewhere, particularly effectively by Glenn Parker, author of *Team Players and Teamwork* and *Cross-Functional Teams*. The following are a few of the rules for making design teams effective:

1. Every team needs a champion. This person may or may not be a member of the team, but you need someone who can handle the

political intrigues that can scuttle a design process. Most champions are from top management and in the best of all worlds he/she would be involved and supportive throughout the design process. With no slight intended to HR/Compensation, the champion should be from a line, rather than a staff position.

2. The leader of the design team needs to be an influential line or executive staff person whose focus is strategic versus administrative.

3. Most of the stakeholders in the organization should be represented. At the same time, it's best to limit the team to from six to ten members. Anything beyond that can minimize effectiveness and create scheduling problems.

4. Teams should not be headed by someone from HR or Compensation but he/she should be included as a team member. The team leader should be someone from the line organization.

5. Always include someone from the appropriate financial departments. You need their expertise. You will be asking them to do a lot of the financial rationale. And at some point you're going to ask *them* to defend the plan, so *you* don't have to. It's always better received coming from "Finance".

6. A representative from MIS is also critical. If you're going to collect data and feed it back to people as measurements, it will be done through the organization's computer system.

7. Include someone from the organizational design or organizational effectiveness departments if there is such a structure.

8. Key line managers are just that. . .key.

9. Find someone who is familiar with computer modeling programs and invite him/her to participate. They need to have simple spreadsheet expertise. If you have any young, bright MBA bushy tails running around, they are perfect for this job. They don't have to be an official member of the design team. Of course, if the MIS representative can do this work, so much the better.

10. Never keep the design process secret. Members should feel free to tell fellow employees what they're up to, with the understanding nothing is certain until top management approves it. You don't want to create false expectations or set the grapevine on fire.

11. Do you need an outside consultant? It depends on how fast you want the process to go. A good consultant will enrich the process and save the team from going down blind alleys or reinventing the wheel. A bad one will show up with a plan already designed.

Once the team is formed, the first order of business is to make sure that everyone understands *why* they have been asked to develop a group incentive plan. If they think it is a compensation plan, designed to pay people more, you have started off on the wrong foot. A group incentive plan is part of the business strategy. It is an integral part of the management system to improve business performance. The rewards are a critical element in the mix, but not the objective.

Members also need to understand that the job doesn't stop when the plan design is approved although their participation on the team may end. *The power of the plan is in the implementation, not the design.* Therefore, the more the design team can keep implementation issues, as well as the plan parameters on the top of their mind, the better off they will be.

ASSESSING YOUR CURRENT PLANS AND CULTURE

The next step is to look at the reward plans that are already at work in your organization and decide what to do with them—keep them, modify them, or discard them. This step may be done in parallel with getting management's direction of primary objectives and desired culture. Assessment can give management more information with which to make those decisions.

You also want to find out what employees really think about how the organization works. If reward plans have a positive effect on the culture of an organization, it is important to know what's not so positive now. Identification of obstacles to success—real or perceived—in the minds of the employees can have some effect on the plan design. The real importance, however, is in how you implement and follow through.

EXISTING REWARD PLANS

You will probably be surprised at the sheer number of compensation and reward plans you will find when you go looking for them. Of course, there are the fundamental ones like base salary with its accompanying merit increases, cost of living adjustments, and benefit plans. There are also rewards for things like attendance, safety, and quality. Rewards, by definition, are anything that is reinforcing to people.

You would think you could go to the HR department to get this information, but they usually don't keep track of all of these plans. They will get you information on base pay, merit increases, COLA*, bonuses, and company dictated perks

There are often people responsible for suggestion plans, TQM, company-wide recognition plans and events, all of which can carry rewards. The heavy lifting comes from each operation. I've found that asking each manager to complete a matrix for those plans he/she controls or funds can ferret out the information in a reasonable time.

*Cost-of-living adjustments.

Here is a complete matrix based on a Midwest manufacturing company:

Plan Name	Objectives	Design & Organization Measured	# of People Covered	% Earning	Average or Median Award Value	Total Cost and Type of Award
Salary	• Attract and retain	• Defined by job • Individuals	4000	100%	$27,000	• $110 million • Cash
COLA	• Attract and retain	• Same % of base pay for all • All non-exempt as a group	2000	100%	$800	• $1.6 million • Cash
Merit Increases	• Attract and retain • Improve individual performance	• Based on performance mgmt; mgmt discretion • Exempt as individuals	2000	95%	$1,750	• $3.3 million • Cash
401k	• Retain	• 50% of all profit over threshold • All employees as a group	4000	100%	$1,250	• $5 million • Cash
Super Heroes	• Role models; retain	• Mgmt nomination • Individuals	3990	1%	$100	• $4000 • Merchandise

The formula for effective reward plans:

Effective Reward Plans =
Direction (Desired Culture + Business Objectives)
×
Power (Awareness + Performance Sensitivity + Value)

Direction
The Motivational Model of Culture

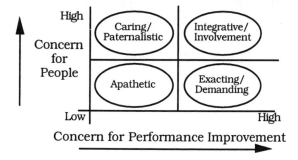

Desired culture is defined as not what the organization is now, but what your management wants it to be.

Business objectives are what management believes are the measures of success.

Awareness is the degree to which employees have the reward plan on "the top of their minds." A plan that has little awareness cannot do much for the organization.

Performance sensitivity is the relationship between the size of performance improvement and the size of the award.

Value is the value of the performance improvement to the organization and to the employees. Low value means little focus.

Assessing Your Reward Plans

Now it's time to assess your existing reward plans against the formula for effective reward plans. Do they support the desired direction in terms of culture and objectives? Are they "top-of-mind," performance sensitive, and valuable? Do they have management support, how much do they cost, and do they get results? An assessment can be as simple as looking at each reward through the filter of these questions and it will give you a snapshot of your reward plans.

Looking at this example, the majority of the cost is in the salary plan. That is to be expected and is a primary target for improvement by forward-thinking HR managers and consultants. For the purpose of explaining the process, let's assume these are all the plans in the organization. It is a *paternalistic* organization (note the employee perceived entitlements of COLA, 401k, and merit increase, and the management discretion driven Super Heroes employee-of-the-month plan). The organization's desired culture, however, is *Integrative/High Involvement*. "Teamwork" is the theme of every corporate communication.

The company's strategic objectives are profit, productivity, cycle time, and new products. The salary plans are paid out every two weeks; the Super Hero recognized monthly; all the rest are annual. Communication is limited to performance reviews, mailing out revisions of the plans whenever they occur, and the company newsletter article on the yearly payouts for the 401k and COLA. Super Heroes are announced each month in the newsletter and their picture is mounted in the Hall of Fame. The design of each plan is pretty standard, except the 401k which is based on a percentage of net profits over the amount necessary to provide a targeted return of equity — something *certainly* every employee understands.

How effective are these plans? Considering what the organization wants, not very effective.

Direction — Desired culture of *integrative/high involvement*. Only the 401k might be capable of supporting that desire since it is a reward for group performance. However, the measure is complex and remote , not to mention the fact that the award is deferred until termination or retirement. That deferral eliminates it as supportive of an *integrative/*

high involvement culture. The rest of the plans, salary excepted, are focused on individuals, not teamwork.

Direction — Business objectives of *profit, productivity, cycle time, and new products*. Again, with the exception of the remote 401k plan, none of the plans are based on any of these specific business objectives.

Power — *Awareness*. The salary plan has passive awareness, but will not affect how people perform. Super Heroes gets the most attention with 1 percent of the people being recognized. The rest have a high entitlement content and draw attention once a year.

Power — *Performance Sensitivity*. Salary is job-based and priced on the competitive labor market. COLA is sensitive only to the Consumer Price Index. Merit increases continually struggle to be individually performance sensitive, but with a pool of funds and subjective measures of individual performance, it becomes a distribution method rather than a performance sensitive plan. 401k is funded on a performance sensitive basis of profit, but it is dulled by the remote, complex formula and the deferral of the award into a retirement account. Super Heroes is a subjective selection process and most of the sensitivity is in those who don't get selected.

Power — *Value*. To the employees, they share $9.9 million in addition to salary, an average of $2475 this year, $1250 of which is put in a deferred retirement account. Forty people get a $100 merchandise award each year. To the organization, the only link to a performance gain is the profit-based 401k. I doubt that anyone would argue there is any connection between profit performance and this rather benign plan. I would characterize these plans as a $9.9 million investment in a "field of dreams" context — spend and maybe they will improve.

Desired culture, objectives, weighting

You have already done an assessment of the organization and have an agreement from top management on their desired culture. *Caring/ paternalistic, integrative/high involvement, or exacting/demanding* are the primary options. I doubt if anyone wants to be *apathetic*. Group incentive plans support *caring/paternalistic* or *integrative/high involvement* cultures, although most are applicable to moving toward *integrative/high involvement*. After getting the objectives and their measures of success from top management, the example matrix may look like this:

Objective	Broad Measure
Financial Performance	Profit or return calculation
Cycle Time	Days - order to payment
Productivity	Output divided by input
Quality	Cost of poor quality
Turnover	% voluntary resignations of total employment

Top management should establish the broad parameters for the plan design. For instance, they may decide what organizational units are to be included — whole company, division, facility, etc. Management may require that one or more specific measures be covered or addressed in the plan.

For instance, they may be very specific about the measure of financial performance being return on net assets or net income before taxes. The matrix then looks like:

Objective	Broad Measure	Weighting
Financial Performance	Profit or return calculation	25%
Productivity	Output divided by input	25%
Cycle Time	Days - order to payment	25%
Quality	Cost of poor quality	25%
		100%

The value of weighting is in the message it sends ("This is what is important around here") and as a distribution mechanism for awards (more about that later).

Where are we in this process?

- Top management has determined the desired culture, objectives, organizational units to be covered, and broad (hopefully) parameters for measures. They have also appointed a design team.
- Either after or in parallel with the step above, the team has made an assessment of the current reward plans and culture.
- Next, the team will determine the
    - measures for each objective
    - level of the organization to be measured and rewarded based on what is reasonable and possible

Measurement

Some key points that apply to group incentive plans are:

1. Be expansive in considering different measurements. Just because top management has given you some guidelines on measurement doesn't mean you cannot be creative. I've found top management to be open to new twists on their ideas about measurement criteria with solid rationale to back up the team's recommendation. Measurement is a lead, operational, or lag indicator of how well the organizational unit is doing against its business objectives. Remember that each objective can have more than one measure. "As measured by" doesn't have to be just one measure.

2. You should not and cannot reward based on every measure you have. Each objective probably has dozens of measures that apply — some more directly than others, of course. Measurement without reward is communication and performance feedback.

3. You have to be able to track the measure in a meaningful time frame. Poor systems can hold up performance feedback. If you are five weeks behind the end of a measurement and payout period, it is too late.

4. You have to be willing to openly communicate all elements of the measurement. That's how employees know how they affect the performance. If you measure productivity as dollars of controllable costs divided by insurance policy serviced and are unwilling to tell the people what makes up controllable costs, you've limited their ability to make a difference.

5. Knowing the historical performance of the measure helps. Most beginning points of payout are based on actual history. Guessing is risky business and should be avoided at all costs.

6. Check out any effects of seasonally or other outside influences (interest rates, supplier or customer changes, etc.) that would cause significant fluctuations in the measurement. Fluctuations will not eliminate the measurement from consideration but will have an effect on the plan design itself. This discussion correlates with base lines that we'll cover shortly. You'll find throughout this paper that the process isn't always linear. There is constantly a need to weigh different parts of the design against each other. Such is the case with determining the value of each measure.

7. Use the Watergate rule: Follow the money. Try to pick measures that will give the organization a financial gain, to be documented by Finance, when they improve. Not all measures will allow you to calculate a dollar value of the gain. Research shows that one of every three to five measures has a financial opportunity. They still are critical to meeting business objectives and can be used for group incentive plans. But try to find a few that all will agree add real value to the gain. This doesn't mean that you should only use financial measures. In fact, operational measures generally give you the best opportunity for putting a dollar value to the gain.)

8. Try to choose measures that can be influenced by the largest number of employees, in or out of their traditional jobs. Beware of measures that can only be influenced by the actions of a few people. Perhaps you remember the quarter that PanAm made a profit. The company sold the PanAm building. If you had been on a profit measuring plan at the time, you would have made some money. But it had nothing to do with the effectiveness of the organization.

9. The acid test of any measure is the question, "Do you want to reward people based on that measure?" (One hint: Don't overreact. As we will learn later, the amount of money available for each measure may be more for awareness than anything else.)

The Critical Design Element – Line of Sight

"Line of Sight" (LOS) comes from the military, describing distance from a target. The farther away you are, the more you have to adjust for the trajectory of the bullet and the harder it is to hit the target. The "further away" the measurement is thought to be from the employee, the longer the LOS and the harder it is for the employee to influence the result. *LOS is the perceived ability of an employee to effect a measure on which rewards are based.*

A very long LOS design, a single profit sharing plan for a 10,000 employee, multi-location organization, ends up just being a method of distribution of funds with little affect on people, except increased awareness. Long LOS plans invariably become entitlements. A very short LOS design, an attendance plan for a work group of 10 people, can be directly influenced by people's behavior. If most of the measures have a short line of sight, it can cause serious administrative and financial risks in larger companies, called cycling.

There is no optimum LOS, just trade-off in the design. LOS concerns usually mean you can't design a single plan that applies to everyone. We will continually come back to this subject as we explore how LOS can work for or against a group incentive plan.

The design affects LOS in four ways: number of physical locations of the organization covered, size of the organization covered, type of measure, and frequency of measurement and payout.

1. **Number of physical locations of the organizations covered.** People relate to their work group, then to their department, then to their division, then to the physical location of their office, and then to the corporation. LOS gets disproportionately long when you combine measurements of one or more physical locations.
2. **Size of the organization covered.** If you have a lot of people covered by one or more organization-wide measures, then you have a very long LOS. How many are "a lot"? No one really knows. Conventional wisdom argues for less than 500 to 600 in a single plan. That seems to be the most people you want covered with one or a set of measures.
3. **Type of measure.** LOS is affected by the employee's understanding of a measure, his/her (perceived) ability to influence it, and the amount of information the organization shares about it. Employees relate to operational measures — productivity, quality, cost control, etc. — much more than to financial measures.
4. **Frequency of payout.** Plans that measure performance and pay out at least a portion of the earnings each month clearly have a shorter LOS than those that measure and pay out annually.

Here are some rules of thumb to consider as you move forward in design:

- Avoid combining different physical locations for measurement and pay out if at all possible.
- It's generally best to define an organization to be measured as 600 or fewer people at a single physical location. If you have a larger number of people at one location, use a mix of measures and move *some* of them lower into the organization, customized to smaller organizational units.
- Have at least one operational measure in the plan.
- If everything else has a reasonably long LOS, try to have more frequent payouts.
- Apart from the plan design, you can shorten LOS by increasing communications, performance feedback, and employee involvement efforts.

What do you measure? The question is really what *can* you measure? First determine what measures reflect the strategic objectives as identified by top management. Theoretically you have a series of strategic objectives with measures connected to them. The team must determine whether or not those are the measures they really want to use.

Management may have explained what they want to measure, but when it gets to the design committee, you may find that management's measurements are not practical. You may discover ringers that management didn't see. The most common ringers are the purity of the measure (it is easily influenced by factors outside the control of the organization measured) and the availability of the information in a timely fashion (you can get the information on monthly performance, but six weeks late). A measurement may mean a lot to an executive but it may not mean anything to rank and file employees. Return on Net Assets (RONA) is a good example. RONA takes a lot of education to make it meaningful to most employees. Even if they understand it, they probably won't feel they can influence it, except in smaller organizations.

So find out what you can measure accurately and quickly at each level of the organization from the top down to the work groups. The measure will probably change as it cascades down the organization. *This is more than a design exercise. Measurement at every level of the organization is the primary performance feedback system for the plan.*

Characterizing measure – Lead, Operating, and Lag

Measures are useful to guide management in how the organization is doing and what it needs to do. Deciding which measure falls into the "lead" category is a subjective process and often dependent on the nature of the business. "Operating" and "lag" are pretty clear categories.

Lead: Customer satisfaction (value), employee satisfaction, sales, market share. (Some would include new product development.)

Operating: Productivity, internal quality, safety, attendance, cost reduction, cycle time, projects, etc.

Lag: Profit, return calculations (RONA, ROE, etc.), economic value added (EVA), and stock price.

There seems to be an optimum number of measures. You don't need to worry too much about this yet, but research shows that plans with three to five measures report better nonfinancial results than plans with more. So, at some point you may need to pare down your list. Three to five measures seem to be enough to give organizations a comprehensive look at their business and customize the plan to fit their needs. Plans with six or more measures probably are just too many to communicate clearly and for effective employee focus. Too many measures are much less effective than too few.

Applying all of this to our example. The objectives, broad measures, and weightings directed by top management and expanded by the design team to be more specific on measurement and level of organization covered are:

Objective	Broad Measure	Weighting	Level of Organization Covered	Specific Measure
Financial Performance	• Profit or return calculation	• 25%	• Company-wide	• Net income before taxes
Productivity	• Output divided by input	• 25% for plants • 0% for headquarters	• Each plant • No measure of headquarters	• Number of pounds shipped per controllable cost dollar
Cycle Time	• Days—Order to payment	• 25% for plants • 50% for headquarters	• Each plant • Headquarters measured on overall performance of all plants	• Days—Order to payment
Quality	• Cost of poor quality	• 25%	• Each plant • Headquarters measured on performance of all plants	• % of labor hours spent on rework and redos

Where are we in this process?

- Top management has determined the desired culture, objectives, organizational units to be covered, and broad (hopefully) parameters for measures. They have also appointed a design team.

- Either after or in parallel with the step above, the team has made an assessment of the current reward plans and culture.
- Determine the measures for each objective.
- Determine the appropriate organizational units to be covered by each measure based on what's possible and reasonable. Now the team will set baselines and goals for each measure.

Setting Base Lines

The simplest definition of base line is "what performance you would expect if you didn't have a plan." Performance above this base line is meaningful to the organization, financially and/or operationally. A base line can be set on any measure. Even a project has a base line: Completed or not? It is the point at which you begin to measure and reward performance improvement.

The best first step in setting base lines is to look at your history with each measure. It could be the last 12 months or several years. If you have a highly cyclical or seasonal business you could use the previous equivalent period.

Base line doesn't have to be an exact match to history. For example, if your measurement is productivity, sales divided by labor hours. You know that you're going to have a three percent price increase increasing sales by three percent. You should include the three percent into the base line. That's known as *packing the base.* Be warned that management can get greedy (or nervous about their financial risk) and over-pack. Over-packing creates a base line that may be perceived by the rank and file as unattainable. It defeats the whole purpose of the plan.

When setting financial base lines it's often important to consider any significant planned changes. If your measurement is return on net assets and you're going to significantly increase assets in the short term by refurbishing your facility, take that into consideration.

Setting Goals (a.k.a., Targets)

Base line is where you start measuring performance improvement. Goal or target is where you think the organization can get if "the plan worked."

Team goal-setting is a powerful process when all of the people covered agree. The fine art of team goal-setting does not apply to establishing a goal for a group incentive plan. It doesn't involve anybody but the design team. It is not a sophisticated process. In this case, setting goals is figuring out what feels reasonable. It's saying, "If this plan works, what could we probably expect. . .." Every measure has its base line and goal. One way to look at it is:

- Base line is what we would probably get without a plan.
- Goal is a 50-50 chance or 5 in 10.

Some people look at the history of peak performance to set goals. They take the average of the best of past performance and make that the goal. Moving the average performance to the previous peaks is reasonable, attainable, and demonstrates real improvement.

Where are we in the process?

- Top management has determined the desired culture, objectives, organizational units to be covered, and broad (hopefully) parameters for measures. They have also appointed a design team.
- Either after or in parallel with the step above, the team has made an assessment of the current reward plans and culture.
- The design team has determined the measures for each objective.
- The design team has decided what organizational units are to be covered by each measure.
- The team has set base lines and goals for each measure. Now the team will

  - Decide the size of award payouts for threshold (if any) and attaining goal in each measure.
  - Agree on who will be covered by the plan and the plan period.

Payouts, Participation and Period

To aid in the discussion, let's use the example introduced in this paper. Remember this example demonstrates process and is not intended to be a recommendation for your plan. I have added base lines and goals, rounded for ease of communications.

Objective	Measure	Weighting	Base line	Goal (% improvement)
Profit	Net income before taxes	25%	$10,000 Million	$10,500 Million (+5%)
Productivity	Units shipped per controllable cost dollar	25%	1.90 lb./$	2.0 lb./$ (+5.3%)
Cycle Time	Days - order to payment	25%	100 days	90 days (+10%)
Quality	Labor hours for rework/redo as a percentage of total hours	25%	15%	10% (+33%)

The Art of the Payout

Payout is initially determined based on "how much" is needed to motivate employees to reach goal on all the measures, assuming proper communications, education, involvement, and feedback. Take a look at the example matrix and think about what percentage of base pay would be necessary to do the job.

386

There is some relationship between LOS and the amount. The longer the LOS, the more you have to pay people if you want them to figure out how to improve upon the measure. There is some relationship between the amount of communications, education, involvement, and feedback and the amount of payout at goal. The fewer the communications, education, etc., the more you have to pay people.

There is also a relationship between the *intent* of the plan and the amount of payout. If the plan is just for awareness, you do not have to pay out as much as you would if you wanted significant improvement in a measure that can be directly affected by the people. If there is a mix of intents — awareness for profit and direct influence on productivity — you may wish to rethink the weighting. You could reduce the weighting on profit and increase it on the others. It is a shell game with lots of variables.

Setting the Payout at Goal

Much like the subjective process you used to set goals by measure, setting the payout for meeting all the goals is more often than not a "gut-feel."

There is some folklore on this subject, some of it helpful, some misleading. There is some research, primarily from the Consortium for Alternative Reward Strategy Research (CARS), and it can save the design team time.

- *Folklore: You have to have pay from 20 to 30 percent of base pay to get someone's attention and be meaningful. Reality:* Rarely. There are two situations when paying 20 to 30 percent may be true. First, if the base pay is quite low, then significant percentages are necessary to develop a reasonable reward-performance linkage and fair and competitive pay. This usually occurs in individual incentive plans, generally piece rate plans, and is considered base compensation. Group incentive plans that have little communication, education, involvement, and feedback and are just asking people to work harder or smarter in their job usually require high payouts at goal.

  The second situation is a function of the employee's level in the organization. We have developed an overwhelming need to make the well-to-do even more so. In the CARS research, we found about 150 plans of the 663 varied the percentage of base pay at goal by type of employee, with the median ranging from 25 percent for top management down to 5 percent for non-exempt employees.

  This median data was consistent for those 40 percent of the plans targeting a payout at goal.

These plans, however, did not perform any better that those with the same percentage of base payout at goal for all employees or those with the same dollar value.

Does this mean 5 percent should be your target? Certainly not. You establish what is appropriate for your culture, the LOS, the degree of communication, education, involvement, and feedback, the types of employees to be covered by the plan, the nature of the measures, and how you set the base lines and goals. The CARS plans reported targets from 3 to 30 percent.

Level of Employee	Target % of Base Pay at Goal
Top management	25%
Middle management	20%
First line supervisors	13%
Exempt professionals	10%
Non-exempt	5%

The research also shows that plans that *target* higher payouts often perform better on their measures and *make* higher payouts. They also report larger gains and better net return on payouts— at least for plan participants at exempt/management levels. These plans also report consistently better non-financial results. It makes sense that by offering bigger earning opportunities, organizations can expect better results.

- *Folklore: The way you determine a payout: Figure how much you are going to gain (save) at goal and pay 50 percent back to the employees. 50-50 splits are a design dictum. Reality:* Put the horse before the cart. The objective is to develop a reasonable payout that will influence people, not just reward them after-the-fact.

Over 50 years ago, the original Scanlon gain sharing plan had one measure, productivity, and was designed to pay out 75 percent of the savings from the improvement to the employees and 25 percent to the company. Variations of the plan have subsequently moved that split to the easily communicated 50-50 split. For PR, it looks and sounds fair. From a design view, it is irrelevant. Most plans have more than one measure, some whose gain can be valued in dollars and some whose can't, but are still terribly important to the company.

If you follow my approach to design, you will end up with some "split" of gains between employee and company, but the design is not driven by a pre-determined split. Group incentive plans are proactive. They are designed to get people to make changes that will improve the measures. That means determine what is necessary for a meaningful payout at goal. Then calculate the value of the gain at goal. Then compare the two for a split — a return on payout. If the return is unacceptable, go back and adjust any of the variables that meet the needs of all those affected by this plan.

The Form of Payouts

Generally payouts are an equal percentage of pay or an equal dollar amount to everyone in the plan. About 30 percent of the plans studied pay an equal percentage. Equal dollar payout is also about 30 percent.

The decision is based on the message the organization wants to send to employees. An equal percentage of pay might reflect the perceived level of each employee's contribution. Equal dollar payouts probably support better teamwork and the sense of equality. For purposes of the payout design step, use an equal percentage of base pay target at goal. It is the easiest way to ballpark your financial exposure at goal. You can adjust the other options rather easily, later.

Does it make sense?

I always suggest a sanity check. Take the targeted percentage of base pay of each type of employee at goal and see if the dollar amount feels right when compared to what you are asking from the employee population. If the majority of your employees are making $20,000 per year, a 2 percent payout at goal is $400 per year before deductions. If you pay out monthly, that would be $33 per month, again before deductions. If there are three measurements, each weighted equally, that's $11 per month before deductions. Is it worth it? Probably not. Do you need 10 percent at goal? That's $166 per month, $55 per measures. Only you know your organization well enough to decide, but make sure you look at the plan from the view of participants.

How about payouts by measure?

Objective	Measure	Weighting	Payout at Goal
Profit	Net income before taxes	25%	25% of 5% of base pay = 1.25% of base pay
Productivity	Units shipped per controllable cost dollar	25%	25% of 5% of base pay = 1.25% of base pay
Cycle Time	Days - Order to payment	25%	25% of 5% of base pay = 1.25% of base pay
Quality	Labor hours for rework/redo as a percentage of total hours	25%	25% of 5% of base pay = 1.25% of base pay

Your top management or the design team weighted each measure. That weighting is applied to the total award at goal to distribute it among the measures. It should be pretty obvious why you don't want more than five measures. It dilutes the payout at goal too much. The same point applies to weighing any one measure less than 10 percent, unless the measure is there just to remind employees of the objective.

When do you begin to pay out?

It's important to determine when to begin payouts. If you reach base line, is that the only point at which you start rewarding people? It depends. Most traditional group incentive plans pay nothing at reaching base line. Employees have to improve over the base line before earning anything. However, if you have been giving out payments on a previous plan that has become an entitlement and you're now converting to a more performance-based plan, then that amount of money might be the amount you would expect to pay out at base line.

When do you stop paying out?

Stretch is the payout cap — the point at which you're no longer willing to pay for additional improvement. Management is often concerned about having a windfall performance, unconnected with what the employees have done. As protection for the organization, they set a payout cap. Depending on the stretch performance level, this could send a negative and misleading message. Base line is the opportunity to communicate what you expect to do without a plan. Goals communicate what you think can be reasonably accomplished. Stretch tells people that there is a limit to what they can earn. It also gives people the subtle message that this is the most management thinks they can accomplish. Finally, it says we are not interested in improving above this point.

Windfalls can occur. If you're worried about windfalls, it's better to exclude the effect from the plan's performance measurement when the data comes in than to have a stretch point that is too low. (If you take this approach, be sure to communicate what you are doing when the windfall occurs. It will reinforce your fair and objective approach for both the employee and organization.) Are stretch points or caps always inappropriate? No, not if they are not high enough.

Who participates in group incentive plans?

If you have a plan that improves business performance, *should* you include everyone? On the surface, the answer looks simple: Involve everyone. It isn't always that easy.

Most organizations already have individual incentive plans for executives that take an inordinate amount of human resource and consultant time. Less time and money are spent on plans for second level management, even less on first-line supervisors and professionals. There is little for the rank and file. Group incentive plans break that mold. Plans reported in the CARS research essentially included everyone in the plan. When there was some exclusion, it was the top manager of the organizational unit.

The best plans include everybody with one exception. People on probation should not be eligible for awards. On an individual performance rating scale of 1 to 5, if 1 is given to a person who should look for another line of work and 5 goes to outstanding performers, 1's and perhaps 2's should not be eligible. This rule tends to tighten up some individual performance reviews and give performance management a bit more teeth.

Setting the Plan Period

Plan period is always pre-announced and defines the plan from starting date to completion date. It's important to make clear to employees in the pre-announcement that at the end of this period one of three things will happen:

1. You will keep the plan exactly as it is with minor changes in the base line or the point at which you measure and pay out. These are minor adjustments to account for the previous year's experience. That's an adjustment of numbers but not of the measurement itself. Some plans announce in advance that they will change the base line on a rolling average, using a three-year period. Each year, the last three years are used to revise the base line.
2. You will change the measurement and/or rules. This is a significant change. Usually organizations add measurements. They seldom get rid of them. This may happen because they have discovered some area of performance that is important to the business that they were not measuring and rewarding previously. People also become comfortable with the plan so adding a new measurement is less problematic.
3. Or, you will kill the plan. Out of the 663 plans in CARS, there were about 80 terminations. We could find little difference between the plans that were terminated and those that weren't. Most of the time they were not getting the performance they wanted. That's good. This is a dynamic process. You don't want to keep running a plan that doesn't work.

On the right side of the model, particularly in group incentive plans, you need plan periods because you never want to suggest that the reward is a guarantee or entitlement of any kind. It must be re-earned every single time.

The most common plan period is 12 months and it tends to dovetail with the fiscal year. There are some exceptions: project teams working on projects that are event driven or have particular schedules will have their own plan periods. These plans are measured at the end of the project or cycle of development. In this case the plan is announced based on what's appropriate for the plans but these are exceptions, not the rule.

391

Where are we in the process?

- Top management has determined the desired culture, objectives, organizational units to be covered, and broad (hopefully) parameters for measures. They have also appointed a design team.
- Either after or in parallel with the step above, the team has made an assessment of the current reward plans and culture.
- The design team has determined the measures for each objective.
- The design team has decided what organizational units are to be covered by each measure.
- The team has set base lines and goals for each measure.
- The team has decided the size of award payouts for threshold (if any) and attaining goal in each measure.
- It has agreed on who will be covered by the plan and the plan period.
- Now the team will forget payouts and start talking about gains with a clean sheet of paper.

Gain is the Group Incentive Plan's Bottom-Line Value to the Corporation

Performance goals are key elements in the design process because they determine a consistent point at which we can measure gain to the organization. Gain can be direct or indirect. It can be visible on the bottom line or it can have an imputed value to the corporation. Valuing gains is the most difficult part of this process and the most critical.

My Watergate rule of "follow the money" plays to the sensibilities of most top managers. We often get buy-in from top management on plans because they make sense or it seems like the right thing to do or it feels right for all the stakeholders. Commitments for more training plans are a classic example of funds committed in good faith and withdrawn at the first sign (or at least the second) of an organization's financial hiccups. A solid, financially justified group incentive plan will not be as subject to managerial shifts in focus as one not so justified.

My Golden Rule: "If you want to get management's attention, grab them by the P&L and their hearts and minds will follow."

Calculating gain isn't easy. . .

We are documented to death on measurement and how to use those measurements as part of a performance improvement process. But the amount written on putting a dollar value to the gain in that performance is pretty limited. That's because it is hard and particularly unique to each application. It is also because we haven't involved our financial friends in the process early enough. I suggest you initiate a "take the CFO to lunch program" when you start this journey. The role of the member of the design team from Finance is to determine the dollar value, if any, of the performance improvement by measure.

Looking at our example:

Objective	Measure	WT.	Base line	Goal (% impvmt)	Payout at Goal	Gain at Goal
Profit	Net income before taxes	25%	$10,000 Million	$10,500 Million (+5%)	1.25% of Base Pay	$500,000
Productivity	Units shipped per controllable cost dollar	25%	$1.90 lb./$	2.0 lb./$ (+5.3%)	1.25% of Base Pay	$130,000
Cycle Time	Days - Order to payment	25%	100 days	90 days (+10%)	1.25% of Base Pay	10 days less cycle time
Quality	Labor hours for rework/redo as a percentage of total hours	25%	15%	10% (+33%)	1.25% of Base Pay	$625,000

So far, we constructed an example based on both operational and financial measures, each with goals and an estimated payout for each. We've assigned a dollar value to each measure at goal.

Where are we in the process?

- Top management has determined the desired culture, objectives, organizational units to be covered, and broad (hopefully) parameters for measures. They have also appointed a design team.
- Either after or in parallel with the step above, the team has made an assessment of the current reward plans and culture.
- The design team has determined the measures for each objective.
- The design team has decided what organizational units are to be covered by each measure.
- The team has set base lines and goals for each measure.
- The team has decided the size of award payouts for threshold (if any) and attaining goal in each measure.
- It has agreed on who will be covered by the plan and the plan period.
- It has determined the dollar value of the gains, expressing those without a dollar value in terms of the objective.
- Now the team will determine if the financial rationale for the plan is consistent with the organization's demands.

Calculating What You Get for Your Money

Return on payout is the relationship between how much money you're going to make as a result of the reward plan and how much you will have to spend. There is a simple way to look at it. Take the dollar amount calculated for gain. Now subtract the amount you will have to pay out at goal, divide by that same payout amount and multiply by 100 to give you a percentage. This is a simple *net* return on investment figure:

$$\frac{\$1,000,000 \text{ (gain)} - \$400,000 \text{ (payout)}}{\$400,000 \text{ (payout)}} \times 100 = \frac{\$600,000}{\$400,000} \times 100 = 150\%$$

plus the additional value from the improvement on performance measures that cannot be given a dollar value:

The *gross* return on payout is $\frac{\$1,000,000 \text{ (gain)}}{\$400,000 \text{ (payout)}}$ or a \$2.50 gain to \$1 of payout.

You spent \$1.00 and made \$2.50, a 150 percent net return on your investment. I realize this is not very sophisticated, but it is as good as anything we have. Compared to many of the capital requests you'll find in major organizations, it is just as logical. I realize capital has depreciation and accounting principles written all over it, but there are dogs and ponies—not to mention smoke and mirrors—in those requests.
Using our example:

Objective	Measure	WT.	Base line	Goal (% impvmt)	Payout at Goal	Gain at Goal
Profit	Net income before taxes	25%	$10 Million	$10.5 Million (+5%)	1.25% of Base Pay	$500,000
Productivity	Units shipped per controllable cost dollar	25%	1.90 lb./$	2.0 lb./$ (+5.3%)	1.25% of Base Pay	$130,000
Cycle Time	Days - Order to payment	25%	100 days	90 days (+10%)	1.25% of Base Pay	10 days less cycle time
Quality	Labor hours for rework/redo as a percentage of total hours	25%	15%	10% (+33%)	1.25% of Base Pay	$625,000

If we assume each measure reaches goal, the payout will be 5 percent of base pay or $625,000 for 500 employees.
The gain would be overstated if we totaled all the gains from each measure, for we would be counting the same dollars twice. Since, in this example, Controllable Costs do not include labor, we could combine the

394

gains from productivity and quality for $755,000. The return calculations are:

$$\frac{\$755,000 \text{ (gain)} - \$625,000 \text{ (payout)}}{\$625,000 \text{ (payout)}} \times 100 = \frac{\$130,000}{\$625,000} \times 100 = 21\% \text{ } net \text{ return on payout}$$

The *gross* return on payout is $\frac{\$755,000 \text{ (gain)}}{\$625,000 \text{ (payout)}}$ or a $1.21 gain to $1 of payout

plus a 5 percent improvement in profit and 10 day reduction in cycle time.

After you have calculated your gross or net return on payout, you can decide if it will be acceptable to management. If not, you can decide to change the payout rates, the measures, or the goals to improve the return. It is an iterative process, adjusting as you proceed, always remembering the plan must be fair to both the organization and its employees.

It's not uncommon to see a broad range of net return on payout — break-even to 300 percent. The 278 CARS plans that were able to put a dollar value on their gains reported a median of 134 percent *net* return on what they paid out to employees or $2.34 gained for every $1 spent.

If your payout exceeds your gain, then you've spent money to accomplish the objectives. It is an investment. In this case, the design team must decide: "Is the expense worth the improvement?" In our example, let's assume the team decided only to use the gain from productivity — $130,000. The plan still met goal in all measurements. Would the net expense — $625,000 in payout less $130,000 gain for a $495,000 net expense — be worth a 5 percent profit improvement, reducing cycle time by 10 days, reducing rework by 5 percentage points and the soft stuff — alignment of employees with objectives, communications, education, feedback, and involvement? Each organization must decide for itself.

Where are we in the process?

- Top management has determined the desired culture, objectives, organizational units to be covered, and broad (hopefully) parameters for measures. They have also appointed a design team.
- Either after or in parallel with the step above, the team has made an assessment of the current reward plans and culture.
- The design team has determined the measures for each objective.
- The design team has decided what organizational units are to be covered by each measure.
- The team has set base lines and goals for each measure.
- The team has decided the size of award payouts for threshold (if any) and attaining goal in each measure.
- It has agreed on who will be covered by the plan and the plan period.
- It has determined the dollar value of the gains, expressing those without a dollar value in terms of the objective.

- The team has determined that the financial rationale for the plan is consistent with the organization's demands.
- Now the team will design the formula for earning — the reward structure.

Creating the reward structure

Creating the reward structure is a simple matrix connecting the performance with the reward. I do *not* recommend a continuous payout schedule, driven by a formula. Here's an example on a continuous payout schedule using our quality measure in the example:

Quality	Labor Hours for rework/redo as a percentage of total hours	15% Base line	10% (+33%) Goal	1.25% of Base Pay Payout

The continuous payout formula would be:

$$\text{Employee payout} = (15\% - \frac{\text{\# of actual hours spent of rework/redo}}{\text{Total Hours Worked}}) \times \frac{1.25\%}{5\%} \times \text{base pay (plus overtime)}.$$

If the organization reaches goal of 10 percent, there is only one payout at the end of the year, and all employees get the same percentage of base pay as a payout. The award for quality only would be (remember the hours are the total for the organization – 500 employees; this not an *individual incentive plan*):

$$\text{Employee payout} = (15\% - \frac{1,000,000 \text{ hours of rework/redo}}{10,000,000 \text{ Hours Worked}}) \times \frac{1.25\%}{5\%} \times \$25,000 = (15\% - 10\%) \times 25\% \times \$25,000 = \$312.50.$$

A continuous formula gives away money. Nobody decides they're going to perform at 11.56 percent of total hours on rework instead of 11.57 percent. Yet, with a continuous payout formula, you are paying for that 0.01 of a percentage point. Again, we are measuring a somewhat imprecise performance measure very precisely.

Continuous formulas eliminate "breakage" for the organization. Breakage occurs when you have incremental steps of performance and payout. If the performance is within the incremental step, the difference between the actual performance and the payout level below it is free. That's breakage. You make incremental payouts and don't pay anything until you reach the next level of performance and payout.

I have no data, but my experience is that performance ends up about 25 percent into the next earning increment. Of course, performance might go 90 percent into the increment, which means the company gets 90 percent of that increment for free. Breakage can amount to quite a bit of improved performance at no cost, depending on number of measures and frequency of payout. The more measures and payout periods, the more breakage.

Here's our quality element in a matrixed, performance-payout step design:

Quality measure = $\frac{\text{Labor hours on Rework/Redo}}{\text{Total labor hours}}$

Base line	Level 1	Level 2	Level 3	Level 4	Level 5 (Goal)
15%	14%	13%	12%	11%	10%
1,500,000 hrs on rework	1,400,000 hrs on rework	1,300,000 hrs on rework	1,200,000 hrs on rework	1,100,000 hrs on rework	1,000,000 hrs on rework
10,000,000 total hrs	10,000,000 total hrs	10,000,000 total hrs	10,000,000 total hrs	10,000,000 total hrs	10,000,000 total hrs
Payout = None	Payout = 0.25% of pay	Payout = 0.5% of pay	Payout = 0.75% of pay	Payout = 1% of pay	Payout = 1.25% of pay

Level 6	Level 7	Level 8	Level 9	Level 10	Level 11
9%	8%	7%	6%	5%	4%
900,000 hrs on rework	800,000 hrs on rework	700,000 hrs on rework	600,000 hrs on rework	500,000 hrs on rework	400,000 hrs on rework
10,000,000 total hrs	10,000,000 total hrs	10,000,000 total hrs	10,000,000 total hrs	10,000,000 total hrs	10,000,000 total hrs
Payout = 1.5% of pay	Payout = 1.75% of pay	Payout = 2.0% of pay	Payout = 2.25% of pay	Payout = 2.5% of pay	Payout = 2.75% of pay

Level 12	Level 13	Level 14	Level 15
3%	2%	1%	0%
300,000 on rework	200,000 on rework	100,000 hrs on rework	0 hrs on rework
10,000,000 total hrs	10,000,000 total hrs	10,000,000 total hrs	10,000,000 total hrs
Payout = 3% of pay	Payout = 3.25% of pay	Payout = 3.5% of pay	Payout = 3.75% of pay

Or for every 1 percentage point reduction in labor hours spent on rework to total hours, each employee earns 0.25 percent of pay.

There is a natural cap on this schedule when no labor hours are spent on rework, resulting in a payout of 3.75 percent of pay. If the performance was measured in an increasing number, you would have to decide if you wanted to cap the performance you're willing to pay for.

Be careful not to make your increments of payout performance too big—only base line and goal, for examples—because people will see that as unfair. It also creates a goal that's perceived to be too high for them to reach. It's important that you reward fairly, so try to find increments that people can relate to; three to five is a good rule of thumb between base line and goal. One increment is too few. Fifty increments is coming close to a continuous formula and is tough to communicate.

Just look at base line and goal measures and see how they break down readily into chunks of improvement. Most design teams try to show the improvement in percentage improvement because it is easier for them to calculate. It is not as effective to communicate percentage improvement as it is to communicate in terms of the measurement itself. Reducing cycle time days in chunks of one day for each level of payout is clearer than a 1 percent improvement.

Express payouts in points

If you have more than one measure and several levels of payout, use points. Points are an extremely flexible tool because you can make a point worth whatever you want: $1.00, 1 percent of base pay, .001 percent of base pay, redeemable for time off or stock or catalog merchandise. They're flexible in another way, too. A point can have a different value depending on the employee's level or organizational unit. If you want to use a non-egalitarian plan in which the CEO makes 25 percent of base pay and the lowest level person makes 5 percent at goal (not that I'm suggesting that) then a point is worth a whole lot more for the CEO than for the janitor.

Converting our quality measure example to points is a matter of deciding what looks easiest to communicate.

Base line	Level 1	Level 2	Level 3	Level 4	Level 5 (Goal)
Payout = None	Payout = 10 points	Payout = 20 points	Payout = 30 points	Payout = 40 points	Payout = 50 points

And so on for all performance levels. In this case a point is worth 0.025 percent of pay. Converting the example to same number of performance levels and payouts in points looks like this:

Objective	Base line	Level 1	Level 2	Level 3	Level 4	Level 5 (goal)	Increments
Profit *Points*	$10 Million *0 points*	$10.1 Million *10 points*	$10.2 Million *20 points*	$10.3 Million *30 points*	$10.4 Million *40 points*	$10.5 Million *50 points*	Each $100,000 increase earns *10 points*
Productivity *Points*	1.90 lb./$ *0 points*	1.92 lb./$ *10 points*	1.94 lb./$ *20 points*	1.96 lb./$ *30 points*	1.98 lb./$ *40 points*	2.0 lb./$ *50 points*	Each 0.02 lb./$ reduction earns *10 points*
Cycle Time *Points*	100 days *0 points*	98 days *10 points*	96 days *20 points*	94 days *30 points*	92 days *40 points*	90 days *50 points*	Each 2 day reduction earns *10 points*
Quality *Points*	15% *0 points*	14% *10 points*	13% *20 points*	12% *30 points*	11% *40 points*	10% *50 points*	Each percentage point reduction earns *10 points*

Try to force an equal number of increments for each measurement. You don't want five steps for one measure and three for the next. You

399

may need to adjust your goal a bit or tweak base line or increments with the objective being to try to make the numbers as round as possible so they're easier to communicate. That's okay. Anything lost in the rounding process will likely be made up through clearer communications and breakage.

Remember, a critical design criterion is finding a balance between a reasonable reward schedule and something that, with a little education, everyone can understand and act upon. Keep asking yourself, "what is the most important message? Where do we want the focus?"

You've just started. . .

The design phase of a group incentive plan is about 25 percent of the effort. Implementation, operation, communications, feedback, employee involvement, promotion, and reassessment is the other 75 percent.

The golden rule of group incentives:

A well-designed plan, poorly implemented, will never do as well as a poorly designed plan, well implemented.

The good news is now you don't have to have a poorly designed plan.

This chapter was adapted from the forthcoming book, **The reward plan advantage: a manager's guide to improving business performance through people***, by Jerry L. McAdams, published by Jossey-Bass, 1996.*

The Consortium for Alternative Reward Strategy Research (CARS) report, "Organizational Performance and Rewards - 663 Experiences in Making the Link" is available from the American Compensation Association, Scottsdale, AZ, 602-951-9191.

About the Contributor

Mr. McAdams is the National Practice Leader, Reward and Recognition Systems, Watson Wyatt Worldwide. He is also the co-director of the non-profit Consortium for Alternative Reward Strategy Research (CARS) and formally vice-president of Maritz Inc., St. Louis. He consults on the effective alignment of strategic objectives and compensation, reward, and recognition plans.

Mr. McAdams served on the White House Conference on Productivity and has testified before the U.S. Congressional Committee studying tax regulations on reward systems. He is a frequent speaker, researcher, and author on reward systems and, in addition, customer satisfaction systems.

He has collaborated with Dr. Robert Mai on *The Learning Partnership* on reward systems and the learning organization, published by Irwin in the Fall of 1995. He contributed to *The Performance Imperative*, Jossey-Bass, 1995, and is presently writing a book on making all reward systems into a competitive advantage, to be published by Jossey-Bass in the Spring of 1996.

Part VII - Team Resources

32

Trust in Teams: An Annotated Bibliography
Liz Teal

The transformation that occurs when a group becomes a team is an exciting process. The different stages and levels within these stages are necessary and predictable. Trust within the team is a valuable element necessary for high performing teams and an outcome of this process. The following list of books and articles can help teams understand the nature of trust from the individual, group, and organizational perspective. This list is not inclusive but discusses trust as it relates to teams specifically.*

Learning how to develop trust is a skill that can be developed by the team and its members. This skill development will enable the team to interact more effectively and resolve issues quicker, thus allowing the group to evolve to a high performing team.

BOOKS

The Wisdom of Teams: Creating the High-Performance Organization by Jon R Katzenbach and Douglas K. Smith, Harvard Business School Press, Boston, Massachusetts, 1993.

The information on trust is scattered throughout the book at the crucial junctions necessary for team success, such as accountability and constructive conflict. Trust is expressed from an overall perspective, which highlights how necessary trust is for effective managerial and group leadership.

Turf Wars: Moving from Competition to Collaboration by Harvey Robbins, Scott, Foresman and Company, 1900 East Lake Avenue, Glenview, Illinois 60025, 1990.

* In addition, please see "Building a Trust Based Organization" (p. 73) and "Trust: The Great Teamwork Enabler" (p. 267) in this Handbook.

Turfism is another way to say "without trust" with regard to business and teams. Teams can benefit from this book by helping them understand the perspective of power and territorial turf: why we need it and how each individual on the team can change behavior. Thus, the team is enabled to be stronger and more cohesive.

Teampower: Lessons from America's Top Companies on Putting Teampower to Work by Clay Carr, Prentice Hall, Englewood Cliffs, New Jersey, 1992.

The chapter on trust expresses the skills, guidelines, and ground rules for creating and maintaining an atmosphere of trust in a teaming organization. Although the approach is from the managers' perspective and how *they* can be a part of the team initializing process, it can give team members insights into the undercurrents that exist when trust is too low or non-existent in their team. The importance of each element and behavior as it relates to the overall big picture of trust in a teaming environment is discussed.

Trust: A New Vision of Human Relationships for Business, Education, Family, and Personal Living by Jack Gibb, Newcastle Publishing Co., Inc., North Hollywood, California, 1991.

Trust is explored from all avenues of human experience and involvement, which makes this a classic on the subject of trust. Chapter Seven, "Emergence of the Group," begins to address areas that apply to teams. Then, in Chapter Eight, Gibb moves into the area of the organization where he discusses the Fear/Distrust cycle and how we work within that destructive cycle. The charts help to explain and clarify points of discussion that can be used in further discussion by the team. Some of this gets into theory, but keep reading, it all makes sense at the end of the chapter. In Appendix B there is a trust measurement instrument called "Diagnosing Your Team," which includes the interpretation of team member responses, both on an individual and team level. It would be appropriate if the team decided to take the instrument as a first step in a process to improve their cohesiveness. The ideas and thoughts expressed in this book are worth the time and effort to discover where you and your team are on the "trust scale."

Cross-Functional Teams: Working with Allies, Enemies, and Other Strangers by Glenn M. Parker, Jossey-Bass Inc., Publishers, 350 Sansome Street, San Francisco, California 94104, 1994.

The lack of trust and open communication limits the sharing of knowledge. This is critical since one of the purposes of cross-functional teams is the sharing of expertise. Cross-functional teams have the typical problems of a team plus the added dimension of people representing different areas within the organization or department. In Chapter 12, "Techniques for Working Together as a Team," the author's list of internal issues that impact cross-functional teams starts with conflict resolution, trust, and communication.

The Empowerment Imperative: Six Steps to a High Performance Organization by Daniel Quinn Mills, Harvard University, Graduate School of Business Administration, Human Resource Development Press, Inc., Amherst, Massachusetts, 1994.

Chapter Six discusses the steps necessary to build trust from a management perspective. This can easily be applied to the team and individuals within the team to check their behavior and attitude with each other. Combined with the chapters on "Empowering" and "Managing Change" this will give team members a slightly different perspective on trust in their group and the organization.

The Leadership Challenge: How to Get Extraordinary Things Done in Organizations by James M. Kouzes and Barry Z. Posner, Jossey-Bass Inc., Publishers, 350 Sansome Street, San Francisco, California 94104, 1987.

The chapter entitled, "Foster Collaboration," brings together the many components of collaboration that lead to a trusting environment. The examples are from both the management and employee viewpoints and can be applied to the team environment very easily. The segment on "Building Trusting Relationships" is especially helpful to everyone.

The Team Building Tool Kit: Tips, Tactics, and Rules for Effective Workplace Teams by Deborah Harrington-Mackin, Amacom, American Management Association, 135 West 50th Street, New York, NY 10020, 1994.

In the chapter on "Problems of Fear and Control" the author discusses the issues of changing to a team culture and how trust fits into that change. Individuals experience resistance due to a loss of control and stress from developing new relationships in a team culture. Both resistance and stress are part of the change process and fears are addressed and replaced by trust. The checklists of behaviors and attitudes can bring new insight into ways of building trust.

Credibility: How Leaders Gain and Lose It, Why People Demand It by James M. Kouzes and Barry Z. Posner, Jossey-Bass Inc., Publishers, 350 Sansome Street, San Francisco, California 94104, 1993.

The authors look at trust as one necessary element if credibility is to be established by a leader. How this element fits into being trustworthy as a leader also applies to a team. The "human dynamics of trust" apply to both leaders and members.

Managing With a Conscience: How to Improve Performance Through Integrity, Trust, and Commitment by Frank K. Sonnenberg, McGraw-Hill, Inc., New York, NY, 1994.

The author discusses at length the basic aspects of trust from the organization, managerial, and employee points of view. These principles can be easily applied to a team perspective. In the chapter on trust a model is used to graphically represent the elements of trust and how they fit together. The effects of positive and negative actions are described through the use of clear examples. Behaviors and attitudes necessary for organizational trust to exist and to be maintained are highlighted.

Leading Teams: Mastering the New Role by John H. Zenger, Ed Musselwhite, Kathleen Hurson, and Craig Perrin, Business One Irwin, Homewood, Illinois 60430, 1994.

Team leadership is a necessary component for the success of any manager. The chapter on "Building Trust" shows the transition from directive to highly participative team management and the critical steps that teams go through to become highly effective. The chapters preceding the 'trust' chapter shows how team leadership can be achieved and how the parts fit together.

Diverse Teams at Work: Capitalizing on the Power of Diversity by Lee Gardenswartz and Anita Rowe, Irwin Professional Publishing, Chicago, Illinois, 1994.

In the chapter on "Relationships" the authors discuss how to build trust in a team through the use of worksheets and activities that can get people to thinking from a different perspective. The worksheets and recommendations for interpersonal problem-solving are excellent.

Building Productive Teams: An Action Guide and Resource Book by Glenn H. Varney, Jossey-Bass Inc., Publishers, 350 Sansome Street, San Francisco, California 94104, 1989.

In this book the author has trust references scattered throughout the text. Note the 'trust cycle' and how this might apply to your team in Chapter Seven on "Improving Team Member Relationships." In addition, the table "Dimensions of Interpersonal Competence" illustrates positive and negative behaviors to effectively manage interpersonal relationships.

The Skilled Facilitator: Practical Wisdom for Developing Effective Groups by Roger M. Schwarz, Jossey-Bass Inc., Publishers, 350 Sansome Street, San Francisco, California 94104, 1994.

As a facilitator, the examples cited are based on behavior and how it might be interpreted by the group you are facilitating. Trust is an important element in the effectiveness of facilitation and group process.

Teamwork: What Must Go Right/ What Can Go Wrong by Carl E. Larson and Frank M.J. LaFasto, SAGE Publications, Inc., 2455 Teller Road, Newbury Park, California 91320, 1989.

This book is good for everyone to read and the chapter on "Collaborative Climate" discusses trust and how it grows in a team. The ingredients necessary to achieve trust are discussed.

Team Fitness: A How-To Manual for Building a Winning Work Team by Meg Hartzler and Jane E. Henry, ASQC Quality Press, 611 East Wisconsin Avenue, Milwaukee, Wisconsin 53202, 1994.

All of the elements necessary to create and maintain an environment of trust within a group are discussed in this guidebook on building a winning team. Trust is not mentioned specifically, but the combination and chemistry of actions and behaviors needed for trust to occur are examined. Through the use of specific exercises, team surveys, and contracts of accountability the team can discuss key issues in a positive, productive way.

Why Teams Don't Work: What Went Wrong and How to Make It Right by Harvey Robbins and Michael Finley, Peterson's/Pacesetter Books, Princeton, New Jersey, 1995.

The "Nine strategies for creating trust" in Chapter 15, "Depleted Trust: Why Should I Trust You?" are very clear with good examples for further explanation. From the perspective of restoring trust and how to maintain trust the approach is down to earth and the information immediately usable. Unnecessary mistakes are explained in terms of why they happened and how to resolve the resulting problems.

ARTICLES

Korsgaard, Audrey M., David M. Schweiger, and Harry J. Sapienza "Building Commitment, Attachment, and Trust in Strategic Decision-Making Teams: The Role of Procedural Justice," *Academy of Management Journal*, 1995, Vol 38, No. 1, 60-84.

In decision-making teams individual commitment to the decision and decision-making procedures facilitate positive attitudes. Perceived fairness by members and the impact on commitment, attachment, and trust are discussed.

Folger, Robert and Mary A. Konovsky, "Effects of Procedural and Distributive Justice on Reactions to Pay Raise Decisions," *Academy of Management Journal*, 1989, Vol 32, No. 1, 115-130.

The article discusses the reactions of manufacturing company employees to decisions about perceived fairness in compensation and pay raises. Interesting information to consider when processing changes in compensation when you are transitioning going into a team structure.

Lanza, Peggy, "Team Appraisals," *Personnel Journal*, 1985, Vol 64, No. 3, 46-51.

This suggests a process to instill trust within the team using the team appraisal system. The article includes an instrument and a questionnaire.

Varney, Glenn H., "Helping a Team Find All the Answers," *Training & Development Journal*, 1991, Vol 45, No. 2, 15-18.

The benefits of a facilitative approach on the part of management and how it promotes a positive, open environment that increases trust in a team are covered in this article.

About the Contributor

Since 1991, Liz Teal has worked at the Center for the Study of Work Teams at the University of North Texas as the Center Program Manager of Education. Liz was one of the key people at the Center who brought about the Center's first Annual Research Theory Symposium in 1991. She has been actively involved in the strategic direction of the Center conferences and the development of conference programs while completing her degree in psychology. She has presented her Team Trust Workshop at the *Effective Work Teams: A Conference for Learning Strategic Skills* based on her extensive research on team trust. Ms. Teal was a member of the Service Organization at the Xerox Corporation for 17 years. During that time, she was both a team member and team facilitator/trainer. She is currently a consultant based in Memphis, TN.

33

Resources in Creating Self-Managed Work Teams
Gerald D. Klein

This article will review a selection of resources available to consultants, staff, managers, and employees to support them in their efforts to establish self-managed work teams. From the large number of resources that might conceivably be of some value, those that are reviewed here are ones *expressly aimed* at the establishment of self-managed teams. As change agents may resort to various media in their efforts to inform and educate, the resources reviewed here include videos, books, and training materials. This article will suggest ways in which these various items can be combined and used in any single system intervention. ***Information for ordering these resources is found at the conclusion of this article.****

VIDEOS

Introduction

It is likely that organizations and organization units will continue to be introduced to the concept of self-managed work teams by knowledgeable presenters. A well-chosen video can serve various functions in these efforts. A video can reinforce and add credibility and detail to a presenter's remarks. Videos can also be used to illustrate alternate approaches and to introduce new issues for group discussion. Videos, workbooks, pair and small group exercises, in addition to straightforward presentation, also introduce variety into an educational experience, which sustains audience interest and energy.

Three videos are reviewed in this section. The first two function as good introductions to self-managed work teams and describe how they can be installed in an organization. Successful applications of self-managed teams are portrayed or shown in both videos. This is important

411

---

*See also the case study by Varney and Diers on p. 171 of this Handbook.

because the actual process of establishing team self-management is challenging; knowing that firms actually succeed at this task can sustain a group through its difficult times as it works toward this goal. The first video, ***Self-Directed Work Teams—Redesigning the Workplace for the 21st Century*** uses terminology and examples that make this resource perhaps most appropriate for use with manufacturing personnel and organizations. The second video, ***Improving Work Systems***, might work better for organizations in the service sector. Featured here is a case study of how a traditionally structured organization in the financial services industry transformed itself into a more successful organization using self-managed teams. The specific activities of a team facilitator from this organization is the focus of the third video, ***Leading a Service Team: A Day with a High Performance Work Team Facilitator***.

The three videos are effective, in part, because each features a well-written narration interspersed with simulated or actual employees describing their experiences, and describing or performing their new roles. Much to their credit, the videos feature employees who are diverse sexually, racially, and ethnically, which permit diverse audiences to identify with those who are shown. On the other hand, none of the videos mention labor unions, who must be prominent players in settings where employees and managers are governed by a collective bargaining agreement. While not reviewed here, there are videos that show labor and management working together to establish self-managed teams.[1]

1. Self-Directed Work Teams—Redesigning the Workplace for the 21st Century

Self-Directed Work Teams makes a strong case for the use of self-directed work teams in contemporary organizations where high performance, high flexibility, high commitment, and constant improvement are essential. This 29-minute video would reinforce or support presentations on self-directed work teams made before a variety of organization audiences. Featuring a straightforward, upbeat, and largely jargon-free narration, this well-done, informative video is likely to prompt constructive questions and stimulate good discussion.

The overall flow of the video is as follows. Self-directed work teams are defined. The narration links many current applications of them to past organizational success in involving employees in quality-improvement efforts. ***Self-Directed Work Teams*** describes in detail the activities of teams and team members and draws a number of useful distinctions between a traditional organization and one structured around self-directing teams. The video pauses periodically to draw these distinctions and does this effectively. The benefits of self-directed teams are identified, as are the results achieved by prominent U.S. companies who have used them. Finally, how an organization can move from a traditionally structured workplace to one built around self-directed teams is described.

Throughout the video the label "self-directed work teams" is used: The terms "self-managed," "autonomous," or "semiautonomous" are not. It is clear from the outset that the focus here is on teams and team members that, to the maximum extent possible, control and direct their own affairs. A self-directed work team is defined in the video as "a team of employees who are responsible for performing a whole task, such as producing a product or delivering a service. The team has all the skills to do the work, as well as to plan, control, and improve the work."

Supervisors, even operating under a new role, are not part of these teams. Their traditional functions of planning, control, and improvement and many belonging to support services eventually become the responsibility of team members, as their knowledge and skills increase. For example, in the area of support services, teams are described as having responsibility for such actions as preventative and light maintenance, safety instruction, and the interviewing and selection of new members. The video describes very well, in my view, the *star system* of distributing these responsibilities among team members. Under the star system each point of a star represents a significant supervisory or support activity. In the video the five points of the star are: production (including planning and scheduling), quality, cost, safety, and employee relations. Three team members describe their star responsibilities in detail and the training they received to help them handle their responsibilities well. Star responsibilities rotate among workers. "Team Leadership" is one of the activities of the team member responsible for the production point of the star. In the video, the current team leader indicates that leadership is actually shared by many members, depending on the issue confronting the team. He says, "People at different star points 'lead' the team" as issues arise under the various star points, such as quality, costs, and new employee recruitment.

In the self-directed work team setting former supervisors exist in the role of area coordinator. An area coordinator oversees the work of several teams (in the video, four), and functions as a facilitator, coach, and trainer of teams and team members. Additionally, the area coordinator, in the words of a team member, "forces the team to look at problems and to find our own solutions. The area coordinator helps get us what we need to do our job right—it's as if he works for us."

An especially effective instructional device that leads to fuller understanding is the frequent use of a simulated self-directed work team. The video not only describes self-directed teams but permits the viewer to see team members in action, including members actually carrying out their star responsibilities. The video immerses you immediately in what we later learn is a daily meeting of team members with star responsibilities. In this early sequence, team members report on results and raise and resolve area problems. Later, team members describe how membership on a self-directed team differs from a traditional work role and, as was mentioned, report on their star responsibilities and how they were prepared to handle them. The individuals playing team members have an everyday, non-actor look about them; they may actually be team members. Because of this, they are credible, even though their individual comments and interaction are scripted.

Similarly effective is the use of an actual manager, who is not identified, to describe the steps taken by his/her organization to shift from a conventionally structured company to one built around self-directed teams. This is an important issue and the video handles it well. The process described would be effective in many settings and includes the following major steps:

- Increasing manager knowledge about self-directed teams through site visits and selected readings
- Formation of a steering committee to oversee organizational change, and the retention of a consultant familiar with implementing team designs
- Selection by the steering committee of promising organization sites
- Providing an overview and orientation to supervisors and employees in those sites
- Selection of an area for a pilot program and forming a design team from volunteers, consisting of supervisors, employees, and staff representatives
- The design team then
    - Carries out a diagnostic study of the current system
    - Creates a vision of how the area would operate if it had fully functioning, self-directed work teams
    - Presents this vision to the steering committee and other area employees for their suggested revisions and approval
    - Prepares a transition plan to guide the area in making the vision a reality

Other more specific design team responsibilities are mentioned and the manager interviewed warns about the dangers of moving too quickly.

It is not reasonable to expect a 29-minute video to "cover all the bases." However, it is important to indicate to the potential user the video's flat sides. Supervisors and managers who view the video are not likely to find enough details about their roles and responsibilities under team self-management. Since this video was made it has become increasingly clear that organizations must address this issue squarely early on; and we know a lot more than we did then about what these roles should entail. Also, it takes a while to realize, and some viewers may never realize, that the employees in the video really represent only a *subset* of a team's members, not an entire team. While it would have been instructive to show this subset interacting with the entire team, this is not done. It is also possible to conclude (incorrectly) from the video that the star responsibilities are carried out by and are rotated among only this subset of team members.

414

2. Improving Work Systems

Prominently featured in another video, **_Improving Work Systems_**, are the managers and employees of the TransAction Services Division of IDS Financial Services, a multibillion dollar subsidiary of American Express. The video documents the transformation of the 300-person, Minneapolis-based division from a conventionally structured operation to one organized around customer teams.

TransAction Services processes mutual funds transactions and is similar in function to the back offices of brokerage houses. Its primary customers are the IDS mutual funds sales force, although the ultimate IDS customers, the purchasers of mutual funds, are also affected by the quality and timeliness of the work done by the Division. The changes made in TransAction Services were prompted by a revenue decline at IDS in 1988 and a desire to improve customer service. Among other things, TransAction customers were waiting too long on the phone and too frequently hanging up, and the company was incurring financial penalties because transactions were not being processed as rapidly as required by statute.

The decision to attempt a complete system redesign followed an unsuccessful attempt by management to affect a "quick fix," which is cursorily described in the video. An outside consultant was also prodding the group toward complete system redesign. An off-camera narrator describes how the change unfolded, starting in 1988. Among the video's strengths is the reliance on the employees of TransAction Services and its consultant, Barry Bateman, from the firm Block Petrella Weisbord, Inc., to move the story along. Employees and managers describe what was done, what they experienced, and their insights at different points in the change process. Most of their comments are offered in 1990, two years after project start-up. Toward the video's end some of the same employees are asked for their perceptions in 1992. Key pre-change and post-change performance data are also presented. It is clear that the system, four years after start-up, continues to show significant improvement attributable to the redesign.

Another strength of the video is that it explicitly describes the process used to bring about the transformation of the Division. Described is the sequence of general steps taken, and a sampling of the activities and mix of individuals involved at each step. A sociotechnical approach, which the video claims has "evolved over 30 years," was used to transform the Division. The sociotechnical approach strives to create a work system that eventually satisfies both organization/client (technical) needs and employee (social) needs. The selection of a sociotechnical approach was likely influenced by consultant Bateman's orientation, yet it is an approach that can be applied widely. A trainer or consultant could productively use this video to prepare a group for undertaking an identical or similar change process.

415

Much of the video describes the change process; less attention is given to detailing worker responsibilities before and after the change, although some of these changes are suggested. In contrast, much of the first video, ***Self-Directed Work Teams***, details team and team member responsibilities under self-management; the process of transforming an existing system is a subsidiary issue. The transformation process used by TransAction Services began with an important Analysis Phase, proceeded to a New Design Phase, which was followed by an Implementation Phase. The Analysis Phase consists of three separate yet complementary analyses. An environmental analysis primarily involves learning more about the specific requirements of a unit's (in this case, the Division's) customers. In the technical analysis an attempt is made to understand how work entering a unit is transformed or changed by unit members. An important goal in the social system analysis is to learn how current unit members perceive the quality of their work lives. The output or results of the three analyses are used to fashion a new, more effective design for a work system. Making this design operational is the goal of the Implementation Phase.

At TransAction Services (and typically), the three phases were managed by a steering committee made up of the vice president of the Division, his direct reports, a representative from the computer systems department, an internal and an external consultant. Following a presentation by the steering committee to all 300 members of the Division, in which the steering committee indicated its openness to radical restructuring, an eleven-member design team was recruited from all levels and functions. With guidance and tools from the external consultant the design team carried out the three analyses and evolved a design for restructuring work in the Division. This new design called for:

- the reconfiguration of all employees into teams of from 25 to 30 members
- teams would be responsible for customers from different geographic regions and team membership would be multifunctional (i.e., each team would contain all the resources and skills necessary to process its work)
- teams members would be fully empowered to make decisions enabling them to process work in an accurate and timely manner
- the teams themselves would perform work previously performed by supervisors
- current supervisors were to become team facilitators and two were to be assigned to each team. Managers/supervisors were to become "strategic directors and boundary managers, managing (obtaining) resources for the teams."

The pace of ***Improving Work Systems*** is slower and the narration more low key than ***Self-Directed Work Teams***, requiring a slightly more attentive audience. Also, unlike the first video, periodic summarization, which is as useful in videos as it is in speaking, is not used.

It is important to note that for a good part of the video the terms self-managed and self-directed teams are *not* used. The reciting of TransAction Services' problems early in the video establishes the need for "work redesign." For much of the video this term is used. A comprehensive assessment of the existing work system undertaken after the "quick fix" doesn't work eventually indicates the desirability of proceeding with self-managed teams.

3. Leading a Service Team: A Day with a High-Performance Work Team Facilitator

Improving Work Systems can certainly be used on a stand-alone basis to illustrate the process of transforming a service setting. A companion video, ***Leading a Service Team***, provides considerably more information on the facilitator's role at TransAction Services. The dynamics between a facilitator and team members are especially well shown. A consultant's or trainer's objectives will determine if one or both videos are shown. (***Leading a Service Team*** would complement nicely two articles by Rollin Glaser, which are described later. These articles are concerned with the facilitator's role.) ***Leading a Service Team*** focuses on the activities of one of the twenty-four Division facilitators, Kathy Sweet. The general responsibilities of TransAction Services facilitators are described and Ms. Sweet compares her former supervisory role with her new role as a facilitator. Clearly seen in the video is how years of performing narrow, specialized tasks does not prepare employees to handle, at least initially, the more technically complex and interpersonally sensitive tasks of supervisors. There are good sequences showing Ms. Sweet coaching a team member in performing a task (negotiating with a sales agent) that previously she would perform; Ms. Sweet overseeing intrateam and interteam interaction; and a team handling a situation never arising before, such as the replacement of a facilitator who is leaving for another opportunity. Also described is the reward system at TransAction Services that rewards team members for overall Division performance as well as team performance.

BOOKS AND RELATED RESOURCES

Introduction

This section will review a selection of books and bound materials that can assist managers and employees in the transition to self-managed teams. Briefer volumes are reviewed here as these can be more easily incorporated into a training experience than the longer, full texts on self-managed work teams that are available.[2] The briefer volumes, some of which feature large typefaces that are reader-friendly, are more suitable for employee groups likely to vary greatly in reading ability. Reductions-in-force and increasing individual workloads in some organizations have also left little time for employees to tackle and master long texts.

1. Four Articles on Self-Managed Teams

The King of Prussia, PA-based firm, Organization Design and Development (OD&D), offers four reasonably priced, individually bound articles on self-managed work teams authored by Rollin Glaser, the organization's president. The articles run in length from sixteen to twenty-two pages and each contains a list of references and additional readings. Two articles are clearly intended for supervisors and managers, in the past a relatively neglected population in efforts to establish self-managed teams. One is directed to team members and the fourth is intended for managers, supervisors, and team members.

Moving Your Team Toward Self-Management is directed at managers and supervisors who lead work groups in traditional organizations. The article assumes little prior knowledge of self-managed teams. The functions or tasks performed by self-managed teams are described, including those tasks that in a traditional system would be performed by a supervisor, such as setting goals and selecting new team members. Other characteristics of self-managing teams are also listed and described, such as the responsibility of teams for a whole and distinct task and the tendency of team members to rotate through many or all jobs. In clear prose, the article touches on the history of self-managed teams, usefully distinguishes between these teams and quality circles, and offers data suggesting that teams are here to stay. The remaining ten pages of the article, which comprise the bulk of the article, confronts squarely (beginning with a section titled, "How Supervisors and Managers Really Feel About Self-Managed Teams") the place and function of managers and especially first-line supervisors in systems that are organized around self-managed employee teams. It argues, correctly, in my view, that developing full team autonomy and team member skill is a process likely to extend over several years in many settings. Until then, managers and supervisors will be challenged by developing in team members the ability to perform managerial tasks. The burden of learning will not be entirely on team members, however. To succeed at developing the team's capabilities, managers and supervisors also will have to learn, as well. Drawing on research by Glaser the article describes six areas of learning required of managers/supervisors:

- learning to become a "facilitative" leader, gradually relinquishing control and responsibilities as team members evidence the ability to handle them successfully
- learning to encourage and empower group members. Developing in team members increasing courage "to think, to challenge, to innovate and to take action" (p. 10)
- learning how to develop in a team and in team members a decreased reliance on external control and the ability to initiate, monitor, evaluate, and correct their own job performance

- learning coping and response strategies for dealing with the myriad of new issues likely to arise as work arrangements are altered
- learning to facilitate the learning of others
- learning to learn from one's own experiences as a team facilitator

The article concludes with a practical checklist of things a manager can do *now* to prepare herself/himself for, and to take the first steps toward, team self-management.

Two of the videos reviewed earlier could productively be used by a trainer or consultant in conjunction with this article and the one to follow, which also addresses issues faced by facilitators. *Self-Directed Work Teams* **shows members of a self-directed team confidently performing functions performed by supervisors in traditional settings—after having been coached and trained to do these. It describes and illustrates well the "star" approach for distributing leadership responsibilities among team members. As was mentioned above, also valuable would be the video,** *Leading a Service Team,* **which follows a team facilitator for a day as she works to train team members in tasks that were previously her responsibility.**

The second OD&D article, ***Facilitating Self-Managing Teams***, furthers the discussion of the facilitator's role begun in the first article. It provides useful elaboration of material introduced in the first article as well as *additional* tools and concepts aimed at helping a new facilitator achieve success in her/his role. Initially, the discussion is structured around a *Self-Managed Team Facilitator Model* which, visually, resembles the familiar Tannenbaum-Schmidt leadership continuum. The model was introduced in the previous article but is examined more thoroughly here. The model reveals how facilitators gradually relinquish their power and control as a team becomes able to successfully handle responsibilities previously belonging to the supervisor. The power and control of the facilitator diminishes and the team's increases as you move from left to right. The model divides the continuum into four stages, compares facilitator and team responsibilities at each stage, and provides rough time estimates of stage duration. More or less complete team self-management occurs in 1 1/2 to 2+ years. The model and discussion assumes a fairly linear process, with a facilitator remaining in place as part of his/her team, with responsibility for just one team. In practice, for good or poor reasons, facilitator/supervisor headcount is reduced fairly quickly, facilitators are pulled out of the teams and are assigned responsibility for two or more teams. This by no means makes the model useless; but actual conditions are usually more chaotic and messy than implied here. Other issues dealt with in this second article include:

- assumptions about people that could either assist or hurt facilitators in their work with teams
- the need to decide with the team how much responsibility the group will have to manage itself. *The Gulowsen Autonomy Scales* (Gulowsen, 1971, 1979) are mentioned as a way of organizing this discussion. A description of these scales and how they can be used is found in the *Exercises* portion of this article, below.
- the interesting idea that a facilitator has to be empowered in order to empower his/her team(s)
- the desirability of self-leadership by team members, and this as a facilitator goal
- the need to become skilled at working with groups or teams and to engage in training if one's skills in this area are weak

Learning to Be a Self-Managing Team, the third article, is intended for employees who are or who will be members of self-managing teams. This article and the first article reviewed above, **Moving Your Team Toward Self-Management**, could be used as a set in any system intervention by a consultant — one article for managers and supervisors, the other for employees — as the overall format and the early portions of both are virtually identical. Like the first article, **Learning to Be a Self-Managing Team** begins with a listing of typical self-managed team tasks and characteristics, a brief history of the origin of self-managed teams and data pertaining to effectiveness. Sections specifically addressed to team members follow. These discuss the personal benefits of participating on a self-managed team, but indicate that they may not be for everyone, and suggest what members have to learn in order for the transition to teams to be successful. Some of the six "categories of team member learning" (p. 7) are identical to the learnings identified as necessary for supervisors as they transition to facilitators. The discussion under each of the six areas describes in detail the learning required and establishes its importance to self-managed work teams. The six areas are learning to:

- cope with change
- accept responsibility for the group's work in addition to one's own work
- develop group dynamics skills
- help the group (and the team facilitator, if one is present) make the transition to a self-managing team
- think critically about work policies and processes
- be a self-directed learner

The article concludes with an employee self-audit of twenty-five questions intended to reveal a person's readiness for team self-management. The audit is intended to provoke thought rather than produce a score (no scoring scheme is presented). Such questions as the following are presented:

- How would you characterize your personal response to organizational change? Proactive in support of change, passive-neutral, or anti-change/pro status quo?
- How prepared are you to learn the new tasks required by this new form of teamwork? Fully prepared, somewhat prepared, not at all prepared.
- Have you ever given feedback to a peer about his/her work performance?
- Have you ever interviewed and selected new members for a work group?

The self-audit questions are very good ones and a trainer or consultant is encouraged to structure a group discussion around this activity. For example, the twenty-five questions could be broken into five-question blocks and scheduled into a multi-day orientation to self-managed work teams. Group discussion of the answers could be used to create a list of team training needs, and to clarify what tasks will continue to be performed by management, at least in the short run, and what tasks will be handled by the teams.

The fourth article, **Helping Your Organization Gear Up for Self-Managing Teams**, is intended for both supervisors *and* employees in organizations either contemplating the move toward self-managed teams or in some early stage of the process. The assumption is correctly made that the concept is so new that confusion can continue to exist among participants who are well into the process. The article starts with a wonderful mini-case featuring Phil, a facilitator of a newly-formed self-managed (or is it self-directed?) team, where each team member is operating under a different definition of what he or she should be doing. Chaos reigns. Under sections titled, "Common Characteristics of Self-Managing Teams" and "Where Did this Radical Notion Come From?" the ground covered in the other articles is covered here. The article addresses in a section the common and obvious question, "If this is self-management, why do we still have a facilitator?" and describes in greater detail than the previous article the transition necessary on the part of facilitators. The article discusses the six major areas of learning required by supervisors transitioning to team facilitators that were described in the first article, **Moving Your Team Toward Self-Managment**. The six areas of learning required by team members, part of the previous article, are discussed here, as well. The article concludes with a discussion of the personal and organization benefits of self-managed teams and a list of "individual actions both team members and team facilitators can take to make the change easier, more interesting, and more likely to succeed" (p. 17). For example, it is suggested that a facilitator frequently ask the group to identify what it needs to learn in order to be more effective.

421

2. Succeeding as a Self-Managed Team

Like the four articles from OD&D, the book by Richard Y. Chang and Mark J. Curtin, **Succeeding as a Self-Managed Team**, and the almost identically titled one by Bob and Ann Harper, **Succeeding as a Self-Directed Work Team: 20 Important Questions Answered**, provide useful orienting and introductory information on self-managed teams and the personal, social, and organizational changes that these require. Both books are reviewed below. To their credit, these books attempt to involve readers experientially. Both volumes contain relatively short and reader-friendly chapters followed by a series of "Worksheets," in the Chang and Curtin book, or "Questions For You," in the one by the Harpers. These sections contain questions for the reader and the overall quality of the questions asked is good.

Using these questions, trainers and consultants could organize, and probably have organized, entire workshops around one of these books. Under the right circumstances, prospective or actual members of self-managed teams, steering committees, design teams and other similar teams, using one of these books, could carry out a "getting ready" or other training experience on their own without the presence of an external resource. A number of training designs can be built around these books. A group could meet once a week to share, compare, and discuss answers to a chapter's questions. In a workshop extending over several days a group could be taken, or could take itself, through the content and questions of one of these books. Alternatively, workshop participants could be divided into small groups, each responsible for working on one or two chapters. Eventually, each would summarize, for the benefit of the larger group, key chapter content and its consensus answers to the questions, seeking larger-group reactions/additions to the latter.

Succeeding as a Self-Managed Team, by Richard Y. Chang and Mark J. Curtin, is a 100-page book and part of the Practical Guidebook series offered by Richard Chang Associates, Inc., Publications Division. Its purpose is to help a traditionally managed work group make the transition to a self-managed team or teams. The authors describe the book as providing "an outline of what to expect during the transition," and doing so "in a logical, sequential and straightforward manner" (p. 1). In this reviewer's opinion *an outline*, albeit a useful one, is largely what is provided. The book contains nine brief chapters and two appendices. The first appendix describes ten ongoing challenges for self-managed teams (e.g., team leadership, intra-team and external communication, peer coaching, and feedback), though these same items were earlier identified in the text as "*skills* necessary for success with self-managed teams" (p. 8, emphasis added). The second appendix contains three reproducible forms introduced and used in the text.

In the first two chapters self-managed teams are described and distinguished from traditional work groups; personal qualities likely related to the success of self-managed teams are listed (e.g., willingness to accept change, to try new things, work responsibly without the need for supervision); and the various personal and organizational benefits, and benefits for customers, arising from self-managed work teams are identified.

Chapter 3 presents a five-phase *Team Transition Model* designed to move a group or department through some of the predictable early issues to the point of achieving initial success operating with self-management. Chapters 4 through 8 each deal with one particular phase of the model, while Chapter 9 is a summary. Each chapter ends with questions, including space for answers, which permit the reader to write down specifics pertaining to his or her setting.

The five phases of the *Team Transition Model* are plan, analyze, design, implement, and evaluate. The first letter of each phase together form the acronym PADIE, used throughout the book. Described under each phase are three or four team tasks to be carried out and, frequently, under a team task several subtasks are listed. Taking one chapter as an example, Chapter 4, "Phase One: Plan," deals with the planning phase. The three major tasks to be carried out during this phase are to *set the stage, clarify your sense of purpose*, and *to determine and communicate the effects of establishing teams on others*, both inside and outside of the organization. Under *setting the stage* a team clarifies why there is to be a changeover to self-managed teams; the likely benefits of this way of working are identified. *Clarifying your sense of purpose* involves three subtasks: developing a team *vision*, a picture of how the team wants to be known in the future; a team *mission statement*, a statement of what the team will do, including the benchmarks that must be met in order for the team to achieve its vision; and identifying team *core values*. Helpful examples are provided in the text that permit readers to distinguish between vision, mission, and core values, items around which there frequently is confusion. The final task in the "Plan" phase is *to let internal and external suppliers and customers know about the changes being planned in the department/group*, because these groups may have to coordinate and communicate with the department/team in a different way.

Collectively, the tasks identified in the book are presented in a logical sequence and can serve as a checklist for groups working to become self-managing. The tasks for the planning phase were covered above. Sampling the remaining chapters of the book (Chapters 5 through 8), two tasks suggested for teams for each of the remaining four phases are:

- Clarify how the various team management responsibilities will be handled ("Analyze")
- To become a team where members are multiskilled, identify what skills members currently have and determine who has the potential to learn new jobs ("Analyze")
- Assign team management and administrative responsibilities ("Design")
- Design the work flow ("Design")

- Create action plans for initial team projects ("Implement")
- Ensure tasks and responsibilities are performed on schedule ("Implement")
- Provide team members with feedback from each other ("Evaluate")
- Gain feedback from important sources outside of the team, such as customers, suppliers, and senior management ("Evaluate")

Among the strengths of the book is the listing of important tasks for traditionally organized groups moving toward self-management; and the clear suggestion that groups approach this transition in a planned way. Another plus are the end-of-chapter questions that permit team members, perhaps with a consultant's help, to do specific thinking about these tasks on their way through the book. Various forms are provided to assist teams in these tasks, and these are helpful, as well. Also, the book explains well how self-managed teams linked directly with customers will permit teams to serve customers better; and it is successful in showing how teams must keep customer needs in mind in all of their activities.

One of the book's important weaknesses is its overly optimistic and perhaps naive view of the ease and speed of a team assuming responsibilities previously belonging to management and supervision. What is described in the text will be true for the rare case only. **The Chang and Curtin text could be supplemented with the first one or two Glaser articles, which provide a more realistic view and more detailed road map, or by the video,** Self-Directed Work Teams, **which does a good job in presenting the "star" model of leadership**.

The text can also be faulted for the things that are not mentioned or provided at certain points. For example, the prospects and fates of managers and supervisors under team self-management are not discussed at all. The discussion of how to form self-managed teams, that is, how to organize or cluster employees, is far too brief, and needs not only to be more extensive but illustrated with examples. Causing some confusion, by the way, is that this discussion occurs in the text *after* teams are directed to establish a vision, mission, core values, code of team member conduct, etc.! The popular "star" approach for distributing managerial responsibilities is not mentioned as an option. Neither is pay-for-skills compensation mentioned in the discussion of cross-training workers, nor are alternative approaches to compensation with self-managed teams. Despite the text's emphasis on the customer, there is no discussion of any simple, yet useful, methods for teams to use to monitor quality. Perhaps this is because these are addressed in other Chang Associates, Inc., publications.

The shortcomings of Succeeding as a Self-Managed Team **can be offset by the decision to use an experienced trainer or consultant along with the text. The overall flow of the text is good; the trainer or consultant could involve prospective team members in the text, providing along the way necessary amplification, additional options and tools, and additional questions for team members to answer.**

Succeeding as a Self-Directed Work Team: 20 Important Questions Answered

At slightly over 100 pages, the book by Bob and Ann Harper, **Succeeding as a Self-Directed Work Team: 20 Important Questions Answered**, is designed to impart in brief, quickly-read form, basic and important information about self-directed work teams. Written primarily for team members but also for managers, supervisors, and team leaders the book is organized around 20 questions. The title of each section is one of these questions. For example, the titles of the first three sections are, "Is This (self-directed work teams) a New Idea?" "What Is a Self-Directed Work Team?" and "How Is It Different From Traditional Work?" Answers to questions average one or two pages although a few run from five to seven pages. Each section concludes with two to four questions for readers that "are designed to help you think through and clarify for yourself some of the most important issues surrounding SELF-DIRECTED work teams and the dramatic changes they bring about" (p. iii). Teams are also encouraged to discuss these questions. Generous space for written answers is provided. For example, at the conclusion of the section that explains why self-directed work teams have suddenly become popular ("Why SDWTs Now?") the following questions are asked:

- What is the compelling reason we are moving to SDWTs now or thinking about doing this now?
- Have the compelling reasons (the "Why are we doing this?") been clearly communicated to everyone?
- Do I agree or disagree with the reasons?

A comprehensive article on self-managed teams would probably cover the same ground as is covered by this book. These questions distinguish the book from an article version and make **Succeeding as a Self-Directed Work Team: 20 Questions** more valuable as a result.

With a few exceptions the questions addressed by the book are arranged in logical order. Following the early sections that identify what self-directed work teams are, why organizations are using them today, and examples of the outcomes achieved where they have been used, subsequent sections deal with the way self-directed work teams operate differently than traditional work groups; the characteristics of self-managed teams that seem to lead to success; the obstacles on the path to success; benefits of self-directed teams for both the employee and the organization; the way self-directed work teams handle the issue of team leadership, and the role of managers and supervisors in the new system; the attitudinal, interpersonal, and technical skills needed by team members; transforming the organization from a traditional one to one built around teams; and the stages self-directed work teams go through. The last section, titled "What Else Can I Read About SDWTs?", is a bibliography of eleven books and no articles, though articles are generally more reader-friendly; and at least three of the books were written primarily for academic audiences.

Some similar information is departed by both the Chang and Curtin book and the one by the Harpers. However, Chang and Curtin's is stronger in providing concrete direction on handling key tasks that are internal to the team while the Harper book is stronger in providing information on the transformation of an organization to self-managed teams. The Harper book also better conveys how important a supportive organization climate is to team success, and does a better job describing the other obstacles facing teams. *Of the two books, more parts of the one by the Harpers would be directly reinforced and illustrated by the videos reviewed above. In contrast, the videos would primarily add new information to the Chang and Curtin text rather than function to reinforce or extend what is there.*

Among the strengths of **Succeeding as a Self-Directed Work Team: 20 Questions**, as already has been suggested, are the many questions requiring readers to write out their reactions, identify and address their concerns, identify potential roadblocks, and so on. The value of a group's or a department's members sharing and discussing their answers could be profound. In contrast with all the other resources reviewed for this article (except the other book by the Harpers, below), labor-management relations are mentioned here in several sections — at least three (sections, 5, 8, and 9) — and the need for these parties to develop a new, cooperative, and mutually respectful relationship is linked to the success of teams. The text also provides teams with various options for handling managerial responsibilities and team leadership, important issues in team self-management; asks team members how these responsibilities will be handled; and asks the reader to answer if he/she is interested or not in leading or sharing leadership of a self-directed work team, and to explain his/her answer.

In terms of negatives, **Succeeding as a Self-Directed Work Team: 20 Questions**, in its quest for brevity, sometimes fails to clarify enough. The answers provided to some questions are likely to raise additional questions in the reader that aren't answered, and even create an inaccurate understanding of what establishing teams involves. For example, in asserting that "quality control and maintenance are part of the team's responsibilities not separate functions" (p. 11) it may be assumed that these functions cease to exist. Workers may well wonder how they are going to perform — and whether they want to perform — all of maintenance's tasks. Also on p. 11, to blunt possible negative employee reactions, some further explanation and justification should be given in addition to merely stating, "The teams schedule which members will do a task; some assign rotating tasks." In the section, "Question 8: What Are the Possible Drawbacks?", one of the drawbacks mentioned is "managers abdicate responsibility" (p. 37). Why this is bad may not be clear: Aren't teams supposed to manage now? Other examples could be given. A more extensive and partitioned bibliography could also give readers access to more information on the brief but numerous examples given of successful company applications of self-managed work teams; union-management cooperation; the distribution of leadership responsibilities in teams; new approaches to rewards that are supportive of teams; organization change processes, and other issues. There is some redundancy between sections, and in the questions asked of readers. A better placement for "Question 10: What Are the Benefits for the Organization?" and "Question 11: What Are the Benefits for the Team Member?" would have been closer to the beginning of the book. The book also argues, on the basis of past organizational experience, the importance of trust and the need to provide team members with job security (pp. 43-45). Few organizations today are trustworthy or willing to provide assurance of continued employment. How companies are handling these issues *today* needs to be addressed.

EXERCISES

1. How Independent Is Our Team? The Gulowsen Autonomy Scales

Members of self-managed teams often have widely divergent beliefs about how much autonomy they have or should have as individuals and as a team. This leads to team member behavior that can differ greatly. Those taking initiative and action are perceived as acting out-of-bounds by those who would have refrained from both in the same situations, and the latter are perceived by the former as too traditional. Differences like this can create real strain in a group and, if group members do not have the skills to address these differences, they can divide a group, morale can plunge, and teams can be abandoned by key team members (Klein, 1991).

An exercise from OD&D permits team members to learn how each member and the team as a whole perceive the autonomy of the team. The inventory, **How Independent Is Our Team? The Gulowsen Autonomy Scales**, can also be used to reveal how much autonomy members and the team believe the team *should* have. The inventory is available with a facilitator guide and is based on Jon Gulowsen's autonomy scales (Gulowsen, 1971, 1979). Both are written by Rollin Glaser, who says, "The results of this inventory should be used to promote a discussion in the group that is aimed at clarifying the group's decision-making authority and identifying changes that could help the group to become more effective in its work, its relationships with each other, and its relationships with other teams" (Glaser, 1991a, p. 10).

The instrument measures perceived (and, with slight adjustment, *desired*) team autonomy in seven areas. A group scoring high in all or almost all of the areas can be described as fully autonomous or self-directed. The seven areas are team autonomy in:

- formulating its goals
- governing its own performance (e.g., determining working hours and authorizing employee absences from work, determining the timing and priority of tasks)

427

- choosing its production method
- distributing its own tasks among the work group
- deciding on its membership, including the ability to choose and dismiss members
- deciding on its leadership, and whether the group wants a formal leader
- determining how individual job operations will be performed

OD&D suggests that the inventory can be used with newly formed self-managing teams, teams that have been operating for a while, or to diagnose as part of a team-building session a group's autonomy before the transition to self-management. ***The inventory could certainly be used in conjunction with many of the materials reviewed thus far. It could be used with the Glaser articles — the work of Gulowsen is, in fact, described in the first two of them; with the books by Chang and Curtin and Bob and Ann Harper; and following the video,*** Self-Directed Work Teams. ***Each of these resources emphasizes the assumption of decision-making responsibilities by teams; the inventory could be used to explore how far in this direction teams have gone or would like to go. Specifically, the inventory could be used as an extension of the third section of the Harper's book, "Question 3: How Is It (working in a self-directed team) Different From Traditional Work?," or preceding the reading of two later sections (Questions 16 and 17) that are concerned with the new technical and team skills, and team training, that are required. (The assumption of more autonomy often requires additional skills.) The inventory could also be used to supplement the "Analyze" or "Design" chapters of the Chang and Curtin text.***

The instrument itself consists of thirty-five items. All items make use of the same five-point Likert response scale where 5 represents, "This statement is completely characteristic of our group," and 1 represents, "This statement is completely uncharacteristic of our group." At points 2 and 4, the word "somewhat" replaces the word "completely," while 3 on the scale means, "I am uncertain about how characteristic this statement is of our group." The following represent a sample of the thirty-five items:

- "Our group assigns work to its own members."
- "Our group can dismiss undesirable members."
- "Management appoints our group leader(s) who handles relationships outside of the group."

Certainly, scores of 5 on questions like the first two indicate that a team has high autonomy. Seven of the thirty-five questions are worded like the last one, above, and are reversed scored: that is, the answer, "This statement is completely uncharacteristic of our group," is awarded a 5 rather than a 1 as it reveals high team autonomy.

Once the inventory is completed scores in each of the seven areas can be quickly calculated by team members. An overall inventory score is obtained when these seven scores are totaled. The manual for participants containing both the inventory and response sheet permits a member to compare his/her total score with the average total score for an entire team. One of the following labels applies to the team depending on the size of its average total score: "Other-Directed," "Semi-Participating," "Participating," "Semiautonomous," or "Autonomous." Each of these labels is defined in the booklet.

The booklet also permits members to compare their scores in each of the seven areas with the average team score for each of the seven, as well. Actually, if the matrix provided in the booklet for recording this data is made into a transparency, and the team is not too large, it can be used to post *everyone's* scores for the seven areas. The participant's manual suggests that where differences are great enough member responses to individual items be examined. Members whose responses differ significantly should offer an explanation or rationale.

When a team has its members use the inventory to identify how much autonomy the team *should* have the participant's manual suggests that

> the most appropriate answer to this question is another question, "What does our work require?" For example, if the group's evaluation of (the item), "Our group interviews and selects its own members," is that it is not a characteristic practice of the group, the discussion might focus on whether or not this really matters to the group's performance. If the answer is that it does matter, then this may be a subject for the group or the group leader to discuss with those who have the authority to change this. . .rule. (Glaser, 1991a, p. 10)

2. Skill Building for Self-Directed Team Members: A Complete Course

Most of the resources for self-directed teams reviewed earlier underscore the importance of team members developing new skills. The video, **Self-Directed Work Teams**, features team members describing the training they received to help them handle their star responsibilities. The articles by Glaser for team facilitators and team members describe the new personal and social skills required, as do the texts by Chang and Curtin, and by Bob and Ann Harper.

The building of team member skills is the avowed purpose of the spiral-bound workbook by Bob and Ann Harper, **Skill Building for Self-Directed Team Members: A Complete Course**. In addition to a focus on skills, its eighteen chapters provide orienting information on self-directed work teams, permit groups to develop plans for transitioning to self-directed teams, and move teams toward agreement on important aspects of team life, such as team ground rules, meeting behavior, and team behavior when there is conflict. (A 19th and 20th chapter contain, respectively, recommended readings and a listing of products and services to support self-directed work teams.) The first eight chapters of this book are, in fact, similar in intent as the book by Chang and Curtin and the earlier book by the Harpers: to create a team infrastructure and team plans concerning such things as the transfer of management responsibilities to team members and cross-training team members that make a successful transition to complete team self-management more likely. Much of the earlier Harper book has been incorporated into this book, especially in Chapters 1 through 8. With the exception of portions of Chapters 1 through 8, Chapters 9 through 18 contain the skill-building components of the workbook and the skill-building exercises. These chapters cover such topics as effective team meetings; listening, disclosure of information, and interpersonal feedback; group skills and group dynamics; decision-making skills; conflict management and quality improvement skills. The chapters generally follow a similar format involving first, individual reflection and assessment, then team discussion culminating in team decisions and commitments. One chapter will be described as an example. Chapter 9, "Effective Team Meetings," begins with a page that describes the benefits and importance of regular team meetings, and offers some suggestions for making meetings more effective. This is followed by a 25-item individual assessment of team meeting behavior. On a five-point scale, where "0" means "never" and "4" means "always," team members evaluate statements about team meetings such as, "Everyone understands the purpose of the meeting," and "We carefully plan the order of the agenda, placing the most important items first." Members total their scores. On a page titled, "Team Exercise: Effective Team Meetings," members are instructed to discuss their answers with the entire team and to answer as a team the following two questions:

1. What do team members see as some of the strengths about your team meetings?
2. What are some areas the team needs to improve? (Make a list of all the suggestions for improvements.)

The following page, titled "Action Commitments," has the following instructions: "Discuss and agree on actions the team feels need to be taken at this time to make team meetings more effective."

One strength of the workbook is that it closely links success with self-managed teams to the acquisition of various team, team member, and team facilitator skills. The skill-building units with their individual and team exercises are more credible and compelling because they follow chapters that describe the personal and social skills necessary if team self-management is to be successful and its many benefits realized. Certainly another strength of the workbook is that it permits teams and team members, whose time might be limited, to quickly get into an area or topic; and in an hour to an hour and a half to experience learning and/or discuss and reach a team decision. Another strength of the workbook is that all chapters attempt to involve team members in an active discussion concerning some aspect of their functioning. For example, the conclusion of the chapter, "Measuring Your Team," lists the following questions for group discussion:

1. How does your team currently get feedback?
2. What does your team currently measure?
3. Are there other dimensions the team should be measuring (teamwork, customer service, etc.)? (p. 57)

The questions posed here and in the other chapters, as in the earlier Harper book, are good ones and, when discussed by a team, are likely to lead to team improvement.

In terms of shortcomings, the workbook offers no active guidance on how these issues should be addressed. Certainly, availability of team meeting time, a scarce resource in most settings, should be devoted to discussing and resolving the most pressing issues. It would seem as if the current table of contents could be supplemented with a second that lists various team problems and the chapters that are most relevant for addressing each. For teams using this workbook on their own, I would not recommend that they start with Chapter 1 and work their way from there to the end. Rather, I would recommend an ordering of the chapters to match the most pressing current needs of a team, including its informational needs.

In addition, since team facilitators and members may lack experience in conducting exercises involving individual sharing, group discussion, and achieving group consensus it is recommended that teams involve an experienced trainer or consultant in at least the initial team sessions that involve the use of this book. There are most certainly skills that are necessary if the promise of the exercises are to be realized. Were a team to attempt tackling the workbook on its own, certainly an important requirement would be *excellent* meeting skills and behavior. If a team was not strong in this area it could conceivably use the workbook to become stronger; this is where it would start.

Finally, experienced trainers and consultants will not be entirely pleased with the coverage, thoroughness, and tools of every chapter. For them, the workbook would function as a point of departure. They would likely find themselves adding information and concepts to what is there, using different individual and team exercises, and modifying or adding to the team discussion questions. While I had these feelings at several points in my review of this resource, it was clear that involving teams in active discussion of the topics covered by the workbook and working to develop team member skills in the various areas identified would, eventually, be of great benefit.

FOOTNOTES

1. See *Redesigning a workplace for self-regulation: The Rohm & Haas Kentucky story.* Philadelphia, PA: Blue Sky Productions, Inc., and Ecology of Work, 1991. Running time: 34 minutes; and *Everybody Leads.* Philadelphia, PA: Blue Sky Productions, Inc., 1991. Running time: 26 minutes. See below for information on ordering these videos.

2. Full texts on self-managed work teams include: E. E. Lawler, III, *The ultimate advantage: Creating the high-involvement organization.* San Francisco, CA: Jossey-Bass, 1992; J. D. Orsburn, L. Moran, E. Musslewhite, and J. H. Zenger, *Self-Directed Work Teams: The New American Challenge.* Homewood, IL: Irwin, 1990; R. S. Wellins, W. C. Byham, and J. M. Wilson, *Empowered teams: Creating self-directed work groups that improve quality, participation and productivity.* San Francisco, CA: Jossey-Bass, 1991; and J. M. Wilson, J. George, and R. S. Wellins with W. C. Byham, *Leadership trapeze: Strategies for leadership in team-based organizations.* San Franciso, CA: Jossey-Bass, 1994.

RESOURCES REVIEWED
(In the order reviewed)

Videos

Self-Directed Work Teams—Redesigning the Workplace for the 21st Century. Spartanburg, SC: Video 2000, Inc., 1988. Running time: 29 minutes.

Improving Work Systems. Philadelphia, PA: Blue Sky Productions, Inc., 1992. Running time: 27 minutes.

Leading a Service Team: A Day with a High Performance Work Team Facilitator. Philadelphia, PA: Blue Sky Productions, Inc., 1991. Running time: 32 minutes.

Videos here and above (footnote 1) are available from sources that include: Blue Sky Productions, Inc., 5918 Pulaski Avenue, Philadelphia, PA 19144 (1-800-358-0022). Blue Sky cannot provide *Self-Directed Work Teams—Redesigning the Workplace for the 21st Century*; MW Corporation, 3150 Lexington Avenue, Mohegan Lake, NY 10547 (1-914-528-0888); and Sagotsky Multimedia, P.O. Box 587, Rocky Hill, NJ 08553 (1-800-921-0999).

Books and Related Materials

Glaser, Rollin. ***Four Articles on Self-Managed Teams (articles sold separately or as a package of four): Moving Your Team Toward Self-Management (1992); Facilitating Self-Managing Teams (1991); Learning to Be a Self-Managing Team (1991); and Helping Your Organization Gear Up for Self-Managing Teams (1991).*** King of Prussia, PA: Organization Design and Development. Available from *HRD Quarterly* (Managed by Organization Design and Development, Inc.), 2002 Renaissance Boulevard, Suite 100, King of Prussia, PA 19406 (1-800-633-4533).

Chang, Richard Y., and Mark J. Curtin (1994). ***Succeeding as a Self-Managed Team.*** Irvine, CA: Richard Chang Associates, Inc., Publications Division. Available from Pfeiffer & Co., 2780 Circleport Drive, Erlanger, KY 41018 (1-800-274-4434).

Harper, Bob, and Ann Harper (1992). ***Succeeding as a Self-Directed Team: 20 Important Questions Answered.*** Mohegan Lake, NY: MW Corporation. Available from MW Corporation, 3150 Lexington Avenue, Mohegan Lake, NY 10547 (1-914-528-0888).

Exercises

Glaser, Rollin (1991). ***How Independent Is Our Team? The Gulowsen Autonomy Scales*** and ***How Independent Is Our Team? Trainer Guide***. King of Prussia, PA: Organization Design and Development. Available from *HRD Quarterly* (Managed by Organization Design and Development, Inc.), 2002 Renaissance Boulevard, Suite 100, King of Prussia, PA 19406 (1-800-633-4533).

Harper, Ann, and Bob Harper (1992). ***Skill-Building for Self-Directed Team Members: A Complete Coursebook***. Mohegan Lake, NY: MW Corporation. Available from MW Corporation, 3150 Lexington Avenue, Mohegan Lake, NY 10547 (1-914-528-0888).

BIBLIOGRAPHY

Glaser, Rollin. (1991a). *How independent is our team? The Gulowsen autonomy scales*. King of Prussia, PA: Organization Design and Development.

Glaser, Rollin. (1991b). *How independent is our team? Trainer guide*. King of Prussia, PA: Organization Design and Development.

Gulowsen, Jon. (1971). *A measure of work group autonomy*. Oslo: Tanum Press.

Gulowsen, Jon. (1979). "A measure of work group autonomy." In L.E. Davis and J. D. Taylor (Eds.), *Design of Jobs* (2nd ed.). Santa Monica, CA: Goodyear Publishing.

Klein, Gerald D. (1991). "A case of semiautonomous teams in a manufacturing setting: The consequences of benign neglect." *Proceedings*, 1991 International Conference on Self-Managed Work Teams. Denton, TX: Interdisciplinary Center for the Study of Work Teams, University of North Texas.

About the Contributor

Dr. Gerald D. Klein is Associate Professor of Organizational Behavior and Management at Rider University. He has a long-standing interest in self-managed work teams, has taught about them virtually since their inception in this country in the early seventies, and has researched and written about these and other forms of employee empowerment. Dr. Klein is a regular and invited presenter at the International Conference on Self-Managed Work Teams and has organized and chaired panels at this conference on the supervisor's role under team self-management and self-managed teams in services. His articles have appeared in such journals as *National Productivity Review, Personnel, California Management Review,* and *Journal of Management Education.*

34

Resources on Empowerment
Victor M. Kline

INTRODUCTION

This article will look at several books, videos, and instruments on empowerment that can be useful resources for those interested in understanding more about the theory and applications surrounding this subject.

Why resources on empowerment in *The Handbook of Best Practices for Teams, Volume I*? For organizations relying on special teams to support strategic initiatives such as manufacturing cycle time reduction, new product development, or mergers and acquisitions, the issue of empowerment is central to the effectiveness of those teams, and ultimately the achievement of the strategic objectives for which they are responsible. Ultimately, empowerment means survival for organizations. As authors Vogt and Murrell state in their book, *Empowerment in Organizations*:

> Organizations built on control and not on an empowering perspective seem to be finding it very difficult to respond to the new challenges of global competition. Often they pay very high salaries but do not reap a commensurate return. They are frequently organizations bloated with layer upon layer of redundant employees competing with organizations with half as many levels of management. They are organizations that hire the best and brightest young professionals, only to see them leave in short order because of their stifling rules and control orientation. They are the organizations being outmaneuvered by young mavericks, savvy foreign competitors with lower labor costs, and their own employees who break away and establish competing firms. Such control-oriented and bureaucratic organizations are not developing either internally or in terms of new markets, and their days are numbered.

For those of us who will be playing a role in creating and supporting empowering work environments, whether as a trainer, team leader, facilitator, manager, senior executive, or colleague, it is important to understand how to use the principles of empowerment to tap the potential of people. Here are some resources that can be of help.

BOOKS

Empowerment in Organizations: How to Spark Exceptional Performance
Judith F. Vogt, Ph.D. and Kenneth L. Murrell, D.B.A.
Pfeiffer & Company, Inc.
8517 Production Avenue
San Diego, CA 92121
(800) 274-4434
© 1991

This is not a trivial, pop-psychology book on empowerment. It is also not a step-by-step "cookbook" for implementing empowerment. Instead, it is a comprehensive treatment of the subject that should be required reading for organization development and human resource development professionals, senior managers, trainers, team leaders, line managers, labor leaders, quality steering committees, and others serious about assuming their roles as change agents around the issue of empowerment in organizations. It will provide implementers with an essential understanding of the complex social, psychological, and organizational dynamics surrounding empowerment, the strategies for organizational change, and a sense of the true potential that can be realized through an empowerment process. It will also aid them in making well-informed decisions about empowerment strategies and implementation steps, and evaluating and selecting resources to support their work. The book has relevance not only for those in business organizations, but also those in the fields of education, health care, law, and government.

The book is divided into ten chapters. In each, the authors develop certain key themes (such as management's power and control needs) which they build on in subsequent chapters. The Appendix contains three empowerment instruments that are reviewed in detail in the "Assessment Instruments" section, of this paper:

- Management Styles Survey: Organizational Culture
- Management Styles Survey: Subordinates' Perceptions
- Management Styles Survey: Manager's Perception

Following are some of the topics addressed in the book:

- How events such as the global energy crisis, or a serious competitive threat to a company, rather than being destructive, can actually serve as catalysts for a transition to a more empowering level of interaction among people

- The need to reconceptualize leadership in organizations toward a concept of shared leadership, what the manager's empowerment role is, and case vignettes to illustrate what each component of that role looks like in practice in real work environments

- The origins of the empowerment movement in the work of Maslow, Carl Rogers, Elton Mayo, and others, including those shaping the fields of organization development and human resource development such as Chris Argyris, Warren Bennis, Jack Gibbs, and Peter Block

- The role of human resource development and organization development practitioners in the empowerment process

- Competencies that change agents should possess, and issues they need to come to grips with before taking on this role

- Case studies illustrating the various ways managers can be empowering to others, and how organizations can be empowering to their people, as well as the role of the effective group as a vehicle for empowering organizations

- Implementation strategies for different settings and different cultures (including a discussion of Japanese versus American models), and cautions for implementers to consider in developing an approach to fit their own circumstances

Applications

The authors should be congratulated for the excellent job they have done in tracing the roots of empowerment and tying together the many threads into a coherent unfolding of our current understanding of its history, its present state, and its potential for the future. They have approached their task with vision and passion and a belief in the true potential that the empowerment process has to offer.

To many readers, however, it will seem like an overwhelming task to integrate all of the complex social, psychological, and organizational factors presented in the book and arrive at a specific plan of action. While it may be easier to turn directly to a quick-fix cookbook, change agents and decision makers helping their organizations embark on the empowerment journey need to understand the complex nature of organizational change and the variables that come into play, and then apply their new insights to the plans they develop for their organizations. The insights gained working through this book will more than offset the time spent.

Zapp! The Lightening of Empowerment: How to Improve Productivity, Quality, and Employee Satisfaction
William C. Byham, Ph.D. and Jeff Cox
Harmony Books
201 E. 50th Street
New York, NY 10022
© 1988

Bill Byham and Ron Cox's book *Zapp!* has become a classic on the subject of empowerment. It focuses on the role of the leader and how his or her actions can either motivate and empower others, or serve to demotivate and suppress involvement, commitment, and creativity.

Presented in the form of a fable with sci-fi elements, the story traces the transformation of Joe Mode, a department manager working for a company where "managers do the thinking, supervisors do the talking, and employees do the doing."

The advantage of using a fable format is that it enables the reader to arrive at insights and conclusions as the tale unfolds, rather than spoon-feeding the conclusions. It also enables the reader to focus on the principles being presented without getting sidetracked by the type of company, type of industry, etc.

Bill Byham and co-author Ron Cox explore the influence of two powerful, opposing leadership forces. The positive, constructive force is called Zapp! and it energizes people. The opposite force is Sapp and it drains energy, enthusiasm, and commitment from people. As the story unfolds, the lead character learns how these two forces work. He jots notes down about his insights and learnings in a notebook and the authors strategically place these pages inside black borders throughout the text to highlight the key principles for the readers.

The prescription for success that develops page by page in Joe Mode's notebook is essentially good leadership skills broken down into easily followed Key Steps such as "Maintain Self Esteem" and "Listen and Respond with Empathy." The principles of delegation, effective goal setting, performance feedback, coaching and development, and even process improvement are also covered. Throughout the story, Byham and Cox provide specific examples of what these skills look like in practice.

From empowering individuals the book moves on to empowering teams.

This is a very easy to read book: Big type, very short chapters, cute story line, and clear, easy to spot profiles of the main points for later review or skimming ahead. No major effort is required to complete it in one or two sittings. It is extremely positive and constructive in its perspective, and should enable managers and leaders to see empowerment as doable.

Applications

Zapp! has been used very effectively as assigned pre-reading for executive committees prior to discussing empowerment initiatives with outside consultants. Plant management teams have read the book and discussed the concepts, and then developed action steps to implement them in their departments. Training departments have developed courses and workshops on empowerment for leaders built around the simple, easy to understand concepts. And copies of the book have been provided to individual managers and team leaders who need to understand how to better empower their people and teams. Human resource development and organization development practitioners, and internal and external management and quality consultants, have even provided copies to clients to spur interest in empowerment, as well as to respond to a need to address employee productivity and team development issues.

Two cautions in using the book. First, experience has shown that the excitement and enthusiasm that is generated by the book fades extremely quickly if there is no follow up to apply the ideas. Merely handing out the book and exchanging comments about how insightful the authors were, "Boy do they have this place pegged!" won't have much of an impact in changing the environment or leader behavior. Change agents and advisors need to structure the use of this book in such a way that the insights for action are captured by the clients, and concrete steps are taken to implement the concepts.

The second caution has to do with the conditions necessary for effective behavior change. In addition to specific action plans to put the concepts into practice, skill training is strongly recommended. There is little evidence that reading a stimulating and exciting book about the principles of playing competent golf, for example, will help you actually play better golf. You need to try out the skills, maybe get some coaching and feedback from a pro, and then practice until you master the steps. Byham and Cox know this, and at the end of the book the enlightened Joe Mode is heard saying to a new supervisor "Well, you might learn the skills to improve Zapp by trial and error, the way I did. But that takes a long time and you can make a lot of unnecessary mistakes. What I recommend is that you build your skills in one of Lucy's training programs so you're more likely to succeed with Zapp the first time you try."

HeroZ: Empower Yourself, Your Coworkers, Your Company
William C. Byham, Ph.D. and Ron Cox
Harmony Books
201 E. 50th Street
New York, NY 10022
© 1994

In 1994, Bill Byham and Ron Cox followed their highly successful book *Zapp!* with the release of a companion book, *HeroZ.* While *Zapp!* was written for and about leaders and their role in creating empowered individuals and teams, *HeroZ* is written for the individual contributor and team member who does not want to wait for their leaders to become enlightened.

This time the fable is set in medieval times. (That is all we are going to tell you about the story line so we don't take away the fun of reading the book for yourselves.) It centers on a work group of three first-line employees, Art, Wendy, and Mac, who "take control of their jobs and relentlessly improve the way they work so that in the end everybody wins."

As in *Zapp!*, the key insights that the trio arrive at in their quest for empowerment are inserted throughout the book as boxed notes that Art posts at his workbench so he won't forget them. These outline specific principles and steps for individuals and team members to follow in empowering themselves and those around them.

The range of topics the book addresses is truly amazing: principles of process improvement; the steps in problem-solving; presenting an idea to your boss and dealing with his or her objections; coaching a co-worker; how to reinforce and praise a co-worker; how to problem solve in teams; how to increase customer satisfaction; how to set meaningful goals; how to develop a charter and mission for your team; how to hold effective meetings. All of these concepts are brought to life through the examples of the growth and development of our three employees.

What this enjoyable book turns out to be is a handbook for the individual employee, team member, and professional for managing the many interactions and processes that are required to be a truly empowered contributor in their organization. It illustrates how anyone can take the initiative to better themselves and their work environment, instead of waiting to be given permission.

Applications

Human resource development departments can use *HeroZ* in assertive skills, development planning, and career management workshops. Managers can hand out *HeroZ* to those people who show the spark of empowerment, and use the concepts in coaching and mentoring discussions to help fan the flame. Change agents and consultants supporting team development activities can provide *HeroZ* as a just-in-time resource when the team is ready, and refer to pertinent sections in team meetings when team and individual member development issues arise. Self-managed work teams can be given *HeroZ* as their survival manual.

Like *Zapp!*, the book is also large-print, has short chapters, and is very easy to read. The only downside is that the authors try to cram a lot of key steps and concepts into the last third of the book. This requires a lot more effort on the part of the reader to work through the final chapters. Facilitators might want to provide some outside incentive or goal to keep people from losing interest and abandoning the book when it is two-thirds completed.

The same cautions about behavior change apply to *HeroZ* as they did with *Zapp!* Understanding the interpersonal skills and concepts necessary to be self-empowering and effective in teams is one thing, being able to develop and apply those skills may require skills training.

ASSESSMENT INSTRUMENTS

Empowerment Inventory
Kenneth W. Thomas, Ph.D. and Walter G. Tymon, Jr., Ph.D.
Xicom, Incorporated
RR#2 Woods Road
Tuxedo, New York 10987
(800) 759-4266
© 1993

About the Instrument

The *Empowerment Inventory* is a self-scoring, self-assessment instrument that measures the degree to which an individual feels empowered by his or her entire job, participation on a team, or work on a specific project, task, or in a specific role. In addition, it provides suggestions for actions that the individual or his/her teammates can take to increase feelings of empowerment. It should take about fifteen minutes to complete and score, plus an hour or so to consider development actions to put the insights to use.

The *Inventory* was developed by Kenneth W. Thomas, Ph.D. and Walter G. Tymon, Jr., Ph.D. Both have had extensive experience developing and validating instruments used in training and human resource development. Dr. Thomas is known for the *Thomas-Kilmann Conflict Mode Instrument*, as well as the *Power Base Inventory* and the *Stress Resiliency Profile*, which he co-authored with Dr. Tymon (all published by Xicom).

Thomas and Tymon define empowerment as an energizing "sense of excitement, vitality and enthusiasm" about a specific role or task. They see empowerment as situational, meaning that an individual can feel empowered in some areas of their work or personal lives and not in others.

The model they developed out of their research on empowerment in managerial populations is built around the *Empowerment Grid*, which focuses on the relationship among four categories of feelings that individuals can have about their work or tasks. Described in detail in the *Empowerment Inventory*, these are: feelings of choice, feelings of competence, feelings of meaningfulness, and feelings of progress.*

443

---

* For more background please see Thomas and Tymon's paper on p. 291 of this Handbook.

The fifteen page *Empowerment Inventory* booklet consists of a questionnaire, scoring instructions, and scoring grids; a guide to interpreting the scores on the *Inventory*; and a section on actions that individuals and/or their teammates can take to increase their sense of empowerment.

The first section of the booklet contains the twenty-four item *Empowerment Inventory*. The person taking the inventory is asked to consider a series of statements and rate the degree to which he or she agrees or disagrees with each of those statements on a seven-point scale from "Strongly Agree" to "Strongly Disagree."

The questions themselves are straightforward and worded in such a way that they should be easily understood by managerial and professional employees. However, the instructions at the beginning of this section of the inventory do not make it clear to the respondents that they must either choose to focus on their entire job, or on a particular role or task, when answering the questions. Given the situational nature of the authors' model, it is important that the respondents have a specific focus when answering the questions. It is therefore suggested that the person administering the *Empowerment Inventory* ensure that those completing it are instructed to have a specific role, task, project, or team in mind when answering the questions.

Answering the twenty-four questions and completing the two scoring forms yields a graph showing how high or low an individual's scores are in relation to the scores of 390 empowered managers the authors used as the comparison group.

Dedicating a full page to each of the four basic feelings, the *Empowerment Inventory* then addresses team actions and personal actions that can be taken to enhance an individual's feelings of choice, competence, meaningfulness, and progress. The range of options should be sufficient to get most people back on track with some good development strategies for helping themselves and their teammates.

A nice addition to this final development planning section would have been an action plan form to provide a written way for people to commit to a schedule for implementing the development actions they selected.

Target Population

The most accurate results from the *Empowerment Inventory* will most likely occur when using the inventory with managers. The reason for this is based on how the scoring is done. An individual will score either high or low on the four empowerment feelings depending on how his or her scores compare with the managers that Thomas and Tymon used as their empowered normative population. Administrators of this survey should be aware that the normal range of scores on feelings of choice, competence, meaningfulness, and progress may be different for other job classifications.

Applications

While no single instrument can apply equally well to all situations, the *Empowerment Inventory* can be an extremely useful tool across a variety of situations.

1. Individual managers, department heads, team members, and team leaders interested in taking the initiative in enhancing their own sense of choice, competence, meaningfulness, and progress in their work should gain useful insights from the *Inventory*.

2. Human resource departments, department heads, team leaders, quality advisors, and consultants can make the instrument available on a voluntary basis to individuals and team members along with some suggestions on its use.

3. It can also be used as part of development planning workshops for individual managers and high-potentials to explore empowerment issues and discuss ways they can gain a greater sense of empowerment in their work.

4. As a team development tool, the *Empowerment Inventory* can help teams address some of the factors that affect the extent to which members get a sense of satisfaction out of their participation on the team, and feel a part of the team process. For example, individual team member scores could be posted anonymously and the team could discuss the meaning of those results and develop specific strategies for enhancing overall member sense of satisfaction with their roles on the team. Or, where trust levels are sufficiently high, the team profile results can be posted by name and the team can have a dialogue about how it can help each of its members by using the "Team Actions" suggestions in the back of the *Empowerment Inventory*.

5. Team leaders or team consultants could administer the survey and use the results in one-on-one coaching discussions with each team member. The purpose here might be to help individual members get greater satisfaction out of their participation on the team. At the same time, having access to the individual scoring profiles and action plan checklists from the team members would help the team leader or consultant identify general factors affecting the team environment that he or she can use to more effectively lead the team and motivate its members.

6. In a one-on-one coaching mode, department heads, managers, human resource development counselors, and consultants can use the *Empowerment Inventory* as a vehicle to structure a productive dialogue with an individual about feelings of empowerment in his/her

445

job, and together arrive at development actions that can be taken to enhance those feelings. The greatest value of the use of the *Empowerment Inventory* would most likely come early in the assignment of someone to a new job, project, or role on a team where it can serve as a checkpoint to evaluate how the individual is responding to the challenges of the job, and where additional support is needed.

7. To track progress, the *Empowerment Inventory* can be retaken and the new scores plotted on the scoring grid using a different color pencil or pen to show changes occurring since the previous date it was taken. Participants should also be encouraged to schedule a date to retake the instrument as a way to encourage follow through on their action steps.

I have one final caution for those administering the *Empowerment Inventory*. The promotional materials from the publisher and the instructions for the inventory both indicate that the inventory can be applied to an individual's involvement in activities from his/her personal life as well as on the job. For example, individuals can assess their feelings of empowerment in their role as a parent. Because the comparison group of managers the authors use in the scoring formula only rated their feelings about their *jobs*, the most valid conclusions will come from comparing an individual's scores with regard to their feelings about work-related activities.

Management Styles Surveys:
(1) Organizational Culture
(2) Subordinates' Perceptions
(3) Manager's Perceptions
Judith F. Vogt, Ph.D. and Kenneth L. Murrell, D.B.A
in the appendix to *Empowerment in Organizations*
University Associates, Inc.
8517 Production Avenue
San Diego, CA 92121
(800) 274-4434
© 1991

Note: 1995 editions of all three surveys are available from B.J. Chakiris Corporation, 250 S. Wacker Drive, Suite 635, Chicago, IL 60606-5834, (312) 258-1222. An updated version of the *Management Styles Survey: Organizational Culture* is also available separately as part of *The 1991 Annual: Developing Human Resources*, J. William Pfeiffer, Editor. It is available from Pfeiffer & Company, 8517 Production Avenue, San Diego, CA 92121, (619) 578-2042. Owners of the *Annual* may reproduce copies of its contents for educational/training events.

About the Instruments

In their book *Empowerment in Organizations* (reviewed earlier in this section), authors Vogt and Murrell show how important the role of management style is in establishing a climate in which employees and teams can be empowered. To assist managers and team leaders in assessing the extent to which their current style facilitates individual and team empowerment, the authors have developed three complementary instruments relating to managerial style. These are the *Management Styles Survey: Organizational Culture; Management Styles Survey: Subordinates' Perceptions;* and *Management Styles Survey: Manager's Perceptions*.

The survey titles give a fairly accurate indication of what they measure. The *Organizational Culture* survey is intended to provide an indication of how those completing the instrument perceive the prevailing climate in the organization *as a whole*, not just their own department or section. The *Subordinates' Perceptions* version shows how a manager's direct-reports view his or her leadership style in the context of empowering behaviors; and the *Manager's Perceptions* version is the manager's self-assessment.

Each survey consists of a thirty-item questionnaire, a scoring form, a grid on which to plot the scores, and an interpretation key to assist in understanding the scores. It should take approximately thirty minutes to complete and score any of the three surveys.

The degree to which managers need to exercise tight control over the use of power plays a key role in the scoring. As a result, these surveys will clearly reveal whether an organization or a specific manager is ready to relinquish control and allow power to be distributed downward and outward in the organization.

In addition, the survey measures the competence of managers in each of six empowerment skill sets:

1. Management-information/communication system skills
2. Decision-making and action-taking skills
3. Project-planning, organizing, and system-integration skills
4. Systems-evaluation and internal control skills
5. Leadership, motivation, and reward systems
6. Selection, placement, and development of people skills

There were some problems with the earlier versions of the surveys that appear in the Appendix to the book. The scoring instructions are not specific enough to guide the respondents efficiently through the scoring steps. In addition, the wording of a number of the questions in the *Organizational Culture* version and the *Subordinates' Perception* version is incorrect. The existing (incorrect) wording is based on how the manager would answer the question, rather than how a member of the organization would answer *about* his or her manager. These errors have been corrected in the surveys that are available through B.J. Chakiris Corporation and Pfeiffer and Company.

In spite of these shortcomings, the surveys are still extremely powerful resources to use in assessing management style and organizational readiness. It would be worth the effort for those wishing to use the surveys to develop their own set of instructions and reword the affected questions, or obtain the updated versions of the instruments.

Target Populations

The *Management Styles Survey: Organizational Culture* would work well in most organizational settings where the intent is to assess the prevailing management style and how it influences the climate for empowerment. Results may be obtained by surveying all members of an organization, or an appropriate sampling of the population.

The *Management Styles Survey: Subordinates' Perceptions* should be used to solicit input from the direct-reports of an executive, manager, supervisor, or team leader. And the *Management Styles Survey: Manager's Perceptions* is a self-assessment instrument that the leader, supervisor, or manager completes.

Applications

Unlike the *Empowerment Inventory*, which deals with the extent to which an individual (or team) feels empowered, these instruments focus on the style of the manager, leader, or managers in general that influences the extent of individual and group empowerment. As such, their greatest value lies in guiding leaders in assessing their current style so they know where to develop their skills to more effectively empower others.

One such application might be as part of an organization's formal leadership development curriculum, especially where empowerment has been raised as a key issue for the organization. Participants can be given the *Manager's Perceptions* version to complete, score, and bring with them to the course, and also be given copies of the *Subordinates' Perceptions* version for each of their direct-reports to complete and return to the manager anonymously. During the course, the empowerment and leadership theories underlying the instruments can be presented, and then participants can evaluate and discuss their survey results and develop action plans for improvement.

As part of executive development programs or large-scale organizational change projects, senior managers and heads of other very large organizational groups might be asked to administer the *Organizational Culture* version of the instrument to a cross section of their organization, score and plot the results, and then present their results at a program or project meeting.

In similar fashion, the *Management Styles Survey: Organizational Culture*, would be a useful resource for managers, organization development and human resource development professionals, quality process advisors, and others involved in the implementation of organizational change initiatives to determine the readiness of an organization to embark on an empowerment initiative.

Finally, in one-on-one development coaching with a manager who appears to have high control needs, or may be stifling the initiative of teams he or she is leading, or merely is looking for ways to more effectively empower his or her direct reports and teams, the self and subordinates' instruments can provide the manager and his or her boss, human resource development professional, or consultant with useful data in a joint assessment of leadership style, changes that are warranted, and appropriate development plans. Vogt and Murrell's book, especially Chapter 3, "Leadership for Empowerment," would be useful reading for the manager in understanding his or her survey results and actions that may be taken to adopt a more empowering leadership style.

TRAINING VIDEOS [1]

The Empowered Team
GEO Group, Inc.
1992. 30 minutes
Includes Facilitator's Guide.
$250 rental/$695 purchase

Produced by the same company that did "Tearing Down the Walls," and also narrated by futurist and author Leland Russell, this program provides an especially well-rounded and concise introduction to the evolution of empowered work teams, and the environment needed to support such teams. It probes questions such as "Why move to a team-based system? What are the obstacles to team development? How do we go about breaking down these barriers? What type of commitment is required by managers and team members? And how long will it take?"

The presentation is divided into three parts, each one addressing a major aspect of team empowerment: Selected management models, tearing down the walls, and team development issues.

The first part traces the roots of empowered teams back to England and Frederick Taylor's Scientific Management movement. Then it shows how the new thinking, which developed as a reaction to Taylorism, called SocioTechnical Systems, provided for the social as well as the technical dimensions of work. It allowed work to be assigned directly to the team rather than to an individual, gave the team group-related tasks rather than repetitive tasks, cross-trained group members, and let the team make the decisions and manage its own work processes.

In part two, Leland Russell reviews some of the obstacles that implementers will encounter, and how to deal with them. The discussion covers the need for specific types of communication, the commitment in time and resources management must make for a successful transition to a team environment, and the need for a collaborative work environment.

449

---

[1]All of the training videos reviewed here are available through Sagotsky Multimedia, P.O. Box 587, Rocky Hill, NJ 08553, (609) 921-8778.

The third part of the program looks at team development issues. We see a manager discussing his transition from command and control, to one in which he adapts his leadership style as his team matures and becomes more skillful, gradually turning the leadership responsibility over to the team as it becomes fully empowered.

A final segment covers the common dimensions of team building (shared vision/mission, shared goals, etc.), barriers to change, training needs, and organizational systems.

The photography is very good and the style varied enough to keep the viewer's interest. Only a dream sequence about being part of a quiz show drags on a bit too long, and may be seen as a bit corny by some viewers.

The program comes with a twenty-eight page Facilitator's Guide, summary sheets for the facilitator listing the key learning points, a master set for making facilitator overheads, and film review note pages for the participants to use when watching the video.

The Facilitator's Guide provides added information on the concepts from the video that will help in introducing the program and facilitating the discussion afterward, and also contains a list of commonly asked questions about empowered teams, such as "Will senior management make the necessary commitment? How will success be measured? How do we get employees to buy in and participate?"

Target Audience

This video is most appropriate for managerial and supervisory audiences, human resource specialists, quality advisors, empowerment and quality steering committees, consultants, team leaders, etc. There might be a problem showing this to employee groups before the launch of an empowerment initiative because of the pointed questions asked in the videotape about management commitment, policies, etc. Until the organization is ready to provide adequate answers to these tough questions, it would be best not to use this videotape with employee populations.

Applications

This program is more comprehensive than any other video training program in the scope of the team empowerment implementation variables it presents. A workshop and a series of follow-up planning meetings could be developed around this videotape for use with a steering committee planning a company's overall implementation strategy, or for individual managers interested in developing empowered teams in their organizations.

It also can be a resource in leadership training programs and team leader training, especially in a discussion of the changing role of leadership and the need for leaders to move through the stages of leadership as their teams become more competent. Most supervisors, managers, and even executives will need help understanding this new role of leader-as-facilitator and coach, and not as decision maker and problem solver. And they also will need help dealing with their natural resistance and insecurity in order for the transition to be successful.

Once the major employee issues and questions have been surfaced, and the organization's systems and responses developed, the video could be part of the launch briefings for work groups to explain what the organization's new team-based systems will look like, followed by an explanation of the implementation plans, and a question and answer session.

Zapp!
Development Dimensions International
1992. 30 minutes
Includes one Leader's Guide and six participant copies of "*Joe Mode's Notebook.*"
$250 rental/$895 purchase

Joe Mode is back, this time in the film version of Bill Byham and Ron Cox's book *Zapp! The Lightning of Empowerment.*

Set in the same eerie, somewhat sci-fi scenario of the book, supervisor Joe Mode struggles to learn what it takes to empower his people.

Joe doesn't have a clue how his own supervisory style is affecting those around him. But with the help of Ralph, one of his employees, he gradually discovers and tries out the key principles of empowerment in fits and starts as he fights his ingrained, autocratic behavior patterns.

These are real-world issues for managers. For many, change is not easy. It doesn't happen instantly and takes time, patience, and persistence. It also takes skills, like listening, that require practice.

For those who have read the book, this will be a delightful reunion with Joe, Ralph, and The Normal Company. However, people who haven't read the book may find the video a bit "goofy," as one viewer noted. This challenge can be handled by preparing the viewers in advance for the cute fable format they are about to see, and assigning them points to look for as they watch the program.

The video does a good job of explaining what empowerment is, what the benefits are for companies, and how it helps individuals and teams perform at their best. It also very effectively illustrates the changes that leaders will have to make in order to create an empowering environment for their people, and how difficult it will be for some to make these changes.

Included with the video is an excellent Leader's Guide and six copies of "*Joe Mode's Notebook,*" a fifty-one page, 2" by 6" pocket text and reference on the concepts, Key Steps, and skills covered in the book *Zapp!* It is included as a participant handout to be used along with the videotape and will serve the participants as a ready-reference on empowerment after the program. Additional copies of the *Notebook* are available for purchase.

451

The sixteen-page Leader's Guide contains a detailed lesson plan, including a script and clear, easy to follow instructions for holding a workshop or discussion session following the video. Utilizing such a discussion session increases the retention of the key concepts and principles from the video program.

The lesson plan is divided into four sections: An introduction on what empowerment is, how it affects people, and the benefits of empowerment for the organization; the Key Principles of Empowerment; the 8 Factors that Create *Zapp!*; and Ongoing Training. The last section of the lesson outline, Ongoing Training, is marked "optional" to allow the program leader to discuss why additional training for empowerment is important and what the organization is doing to make that training available to leaders.

Target Audience

This video is for those with leadership responsibilities, including managers, supervisors, team leaders, lead operators, and section heads; as well as those who need to understand the leadership principles involved in empowerment in order to support empowerment initiatives.

Applications

As part of a leadership development curriculum, team leader training, quality facilitator training, etc. *Zapp!*, the video, can be used to introduce the concept of empowerment, the leader's role, and the skills needed to effectively empower others. At sessions with a senior management team or steering committee to determine organization readiness for empowerment, or at an assembly of all leadership personnel in an organization as part of the roll-out of an empowerment initiative, it can sensitize the organization's leaders to the role they will have to play, and skills they will have to master in creating an environment that will support empowerment.

EMPOWERMENT SKILLS PACKAGED TRAINING PROGRAMS

When you do get to the issue of skills training, be aware that we are talking about basic interpersonal, leadership, and group skills applied within the paradigm of empowerment. Zenger-Miller, Inc.[1] and Development Dimensions International[2] are two examples of established international training firms that have developed extremely powerful and effective packaged training programs for individuals, leaders, and teams that will support their efforts to be more skillful in empowering themselves and in interacting with and empowering others. There are

---

[1]Zenger-Miller, Inc., 1735 Technology Drive, San Jose, CA 95110-1313, (800) 866-2438.
[2]Development Dimensions International, 1225 Washington Pike, Bridgeville, PA 15017, (800) 933-4463.

also other companies and educational institutions around the world that specialize in delivering skill development training programs for organizations and individuals.

There is one training program marketed as a training video that we have selected to review under this section on packaged training programs because of its usefulness and value.

Team Player: Together Everyone Accomplishes More [1]
American Media Incorporated
1992. 21 minutes
Includes trainer's "Course Materials Guide" and a set of "building blocks" for workshop exercises.
$175 rental/$650 purchase

This video-based training program doesn't have the word "empowerment" in its title, but there are still some good reasons for including it in this resources section. First, it is about teams. Second, teams need some basic group process skills in order to be able to function effectively. Third, the video comes with a dynamite leader's guide for running two, four, six, or eight hour team development workshops, and workshop follow-up sessions. And finally, this particular video is about a group of people thrown together by their management with only a project objective to guide them, yet they learned how to operate effectively together as a self-managing ("empowered") team.

In addition to the videotape and a "Bridging the Gap" interactive game, this program comes with such an outstanding leader's guide that it actually can function as a self-contained packaged training program for teams. This makes it an excellent value as well as a useful resource.

Set in an insurance company, six people from different departments and levels in the organization are told by their management that they are to be part of a permanent customer service team. Their first assignment is to present a plan to management to reduce the excessive claims processing time that is causing the company to lose customers. They are given no other instructions, no preparation, no training, no facilitator, no one in charge.

We watch as these people wrestle with their frustrations, take responsibility for pulling themselves together, and develop from a group of individuals into a team. Along the way, they learn some basic lessons about how to function effectively as a team:

- The need for and how to set ground rules for participation and meeting management
- Why consensus decisions may be better than majority-rules voting
- The importance of structured problem solving and determining the root cause of a problem before jumping to solutions
- How to encourage everyone to participate

453

---

[1]This is also available through Sagotsky Multimedia.

- Why it is sometimes better to take a bit more time and do it right, than to rush in order to get it over with
- How to be a better team member

The team members in the video voice frustrations that people at all levels and in all occupations have experienced at one time or another: "We're not a team. We're just a bunch of people who get together once a week to have stupid arguments or talk on the phone and do other work!" To their credit, they work through the issues that come up, and through this video, serve as a model from which other teams can learn.

The highlight of this package is the Facilitator's Guide. It is divided into four sections. The first provides a background on the program, how to plan your team training session, and what is covered in the videotape. It explains how to decide whether to offer an eight hour program, or one of the shorter length designs in the manual. And it also contains a sample memo to send to the participants announcing the workshop entitled "Team Player: A course on working together."

The second section contains detailed, step-by-step lesson plans for the two, four, six, or eight hour program versions. There are learning objectives and agendas for each version, overhead masters, and complete lesson plans. The lesson plans guide the instructor through each segment of the presentation, discussion questions to ask, breakout group exercises, exercises in setting ground rules, the "Bridging the Gap" team exercise with the building blocks that come with the program, even notes to the instructor about audiovisual materials, flipcharts, etc. needed for each segment.

The third part of the Facilitator's Guide contains a master set of the participant's materials, ready for duplicating. And the fourth section contains "reinforcement materials."

This "reinforcement materials" section contains some very effective follow-up suggestions. For example, it has a draft memo the instructor can send to the participants' managers to have them follow-up with their people to discuss how they are applying what they learned. It has three ready-to-use instruments: A *Team Function Assessment Survey* that can be used to evaluate the way the team is working; a *Team Player Feedback Survey* to provide feedback to the individual members of a team on how their teammates perceive them as team players; and a *Team Meeting Critique Form* for the team to use in evaluating its meetings. It even has a draft memo and data form that the instructor can use to report the survey results back to the team members.

Target Audience

This program could be used with intact teams or at workshops for members from different teams and should be well-received by audiences at most levels in an organization and in most occupational settings. The producers also have a "British dialect" and Swedish language version. The video is closed-captioned for the hearing impaired (when a decoder is used).

Applications

Out of the box, this program is ideal for intact work groups, new or existing cross-functional teams, leader-led teams, and self-managed teams. For newly formed teams, it would be a good way to launch the team and get it off on the right foot. For established teams or work groups that are struggling, it is a way to provide some tips to get them back on track.

The videotape by itself can be used in a wide range of team training programs, quality work group training, task force training, and even as part of courses on the individual's role in effective meetings. Or, with some modification to the supplied lesson plans, a course on being an effective team player could be designed around the video and offered to all employees in an organization moving toward a team-based environment.

In using this with either existing or newly formed teams, be aware that the program does not address the aspect of the organization's responsibilities in convening a new team, for example the team's authority, if it has the right membership, its relationship to other teams, or resolving conflicts between one's functional job responsibilities and one's role on the team.

APPLICATIONS FOR TEAM BUILDING

The following are examples of applications using some of the resources on empowerment reviewed in this section of *The Handbook of Best Practices for Teams*.

Holding a Team Development Checkpoint: The team leader, consultants or advisor to an established team may want to assess the effectiveness of the team as part of a routine timeout from task-related activities, or in response to indications that the members of the team may not be functioning up to their fullest potential. To illustrate how to approach this with the aid of an instrument, we will use the *Empowerment Inventory*. Regardless of the instrument used or the model for analysis, the greatest value will come from the self-assessment the team goes through, and the constructive dialogue around improvement actions.

Step 1: Discuss the process you have in mind with the team, why it can be of help to them and to you as the leader/advisor, and get their buy-in. Also, depending on the degree of trust among the team members, agree on how the data from the *Empowerment Inventory* will be reported back to the team, anonymously or by name. Set a date/time for a meeting to review and discuss the results. (Suggest two hours to review the data and develop action plans.)

Step 2: Distribute the *Empowerment Inventory* and instruct the team members to answer the questions with their role on the team in mind, and try their hand at the action planning section of the booklet. Have them write their names on the top of the scoring form and return the form to you at least a week before the feedback session.

Step 3: Make a master chart of the team's scores on an overhead transparency or flipchart. If the team prefers to have the scores reported anonymously, replace the names with "A," "B," "C," etc.

Step 4: Analyze the results and identify strengths as well as issues for the team, and the issues for you as the team leader to address. Develop a strategy to deal with the team issues, and a strategy for you to deal with the leadership issues.

Step 5: Present the results to the team at the follow-up meeting. Go over the Empowerment Grid model and definition of the four categories of feelings using the interpretation guidelines in the *Empowerment Inventory* booklet, and then lead a discussion of what the team sees as their strengths and areas for improvement. Work through the "Taking Action" pages of the inventory booklet with the team and select Team Actions and Personal Actions to work on. Set specific target dates and assignments for each action item, and a follow-up date to check progress.

Step 6: Re-administer the *Empowerment Inventory* in ninety days and discuss the results with the team. Take any additional actions necessary to maintain the momentum.

Attachment 34-A shows an example of the Empowerment Inventory scores for a cross-functional team. The team is responsible for the development and launch of a new consumer product for its division. The team has been in place for almost a year and Susan, the team leader, senses that the team is getting bogged-down and the members somewhat frustrated over the team's lack of progress. She has proposed to the team that they schedule a timeout to assess their progress and discuss ways to improve their working together.

With the exception of Ted, the scores show this team to be a highly motivated and empowered group of people who are experiencing frustration over their lack of progress in achieving their objectives on the team. Susan, the team leader, can take the team through a discussion of where these feelings of a lack of progress are coming from, and what they can do to correct the underlying causes. The action planning checklist "Building Feelings of PROGRESS" at the back of the *Empowerment Inventory* can help the team identify both individual and team actions to improve the situation.

ROCK & ROLL BRAND TEAM

	Choice	Competence	Meaningfulness	Progress
Susan	38	42	39	24
Bashir	34	41	38	30
Ted	18	39	24	20
Victor	38	40	39	21
Rose	42	42	38	18
Charles	32	40	42	18
Normative Ranges				
High 25%	>35	>39	>36	>35
Middle 50%	25-35	34-39	29-36	29-35
Low 25%	<25	<34	<29	<29

Empowerment Inventory results for a cross-functional team

As for Ted, there most likely are issues that extend beyond his role on the team that will need to be addressed. This should be a cue for Susan that a private discussion with Ted might be of help to assist him in working through the factors negatively affecting his feelings of empowerment. Here again, the "Personal Actions" checklists on choice, competence, meaningfulness, and progress in the inventory can be used to guide Susan's coaching session with Ted. They may also provide Ted with a starting point for a discussion with his department manager on ways he can get greater satisfaction out of his work with the company.

Because the members of this particular team have been extremely candid with each other and supportive in their interactions, the team decided not to have the scores reported anonymously. Ted's colleagues, in recognizing his low feelings of empowerment, can use the inventory's Team Actions checklists to identify specific ways they can provide him support. If there was not this level of trust among the team members, revealing Ted's scores to the team might be embarrassing for him and counterproductive as a team-building effort.

Supporting a Self-Directed Work Team

Creating a new self-directed work team, or facilitating the transition of a traditionally supervised team into a self-directed team, are two of the most challenging of team development projects. In the following example, we will see how a company helped an existing team become self-directed:

In their quest to achieve world-class customer service, the Executive Committee of this company, working with an outside consulting firm, formed two task forces to come up with ideas for increasing customer satisfaction. One was a cross-functional group, and the other was composed of the company's five customer service representatives. Both task forces were given written charters spelling out their mission, membership, etc., and were assigned process consultants to help them get started on their missions.

The manager in charge of the Customer Service Department was a very controlling, old-school autocrat with twenty-five years service at the company. Her boss, the company's Vice-President of Finance, felt that her participation on the customer service task force would stifle her people's initiative. So to maintain her self-esteem, she was asked to sit in with her boss at the Executive Committee meetings on this pilot project, rather than being part of her employees' work team.

At the same time the two task forces were getting started on their projects, the consultants gave the members of the Executive Committee and the Customer Service Manager copies of the book *Zapp!* to read, and they discussed the concepts at one of their meetings. Their assignment was then to apply as many of the concepts from the book as they could, and report on progress at subsequent Executive Committee meetings. (The Customer Service Manager's boss spent a lot of time coaching her in the application of *Zapp!* to her on-the-job situations.)

Over a three-month period, the outside consultant worked with each task force to give them just-in-time coaching, and help them get rolling. He gave them each copies of *HeroZ* to read, had a discussion session to capture their insights, and would refer to various sections of the book for tips on problem-solving, process improvement, running effective meetings, etc. when it was appropriate. He also presented additional materials to them on process mapping, shared-leadership at meetings, etc. and showed them the video "Team Player: Together Everyone Accomplishes More" to help with the leadership of their meetings. Little by little he cut back on the meetings he attended as they began to share the leadership of their group until they were running it on their own with the help of their *HeroZ* handbook.

This, of course, was an especially challenging time for the Customer Service Manager who was used to handling important decisions herself. But to her credit, she followed the guidelines in the book and the suggestions her own boss provided to give her people the autonomy their charter and mission required. Likewise, to their credit, the five customer service representatives followed the tips in *HeroZ* to get her buy-in, as well as that of others, before finalizing any changes in procedures.

After four months of stellar performance for both teams, an interesting opportunity presented itself. The Customer Service Manager announced an early retirement due to a family illness.

By this point, the customer service representatives were able to make so many significant improvements in work flow, company order processing procedures, and shipping and receiving cycle time reduction, managing team. The decision was discussed with the team, and the team members were given an across the board 10 percent salary increase with the promise of another review in six months.

Silence. No "thank you's." No "we're thrilled with your confidence in us." Not even any questions. The two executives thanked the team, and ran to call the consultant.

After talking with the team members individually, the consultant found out that they were concerned about who would talk to someone who didn't do their work. What if someone was out sick, who would decide on coverage? When the manager was still there, there was always the authority figure available, even if she was never called on to intervene. Now, the team members had to deal with the delicate issue of giving each other constructive feedback, dealing with conflict, and coaching co-workers who needed help. And they were scared to death at the prospect.

So once a week for two and a half hours per session the consultant put them through a half dozen of the Zenger-Miller *Working*[1] program skill units. They read the principles and steps involved, saw the demonstration videotapes, and practiced using the feedback and coaching skills with each other. They even handled some personality conflicts back on the job using these skills only a few weeks into the program. They were finally back on track with the skills to manage their own performance.

Recently, two clerical people were moved into the department as a result of a process improvement suggestion from the team. And the team itself is training these people, sharing the responsibility with each other for their development, and handling their supervision until they can become equal partners.

The team is also working on a team-based performance appraisal and compensation system design for their department. They weren't totally happy with everybody getting the same 10 percent increase last time and wanted something to reflect individual initiative. So the Executive Vice-President told them he would be open to another way of doing it and to suggest something. And they will. The consultant gave them information on various approaches to performance appraisal and compensation. Now the choice of appraisal/compensation model and the rest of the work is up to them. They took ownership.

---

[1] *Working* is Zenger-Miller's packaged interpersonal skills training system for nonsupervisory personnel. Twelve modules cover subjects such as listening, giving feedback to others, participating in group meetings, resolving issues with others, being a team player, etc.

About the Contributor

Victor M. Kline is a senior organization development consultant with over twenty-five years experience supporting large-scale organizational change interventions and team development initiatives. He was Corporate Manager of Organization and Management Development for Engelhard Corporation where he started the human resource development function in this multinational corporation, and he served with Johnson & Johnson Corporation as Director of Organization Development and Training at McNeil Consumer Products Company, their highly successful Tylenol division. He holds a masters degree in interpersonal and group communications and did his postgraduate work in psychology and doctoral work in management at Rutgers University. He is currently head of Princeton Consulting Associates, a New Jersey-based organizational effectiveness consulting firm.

Part VIII - Contributors

CONTRIBUTORS TO THE HANDBOOK

Michael Beyerlein
Center for the Study of Work Teams
University of North Texas
P.O. Box 13587
Denton, TX 76203
817-565-3096

J. Thomas Buck
Prism Performance Systems
37000 Grand River, Suite 230
Farmington Hills, MI 48335
810-474-8855

BJ Chakiris
BJ Chakiris Corp.
250 South Wacker Drive
Chicago, IL 60606
312-322-1222

Kenneth N. Chakiris
BJ Chakiris
250 South Wacker Drive
Chicago, IL 60606
312-322-1222

Dan Dana
MTI Publications
10210 Robinson Street
Overland Park, KS 66212
913-341-2888

Dan Diers
Rockwell International
350 Collins Road NE
Cedar Rapids, IA 52498
319-395-2685

William G. Dyer
Dyer Consulting Group
3077 Mojave Lane
Provo, UT 84604
801-374-5741

Sue Easton
Easton & Associates
729 Palmer Court
Lake Mary, FL 32746
904-383-4425

Patricia Kay Felkins
BJ Chakiris Corp.
250 South Wacker Drive
Chicago, IL 60606
312-322-1222

Nancy J. Finley
Prism Performance Systems
37000 Grand River, Suite 230
Farmington Hills, MI 48335
810-474-8855

Deborah Harrington-Mackin
New Directions Consulting
P.O. Box 788
N. Bennington, VT 05257
802-442-3631

Lois B. Hart
Leadership Dynamics
10951 Isabelle Road
Lafayette, CA 80026
303-666-4046

David Jamieson
Jamieson Consulting Group
2265 Westwood Blvd.
Los Angeles, CA 90064
310-397-8502

Amy J. Katz
Zenger-Miller, Inc.
1735 Technology Drive
San Jose, CA 95110
408-452-1244

Gerald D. Klein
Rider University
2083 LawrencevilleRoad
Lawrenceville, NJ 08648
609-895-5561

Victor M. Kline
Princeton Consulting Associates
6 Melvina Drive
Lawrenceville, NJ 08648
609-896-3559

Bette Krakau
Krakau & Associates
255 Sheringham Road
Columbia, SC 29212
803-781-8405

Richard P. Kropp, Jr.
The Davies Group
3-J Taggart Drive
Nashua, NH 03060
603-891-1333

Jerry McAdams
Watson Wyatt Worldwide
8182 Maryland
St. Louis, MO 63105
214-978-3400

Larry Meeker
Advanced Team Concepts
2312 Brennan Drive
Plano, TX 75075
214-964-1083

Linda Moran
Zenger-Miller, Inc.
6 Apple Lane
Simsbury, CT 06070
860-651-7633

Stu Noble
Block Petrella Weisbord, Inc.
1207 Claridge Road
Wyndmoor, PA 19038
215-836-2401

Maureen O'Brien
OB Management Consultants
P.O. Box 20038
Myrtle Beach, SC 29577
803-650-3183

Sylvia Odenwald
The Odenwald Connection
30010 LBJ Freeway
Dallas, TX 75234
214-221-5793

Glenn M. Parker
Glenn M. Parker Associates
41 Woodlane Road
Lawrenceville, NJ 08648
609-895-1920

Steven Phillips
Phillips & Associates
23440 Civic Center Way
Malibu, CA 90265
310-456-3532

Gayle Porter
Rutgers University,
School of Business
Third & Penn
Camden, NJ 08102
609-225-6216

Mary Rahaim
Amoco Production Company
P.O. Box 3092
Houston, TX 77253
713-368-6567

Lilanthi Ravishankar
Zenger-Miller, Inc.
1735 Technology Drive
San Jose, CA 95110
408-452-1244

Ed Rose
Harris Semiconductor
P.O. Box 883/MS 59-042
Melbourne, FL 32902-0883
407-724-7560

Lee Royal
SHL Systemhouse
1460 Roundtable Drive
Dallas, TX 75247
214-689-7124

Darlene Russ-Eft
Zenger-Miller, Inc.
1735 Technology Drive
San Jose, CA 95110
408-452-1244

Peter Scholtes
Scholtes Seminars & Consulting
131 West Wilson Street
Madison, WI 53703
608-255-9789

Liz Teal
Team Trust Consulting
3307 Brookmeade Street
Memphis, TN 38127
901-353-0467

Silvasailam Thiagarajan
Workshops by Thiagi
4423 Trailridge Road
Bloomington, IN 47408
812-332-1478

Kenneth W. Thomas
Naval Postgraduate School
26 Antelope Lane
Monterey, CA 93940
408-647-9382

Walter G. Tymon, Jr.
Villanova University
810 Robert Dean Drive
Downingtown, PA 19335
215-873-2914

Glenn Varney
Management Advisory Associates
P. O. Box 703
Bowling Green, OH 43402
419-352-7782

Dominick Volini
Block Petrella Weisbord
1009 Park Avenue
Plainfield, NJ 07060
908-754-5100

Lynn Wilson
Amoco Production Company
550 Westlake Park Blvd.
Houston, TX 77079
713-366-3163

Zenger-Miller, Inc.
1735 Technology Drive
San Jose, CA 95110
408-452-1244

Jack Zigon
Zigon Performance Group
604 Crum Creek Road
Media, PA 19063
610-891-9599

IRWIN
Professional Publishing®

1333 Burr Ridge Parkway
Burr Ridge, IL 60521
(800) 634-3966

About Irwin Professional Publishing

Thank you for choosing Irwin Professional Publishing for your business information needs. If you are part of a corporation, professional association, or government agency, consider our newest option: Irwin Professional Custom Publishing. This allows you to create customized books, manuals, and other materials from your organization's resources, select chapters of our books, or both.

Irwin Professional Publishing Books are also excellent resources for training/educational programs, premiums, and incentives. For information on volume discounts or Custom Publishing, call 1-800-634-3966

Available from Irwin Professional Publishing or from fine bookstores everywhere

GLOBAL SOLUTIONS FOR TEAMS
Moving from Collision to Collaboration
Sylvia B. Odenwald

Includes groundbreaking strategies that multinational workgroups can use to overcome distance as well as cultural differences to help better accomplish common goals and develop higher productivity. (195 pages)

ISBN 0-7863-0476-6

LEADING TEAMS
Mastering the New Role
John H. Zenger, Ed Musselwhite, Kathleen Hurson, & Craig Perrin

Focuses specifically on the role of the leader as the key to long-term success, showing how managers can care an enduring, vital position for themselves in a team environment. (275 pages)

ISBN 1-55623-894-0

DIVERSE TEAMS AT WORK
Capitalizing on the Power of Diversity
Lee Gardenswartz and Anita Rowe

Diverse Teams at Work shows how to manage the many differences inherent in today's teams, and provides an analysis of the primary dimensions of diversity and how they shape expectations and team behavior.

ISBN 0-7863-0425-1

BUILDING TEAM POWER
How to Unleash the Collaborative Genius of Work Teams
Thomas A. Kayser

Building Team Power offers easy-to-implement ideas, tools, and techniques for increasing team productivity in an environment, whether public or private sector, profit or nonprofit, or service- or manufacturing-based.

ISBN 0-7863-0302-6

WHY TEAMS CAN FAIL AND WHAT TO DO ABOUT IT
Essential Tools for Anyone Implementing Self-Directed Work Teams
Darcy Hitchcock and Marsha Willard

Why Teams Can Fail identifies the most common problems faced by teams, offering specific suggestions for spotting and solving the problems and creating teams that really work.

ISBN 0-7863-0423-5

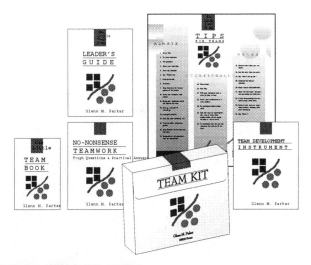

INSIGHT INVENTORY
Understanding Yourself and Others

INSIGHT Inventory is a comprehensive, self-scored behavioral style profile. It provides users with a quick way to learn about their behavioral characteristics. Each inventory comes with detailed directions and skill development activities.

Use INSIGHT for:
- Team Building
- Conflict and Stress Management
- Leadership Training
- Interpersonal Skills, Sales, and Customer Service

Key Features of INSIGHT
- **Easy to use**—participants complete, score, and chart their own profiles in minutes.
- **Valid**—reliability and norming studies are based on thorough testing at a major university using heterogenous groups and following strict APA guidelines.
- **A perfect bridging activity**—use as an important skill building element for a variety of training programs

FREE OFFER!

Take an INSIGHT Inventory *on us!* Call 1-800-366-4401 (extension 14) to get a **free** sample inventory and a descriptive brochure.

INSIGHT with 6-page interpretive guide	**$5.95**	(Code … IIFB)
INSIGHT with 16-page skill-building booklet	**$11.95**	(Code … IIFA)
INSIGHT Training Manual with 59 minute video	**$195.00**	(Code … IITM)

THE TEAM KIT
Glenn M. Parker

Finally a comprehensive resource with practical solutions to a variety of common team problems. Glenn M. Parker, the noted writer and consultant, has researched the most common concerns that team members and leaders face on a day-to-day basis, and developed this collection of useful tools to help your teams function more effectively.

The Team Kit includes:

The Little Team Book—Team members will use this job aid as a daily reference on such topics as: team vision, conflict resolution, and how to give feedback. Assessments are included to help team members evaluate themselves and the team. (64 pages, $6.95)

The Leader's Guide—Prepare a team mission statement, write objectives, manage team meetings, and more, with this complete leader's guide. It provides how-to information on team development and maintenance, reproducible assessments, and job aids. (96 pages, $29.95)

Tough Questions and Practical Answers—This booklet provides helpful, practical answers to the 60 most frequently asked questions regarding the effective functioning of teams. It is an every day team problem solver in a handy question and answer format. (96 pages, $29.95)

Tips for Teams Wall Poster—A handy reminder of the do's and dont's of successful teams. (20"x24", $12.95)

4 Team Development Instruments—The *Team Meeting Survey* is a 44-item instrument which assesses the planning and implementation of your team meetings. The *Reality of Self-Direction* instrument assesses your team's level of readiness to become a self-directed team. The *Self-Directed Team Culture Survey* assesses the degree of support for teamwork both within your team and the overall organization. The *Organizational Weather Report* details the extent to which your team is oriented toward achievement and power. (set of 4 Instruments, $19.95)

Team Kit Special Offer! $115.00
Save over $25.00 and get a FREE team tote box!

Includes 8 copies of the *Little Team Book*, a Leader's Guide,*Tough Questions and Practical Answers*, a set of 4 instruments, one poster and a team tote box.
(Code … NTK)

HRD Press • 22 Amherst Road • Amherst, MA 01002 • 1-800-822-2801 • Fax 413-253-3490

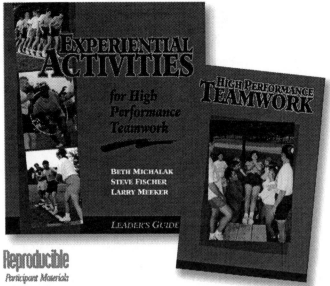

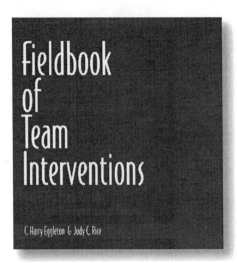

Reproducible
Participant Materials

EXPERIENTIAL ACTIVITIES FOR HIGH PERFORMANCE TEAMWORK

Beth Michalak, Steve Fischer & Larry Meeker

Develop your teams with these experiential techniques that combine physical and mental challenges. This manual provides research-based strategies to strengthen seven key team skill areas. The issues covered in this book are crucial to the success of all types of teams—operations, engineering, management, and support. Trainers and facilitators will find it simple to adopt these ready-to-use activities to add new interest to existing programs. Engaging, motivational participant booklets are included as follow-up support materials.

Training Objectives
- Develop new teams and build team cohesiveness
- Integrate experiential learning into existing programs
- Improve team motivation

Selected Contents
- The Power of Experiential Team Building
- Team Development • Building Effective Communications
- Problem Solving • Leveraging Diversity • Establishing Trust
- Strengthening Cooperation • Creating Effective Teamwork
- Building Team Spirit • Team Training Curriculums
- Summary of Findings and Results

Training Package Includes:
- Leader's Guide with reproducible activities
  (175 pages, 3-Ring Binder)
- 5 copies of *High Performance Teamwork*
  (48 pages, Paperback)

Complete Package   **$99.95**   (Code ... EAHP)

**Additional *High Performance
Teamwork* Books**   **$5.95**   (Code ... EAHPB)

Reproducible
Participant Materials

THE FIELDBOOK OF TEAM INTERVENTIONS
Step-by-Step Guide to High Performance Teams
C. Harry Eggleton & Judy C. Rice

With this well-organized fieldbook, implementing successful team interventions is a simple matter of following a set of detailed, readable steps. Within minutes you can identify an area for team enhancement and have an array of proven intervention options to choose from. Throughout the fieldbook you'll find examples, hints, and comments that make the interventions accessible, approachable, and, most importantly, effective.

These team interventions have been field-tested and reviewed by leading practitioners in the HRD field to ensure that they are understandable and clear. Each one is described in a practical, user-friendly format covering when to use it, its purpose and overview, time required to complete it, and a detailed guide which includes scripts, flowcharts, and reproducible masters on disk.

Contents
Team Performance
Clarity of Goals
Commitment
Leadership
Role Competencies
Norms
Decision Making and Problem Solving
Support and Influence

350 Pages   **Paperback**   **$49.95**   (Code ... FTI)

HRD Press • 22 Amherst Road • Amherst, MA 01002 • 1-800-822-2801 • Fax 413-253-3490

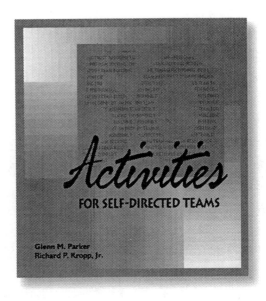

TEAM BUILDING BLOCKS
Practicing Group Collaboration
Carmine Consalvo

Renew your teams with this stimulating, hands-on training tool. *Team Building Blocks* gives your teams an easy-to-implement, effective, and enjoyable opportunity to practice and refine their problem solving and communication skills.

Using the set of 14 polished wood blocks, participants work together in performing these engaging exercises. Your teams will be motivated and stimulated by solving problems, reaching consensus, and resolving differences while involved with these experiential puzzles. The game comes complete with 14 wooden blocks and an 84-page activity manual, which includes 18 detailed activities, facilitator notes, post-activity commentary, and solutions.

Exercises Cover
- Risk taking
- Diversity
- Coaching
- Information sharing
- Logic and spatial relations
- Trial and error learning
- Inter-team consultation
- Time management

Training Objectives
- Illustrate the principle of "coopetition"—the competitive and cooperative nature of teamwork
- Highlight the importance of information sharing and collaboration between teams
- Demonstrate the negative impact of distrust among team members

Complete game set	$149.95	(Code ... TBB)
Additional set of blocks	$59.95	

50 ACTIVITIES FOR SELF-DIRECTED TEAMS
Glenn M. Parker & Richard P. Kropp Jr.

Implement successful self-managed teams in your organization. This collection of proven training exercises has been tested and refined in actual team training sessions, and covers all aspects of team development, including mutual goal setting, managing team stagnation, and developing team norms. The activities encourage active participation and feedback from participants and come complete with all the necessary questionnaires, exercises, and handouts.

Training Objectives
- Determine if empowerment fits into an organization's current culture
- Assess a team's readiness for self-direction
- Motivate a team and set it into action
- Prepare a team to receive delegated authority

Training Methods
- 20 ready-to-use questionnaires for assessment of key team skills
- Written exercises which reinforce team building concepts
- Group discussions which encourage active participation and feedback

Activities Cover
- Building Trust
- Resolving Conflict
- Intergroup Team Building
- Team Meetings
- Team Effectiveness
- Group Problem Solving

250 Pages	3-Ring Binder	$139.95	(Code ... 50SDT)

HRD Press • 22 Amherst Road • Amherst, MA 01002 • 1-800-822-2801 • Fax 413-253-3490

Reproducible
Participant Materials

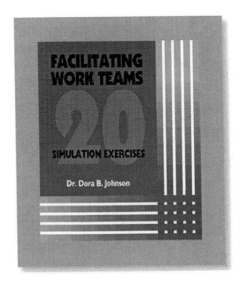

FAULTLESS FACILITATION

Lois B. Hart, Ed.D.

Use this practice-oriented workshop to teach team leaders and group facilitators the key skills for leading productive team meetings. This workshop contains everything you need to teach others how to facilitate; it comes complete with background material for the trainer and participants, and handouts for evaluation.

The Instructor's Manual offers 27 in-class learning activities and optional training designs (1, 2, 3, or 5-day) to go with the best-selling *Faultless Facilitation Resource Guide*. The Instructor's Manual lays out exactly how to plan, run, and evaluate skill-based training for inexperienced facilitators.

The Resource Guide includes "how to's" on group leading and problem solving for new facilitators. It covers everything from agenda setting to selecting the right problem solving tools. Use it as a participant coursebook with the training program, as a self-study option, or for managers who need to understand more about the facilitator's role.

Contents Include

- Warm-up and agenda setting
- Observing, listening, and questioning skills
- Problem-solving methods
- Dealing with problem people
- Setting team guidelines
- Creating a Vision
- And much more!

Instructor's Manual
3-Ring Binder	256 Pages	$99.95	(Code ... FFI)

Resource Guide
3-Ring Binder	184 Pages	$59.95	(Code ... FF)

Buy Both Volumes and Save! $139.95

Fully Reproducible

FACILITATING WORK TEAMS
20 Simulation Exercises

Dr. Dora B. Johnson

These 20 fully reproducible simulation exercises provide opportunities for facilitators to practice the skills they've learned in facilitation training. They give facilitators a chance to test their team facilitation skills in a supportive environment where they can benefit from the constructive feedback of their peers.

The exercises are based on extensive field research and interviews with veteran trainers to ensure that they accurately reflect the most important issues facing today's team facilitators. Each is presented in a realistic team scenario which encourages stimulating and productive interaction among participants.

These exercises can be easily integrated into an existing facilitator training program for cross-functional, self-directed, or quality teams. They each come complete with notes for the trainer, briefing and debriefing worksheets, and suggested variations of the exercise.

Training Objectives
- Provide opportunities for facilitators to practice skills
- Identify the processes of facilitating a team
- Demonstrate techniques to evaluate team effectiveness
- Present methods to effectively resolve team conflicts
- Develop a realistic time frame for action plans

300 Pages	3-Ring Binder	$89.95	(Code ... FWT)

HRD Press • 22 Amherst Road • Amherst, MA 01002 • 1-800-822-2801 • Fax 413-253-3490

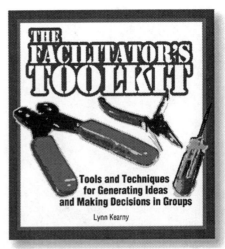

Fully
Reproducible

50 ACTIVITIES
FOR TEAM BUILDING
Volumes 1 & 2

Create high performance teams with these collections of fully reproducible activities. All the activities employ the principle of "learning by doing" to ensure that the skills the participants learn can be applied to real work situations.

Volume 1 contains creative training activities which focus on the building blocks for teams such as communication, leadership, conflict resolution, and decision making. Volume 2 offers 50 additional activities for team development and provides practice on cooperation, balancing roles, and defining team objectives and goals.

These activities are ideal for team leaders who are looking for creative activities to energize their teams but do not have the time to develop them. All of the activities are ready-to-use and are fully reproducible; with little effort you can implement them into an existing training program. Each volume comes with detailed trainer's notes, clearly stated objectives, and a quick reference index to the activities.

Training Objectives, Volume 1
- Improve inter-team communication
- Assess the effectiveness of a team
- Establish team missions and goals

Training Objectives, Volume 2
- Encourage continuous team improvement
- Develop a mutual support network
- Create balanced team roles

Vol 1: 236 Pages   **3-Ring Binder**   **$139.95**   (Code ... 50TB)
Vol 2: 248 Pages   **3-Ring Binder**   **$139.95**   (Code ... 50TB2)

Fully
Reproducible

THE FACILITATOR'S TOOLKIT
Tools and Techniques for Generating Ideas and Making Decisions in Groups
Lynn Kearny

Everything you need to effectively lead a team, plan group meetings, and foster team decision-making is now available in one handy toolkit. This collection of fully reproducible activities and techniques will benefit training specialists, supervisors, managers, team leaders and anyone else whose job success depends on the results produced by groups. It includes practical guidelines for managing every aspect of a group or team setting.

If your organization is relying on team and group work to improve business processes, define needs, even reengineer the organization itself, this collection of activities and techniques will get you the results you need from your teams.

Contents
1. Creative Thinking with Groups
2. The Map—Specific directions for leading a group from idea to decision
3. Six Basic Group Needs—How to troubleshoot a group that's stuck
4. Managing Process—Tips on keeping your group focused and goal-oriented
5. The Toolkit—Includes 49 fully reproducible tools and activities for developing ideas and solving problems with groups, including:

• Brainstorming	• Gantt Chart
• Force Field Analysis	• Data Dump
• Manipulative Verbs	• Ideaweaving
• Map the Territory	• Poll the Group
• Upward Delegation	

6. User's Guide for Selecting Tools

300 Pages   **3-Ring Binder**   **$125.00**   (Code ... FT)

LESSONS IN TEAMWORK
Computer-Based Training Modules
Kimberly Mullins

This innovative software program enables you to conveniently offer interactive team building training to individual team members without scheduling time-consuming training sessions. It presents eight stimulating lessons and activities on effective teams. The complete CBT program includes more than 2½ hours of self-paced instruction complete with engaging assessment exercises and interactive feedback. Use *Lessons in Teamwork* for: on-the-spot training for new team members, refresher training, and training team leaders on specific skills.

Lessons include:
- What is a Team?
- What Makes a Team Effective?
- How to Evaluate and Reward Success
- Motivation and Commitment
- Team Roles
- Effective Communication
- Positive Conflict Resolution
- Participative Management

64-Page Paperback with 3½" disk   **$95.00**   (Code … LT)

Please call for pricing on multiple copies.

Hardware requirements: IBM PC or compatible, 386 or higher, 640K RAM, DOS 3.1 or higher, Hard Drive, VGA monitor, mouse (optional).

TEAM LEARNING SYSTEM
for Windows™
John E. Jones, Ph.D. & William L. Bearley, Ed.D.

This user-friendly software program assesses team performance on two vital dimensions: 1) each individual's effectiveness as a member functioning within the team structure; 2) the group's overall performance and how well they engage in productive team behaviors. The System measures these conditions of group functioning with the aid of two reliable survey questionnaires. The questionnaires produce clear reports based on individual and group responses. This information allows group members the opportunity to engage in concrete action planning for improving team performance.

About the Questionnaires
- *Right Things Right* is a quality-improvement questionnaire that the team uses to identify its opportunities for continuous improvement. The reports generated categorize the team tasks on which there is group consensus, or disagreeing opinions.

- *The Team Player Assessment* supplies essential feedback to members by illustrating how personalities and behaviors affect team performance. Members quickly learn if their self-perception matches how others perceive them. A feedback report is generated for each member indicating individual strengths and opportunities for growth in interpersonal and task behaviors.

User's Manual and 3½" disk   **$95.00**   (Code … TLS)

Please call for pricing on multiple copies.

The *Team Learning System for Windows*™ runs on IBM PC or compatible computers. It requires Windows™ 3.0 or later, 4 MB of memory, 1.3 MB of hard disk space, and a mouse/pointing device.

HRD Press • 22 Amherst Road • Amherst, MA 01002 • 1-800-822-2801 • Fax 413-253-3490

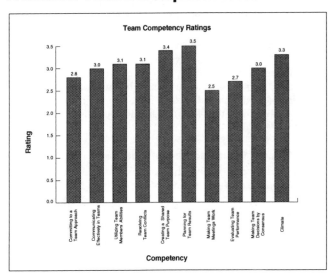

Performance Skills Teams Workshops
A Fully Inclusive and Adaptable Team Building Curriculum

Each Workshop Includes
- Instructor's Guide
- Participant Coursebook
- Lesson plans and activities
- Transparency masters

Workshops	**$79.95 each**
3-Ring Binder format.	
Additional Participant Coursebooks	**$9.95 each**
You will need one coursebook for each participant.	
Site License	**$195.00 each**
Includes all workshop materials on diskette and permission to customize and print unlimited quantities at your site.	

1. Committing to a Team Approach   4½ hours

Energize your newly formed teams with this workshop that helps participants explore different team roles as well as four critical stages of team development. By learning through experiential exercises about the behaviors that occur at each stage of team development, members will preempt resistance to the team approach.
Order Code … TCTA

2. Communicating Effectively in Teams   4½ hours

Improve all key communication skills within the context of achieving team goals. This workshop systematically presents core communication skills such as active listening, giving and receiving feedback constructively, and reacting to others' ideas. Order Code … TCET

3. Resolving Team Conflicts   3 hours

This workshop focuses on resolving the types of conflicts that commonly occur in teams. Participants determine their natural conflict management styles through the use of the *Conflict Style Inventory*. They learn techniques for assessing conflict situations and applying the most appropriate conflict management style for each situation. Order Code… TRSC

4. Creating a Shared Team Purpose   2½ hours

The ideal starting point for creating a fully functioning, high performing team, this workshop will help team members establish a mission that can be used to guide the formulation of goals and objectives. A series of skill building exercises will get everyone working toward the common goal. Order Code…TCST

5. Planning for Team Results   3½ hours

This workshop enables team members to set goals and objectives that are in direct support of the team's purpose. Team members will learn to compose goals that are supported by specific measurable objectives. Order Code … TPTR

6. Making Team Meetings Work   2½ hours

Meetings are the hub of team communication and decision making. This workshop addresses why meetings should be called, how to prepare for them, and most importantly how to conduct them effectively. Order Code …TMTW

7. Evaluating Team Performance   2½ hours

This workshop provides team members with an analytical framework for thoroughly evaluating nine critical dimensions of team effectiveness. Participants will gain a clear understanding of their team's strengths and weaknesses, and will develop a process for improving team performance. Order Code … TETP

8. Making Team Decisions by Consensus   2½ hours

When working in teams, it is critical to make decisions that all team members agree with and support. In this workshop, team members learn four basic decision making approaches and identify why consensus decision making is most beneficial in a team setting. Order Code … TMTD

9. Solving Team Problems   3½ hours

In order for teams to be successful, they must be able to solve everyday problems decisively and effectively. With this workshop, teams will learn to do so while working on an actual problem the team currently faces. By the end of the workshop participants will be ready to implement solutions.
Order Code … TSTP

10. Utilizing Team Members' Abilities   4½ hours

This workshop provides a framework by which teams can identify individual team members' strengths and reorganize to more efficiently achieve team objectives. Teams complete this training by developing an action plan to implement improved utilization of team human resources. Order Code … TUTM